THE FRENCH REVELATION

THE FRENCH REVELATION

by

N. RILEY HEAGERTY

www.whitecrowbooks.com

THE FRENCH REVELATION

Voice to Voice Conversations With Spirits
Through the Mediumship of Emily S. French

Witnessed, Tested and Documented by the Celebrated
Buffalo Attorney, Edward C. Randall

The Complete Works Compiled, Researched & Edited by

N. Riley Heagerty

All Spirit Words In This Entire Work Are Illustrated in **Bold Print**

Try to imagine yourself sitting in a completely darkened room, just you and the psychic medium. Suddenly, from the breathtaking stillness and apart from the medium, a voice, one that you know and recognize, manifests from the thin air and addresses you by your name. This very voice is coming from an individual you positively know left the physical world. Besides speaking, the voice, when replied to, answers back, which proves that it can also hear besides speak, and a conversation ensues, one 'betwixt' two worlds. This is the phenomena of Independent Spirit Voices, the phenomena of the medium Mrs. Emily S. French. If you believe in the written word, and trust in the unimpeachable character of those who lived and documented the experience, then you will believe the evidence for life after death and spirit communication contained within.

THE STORY IS TRUE - THE CHARACTERS ARE REAL - NO NAMES CHANGED

ONE OF THE MOST EXTRAORDINARY PSYCHIC EVENTS OF THE 20TH CENTURY

"THE DEFINITIVE WORK ON LIFE AFTER DEATH... A MASTERPIECE."

-George Cranley, Past President of the Noah's Ark Society for Physical Mediumship, England

The French Revelation

Published and printed in the United States of America and the United Kingdom
by White Crow Books; an imprint of White Crow Productions Ltd.

For information, contact White Crow Books
at 3 Hova Villas, Hove, BN3 3DH United Kingdom,
or e-mail to info@whitecrowbooks.com.

Cover Designed by Butterflyeffect
Interior design by Velin@Perseus-Design.com

Paperback ISBN 978-1-910121-46-7
eBook ISBN 978-1-910121-47-4

Non Fiction / Body, Mind & Spirit / Death & Dying

www.whitecrowbooks.com

TO CAROLINE
MY SHINING LIGHT
You Have Illuminated my Heart Forever

"The realities of the spirit world are beyond description. I might spend hours telling you of it and not reach your minds with any conception of its glory, its greatness, it's grandeur. It is so vast in extent, so marvelous, that any attempt to give you more than a faint idea would be futile."

A spirit speaking in their own independent voice at a séance with Mrs. Emily French

In the beginning, a spirit speaking to Edward C. Randall said:

"I find about you, Mr. Randall, a crowd of earnest spirit people who are bending all their thought upon this which you are about to undertake. They will help you, when writing, by their suggestions, and, as the little book begins its journey to find the hearts of men, they will open many doors, and guide it to many darkened homes. The light illuminating every page will be the beacon for many in distress, and we in spirit do most sincerely thank you for your efforts to bring these great truths to all people.

"We see so many entering spirit-life who have lived and died ignorant of this natural law, and we know so well the importance of knowing and living according to that law, that we rejoice over this book of knowledge and we will speed it on its helpful journey with eagerness and with pleasure."

"The Direct Voice is the highest psychical phenomena yet discovered, and it is the most convincing besides being quite the most wonderful. All of the discoveries of man fade into insignificance when compared with this great discovery."

J. Arthur Findlay (1883-1964) Recipient of the Order of the British Empire; renowned author, psychic researcher and authority on Religious History.

"The work of the American attorney and psychic researcher, Edward C. Randall, with the Independent Voice medium, Emily S. French, spanned more than twenty-two consecutive years—an unprecedented feat in this field of study—and produced five books, all predating by many years what was considered to be the most definitive work of its time on the subject, *On The Edge of The Etheric*, by J. Arthur Findlay. Now, with Heagerty's extraordinary book, *The French Revelation*, we not only have all of the work of Randall and French presented as one complete edition, but can also celebrate the fact that these valuable findings have been rescued from total obscurity and marched straight to the forefront of this vital field of research where they rightfully belong."

Tony Ortzen, Editor, *Two Worlds Magazine*, England

"I have always maintained that lawyers, barristers, and judges are far more qualified to assess evidence of survival of death than magicians, psychic researchers, etc., and this book amply confirms my view. Bringing his acute legal mind to bear, Randall was able to ask the spirit visitors the most searching questions about the continuity of life and the conditions that await all who inevitably will pass into the world of Spirit. In compiling this great work, and making it available to the general public, Riley Heagerty has performed a great service to humanity. It is often written that this book or that book should be on the shelf of every Spiritualist or Survivalist, often without justification, but in this case we have a book which will stand the test of time and one which Emily French and Edward Randall can feel justly proud. *The French Revelation* is a must for every bookshelf."

George Cranley, Researcher, past President, Noah's Ark Society, England

"The knowledge Edward C. Randall acquired in these séances and, most importantly, how it was delivered by the Independent Voice, spoken directly by the spirits, is incontrovertible and conclusive proof of life after death."

BARBARA THURMAN, LATE PRESIDENT, NATIONAL SPIRITUALIST ASSOCIATION OF CHURCHES, USA.

"*The French Revelation* is destined to become a classic of Psychic & Spiritualist literature for which N.Riley Heagerty must be congratulated."

COLIN FRY, INTERNATIONAL SPIRITUALIST MEDIUM AND STAR OF "THE SIXTH SENSE."

"Mr.Heagerty has placed all students of psychic research greatly in his debt with this new edition of material, much of which has never been seen by historians of Physical Mediumship."

LESLIE PRICE, EDITOR, PSYCHIC PIONEER PROJECT

"This account is a unique record of Independent Voice mediumship as it was practiced by Madame French in the early days of Spiritualism in the country where it all began, documented by the investigator for 22 years, Edward Randall himself, in the beautiful prose of a more leisurely age."

GRAHAM JENNINGS, EDITOR, *TWO WORLDS MAGAZINE*

"When asked what one book he would want if stranded on a desert island, G. K. Chesterton, the English author and philosopher, selected" *A Practical Guide to Shipbuilding.* "I sometimes ponder that question and, not being much of a carpenter, have leaned towards books which might give me a better idea of survival beyond the physical realm. Such books while giving me hope for a future life, also tend to make the current life more bearable, at the same time giving new insight and renewed fortitude into surviving this one. Thus, *The French Revelation* would receive strong consideration as the book I would select to have along on the desert island. Having read more than two hundred books on mediumship and spirit communication, I cannot recall a single one offering more wealth of credible wisdom, guidance and thought provoking information than this book."

MIKE E.TYMN, RESEARCHER AND AUTHOR OF *THE AFTERLIFE REVEALED, TRANSCENDING THE TITANIC: BEYOND DEATH'S DOOR,* AND *THE AFTERLIFE EXPLORERS, VOLUME I.*

"Riley Heagerty's The French Revelation is the most inclusive written record of the testing of Emily S. French-the phenomenal independent-direct voice medium. A must read for any serious investigator of Spiritualist phenomena."

RON NAGY, LILY DALE HISTORIAN, AUTHOR OF *SLATE WRITING, INVISIBLE INTELLIGENCES,* AND *THE SPIRITS OF LILY DALE.*

"There have been few books on the relatively rare phenomena of the direct-independent voice in that class of Spiritualism literature spanning the last century; many have been unfortunately lost over time. The works of Edward C. Randall, of which few copies exist, outshine them all, and would have also remained submerged if not for the efforts of N.Riley Heagerty. In a truly scholarly feat of determination, Riley has compiled and presented the most significant of Randall's investigations and eyewitness accounts of the medium Emily S. French. I was blessed to have found this book ten years ago, and have returned to it again and again with gratitude, always finding new insight into the world of spirit."

AUGUST GOFORTH, CO-AUTHOR, *THE RISEN: DIALOGUES OF LOVE, GRIEF AND SURVIVAL BEYOND DEATH.*

ACKNOWLEDGMENTS

However large or small their contribution to *The French Revelation*, thanks are due to the following for their help along the way:

My Parents, for Everything; Brothers and all Family Members; my beloved Kiwi, Little G, Midi Pantaloon, Little Bittle and the Attic; Abraham, John King, Jean, Macbeth and all the Spirits; the Fords, and Riverside Cemetery; The Oswego Public Library-Carol, Martha and the staff, Oswego, New York; Penfield Library at Oswego State University, Mrs. Mary Bennett; Edward A. Mervine, Attorney at Law, Oswego, New York; Onondaga County Public Library, Syracuse, New York, Mr. Chris Cox, I.L.L.; Buffalo and Erie County Public Library-William H. Loos, Curator/Grosvenor Rare Book Room, Buffalo, New York, who supplied me with, over the years, invaluable biographical information on Edward C. Randall; Buffalo and Erie County Historical Society; University of Rochester, Rochester, New York; Rochester Public Library-Local History Division; Rochester Historical Society; Erie County Surrogate's Court, Buffalo, New York; Middle Earth Books, Paul B. Hudson, Michigan; The Lily Dale Spiritualist Assembly and The National Spiritualist Association of Churches, Lily Dale, New York; Ron Nagy, Historian, Lily Dale Assembly; Library of Congress-Rare Books and Special Collections Division, Washington, D.C.; The Eileen Garrett Library, Joanne D.S. McMahon, PhD., Parapsychology Foundation, New York, New York; University of Buffalo-Charles B. Sears Law Library; Allegheny College-Lawrence Lee Pelletier Library, Meadville, Pennsylvania; Stanford University Libraries, Elizabeth Green, Stanford,

California; The New York State Library, Cultural Education Center, Henry Ilnicki, Albany, New York; The American Society of Psychical Research, New York, New York; The Blue Dragon Bookshop, Ashland, Oregon; Berry Hill Book Shop, Deansboro, New York; Chester Valley Old Books, Frazer, Pennsylvania; The Book Mark, Rittenhouse Square West, Philadelphia, Pennsylvania; Yankee Peddler Bookshop, Rochester, New York; Bettman Archive, New York, New York; Health Research, Mokelumne Hill, California (original store), and now Ben Roberts and Nikki Jones, Pomeroy, Washington; Mrs. Ellie Tritchler, genealogist, Buffalo, New York; Mr. Roy D. Goold, genealogist, Brockport/Rochester, New York; The National Archives Trust Fund, Washington, D C.; Virginia W. Common, granddaughter of Edward C. Randall; Mrs. Marylyn Graham, wife of the late Thomas H. Graham, grandson of Edward C. Randall, and lastly, for its dedication, loyalty and integrity of purpose, the home circle, and all those who have contributed to its development in this world and the next; England: The Noah's Ark Society for Physical Mediumship, the committee, staff, mediums and members; The Society for Psychical Research, London; Harry Price Library, University of London; College of Psychic Studies, London; Marion Hancock, Bookseller; The Spiritualist National Union, Essex, Publication Committee, for permission to use the quotes of Arthur Findlay from "On The Edge of The Etheric," and "Looking Back." Australia: The University of New England, Department of Psychology, Armidale; Melbourne Theosophical Society, Melbourne, Victoria; The Australian Institute of Parapsychological Research; La Trobe University, Dr. Al Babay, Department of Humanities, Bendigo, Victoria; State Library of New South Wales, Sidney; State Library of Victoria, Melbourne, Victoria. The rare, elusive unpublished material of Edward C. Randall could not have been located and included in this work were it not for some good old-fashioned determination and the help of my Australian friends. And finally, to Diane K. Rossell, whose untimely passing from the physical life was the awakening that led me to investigate life after death and spirit communication.

LIST OF ILLUSTRATIONS

Illustration 1: Photograph of Emily S. French (seated), circa 1912, taken shortly before her death, with her daughter Ella French Oberst (1855-1940), standing to her left dressed in white; her granddaughter Louise Oberst Angell (1882-1958), standing behind her and, on her lap, her grandson Alan Scott Augell (1909-1963); four generations represented.

Illustration 2: photograph of Edward Caleb Randall, Men of Buffalo portrait, circa 1904.

Illustration 3: Photograph of Edward C. Randall, the Courier Express, circa 1934.

Illustration 4: Photograph of Emily Sophia McCoy French, age 40 years, taken in 1871, seven years after the untimely death of her husband Lieu't James H. French in the Civil War (see appendices), and nineteen years before meeting Edward C. Randall. As a symbol of her state of mourning over the loss of James in 1864 and her young son William H. French, "Willie" as he was called, at age 26 in 1881, Mrs. French wore the color black until her death in 1912.

Illustration 5: The house at West Ferry Street, city of Buffalo, New York, former home of the Edward C. Randall family as seen in modern times, where the psychic experiments with Emily S. French took place. The Tower Room was built into a remote section of the third story of this stately home, used specifically for their séances. The Randall family was in residence at this location from 1899 to 1921.

CONTENTS

INTRODUCTION

"Nothing is too wonderful to be true." –FARADAY

Audacious, startling and incredible would be mild characterizations of the assertions that were contained within the first published work of Edward C. Randall entitled *Life's Progression; Research in Meta-psychics* (Henry B. Brown Company: Buffalo, New York, 1906.), which he suddenly and unexpectedly dropped like an atom bomb of controversy into the religious world. His announced object in publishing the work, which he said represented fifteen years' research in meta-psychics, a comparatively unknown field of study, was to illuminate, but he also knew that it would produce a fire storm of heat as well as light.

"There is no death; there are no dead."

These words stood out on the cover of the book, and in its foreword he asserted the following: "I have no need of creeds nor use for faiths. Positive knowledge has displaced them both and I have come to know there is no death; there are no dead. That change is one step only in life's progression, in the unceasing march of evolution, in which neither identity nor individuality is lost, and that life goes on and labor continues as the soul works toward perfection, for progress is an absolute law that nothing can resist."

His words were a direct challenge to orthodox thinking and through all the pages of his work ran this disconcerting challenge to those whose idea of God, of heaven, hell and a future life were based strictly on the Bible. If there is no death, if there are no dead, what then would become of the resurrection morn; where shall we look for the great White Throne, where for the One who shall intercede for the sinful; where shall the separation of the goats and sheep take place; where are the streets made of gold? Mr. Randall's findings annulled these widely accepted teachings. He was convinced that every man must, and will, stand as his own redeemer. He was not inferring by his statements that he did not believe in the life hereafter, nor in the universal power and controlling force which is denominated God and which is thought by some to be clothed with a personality and by others considered the essence of good; the true spirit of love, only not embodied. He did not contend the existence of these things. He did believe in a heaven, not a heaven of idleness and exclusiveness, but a heaven peopled by active, progressive and hard-working spirits. Mr. Randall likewise believed in hell, only it was not a hell where punishment is meted out in an atmosphere of flames and sulfurous fumes. In this modern day, belief in a hell of fire and brimstone may seem outmoded, but there are some, rest assured, who still look upon hell as a place of physical torment. Many conceive hell to be a place apart from heaven where the wicked have gained admission by their actions while on earth. There is also the steadily growing belief that hell is a state of remorse of the spirit, and this view comes extremely close to Mr. Randall's hell.

The author of *Life's Progression* published four more, equally startling books which together embodied the results of his psychic research. The works were the outcome of what Mr. Randall termed his positive knowledge, yet he never claimed that he was the only one that knew or could know. This certainty, in the year 1906, was remarkable of psychic literature. Many books had been written previously about the life hereafter; men of many minds had reasoned from many viewpoints as to what might be seen beyond death's mysterious door. These speculations began in the very early ages and have continued right up until this present day, but at the turn of the century, few books, if any, had been written which purported to give exact and definite knowledge of the life that is beyond the Everlasting line.

And where did Mr. Randall get his information? His answer, always direct and without equivocation, was: "From those that are living that life" he said, "from spirits with whom I have talked voice to voice, for many years," and he meant "voice-to-voice" literally. Commenting on the reasons for publishing his research, he further stated:" I do so in the hope that the fear of death may pass, that those who mourn may find consolation, and that all may find understanding. All the facts that we know and can gather—the miracle of death; each new birth; all teachings from the great beyond, and here; all discoveries and inventions; all the wondrous paintings, miracles of form and color; the marvelous marbles that seem to live and breathe; the secrets told by winding stream and desert sand; the record of all events evidence a Directive Force that we call God, that finds expression not only on this poor earth of ours, but in the planes beyond, where all at last must go. I have come to know something of the plan, purpose and operation of the Directive Force, not only here, but in the planes beyond. Having come into touch with those who live there, we have discussed these questions, and their teachings, faithfully recorded, I have given to you as they were given to me unaltered and unchanged."

The world seemed to stand at attention when Mr. Randall made public the results of his research and soon after, his works attracted the following of the two foremost American psychic researchers at the time, Dr. Richard Hodgson and Prof. James Hyslop, and also, England's leading experts of psychic research, J. Arthur Findlay and Vice-Admiral W. Usborne Moore (see Appendices and Reading List). This was, after all, no ordinary man making these astonishing assertions concerning the very nature of man's destiny; Mr. Randall was an esteemed member of the highest echelon of society, one of the most powerful leaders of business in the United States, and, furthermore, a celebrated trial lawyer, well known for his abilities of sifting evidence and interrogation of witnesses on the stand. His very presence within this body of research was, in itself, a proclamation of its seriousness.

Edward Caleb Randall was born in Ripley, New York, in 1860 and obtained his preliminary education in the district school and academy of his native place. He was prepared for college under private tutorship and he pursued his classical studies at Allegheny College in Meadville, Pennsylvania. In 1883 he was admitted to the bar, having been practicing at Dunkirk since 1879. He married Maria Howard of Buffalo in 1897. At the time of his death in 1935, he was the president of the American Super Power Corporation, Super Power Syndicate Inc., Niagara Terminals Buildings Inc., Cataract Development Corporation, South Buffalo Gas Corporation, vice-president of Eureka Smelting Company, and director of Prest Air Corporation.

Mr. Randall stated when he began his investigations into psychic research, he had absolutely no place in his mind for even a conception of a spiritual existence, or for any agencies in the universe other than matter and force. For this famous trial lawyer and astute businessman, his days of agnosticism and conjecture ended and a wondrous journey of transformation began with his introduction to a quiet little woman who lived on Tremont Street in Rochester, New York. She was a psychic medium, her name, Mrs. Emily S. French.

Emily French And the Direct-Independent Voice Phenomena

> "For to one is given by the Spirit the word of wisdom; to another the word of knowledge by the same Spirit... To another the working of miracles; to another prophecy; to another discerning of spirits..."
>
> - First Epistle of Paul the Apostle 1 Corinthians, Chapter 12

Arthur Findlay, in his classic book, *Looking Back,* published in 1961, mentions that when he visited Mr. Randall in 1923 and asked him how he became interested in the phenomena of Direct-Voice, Mr. Randall responded by saying that in 1890 he had been approached by a number of his associates who requested him to investigate the practices of a lady named Mrs. French since, reportedly, she was a magician of the highest class and the cleverest fraud in America. It was assumed that Mr. Randall, being a master of detecting fraud on any level, was the last person who could be bamboozled by any charlatan, especially one pretending to be contacting the so-called dead. He stated, "I went (to Mrs. French's home in Rochester), and found there two others, both men of national reputation. We sat in a dark room for two hours, and heard what purported to be voices...we found Mrs. French far along in years, of rare refinement, a beautiful character, and we were satisfied, a perfectly honest woman." He quickly realized that the accusations made previously by his associates were absurd. Without exception, Mrs. French was held in the highest regard by her acquaintances and, most astonishingly and of the highest evidential level, took no money for her services. That she inspired trust is evident in the wondrous reports about her, some of which are given by those with weighty names and marks of scholarship. Mr. Randall was to eventually consider this unassuming woman from Rochester the greatest living psychic in America, if not in the entire world. His deep and unalterable conviction of the extraordinary nature of the case led him to experiment with and investigate the phenomena attending Mrs. French for twenty-two consecutive years; phenomena so marvelous that such occurrences would be impossible to apprehend unless an individual be familiar with the experience itself or the literature which deals with it.

In the presence of the medium, Mrs. French, but quite apart from her, *voices,* claiming to be those of deceased people would speak, and, when replied to, would answer back intelligently, which proved that not only was a mind behind the voice, but also that the speaker was able to hear as well as speak. Isolated voices manifesting from space without visible source of agency, could something be too wonderful to be true? Absolutely not, according to Mr. Randall. The proof, he said, was incontrovertible and conclusive, brought about by the sheer weight of evidence resulting from his many sittings and exacting experiments in which he tested the powers of Mrs. French in every conceivable way he could devise. The evidence was spoken; it was established through the attestations of men, women and children who had experienced the drama of death and who had come back by way of the direct-independent voice to share their experiences with those still living in the physical world.

Concerning the actual mechanics of speech, the following was spoken to Mr. Randall during one of the earlier séances:

> **"There are in our group,"** the spirit replied [after being asked by Mr. Randall to tell of the conditions which enabled them to speak], "seven people, —**all expert in the handling of the electric and magnetic forces, and when you and the psychic, Mrs. French, meet, the vital force that emanates from her personality is gathered up. We also take physical emanations—substances—from you and the others with you, while we contribute to the mass a certain spirit force. Now, that force, which we gather and distribute, is just as material as any substance that you would gather for any purpose; it is simply higher in vibration. We clothe the organs of respiration of the spirit who is to speak, so that his voice will sound in your atmosphere, and when this condition is brought about, it is just as natural for a spirit as it is for you. You then have what is known as the direct or independent voice, that is, the voice of a spirit speaking as in earth life."**

Although very little information is obtainable on the early life and biographical background of Mrs. French, some insight into her person and practices may be gleaned through the following passages.

This information was taken from a letter written by the secretary of the Rochester Art Club, Mr. A.W. Moore, dated 1905:

With a newspaperman's soul, I found out something about the lady's antecedents. She belongs to the American branch of the Pierrepont family, the head of which is the Earl of Manvers, whose principle estate is at Holme Pierrepont, Nottinghamshire, England. I borrowed a book giving the history of the American branch, in which there is a list of the members of the family then living in the United States. In the list I found the name of the late Judge Pierrepont, one time minister to the Court of Saint James, London, and at the very end, I found the names of Mrs. French and her only child, Mrs. D. Oberst. Mrs. French is the widow of the late Lieut. French of the United States Volunteers, who lost his life during the war of the Rebellion. She draws a pension of an officer's widow. For many years she has made her home with her daughter, and her chief pleasure in life is administering to the comfort and education of her grandchildren. She is a lady of refinement and possesses the charming, unassuming and gentle manners of a well-born race.

From *The Encyclopedia of Psychic Science:*

> Mrs. Emily French (1831-1912), of Rochester, a relation of President Cleveland, excellent American direct-voice medium. She was investigated for more than twenty years by Edward C. Randall of Buffalo. Isaac K. Funk and Prof. Hyslop [see Part III and appendices] also conducted remarkable experiments and proved that the voices did not originate in the vocal organs of the medium. "Red Jacket," her Indian guide, had an exceedingly loud, masculine voice which could have easily filled a hall with a seating capacity of two thousand people. The medium at that time, was a frail old woman, with a weak and irregular heart and very deaf. Yet the communicators-the spirits-could hear every remark of the sitters at the séances.

As a superb example of a completely spontaneous situation involving the phenomena attending Mrs. French and one with the highest evidential value, I include the testimony of Mrs. French's personal physician and friend, Dr. Jane M. Frear, who lived at 21 Orton Place, Buffalo, New York; it is dated 1907:

"My father [and I] at one time were talking with her, we standing on opposite sides of a doorway. The light from the next room made Mrs.

French's face plainly visible to me. I was looking at her and talking to her when the loud voice known as "Red Jacket" *spoke to us from the top of the stairway,* which was in the dark. I have also heard a voice beginning to speak while she was talking. This has happened on several occasions while I was chatting with her-her deafness prevented her from catching the first vibrations of the other voice or voices. I have also heard two voices singing at the same time-she does not sing. These voices were male voices."

Emily French was 80 years, 11 months and 12 days old when she quietly passed away on June 22, 1912 at her home at 227 Tremont Street in Rochester, where she had spent most of her adult life. She was buried in Mt. Hope cemetery in that city.

The Complete Work of Edward C. Randall
with Emily S. French

"Seek, and you will find; for you have aids from Nature for the discovery of Truth. But if you are not able yourself, by going along those ways, to discover that which follows, listen to those who have made the enquiry."
–Epictetus

Ninety years after his first published work startled the world, I present to a new audience as one edition, the complete Meta-psychic research of Edward C. Randall with the spiritual medium, Mrs. Emily S. French. Included, in edited form, are his five books, published between 1906 and 1922, and never before published, rare excerpts from his last unfinished manuscript, written in 1926, which I was fortunate enough to locate in Melbourne, Australia. Most importantly, all of the words spoken by the spirits and stenographically recorded by Mr. Randall and published by him are included in *The French Revelation.*

To all those who are interested in life after death and spirit communication, or to those who are uncertain of their beliefs, the case of Mrs. French cannot be denied as one of the most evidential cases in psychic history. Greed and notoriety played no part in Mrs. French's life. There was no media frenzy, sensationalism or Internet back then. She refused money from anyone, and wanted nothing in return, except that all who experienced her mediumship would gain from it, and gain they did. Total selflessness was at the core of her spirituality. Many books have been published on the various types of phenomena manifesting in the séance rooms all over the world and many of these are classics, (see Suggested Reading List), but few, are infused with direct, in depth, specific teachings from the world of spirit. Teachings that help us to understand the meaning of life itself, here and now, and in the afterlife where all, without exception, are headed. Compiled into one solid edition at last, this body of work is truly the Magnum Opus of Emily S. French and Edward C. Randall and one of the most important works ever recorded.

The Spirits have said:

> **"We communicate with you not merely to prove survival but to attract attention to the important truths connected with it. We are anxious to show mankind that earth-life is not complete in itself, but contributes to a larger order, that it is an episode in a stupendously larger drama."**

God does seem to work in strange and wonderful ways. After having finished compiling *The French Revelation*, I found in a musty-smelling little sequestered nook in his hometown library, yet another faded obituary notice for Edward Caleb Randall, and in it was a statement from his memoirs which he completed before his death in 1935. He had written that the world would not be sufficiently advanced for the theories set forth in his work until another half century had passed; at a time when, as he expressed it, "the world is ready." It was precisely fifty years later, in 1985, when I came upon, quite unexpectedly, Randall's great classic, *The Dead Have Never Died*, and determined shortly after reading it to try and locate what other research he may have done and compile it into one complete edition. My entire mission has now come to pass, and I bow in thanks to the Infinite Intelligence who, it seems, has allowed me to have played a part, however large or small, in fulfilling the futuristic prophecy of this great American researcher, Mr. Edward C. Randall, with the psychic wonder of the world, Mrs. Emily S. French.

May these glorious truths, given to the world by these two tireless explorers into man's greatest mystery, now infused with new life and set on its course once again, provide a more clear and rational understanding of life's progress, and by so doing, enrich the world; complimenting God, natural laws, universal Truth and substantiate to a profound degree, man's rightful place in the unceasing march of evolution.

N. Riley Heagerty, New York, 1995

CHAPTER 1

FROM AGNOSTICISM TO BELIEF

BY EDWARD C. RANDALL

> The wise are instructed by reason; ordinary minds by experience; the stupid by necessity; the brutes by instinct.
>
> —CICERO

To understand things as they are the world must have truth. While it has made gigantic strides in all the arts and sciences, hardly a step has been taken in the way that leads to a knowledge of man's ultimate end.

In the presence of death, faith, belief and creeds wither and decay, and doubt goes hand and hand with grief. In such a presence we feel what speech cannot tell, and hope that what seems night here is somewhere else a dawn. In the majesty of this silence, how acts and deeds burst into perfect form. When loving hearts are breaking, and heads are bowed above an open grave, how dare any priest presume to tell what he does not know?

Belief will not change natural law; Faith will not save or condemn one; Ignorance will not excuse one; Traditions stay progression, while doubt is the dawn of reason. Why not find out now, if possible, some solution of this problem and what this life leads to? Little at best can be known of the afterlife, so boundless is its scope; yet enough can be learned while in the body, to dispel the awful fear and to lighten the sorrows that fill the human heart, as well as to make men lead better lives because they can live more intelligently, and so enrich the world. That I may increase this knowledge, I have investigated every natural law that I have had the opportunity and ability to study, and now, owing to present freedom of speech, I publish the results of my investigations without fear. In many ways I have sought the thought of men, both in and out of the body, ever drawing my own conclusions, and making my own deductions. I have felt the thrill of success in the discovery of new laws and in the proving of new facts.

The bridge of death no longer rests upon clouds of hope, but upon the great piers of knowledge. Every act is but the product of conditions, and the heart applauds the brain when one works to increase the force of universal good.

I know that matter is eternal and that only form is new, and that one who but yesterday in the flush of health faced the storms of life with splendid courage, and whose body lies tonight in the embrace of mother earth, is no exception to the rule. All that was matter, as we use the term, the outer garment, all that gave him physical expression, will mingle with the substance from which it was formed: but his spirit is eternal, his progression will be unbroken, and his horizon will widen, as he reaches the sphere of psychic discovery.

I know that to the limits of that plane in which he lives at first, the human voice will carry, the thought will reach. The so-called dead live here about us, know our sorrows and grieve with us. They share our happiness, they know our hopes and ambitions, and, by suggestion, through our subconscious brain, they influence our daily conduct. I know that there in the after life they have feature, form and expression, and, therefore, bodies composed of matter, for there cannot be form without substance. The substance that forms the bodies of spirit-people, vibrating more than five octaves higher than the violet ray, few in earth-life ever see, though spirit people see and talk with each other, and with mortals when necessary conditions are secured. I know that every hope, ambition, and desire of earth are continued beyond this life, as is also the burden of wrong. I know that we are as much spirit now as we ever shall be; that in death, so-called, we simply vacate and discard the gross material that gives us expression in this physical plane. All about this matter world of ours, there exists, in fact, the psychic or spiritual universe, more active and real than this, peopled with all the countless dead, who, no longer burdened with a physical body, move at will within the boundaries of their sphere, in what appears as space to mortal man.

Long ago I became satisfied that nothing ever dies, that those who in death pass from this earth-plane still live, and that, if the conditions were made right, they could talk with us voice to voice. Now, after fifteen year's scientific research and experiment, I have made a condition so perfect that, with the aid of Mrs. Emily S. French (whose psychic powers have been developed), I am able to carry on freely conversations with spirits out of the body. Thousands who have passed through the change called death, who live and labor in the world of thought around and about us, have told me something of the laws that govern all life beyond, what they find, how they live, have talked of their occupations and their progression. Their life is an active one. All the new conditions, all the great laws by which they are to be governed, must be learned, and only by individual effort can they live intelligently and well. I know that a wrong act in the earth-life must be lived over again in the next sphere, and lived right, before advancement is possible; that labor is often long, but that families and friends are, in time, reunited and take up the thread where it was broken. I have heard them talk amongst themselves, and to me, and many eminent men and women, upon my invitation, have heard the same that I have heard in the material conditions that we have made.

I do not seek to prove that soul-life follows death—that is self evident to all intelligent men and women-but to give some information of the character and condition of that life among the spheres of progression. I would reach the thinkers, those who reason. Pearls of thought are for those who dive deep; in the shallows one finds only pebbles. These pages will not appeal to those who fear damnation as the penalty for searching for truth. But there are many who, working in the fields of knowledge, will welcome a co-laborer. Such would I join, bringing with me these teachings from planes beyond.

I know something of the democracy of death, and all that mankind is beginning to hear and march to the silent music of reason. I know, to, that the highest duty of everyone is to contribute what he can to the prosperity of the many, who though rich in material goods, are mentally poor in the land of opportunity, and that this individual life of ours, whether it has had birth within the palace or the hut, no matter how it turns and curves and falls among the hills as it courses from the mountain-tops, through valley-lands, or, lies at times in stagnant pools of ignorance and vice festering in the sun, must some day reach the great ocean of eternal life, from whence it came, clean and pure. I am told that:

> **"Beyond the life men call material, is another so much more real, so much more vital and interesting, that, when you enter into its fullest harmony, the little lives you led on earth will fade into the dim reality of a dream-like past."**

We cannot in the nature of things know much of the everyday life of spirits who people what to us is infinite space, because we are unable to grasp, to any great extent, the realities of their conditions. All can learn a little of matter and laws that control it beyond the physical plane, and to that extent can reason from cause to effect, without which there cannot be any rational conclusions.

I know that the tendency of all people is to do right, and that an invisible world, peopled by the so-called dead of all ages past, is interested in and is aiding our progression, that it speaks to our dull ears with silent voices; and I know that the great desire and hope of those beyond is to bring the world to an understanding of what death means and of what follows so-called death, so that, knowing these two things, they may learn how to live the earth-life well.

It is time that men who know that those out of the body can and do talk to men, put away fear of the speech of people, and lend the weight of personality to this philosophy of truth. The age of faith is past. The teaching of the church no longer satisfies the hunger of heart and brain. This is an age of fact. The present calls upon men to think, not to believe; the torch of reason has been lighted, and its day is here.

I have no need of creeds nor use for faiths. Positive knowledge has displaced them both, and I have come to know there is no death; there are no dead.

I have written these pages with the hope that some heart, heavy with sorrow, may come to comprehend the truth about death, and to know that those called dead are alive, and that all is well with them. We should ever look with eager eyes for gems of truth, and what we find, we should have the courage to express. I know better than anyone can tell me, how incomplete is this Meta-psychic philosophy, but bear with me: I have gone, in my research, beyond physical laws and the books of men, out into the wilderness of fact; beyond the beaten path into another world, and what I have written, incomplete though it may be, 'are facts' and 'they are true.' Without arrogance, prejudice or preconceived notions, I have sat at the feet of learning, and, with eager and receptive brain, have listened to the teachings of splendid minds beyond the physical sphere and have weighed carefully each word in the light of reason and experience.

I know that origin and destiny are no longer beyond the grasp of the human mind: that spirit which is human life, when clothed with material, is visible to the physical eye; when separated is invisible; that dissolution is not annihilation, but liberation and opportunity.

I know that man has no Redeemer but himself; that God is universal good and dwells in the heart of all mankind. Now we sail the intellectual seas, making soundings and charts on the farther shore. We are coming to understand and master the blind forces of Nature, as we open the windows in the chamber of thought, and to comprehend the economy of Natural Law.

Some mortal lives are so lived that they stand out like trees aflame along the green and wooded shore where waters beat with endless wave; others, like undergrowth within the endless forest, remain unknown, but each must, according to the immutable laws of progression, at some time, obtain perfect development, which is the heritage of all; this is the law of life.

I have submitted this manuscript to a large number of advanced thinkers both in America and Europe, and the general criticism has been that it is so in advance of experience, so different from the old teachings and beliefs, that few will grasp or understand the new propositions presented.

This is without a doubt true, but the facts as I have gathered them cannot be changed; truth is infinite. Volumes have been written by the world's foremost writers to prove the possibility of communication between this plane and the next, though few have been privileged to enjoy direct and independent speech to the extent that I have.

Those who read the pages that I have written must assume that speech is possible and that I have had the experiences narrated. I do not attempt to enter the elementary field; others have covered that branch. I have tried to transmit facts as they have been given me, and I expect many to accept them because they are in accordance with Nature's Law and appeal to reason.

It is a great privilege to be evolved out of the great mass of life, to obtain individuality with all its possibilities not by a miracle, but through positive law. But that privilege brings responsibilities, among them the necessity of living a clean life, of developing character to the utmost, of doing something to make others happy, and of making the world a little better because we have lived a day within its confines. These things are not difficult to accomplish if we are unselfish. To the new thought, to the progress of the world, each may give something. Great truths come from the obscure. The night brings forth the stars.

Night after night Mrs. French and I sat and talked and listened in darkness. Why in darkness? do you ask. Because in light there is motion. In order that the spirit may talk with audible voice it must, for the moment, be clothed with material. Motion disintegrates matter. Everything that ever lives was born in the dark. In this condition, then, the whispers came more distinctly. Words were uttered, sentences formed, until in time, out of the darkness, in my own home, surrounded by conditions that I myself made, voices full and clear came, filling the room, reverberating through the whole house—Metapsychic voices which any could hear as well as I myself, and which many have heard. With these voices came splendid speech, great lectures, much knowledge. We were told that in space and from the beginning there have been "two elements." One we call "spirit" the other "matter." Spirit lives and feels and never dies. It struggles constantly after knowledge, and uses matter to aid its development. In our individual inception, according to natural law, an atom of life force from the great universe, which is all life, is clothed with material, and thus becomes an individual conscious spirit, ever growing, ever changing, ever developing, according to the unwritten laws of evolution and progression. Death is but one of the natural changes in the march.

The room in which we hold communication with the spirits was constructed as directed by our spirit band. It is consecrated to this work, and naught but harmony enters. In the day, the sun, so essential to life, floods it, and in the evening, when our labor begins, the curtains are drawn and darkness fills the room. Cloudlike substances form and change, evidence of gathering spirits. Magnetic and electric lights float and fall, but give forth no illumination. Then they greet us, and we them, with words of welcome and fellowship, as do guests and host in any home. Usually, someone advanced in the other life is introduced, and he speaks on some special subject. In this manner, we are taught. We may ask for a lecture on any subject; and the same evening, or at a subsequent time, it will be given by a master-mind. I have never heard such teachings and magnificent discourses in the material world. Our circle is known in that other life, and thousands are always waiting to come within the vibrations that have been formed. They seek to throw off material conditions that still impeded their progress. (see Mission Work) Our co-laborers bring those who are in a state of unconsciousness to awaken them beyond the grave through the material vibrations made. Hundreds in the same mental attitude are gathered at a time. One, two, or more, the best qualified, are selected who, taking on the proper condition, talk with us and with the band working with us; while the many wait, watch, listen, and so obtain the same lesson and the same help that the spirit speaking does.

In this branch of the work, a voice comes out of the darkness, in greeting, often bewildered. Many a spirit knows nothing of the flight of time. It grasps the thread where it was broken, and I have heard a sentence finished that was apparently started when death came. The thought that was uppermost when the shadow fell is the dominating idea when the awakening comes. Then, with all the gentleness and patience, we guide the thoughts to the new surroundings. The spirits tell us that death nearly always comes before they are ready. It seems that those who belong to "this class" are so material, that we who are in like condition alone can penetrate the wall of darkness that they have unknowingly built about their mentalities, and so, reach them. When this is done, and they realize what and where they are, they look about and see those long mourned. Then come the joyful greetings. Hands clasp hands, and many voices speak words of welcome and courage. I have heard a man who, seeing the face of one whom he has wronged, cry out in agony and fear. I have heard words of happiness when a mother clasped a long-lost child; or husband, a wife. I have heard the trembling language of old age and the prattle of little children.

My instruction has been splendid. Among the teachers have been such spirits as Channing, Beecher, Talmage, Ingersoll, Hough, Dr. Hossack, Segoyewatha, and hundreds of others. Lectures from such men, speaking in their own independent voices, materialized for the time, leaves no doubt as to what follows death. I have never heard such matchless oratory, such sermons, such thought expressed by the living as I have from the so-called dead. They tell me that we are as much spirit today as we will ever be. We are not all that we can become; but there will be no sudden acquisition. Death itself will add little to present knowledge; nor will it enlarge our opportunities to any marked degree. Opportunities are just as great with us here as they ever will be. Here and there all depends upon individual effort. Labor is endless. The goal recedes as we approach. There was no beginning, there is no end, and on through eternity there will be something for us to do. There will be greater heights to climb, greater knowledge to acquire, or work to do, we might then, in the interpretation of the Church, become gods.

According to my instruction, death is a moving out, a vacating of the earthly habitation, a separation of the spirit from the body. As it is, then, a natural incident, it is painless, sometimes conscious; but more often unconscious, and the awakening is like the coming from bewildered sleep. We were the same last night before sleep as we are this morning, and we have the same surroundings. We shall be the same after death as before, and probably we shall be in the same place.

Death is like birth, with this exception: In death one takes with him the knowledge and development acquired in this "material existence" which we are told is a period of preparation for eternity, as we call it, the preface to the book of life. There is no break, there is only progression to greater possibilities.

Reasoning from material laws, it is hard to comprehend what spirit is. I am taught that it is conscious, visible thought-soul-life.

If this life has been lived in harmony with natural law, if one has done right, and, hearing the voice, followed the dictates of conscience (which is the spirit of God), if he has been just and considerate among men, and has done the best according to his understanding, then those who have gone before are able to reach and greet him with words of comfort and consolation. He sees and recognizes old friends, and they explain to him the laws and conditions that henceforth must govern him, under which he must live and work. They become his teachers. He comes to himself. He appreciates and sees that all solids here possess life and conscious individuality. He learns that all life, like man, has language, or means of communication. He learns that the rocks, the trees, the flowers and growing grain, all animal and vegetable matter, continue to live, and in the spirit-world there is the conscious spirit of everything that we have and much that we know not of, that death is not the end. The spirit freed from material can climb the heights, like our thoughts, can speed over mountains of ice and snow, through the valleys, over oceans, through foreign lands, can circle the globe, and in time, in ethereal regions, go to the other planets, can soar through unfathomable heights to the stars; for in spirit, as in thought, there is no space or time.

Mrs. French, the finest psychic in the world today, has been a co-worker with me throughout the entire part of my investigations. This splendid woman of culture and refinement, now 76 years of age, (1908) has, without compensation, devoted the evening of her life to aid me in solving the great problem of death.

She contributes to the experiments such psychic force as is required, while I give the physical force that makes speech possible.

Mrs. French and I simply go into this room, already described and sit in darkness, with the small table only between us. The occasion is not solemn; nor are the surroundings gruesome; rather it is a school-room and the lecture hour devoted to the unfolding of nature's simple laws.

One morning, when Mrs. French and I were in this room talking to a physician who lived in the time of Alexander Hamilton and was one of his friends, a member of my family raised a window-shade in the attic, allowing sunlight to flash all over the room. The rays were reflected through the ventilator in the ceiling, partially lighting the room directly over where a spirit being stood talking. I saw his form perfectly. Without a break in his discourse, he stepped to one side toward the corner where it was darker, continuing his discussion, simply saying as the place where he stood became partially lighted:

> **"We have promised the time should come when you should see us, but we scarcely expected it would be this morning."**

He stood there in full materialized form, else how could I have seen him? He was a spirit, for Mrs. French and I were in the room alone, and no other man could have come in without opening the door and letting in the full light of day. I not only saw him, but I heard his spirit-voice, as I have heard it many times since. This is a fact: I saw, I heard, I know.

On another occasion, Mrs. French and I were alone, the shutters were closed and the room was darkened; but outside the sun was shining. A spirit whose voice I recognized, said:

> **"When I say 'now,' let Mrs. French stand, reach both her arms across the table, and you take hold of them firmly, regardless of what happens."** The voice soon said, **"Now."**

Mrs. French arose; I took both of her hands in mine, determined to hold them with great firmness, which I did, with senses keen in anticipation, but with no intimation of what was to happen. So firm was my hold on those hands that I knew, whatever happened, her hands could not aid in the demonstration. Soon the room was filled with the perfume of fresh flowers; one swished in the atmosphere and fell at my feet; my grip tightened on those frail hands. There was no movement of Mrs. French's body, but flowers came apparently from every direction, even from the ceiling, striking me on the head, face, chest, back and side, falling on the table and around us in great profusion. I immediately opened the door and hurriedly called others of my household to see the display. We found upon the table, chairs and carpet, upwards of one hundred pure white sweet peas, fresh, with dew sparkling in the petals. The stems had been twisted off. At a later time, I asked how such a demonstration, so at variance with physical laws, was possible. I also asked whence came the flowers? I was told that no law had been violated, but that physical laws which mankind has not yet discovered, had been used, that spirit people took sweet peas from a garden where they grew in too great abundance, changed their vibratory conditions, as we change water into steam, conveyed them in this state into the room, altered the vibration back again into its primary stage which restored the flowers to their original condition and color; then they threw them on and about me as I held Mrs. French's hands. They did this to show me their strength and to demonstrate a vibratory law. To this day I have kept some of those sweet peas given by those spirit people.

At other times when alone with Mrs. French, I have been told to take both her hands and to hold them firmly, during which time spirit-people have come in full physical form, stood beside me, and put their hands on my head. Their hands are warm and firm, but the touch is strange because they are in a state of intense vibration; they do not tremble or shake, but they seem to pulsate with a rapidity that I have not words to describe.

I can sit in this room with no one present but Mrs. French, one hand upon the table, her mouth upon the back of that hand, my other hand on top of her head, holding it firmly so as to prevent the possibility of her speaking or moving her lips, and hear the spirit-people telling of life as they find it in the land of silence, as it is called.

At the demand of science, at one time, I permitted Mrs. French to go under test conditions. They wanted to apply what is known as the "water-test," that is, filling Mrs. French's mouth with water, to see if spirit-people could speak while she so held the liquid. At my request she consented. A man of science was chosen to make the experiment. He came and I gave him the key to the room in the afternoon, so that he might prepare his own conditions. In the evening, this learned professor, Mrs. French, and I, without lighting the room, and without any knowledge on our part of what condition it was in, entered. Mrs. French was given a certain quantity of liquid which this man put into her mouth. I could hear her breathe with difficulty. A moment's silence, and then a voice came in the darkness, unusually loud and strong, saying:

> **"You see we can speak under the conditions you have made." I turned to the professor, asking: "Are you satisfied?" and he said, "I am." Then I said: "Remove the liquid; please measure it, and see if the amount expectorated is equal to the amount put in, and of the same color. I did not know the color or the amount. Upon examination, both were found intact. The test was evidential.**

This man declined to publish this fact, saying it was in advance of the times. He was afraid that science, so-called, would not accept his statement. In view of such conditions I made arrangements some four years ago, for Mrs. French to go to New York at the request of Dr. Isaac Funk and his associates. (See Chapter III., Ed.) She sat with him for eleven nights, the record of which is published in "The Psychic Riddle." Results similar to my own were obtained, and at a later time, Dr. Funk, at Rochester applied the water-test again, and spirit-voices spoke to him while Mrs. French's mouth was filled with liquid. Such conditions demonstrate: (a) that Mrs. French does not do the talking, for her organs of speech are not used; (b) that the voices are independent. By that I mean that spirits use their own vocal organs.

Such facts convince me that people I have known in the body continue to live when the physical has gone back to dust, that they have the same individuality, the same continuity of thought, and the same characteristic speech in the afterlife as this.

By such experiments it is proved to be a fact that life continues after death; that death is only a change of vibratory conditions; that the soul, mind, thought, by whatever name you choose to call this ego that thinks, reasons, and is, in no way changed, only its actions is governed by new laws controlling in the higher vibration of which they are a part. They are the same person as before; and, given the required conditions, can talk just as well as ever. This requires no deductive reasoning; it is a fact proved and by many accepted.

One in spirit-life said to me, in discussing this subject this day:

> **"You know because you ask, and fact and reason answer. It is so even now, that few truths reach the intelligence of men which are not bought in wrappers of superstition, tied with baffling unreality. All creeds, founded on the little ambitions of a sect of men seeking their own renown, are being swept aside, and the**

truth, naked and unafraid, founded on nature's laws, is coming to be understood.

"Nature does not hide her laws, but holds them subject to the call of men, asking only that man shall qualify himself and know how to use and apply them intelligently, when they are unfolded to him. Nature is no wiser, but is ever ready to give of her abundance."

When we meet to continue our investigations, a period of ten to twenty minutes elapses before spirit-people speak, during which time I feel as though some great power was in some indefinite way drawing upon my physical strength, at times almost to the point of pain; then the hush of expectancy; then the greeting, as in any drawing room, and quite as natural, as they come in one by one.

Working on the spirit-side of life, aiding this work, was originally a group of seven persons, who built up conditions every time we conducted experiments, the most important of which is the chemist, for he must know at once what conditions will harmonize, and what elements can be used and applied to different spirits to enable them to use their organs of speech so that their voice will reach our ears. We contribute, as I have said, physical vibrations, while spirit-people bring spiritual, that is a higher vibratory state, which the group manipulates. The condition under which we get these voices, is a utilization of both.

Certain of the spirit-group arrange these requisite conditions, while others direct the work.

So mighty is the force of human thought, and so delicate are the conditions of a spirit's body when it has taken on material in preparation for speech, that, by word of command or even by thought-projections, I can break down its conditions and prevent speech. This is why those who oppose this philosophy so often get negative results when they seek demonstration; by their mental attitude or thought-conditions, they make impossible the very thing they seek; they so intensify their thought-substance that spirit-people are not able to break into the conditions they make for the occasion.

Here is another piece of evidence which proves that the voices are not those of mortals. Spirit-people in speech with me, while using their organs of respiration, do not breath as we do. I have often heard a lecture twenty minutes in length, without a break, the voice rising and falling in inflection, speaking with great force and clearness but not drawing one breath in all that time. This is a physical impossibility for any mortal man.

Each voice has individuality. When a new spirit comes for the first time and takes on the condition of vocalization, there is often a similarity in tone quality, but this soon passes away, as they grow accustomed to speak, never change, and are easily recognized. Of such we never ask their names, for we know. There is no similarity of thought or words; these differ in different people in that world as in this.

The strength of the voices varies greatly; one of our group speaks with sufficient volume to fill easily a great auditorium, and his lectures ring through the whole house. Another whom I have in mind, always comes with great dignity and courtesy, is careful in speech and considerate; but his voice, while very distinct, has not great volume. The voice of another, who was very near to me in earth-life, is as clear, strong, and natural as in the days when we discussed this philosophy, or walked in the forest trying to understand and come in touch with the law of life; and we have since his going talked as much, and with as great freedom, as in the latter years before his going. There has been no subject of knowledge common to us both, that he ever hesitated to discuss in all its minutest details. This friendship of many years is continued without a break, and I enjoy his presence and our talks as I never did before.

One night, a voice of great volume and strength came out of the darkness, clothing thoughts with such speech as only one man has ever used, telling of life as he, who was one of the world's great agnostics, found it after death; of his life-work and duties there, and something of the environment of a spirit and the possibilities of progression, closing by saying,

"I am Mr. Gordon."

I said to him: "It is one of the rules, long in practice in our work, that when one comes as you have, teaching philosophy, identity shall be proved. Can you do this?"

> He said: **"I think that can be done without difficulty."** I replied: "Did you ever meet me?" He said: **"Yes."** "Where?" I asked. **"At the Niagara Hotel in your city."** "When was that?" He said: **"I don't now recall the year, but it was when I gave a lecture on Progress at the request of the Real Estate Men's Association."** "What was the date of the lecture?" He replied: **"I don't recall, but it was in**

> **the early nineties."** "Where was the meeting?" **"At the Music Hall, as I now recall."** "Do you remember who sat in the box at your left that evening?" **"My recollection is,"** he replied, **"that my wife and daughter did, with others."**

This was proof; it was all true. This is one of the ways adopted to prove identity; and this man stood the test to my entire satisfaction.

Hundreds, yea thousands, have come and talked with me, and to many whom I have invited to participate in the work, -thousands of different voices with different tones, different thoughts, different personalities, no two alike; and at times in different languages.

No spirit ever feels at liberty to come into our sessions without the invitation of the spirit-group or of myself any more than a stranger would come into my house for social purposes without an invitation. The same laws of privilege and hospitality which operate in the earth-life, prevail in the spirit-world.

CHAPTER 2
SPIRIT VOICES

Documented Spirit Conversations and Discourses Stenographically Recorded, Collected Materials and Séance Memoranda.

> "Read not to contradict and confute, nor to believe and take for granted, but to weigh and consider."
>
> –Bacon

Thought and Mind

There are certain expressions and sentences in our language which are, at present, substantially meaningless, because the mind is unable to grasp what it cannot analyze. That "thought is substance," and "mind is matter," mean but little to mortal man, notwithstanding his wonderful progress. Perhaps I can deal with this difficult proposition in no better way than to quote what spirit-people have told me concerning the question.

> **"Back in the past centuries, when the world of spirit had not its present development, there was little original inventive thought. Man built a shelter, killed his food, and fought his enemies, as any animal does. As the spirit-world progressed, and became more intelligent; as it obtained greater understanding, and grasped, with greater power, the life forces, or, in other words, more power of thought, and more ability to help mortal development, then, by**

reason of spirit-suggestion, acting through man's sub-conscious mind, he began to feel an awakening for something better, and the process of civilization began."

This statement emphasizes the fact that all life in every sphere ever has been, now is, and ever shall be, progressive; that there was a time in spirit-planes, as well as on this plane, when they did not possess the intelligence, comprehension and power that they do today, not nearly as much as they will in time to come.

Of what lies beyond the next, or first spirit-sphere, those who live there know but little. Knowledge is acquired only by effort, there, as here; and only as we comprehend the economy of natural law and mind power, do we progress.

Again this spirit said:

"Beyond and before everything is mind; that is, understanding. Mind is matter, as you use that term, with this difference; it is carried beyond the physical into a higher vibration. Let me illustrate in this way: Good thoughts have a higher and more rapid vibration than bad thoughts, and bring us into closer harmony with spirit-intelligences. There is no barrier to thought; it carries us to the uttermost parts of the earth; to the heights of perfect joy and to the depths of woe. The people of earth are just beginning to gain some knowledge of this force for good within themselves. Once let that fact be understood, and mortals will come nearer to understanding their destiny."

Another said:

"Mind is the aggregate of all thoughts. Mind is the universal thought. As a drop of water signifies but one infinitesimal part of the great ocean, so a thought is but one infinitesimal part of the great ocean of mind. Thought is creative energy, the essence of all things, and expresses itself in form. The vibratory energy of thought waves produce form, sound and color, though they are never perfectly expressed in the physical plane. Not until men have arisen out of the physical condition can they come to an appreciation and comprehension of matter so refined as to be known as mind. Thought belongs to the universal man; mind to the race universal."

Words are but symbols used to express thoughts. There is nothing in a word except that it conveys an impression or ideas to the mind. They are coined as new conditions arise. When Newton discovered the law of gravitation, he had difficulty in finding words to describe the fact, so new was the proposition. So it is with Metapsychics, that is the philosophy of life beyond the physical; this science is so new and so little is known on the subject, that words have not as yet been adopted that will allow of exact detail or comprehensive report.

I said to a spirit who in earth-life, was the foremost scientist of his time, "What is ether, and what is mind?" and he answered:

> **"Ether is simply atmosphere in more intense vibration than which surrounds the earth. Ether surrounds spirits unless they go into the earth-plane. Mind, I mean the thought, not the habitation of thought, when the earth-life is over, becomes the entire being. It is the only part in man that is of such vibration that it can enter in and progress to spirit-life. The brain is so constructed that there is an opening for spirit-force or suggestion; consequently, it proves that the entire mind is of such vibration that the spirit-force can reach it; otherwise suggestion would be impossible.**
>
> **"Mind is the essence of being, —the ego. It is material, but differing in vibration from the body. Spirit-force surrounds the flowers, teaching them how to grow and bloom, but they have no conscious original thought."**

And so we find matter rising higher and higher in vibratory action. First the earth, then water, then atmosphere, then ether, and finally mind, which is matter as much as the earth is matter, yet it directs and controls all substance in a lower vibratory condition.

One of my co-workers said:

> **"Be tempted to one extravagance only in this book of ours. Use every argument and all the forcefulness you can, to show what a little thing, a tiny span, the earth-life is. Real life begins when the heavy, material body is left behind, and the soul springs upward into the unlimited regions of thought-life. There all grows, learns, expands into perfect fullness of being until one becomes a perfectly developed spirit, able to blend with other spirits similarly developed and perfected. There is no beginning**

and no end, then, to the heights he can ascend; no joy that is unknown or untasted; no wonder of the universe of which he does not become a part. It is being, then, that state which cannot be defined to unthinking and incomprehensive minds. But try to grasp this idea, for it gives such an interest and zest to everyday life. Some day each shall be a part of the great force that makes all things work in unity. Before the force was so strong, there was not so much good working among men. They were cruel, barbarous and uncontrolled. Much has that mind-force, working silently but constantly, achieved in the past ages, and much more will it achieve, now that mankind has become receptive to our suggestion.

"Thought is the expression of mind; it is partly caused by spirit-suggestions through the subconscious mind, and partly an expression of oneself. Deeds are thoughts grown to maturity, and yet a thought unspoken or unlived, will exist through all the ages, as though expressed."

Another spirit speaking on this general subject has said:

"You all give off an aura, and if you knew the conditions emanating from some people, you would very quickly eject them from your home. In those whose lives are not strictly upright we find the aura very bad, mixed, cloudy, confused. The emanations of people of good health vary in shade from white, pale pink, to rose color. When the auras approach the dark colors, browns, greys, and blacks, we know that the person is wrong in some way. Now this aura is influenced by passions such as hate, envy, malice, evil speaking, anger, and when one sets out to do an injury to another, let me assure you that he injures himself far more than the other person."

I have been told that a clean, highly developed thought goes out into the ether with the appearance of a search light, starting from a central point and radiating through space. Once again, mind is matter, and thoughts are things, and so wonderfully active is the operation, that we are continually forming our mental creations in such refined substance.

With all our development, and it has been great, we are able to hear only a few of the sounds that vibrate in our atmosphere. With all our achievements we are unable to see motion except it be slow in movement and in physical garment. On this subject one said:

> **"We can also read the thoughts of another—conditions being favorable—as readily as you can gain a knowledge of a language not your own. Thoughts being motions of the mind, assume specific and definite forms, and when distinct in the mind, can be clearly perceived and understood by any spirit who is in sympathy with the mind in which they are generated."**

On turning once again to the lectures from the more advanced minds in the next expression of life, I find the following:

> **"Thought is a wonderful force and even we cannot grasp its magnitude, nor understand all its power. It is a living, vital thing. A thought born in your mind is for good or evil, a thing to be reckoned with again, when it will confront you face to face and claim you as its author. The best thoughts are those born of Nature in its beauty, rather than those that have had the touch of material hands. I would like to say something, too, about the beauty of pure thought, how it returns to one after earth-life, laden with sweetness and intensified tenfold. You cannot realize all each good, generous, noble thought will mean to you someday, even if it never grows into an act. Evil thoughts breed darkness and despair, cling to the soul, go with you into the afterlife, and become your close familiar friends. You are never rid of them a moment until you have taken them up one by one and lived them over again. The power of suffering for evil is increased on this side of the vale, just as joy is intensified beyond anything you can feel. Such joy you have from your good thoughts and deeds. A thought can have many branches, but the parent stem is planted deep in your own soul, and only your hand can remove it in the future. If it be good it will bear richer fruit each year. When you have traveled and especially enjoyed any scene, you have a picture of it in your spirit-home, just as books you own are found on the shelves. Music will fill the home of the sensitive, and so on indefinitely. This is the home of which spirits speak. It practically becomes your house. Your thoughts do not look to us like anything in a material sense. They are felt. They create an atmosphere that is like a cloud around you, and this condition is easily discernible by us and felt by sensitive spirits in the body. All thoughts are not**

> **necessarily known until the spirit himself is confronted by them. Then they stand out prominently to him. But even then, others may be only conscious of his character by the conditions he is forced to undergo before he can overcome the evil ones. We may know the thought when it is formed, and then, again, we may know it by the condition made in spirit-life. Thoughts are around the persons who create them, but they are not confined there, for they go as well to build the home in the spirit-world. While it is true that they are stored in millions of brain cells, they are also all about one, forming an aura. This is the influence one feels when he comes into the near presence of strong mentalities. Sometimes it is pleasant, often, not. This is the spiritual part of the thought. What is in the brain is more material, —of a consistency that is easier for man to use, if he desires to retain knowledge of any kind. These ideas are hard to put into words. They are subtle. There is a color, a note of music, a perfume, a spirit all in each close harmonious thought. A chord of music will cause the color vibration that belongs to it; the perfume that belongs to that same vibration can cause the same color, and the perfume can cause the harmonious thought. You can truthfully say that thoughts are different notes of sound."**

Dual Minds

It is now known that we have two minds as well as two bodies. The subconscious mind functions in the etheric brain of the inner body; the conscious mind functions in the physical brain of the outer body. The subconscious is the mind that survives dissolution, carrying the imprints made on it by the conscious mind, which does not survive, but which perishes with the physical body. The subconscious mind, the real mind, suggests to the conscious mind, although often the prompting of that still small voice is unheeded. Now the conscious mind is mortal; the subconscious is immortal.

It has been my privilege for many years to hear great lectures from learned philosophers and psychologists, long inhabitants of the next state, of which I have the stenographic reports. I quote from one of these lectures of the spirit psychologist:

> **"It has always seemed to us that the subject of mind, or minds, is one which your people have been little interested in. It is difficult**

to conceive of a more essential subject. I dare say, speaking conservatively, there are in your world few who know that they have such a thing as a subconscious mind. We do not care particularly for the term 'subconscious.' It is a misnomer and we object to the nomenclature, because this mind is not really subconscious; it is super-conscious.

"If mankind had an understanding of the importance of the relationship between the conscious and the subconscious minds, it would make a great difference in the courses men would lay out for themselves in earth life, as well as in their lives after the transition.

"Perhaps it is well to speak first of the conscious mind, which, to most people, is the only mind they have, that mind which makes or creates a cause, of which actions are the effect, that mind which controls the voluntary actions and the muscular contractions of the individual.

"Now then, the conscious mind is something else besides being a center of nerve impulses controlling the actions and movements of the body. It has a far greater relationship to the universe, to our fellowmen and to God. The mind is the dynamo that is constantly generating thought forms. These thought forms have shape, size and color, and potentialities appalling to those who understand clearly the functions of the conscious mind.

"These thoughts that emanate from the minds of mankind are at a fixed rate of vibration, going forth into the universe at the same rate as that of the mind which gave them their impetus. They are constantly impinging against the receptive minds of earth-people and also of disembodied people who are in what is known as the spirit world. They may be uplifting; they may be charitable, sympathetic, kindly; on the other hand they may be destructive, causing injury, exciting conditions which often results in actions sad and distressing indeed.

"The sub-conscious, or super-sensitive, mind, which so many people know not, although they possess it, is a fourth dimensional mind, or the mind of the astral body, contained within your three-dimensional, physical body. The sub-conscious mind, being fourth-dimensional, is subject to that unerring law of accuracy which is dominant in the fourth-dimensional or etheric plane. Therefore, the sub-conscious mind, because it is accurate, should dominate the conscious mind, which is likely to be inaccurate because it operates only in the third dimension and is subject to the desires of mankind, limited by environment and by all sorts of conditions.

"When man is sleeping, when he is tired, it is the subconscious mind which builds up the will-forces in the body, sees that everything functions smoothly, supervises the beating of the heart, regulates the respiratory functions, and makes it possible for you to exist.

"The subconscious mind is very much higher in vibration than the conscious or objective mind, the three-dimensional mind of the physical body. Now, then, it develops upon mankind to accelerate the vibrations of the conscious mind so that it may be in unison, or nearly so, with the vibrations of the subconscious mind, which alone survives.

"The subconscious mind is always right. From the subconscious mind comes the 'still small voice,' that thing which people know as the conscience. The conscience is a definite manifestation of the subconscious mind, trying to dictate to the conscious mind that it is in some way or other in error.

"The conscience is a manifestation of the subconscious mind, registering encouragement or protest on the conscious mind. The subconscious is always present. Sometimes—a great many times, I am sorry to say—it is dominated by the carnal, or conscious mind, but it is always there, ever active in its endeavor to lead mankind aright."

I had long known that we are here and now possess two bodies, but the suggestion that we also, here and now, have two minds was new. I did not accept it when made—it troubled me. I knew that spirit people were as prone to error as mortals, and I have ever rejected statements from that source, as from a physical source, that did not appeal to reason.

Troubled with the proposition, so new and original, I took the question up with Dr. David Hossack, whom I have already quoted. Dr. Hossack has been an inhabitant of the spirit world for more than a century, with him I have been in communication for thirty years and more, and whose statements I have ever found reliable. I asked him this question:

"Is it a fact that we possess two minds as well as two bodies, and that the conscious or material mind does not survive?"

This was his answer:

"As you have two bodies, the material and the spiritual, so you have two minds. The spirit mind is that which comes from the infinite, and is clothed with the material at conception. It is life-force, and cannot be destroyed. This etheric soul or mind is the force for good that is in each of us; it is in embryo during earth life, finding full development only in the spirit world.

"The material mind is the conscious mind. It functions through the direction of the spirit mind, unconsciously, of course, as the spirit mind, in the majority of men, enwrapped so closely with gross material folds that it is rarely discernible. However, the two are as separate and distinct as your two bodies.

"You do not take the material mind with you into this world, any more than you take the earth body. The conditions here are such that you could not bring either with you. Yet the soul is the mainspring and the compelling force of both bodies and both minds. The spirit mind is the only conscious mind. By that I mean that it is the only real, living, eternal Mind. As your earth progress goes on, this spirit mind is the life-force which you feel and know as the real part of your existence. Your conscious, earth mind is only the storeroom for the subconscious spirit mind to build on and grow within you.

"When you pass on, you take the wares from this storeroom with you, but earth consciousness is transitory and not real; only the inner richness is carried on and becomes part of you when, in dissolution, the two are finally separated."

The Spiritual, or Etheric Body

> "It is sown a natural body; it is raised a spiritual body; There is a natural body and there is a spiritual body."
>
> -1 CORINTHIANS 15: 44

Man's Etheric Body

The ancients thought that ether filled the sky, and was the home of the Gods. It was contended by Aristotle that it extended from the fixed stars down to the moon. Modern science has heretofore contended that all space is filled with a substance having rigidity and elasticity, with a density equal to our atmosphere at a height of about 210 miles—easily displaced by any moving mass—compared to an all-prevailing fluid or derivative of gases through which heat and light are constantly throbbing.

In "Modern View on Electricity," Sir Oliver Lodge, speaking the last word concerning ether, says,

> "It is one continuous substance filling all space; which can vibrate as light, which, under certain unknown conditions, can be modified or analyzed into positive and negative electricity; which can constitute matter; and can transmit, by continuity and not by impact, every action and reaction which matter is capable. This is the modern view of ether and its functions. The most solid substance in the world is not iron, is not lead, is not gold, is not any of the things that impress our sense as extremely dense. The most solid thing in existence is the very thing which for generations has been universally regarded as the lightest, the most imperceptible, the most utterly tenuous and evanescent beyond definition or computation; it is the ether. The ether is supposed to permeate everything, to be everywhere, to penetrate all objects, to extend throughout all space. The earth moves through it; the sun and all the stars have their being and their motion in and through the ether; it carries light and electricity and all forms of radiation. Nobody has ever seen it, or rendered it evident to touch or to any other sense. It escapes all efforts to feel it, to weigh it, to subject it to any kind of scientific experiment. It plays no part in mechanics. It neither adds to nor takes away from the width or substance of any known substance. We are assured by some of the highest authorities that

the ether is millions of times more dense than platinum, one of the most solid metals known."

(Sir Oliver Lodge (1851-1940): World famous mid 19th-century British physicist, author, lecturer, and fearless champion for survival of death.)

I am assured by those versed in the physics of the afterlife, with whom I have speech, that all life, down to the atom, and beyond, has etheric form; that every atom that makes up mass of rock; that every molecule of earth that covers the barren stone; that every grain of sand that forms the ocean shore; that every seed, and plant, and shrub, and tree; that every drop of water that flows in creeks, falls as rain, or constitutes the lakes and seas—all have etheric form.

Another, speaking on this matter said:

"It is the etheric body that sees, hears, feels, smells and tastes, evidenced by the fact that the physical body has none of the five senses when separated from the etheric. The ear, for instance, with its complicated chamber and auditory nerves, really hears through the etheric brain. Sever the nerves, destroy the tympanum, and you destroy the communication; put any of the very fine mechanism of the auditory chamber out of commission, and you either cannot hear at all, or at best, very imperfectly. Every concussion causes an ever widening circle in the atmosphere, that is, in the ether of the atmosphere, which at least reaches the auditory chamber, an ever widening circle in the atmosphere, that is, in the ether of the atmosphere, which at last reaches the auditory chamber, communicates with those fine nerves and with the brain. By that wonderful process we understand the difference between harmony and in-harmony, between sweet sounds and discords. Similarly, through a disturbance set up in the ether we understand language."

The Inner Spirit Body

"There is a natural body, and there is a spiritual body." Those words have fallen from the lips of priests, over the bodies of the so-called dead, for thousands of years, yet not a single minister who uttered them, nor one among the millions of mourners, who for centuries past heard them, ever formed any rational conception of what they meant—and for ages the world has been filled with sorrow.

I have seen spirit bodies materialize, have touched them and found them as the natural. I have heard them speak and tell over and over again that they had bodies, the same bodies as when they lived the earth life. Still I was not satisfied, and sought to know the character of the two, how they blended, how they worked as one, what natural law was involved, what happened in the dissolution process, why two were necessary, to the end that I might comprehend the fact, for until such knowledge was acquired I had only a very hazy idea, if any, of the situation.

As fast as I was able to comprehend the facts, they were given me, and lo and behold, like all natural laws, I found all simple.

I asked this question of Dr. David Hossack, who, as I stated before, has been in spirit life nearly a century:

"Is my understanding correct, that here and now we have, and possess, an inner etheric body, which, divested of its flesh garment, passes intact into the spirit world?"

In reply he said:

> **"There is an inner, etheric body, composed of minute particles, of such substance that it can, and does, pass into spirit life. Your outer bodies are too gross and material to effect the change. The inner body is but the mind, the thought, the soul of the person. It is in the semblance of the material body, but whether beautiful or ugly, strong or weak, depends upon the inner life of the person to whom belongs that particular spark of the great radiance called life, or God. Some there be who build a fair body, and some there be who come into this life with a body so misshapen and sickly it takes much effort to effect an upright, clean one. They all come with bodies naturally, as all things have minds, after one fashion or another; but the conditions of these bodies are very different. Naturally, the mind, being the reality of man, is that which lives on, —beautiful or disfigured by good or evil thoughts, as the case may be. The only comfort is that everyone has opportunity here to work out the change in himself, and sometimes those changes are very rapid."**

Another said:

"In earth life I gave all for wearing apparel; and when I reached the spirit world, I did not have rags enough to cover me, and the beauty of my form had vanished. I was misshapen and distorted. At first I could not understand that it was my spiritual body that was so deformed, for I had not given the spiritual part of me a thought while on earth. In fact, the earth was all in all for me, and I did not trouble myself to think of another life, deeming the time better spent in enjoying the things I knew I possessed. A spirit came and offered to clothe me, but no sooner did the garments touch my body than they were discolored. My progress has been slow, but after many years of suffering I have developed my spirit and restored its beauty, but it is different from what it was in the life below."

But evidence of all things spiritual must, of necessity, come from those who live there. Their condition is different, their laws are different, for they live in a world invisible to our eyes, and we cannot insist, if we could understand their life, on applying physical laws and methods. It is from spirit people that I have sought knowledge, and from them, and through years of investigation and research, I have come to know as a fact that "there is a natural body and there is a spiritual body."

God, Creation and Force

"Poise the cause in justice' equal scales,
Whose beam stands sure, whose rightful cause prevails."

William Shakespeare

Spiritual Conception of God

In order that one may have some idea of the character of my work, I give in this chapter a report, word for word, of a discourse given me on God. The spirit who gave it has aided me much by his teaching of the higher life. He said:

"I have some ability and am given much thought. I was interested in Metapsychic philosophy, and naturally I was in very bad repute

among those who thought they knew life and its problems. I could and did receive inspired writings, but they were destroyed after my death by a sister. I knew something of spiritual law, and I practiced it to the best of my ability. I appreciated the need of helping others. This led me to establish a harbor for the sick. (Heriot Hospital, Edinburgh.) Someone sent me the thought that I was needed here, —I do not know who it was, but it was my desire to be with you. I am interested in your work, because my own life was so much given to this thought. I did not have much enlightenment save from phenomena, but it was enough to make me ready for the change. Yet I was dazed at first, it was all so beautiful. I found a dear younger sister waiting for me, and together we have climbed to great heights.

"Progression is unlimited. It stretches away into the vast future. One may climb and soar, but never reach the end of all that can be done to make oneself a perfect being. I understand that there are seven spheres. I am in the Fourth, but the last is without limit. Each plane is more ideally beautiful than the preceding; each, harder to tell about to earth's ears. I cannot describe the wonderful sounds we call music; they are so rich, so harmonious; they find an echo in the deepest places of the heart; they create beautiful thoughts, and help one's development in every way.

"The fields are blazing with posies, and filled with songbirds of brilliant plumage. Everything the heart or eye can desire is there, only enhanced in beauty beyond our comprehension, and as we pass from plane to plane we are always astounded. It becomes sublime. When one is away from the earth-plane there is no more mixing with the lower classes, except as your work takes you among them when they need help; but you live among your own kind and often meet them as neighbors through many planes, if your progression is about the same.

"In coming back to you we pass through all the planes below us, taking on their different conditions as we come, taking on a little more material in each one. I can explain it only in this way, although, of course, it is not material, a little less spiritual would be a more correct expression. It is not difficult to come back, but it is a little strange. To go into the lower spheres seems like taking a plunge into muddy water. As a rule, each plane helps those directly below it, except in special cases like this. I think many of your friends have not progressed as far as I have, and I was sent for because it was thought that I could explain further. Those in the lower plane have only to come near, for that is the earth-plane. You are on the material plane, which is lower still, and does not count among the spirit ones. Our home may be said to be space and what thought makes it. We simply create the different conditions about us by thought. A spirit in the earth-condition, can, by his better thought, change the conditions that exist where he is, and be able to see different good spirits about him.

"I would give this message to the world: Be clean, faithful, and strong, and your progression here will be rapid. I would add to this: Be tender of the weak, and, even if you understand nothing of the future life, your progress will be good. You ask me who and what is God? I answer, God is universal good. I mean the spirit of good that is in every man's heart, tho' it is sometimes covered with dust and dirt. I said universal, because I know it is there. Sometimes it will grow and blossom. There will come a time when man will know he is a part of the great scheme of the universe, and will realize that this scheme is good. More of God will come into his heart, the dust will scatter and the bud will grow. God is the life, the spirit entity of each man, all the better part of him. God is the spirit that permeates all the best in man and matter. The word 'God' is used by us. It is the thought-term of good. The Christian Savior was simply a type such as all religions have, —a symbol of a perfect man. Each one should lead a good life, the best his conception suggests; then he will know that good is a blessing, more lasting than riches and renown. One cannot talk to the Church, my friend, but to individuals, and through them hope to reach the Church itself. Through the shepherd, you reach the flock. The change is very disappointing to many. They expect to find something very different, and cannot make up their minds that they are not to throw all their burdens upon someone else. As I have said, when people have been conscientiously good, they are very easily taken into their right place. Sometimes they are stubborn for a while, but it all comes right in time.

> **"The best any can do is to try to make the world realize that the best in everything is most desirable, and that everything filled with good is best and lives on when evil is found despicable. One is happy when good, fearful and miserable when bad. Nature is God, is always good, always smiling even in her storms. Nature is but fulfilling her promise of future plenty, as a mother goes through the storm of childbirth, that she may replenish the earth. Be not wiser than Nature. Follow her as closely as you can. Nature is natural in all her changes. The God-spirit is breathing through every fold of the rose, every leaf and ear of corn. Let the sunshine pour into your heart, and be generous, natural, and abundant with your goodwill and cheerfulness. The rains will come when they are timed. They will replenish the green of the harvest and make it richer. The storms of life may beat upon you, but you will find they only break down the dead branches and you will be more straight and fair for their passing. God is in all this, and if you but open your heart and let into it all the good there is, you will find peace and exaltation. I will come again. Good night."**

This is what is now coming to me from a little beginning, and I give these words to you as I received them, unaltered and unchanged.

Origin of Man

The subject next in importance to the future condition or state is the origin of the spirit or soul of man. Darwin, Huxley, and many other great naturalists, biologists, and scholars, have reasoned and speculated on this theme with great force and logic. They do not claim to be authoritative, and they offer to the expectant world no definite, tangible facts. All is theory.

A spirit speaking from the higher state has said:

> **"When matter, according to natural law, becomes receptive, it is impregnated with this life-force of the universe, and with the help of material nature develops a soul. This overpowering spirit-force, so strong and harmonious with Nature, is able to enter into the seed and give the power to live. It is like the touch of a hand that starts a machine into motion. The great spirit of life, called God, is the match to light the fire. Material must be laid ready,**

for spirit cannot create in earth planes. It is not reincarnation, because individual spirit does not enter. Only the touch that generates life in the material seed is given."

The spirit of man comes from the Sphere of God, or Universal Good, and it returns sometime, enriched and glorified, through the spheres and planes of progression.

Creation

Though we talk freely, when all conditions are at their best, with men and women after they have passed through the change called death, though we find that they retain consciousness and individuality, and are told much of their occupation and environment, many problems still remain. The spirits do not solve them, because they know little more of the solution than we do. They, like mortals, know what they have been taught only.

One who has worked with the American branch of the Society for Psychical Research and its great thinkers, who has himself made this thought the study of a life-time, read some of these chapters, and asked me pertinent questions, which I submitted to spirit-intelligences. In answering, I use the words given me by spirits as are included within marks of quotation.

What of Creation?

"The beginning of things was brought about long before this world existed. The universe was in a chaotic state for many centuries, while this solar system was gradually forming and becoming perfected. The great forces were very slowly evolved. The original propelling force came from a mere atom of good, that permeated seething, massing material. This held the tiny element of upliftment. Very slowly light came where there was darkness. Worlds were gradually fashioned. Finally, life began to take on form, —first in vegetable; second, in the lower animal; third, in man. All these simply came from an element of progress, impossible to understand or resist."

What of the personality of God?

> **"We have tried to explain the personality of God to you before. We have said that we do not know absolutely. Many spirits think that God has personality; others, that God is but the combined souls of men, risen to the sublime height that makes them one with the universe. Spirits, just as mind on earth, form ideas from experience. I, myself, do not think there is a God other than this great united force of good."**

I cannot conceive of a man-God, with personality. The universe is so vast, and this earth and all thereon so small in comparison, that I cannot understand how such a conception could be possible. But, comprehending in some little way the power of one man's mind over matter, I can appreciate the power and force of all minds in the universe working in perfect harmony. I can see God as a principle working universal good. I do not know what God is beyond what is told me. I cannot grasp the infinite; neither can spirits, until they become one with it.

What of the Christian Savior?

> **"Christ was a wonderfully spiritual being. His communion with spirits was unlimited and he lived His life in an exalted state, which made Him seem different from other men—that is, of course, believing his life was not a mere legend. If He did live, He could, since He was so spiritual, have risen rapidly to the highest sphere and mingled with those other souls—exalted through gradual purification, —and so fulfilled His inspired promises to mankind. From time to time you have such unusual spirits among men. Religions have been evolved from their lives, all tending to uplift men. Christ was the highest type that has come to us, and the influence for good in the story of His life is still unlimited."**

Why, then, is there conflict between spirit revelations?

Why ask a spirit to tell us now that which he, himself may not learn for a thousand years? Spirits do not know what is beyond them any more than we know what is beyond us. If life is endless progression, how can they? From actually living in the next spheres, they form opinions, based on such information as they have obtained, just as we do on economic questions. Those ideas may be honest, but may differ in conclusions.

I have positive knowledge.

Force is Life! A Mystery Difficult to Comprehend

> **"Force, wherever found or however expressed, is life."**

These words fell from the lips of a profound spirit psychologist who was talking with me many years ago. I have ever since been trying to comprehend them, but so tremendous is their import that I have not made great headway. I can appreciate that there is force in all matter, and that life is in all substances. What would keep the atoms in touch with each other unless it were the force of attraction? Can we imagine force without matter, or matter without force? Force must be attached to something. We cannot conceive of life in any form except expressed in matter, for we understand that life in every form is governed by law.

Again, there can be no destruction of force. If it disappears in one form, it appears in another form.

Another, speaking on this matter said:

> **"There is no limit to space. Time is nothing in the universe. All creation is united, but erected by multitudes of individual atoms, the physical builders of the universe.**
>
> **There are three physical laws in matter: repulsion, which tears down; attraction, which builds up; and arrangement, which produces form. All life, within a prescribed limit, is destined to be torn down, but all life that passes through the tearing-down limit is destined to continue forever."**

"Where is the line of demarcation in individual survival and non-survival?" I asked a learned Etherian. He answered:

> **"Every atom that makes up your globe has life-force and personality, but it is only when that life-force has progressed according to Nature's laws, until the individual atom is clothed with material finer than earth substance, that it will have continuity. All life-force below that vibration will reform, to produce, clothe and protect man, the highest expression of life on**

your earth. All Nature is working to this end. All life-force which functions on your earth in a flesh garment survives."

I then asked:

"If you have within our cosmos a part of that living God-force, so that ultimately we shall become a part of that directive force, are we here and now in reality mortal "Gods?"

He replied:

"Embryo Gods! But in the end all will work as one, creating new worlds and peopling them, so that the infinite creative life-force may be increased. Such is our understanding. Nature can no more stand still than the individual. If it did stand still it would begin to decay, for stagnation means dissolution. New stars and constellations are being formed from time to time, as your astronomers know, which ultimately will become peopled, for progress extends throughout the universe.

"The minds of all who in ages past have inhabited your earth are even now journeying back to the source from which they came, and will function ultimately in and with that infinite creative force. Destiny is really beyond our comprehension as yet, but the privilege that is ours and yours we should ever have in mind, so that we may make ourselves able to develop to the utmost, wherever we are.

"Force, then, as you use that term, is the evidence of life as it functions physically. In fact, force and life are one and the same. All life-force is intelligence and dominating good. The elements are made up of all the right influences, motives, and deeds of all the spirits of eternity. This force grows as the spirit-force is increased, and that force is increased continually by atoms of this force being brought into earth-life through natural conceptions. This is necessary that the cycle may constantly expand, one within another, an endless chain, the greater cycle being that outside an enveloping lesser cycle."

The Drama of Death/Leaving the Physical World

"And he showed me a pure river of water of life clear as crystal."

-REVELATION. XXIII

The First Condition

The first step in progression is so earth-like it is at first difficult of comprehension. We have been so long taught that the death change is so marvelous, a spirit is reluctant to accept the simple situation. It has been compared to the going from one room into another. While surroundings are changed they are similar; like, yet unlike; but the thought and individuality are in no-wise altered. These are identical; the mode of expression and the touch only are different. This is not what is ordinarily expected, therefore it is oftentimes reluctantly accepted.

I have had many descriptions of life and conditions from those in the next world, among them the following:

"I have no recollection of my transition. I awoke and saw the smiling face of Grandmother. It seemed natural, and was intensely real. I had in my illness no thought of dying, so that it did not occur to me at first that she had long before made the change known as death. I had been very fond of her. She met me with words of tenderness and love, and gradually explained just what had happened.

"I will not speak of the shock it was to me to witness the grief of my parents. I wished to get up from my bed; with the desire, I was out of it and felt loving arms about me, heard joyous words of welcome, and behold, I was clothed with soft white raiment—this without volition of my own. I was taken to her home, a cottage surrounded with wall and garden where flowers grew in abundance. There I found, in his young manhood, a brother who had passed on in infancy.

"I had much to learn, but there were many to help. I marveled at what could be done by thought. The home and its environment were thought creations, and in a little time, by concentrating

> **my thought and visualizing things desired, they took form and appeared, seemingly out of the invisible, but to me tangible and real. Thus I furnished my room, and hung on the walls thought pictures of those I love.**
>
> **"But do not imagine we have any magic wand that will enable us to fashion everything desired. We have our limitations, the same as you do. I have now just such a home as is suitable to my condition, but by work I can change, improve, and beautify it. Some people who, in earth life, lived in palaces, now live in hovels, under conditions most deplorable.**
>
> **"Until now I never knew what it was to be absolutely well. A vitality is within me I had never before known. I feel no weariness with the work I am doing. Another condition that impressed me was that all time is now, and all distance annihilated. We live in the present always, and if we desire to enter another condition within our zone, or go to a place on your plane, we concentrate our thoughts, and we are there. This is to me, even yet, most marvelous.**
>
> **"You ask of my friends here. The most wonderful thing about this life is the way harmonious spirits get together. The communion of souls spoken of in the Bible is a literal phase of life here. It is the finest and most satisfactory companionship I have known, and so enduring. You just seem a part of them and they of you, for the law of harmony holds you together and makes a perfect union. There is nothing physical about it, of course; it is finer than any physical thrill you have ever known. One feels so contented with this perfect understanding and mingling together. I do not seem to get lonely anymore. I am busy and interested; life on your plane seems like a dream, and now the only time I have really lived."**

"What of your occupation and work?" I asked this spirit, who left this world in the dawn of young womanhood, and whom it was my privilege to know. She replied:

> **"There seems no end of things to do. There are many crippled children here who have never walked, and I have been impressing them with the thought that they are no longer crippled. We have no bodily imperfections, you know, and I am teaching**

them little dance-steps, and observing their joy as they realize that they can use their legs. I am also going to classes in higher ethics, to understand the way motives and thoughts are power for good or evil. The mind is so powerful, and one's thought react through eternity. The minds of many people are really deplorable. The days fly, and I am very active. The forces are such that one has to work and do something all the time, and comes the satisfaction of accomplishing things. I find more and more congenial people. Life is free and lively, with no restriction in space, time, or energy. If we want to do some particular thing, we seem to have all the energy imaginable to put it through, and we get so much out of it.

"There are those who are constantly influencing people in earth life. I am intensely interested in their work, although I never believed much in it when I was with you. But now I can see the results of wrong thought and I find I can at times prevent a little, and it is interesting to do that. I am going to make a big change in my life here very soon. I mean that I am going to progress a little further; so I am doing more to express myself. That is the great joy of being here. When you get to the stage of self expression, you feel the great thrill of creation, because you are creating yourself and becoming one with the great Power, instead of being moved by higher laws. I do not mean that we are not governed by higher laws. We all are so governed, but progress is an expression of the force of creation, so that when you advance, you feel that you belong to the higher forces and working with them."

A Soul's Awakening

Experiences and Surroundings Described.

"First of all—I awakened free from pain, care, and toil; no grief, no cold or heat, no thirst or hunger; and above all, the pleasure of being reunited with those I love. Tender arms enfolded me, and I heard the tones of well-remembered friends, long lost, almost forgotten, whispering words of welcome. I gazed around and saw a brilliant, happy circle of loved and loving friends, companions and kindred, beckoning. No more parting, no more death, no more sadness.

"I saw white, spirit cities, long bright roads, embowered in groves and waving trees, and outstretched flowery plains, all full of lovely, happy, busy people, radiant with joy and life. Such was my awakening; such the rest my tired spirit encountered.

"It is only when I return to the earth-plane, and come in contact with grief and sorrow, that I take on earth conditions. I feel no sense of weight. I sped like the lightning's flash through space, on the buoyant waves of ether; I see the dull round globe, at times, far, far below, with its canopy of clouds, and mankind, insect-like, swarming upon the surface. I look up through happy tears to the heavens, so dim to earth, but so gorgeously bright to me.

"Vain would be the effort to speak of things and scenes, modes of life, for which earth has no language or parallel. Some few conditions of this better land of ours I may describe in human speech; more we are not allowed to give, lest it tempt many to end earth life, with work undone.

"Our home is the place where our loved ones cluster, to which our divergent wanderings tend back again. Home is the place where all our tastes find expression, where one may rest, grow, and exchange glad greetings with all he seeks or loves—a place to think in, until we grow ready for another advance. Every spirit has a home, a center of love, rest, and ingathering of new powers and forces—a place where all one has desired, most wished or longed for, takes shape and becomes embodied in the soul's surroundings.

"Sometimes a spirit gravitates as mine did, to some lonely, church-like hall, a quiet place of inner rest and contemplation, where the past resolves itself into shadowy pictures which come and go, mapping out the minutest event, thought, or word of past earthly life. I saw that ineffaceable record, which every soul must read again and again, as the past returned with its appropriate judgment.

> "Many events for which, at the time of their occurrence, I felt regret, I found as inevitable results of previous acts, without which my life would have been incomplete. Deeds and actions on which I had prided myself now showed the littleness from which they sprang; sorrows, which had wrung my spirit, appeared as blessings; and thoughts which I had once lamented, I find to have been inevitable effects. I saw myself to be, as it were, a chemical compound, made up of what I have been, or what I had done, said or thought.
>
> "All things appeared in judgment, and, stranger yet, all that I had and all that I possessed, enjoyed, or saw, the very air I breathed, was tinctured by myself; so that I saw, felt, heard, and enjoyed only as my inner nature colored my surroundings. All things are real around me, but my capacity to know and use them has sprung from my inner self.
>
> "In our land, ideas are all incarnate realities and living things. Nothing is lost in the universe. All that ever has been, can be, or shall be, is garnered up in the ever-present laboratory of being. It is a glorious privilege to roam throughout the endless corridors of time, and still to find an eternity in which to progress."

The Death Change

What happens at death? What are one's sensations, and what meets the vision on awakening? This has been described thousands of times, and I quote from my records something of what I have been told on the important subject:

> "It is a privilege to tell you of my transition. The last physical sensation that I recall was one of falling, but I had no fear—it seemed so natural. At the same time I heard voices speaking words of encouragement, voices that I recognized as those of loved ones that I thought dead. For a time I had no recollection. Then I awoke in this spirit sphere, and never will I forget the joy that was mine. I found myself, saw my body, which appeared as usual, except lighter and more ethereal. I was resting on a couch in a beautiful room filled with flowers. I looked through a window and saw the

landscape, bathed in rose-colored light. There was a quiet that was impressive, then music, the harmonious vibration of which seemed to rise and fall softly. Then one appeared, and, though she spoke no words, I seemed to understand and answered. In this thought language she told me that she had been my guardian while in the old body, and now that I had been released she would take me over the home that I had in my life been building.

"She said: This room so beautiful is the result of your self-denial and the happiness you brought to others, but there are others not so pleasing;' and we passed into another that was dark and filled with rubbish; the air was heavy. This,' my guide said, 'was built through my selfishness.' Then to another, a little better lighted. I was told that every effort to do better created something brighter. Then into the garden where, among beautiful flowers, grew obnoxious weeds, the result of spiritual idleness. The house must all be made beautiful,' she said, 'the weeds of idleness uprooted; and this can be done by yourself, through work in the lower planes, by helping others."

My father's experience he described to me as follows:

"You will recall the day of my dissolution. I had been in poor health for some months. That morning the air was so soft and warm, and the sun so bright, I wanted to be out in it, so I took my horse and buggy and started for a village about seven miles distant. As I drove along, a weakness seemed to come upon me and I partially reclined upon the seat. Even then, though seventy-six years of age, I had no thought that my passing was near. As I arrived at the house where I was going, the sensation of weakness increased, but I was able to walk in unaided and sat in a chair. The faintness increased, and, raising my eyes, I saw your mother standing in the room, smiling. Startled, I arose to my feet, and my last earthly sensation was falling—and, as I now know, I did pitch forward on my face. I do not recall striking the floor, or pain in my death change. When the separation came, I was like one in sleep. The next I recall was awakening in the same room, with the leader of your spirit group holding my hand, helping me up. I had heard his wonderful voice many times when I was privileged to come into your work, but it took me some little time to realize

what happened to me. I saw my body on the floor. This startled me, for the body I then had was to my sight and touch identical with the one lying so quiet. I saw people hurrying, and heard the anxious talk, not yet comprehending my separation from the physical body. I turned to your old friend, and mine, and asked him what had happened. He answered:

"Have you not been told when you talked with us in your son's home, that death was the separation of the inner from the outward body?'

"I recall that statement,' I replied, 'but I never comprehended it.'

"You have just made that change,' he said; "you are now an inhabitant of the spirit world and one of us."

"I was deeply impressed with what he said, but dazed. I could not realize that the something called death was behind me and that in me there had been no change, for I was the same in appearance and thought as before. Then memory quickened, and I commenced to think of what it meant. I could not think clearly, and my guide said, 'Come with me for a little time and rest, and all will be well with you.' I went with him, and those I saw and what I was I will tell you another time."

This is another's description.

"I remember seeing about me those that had been dead for a long time. This impressed me greatly, but I did not realize it fully. Then I felt a peculiar sensation all through my body. Then I seemed to rise up out of my body and come down quietly on the floor.

"I was in the same room, but there seemed to be two of me, one on the bed and one beside the bed. All about were my family in deep grief, why I could not tell, for my great pain was gone and I felt much better. Some of those whom I recognized as persons who had died, asked me to go, and with that thought I was outside and could apparently walk on air. My next thought was that it was a dream and that I would awake and feel again the terrible pain. I was gently told what had happened, and I felt that God had been

unjust to take me when I had so much to do, and when I was so needed by my family. I was not satisfied with the place I was in. About me there was a fog, and I started to walk out of it, but the farther I walked the more dense it got, and I became discouraged and sat down by the wayside in deep grief. I had ever tried the very best for those dependent on me. Where was my reward? Then some one approached, came as it were out of the fog, and I told him of my life work and complained of the condition I was in, and questioned the justice of it. He replied, "Yours was a selfish love; you worked for self. You should have made others happy as well as your own."

"He promised to help me in my great trouble, if I would help myself. Together we have worked, and now all is well; it is light and glorious. But that first awakening was not all that could be desired. My greatest disappointment after my awakening was when I returned to my old home, for I discovered that none could see or feel me and all grieved for me as one dead, and their sorrow held me. I wept with them, and could not get away, until time healed their sorrow."

How terrible it is that the world that has made so much progress in many things knows little of this greatest change, and the little it does know has almost been forced upon it by a few that know this truth and have the courage to stand for it.

These descriptions, as I review what I have written, do not give a fair idea of an average death change, and looking through my records I find another more normal:

"I left the physical world rich. I had little money, but day by day, during a fairly long life, by some act I made others happier, and so spiritualized and uplifted my spirit. Such was my only religion.

"When the separation approached, though I had no actual knowledge of what was to come, I had no fear. I had been very sick, felt greatly exhausted, and longed for rest. I realized the presence of my family and their grief. There came to my senses harmonious vibrations that sounded afar off, like string and reed instruments played by master hands. It seemed to approach and then recede, and was lost. It soothed and comforted me. Then I realized that

others were in the room. I could not see their faces distinctly, and wondered at strangers coming in at such a time. Some one spoke, and, rousing up, I saw more clearly and recognized many of my friends whom I had thought dead.

"I was not startled or frightened—it was all so natural. They greeted me cordially and asked me to go with them. Without effort, other than desire, I arose and joined them and went with them, for the moment forgetting the grief of my family. I seemed to travel without effort. Then I met a great company of men and women with radiant faces, clothed in white and blending colors. Their greeting was one of joyous welcome, and happiness was in everything. It was like meeting old friends that had been gone for a time; it was simply glorious and so intense that for a time I gave no thought to the tremendous import of it all. Then I looked about. There was harmony in everything. I was in a new country. About me I saw great variety of landscape, most picturesque mountain ranges, valleys, rivers, lakes, forests, and the corresponding vegetable life of all that I had known. It was suggested that I go to a rest house, where my strength would be restored. I did and seemed to fall into a deep sleep almost immediately. After a time I awoke, when some one whom I knew and loved said, 'Come with me now and view your inheritance.' I went, and the glory of it was, and is, beyond my power of description.

"I should like the privilege some time to tell the world of the beauty in which I live, and the pleasure I find in the work allotted to me. This plane, and all planes, I am told, is governed by law—Nature's law, the same as yours—and it is the privilege and duty of everyone to develop the spirit by study and helping others. There is so much I should like to say of my return to my family, but, as I am asked only to describe my spirit passage, I will leave that and tell you more concerning the joy of the spirit at some more opportune time."

There are those in the next life who have qualified for, and are assigned to, the reception department, whose duty it is to solace and comfort such as are grief-stricken because of the sudden severing of social ties, as it seems to those taken suddenly out of the mortal. This is a description:

"I am here to describe as well as I can the actual scenes over here, as the new born spirits, divested of their physical bodies, come over. They come to us, not one or two or three, but in crowds, by thousands and more, some not awakened to consciousness, some just waking, some fully conscious. Few realize for some time that they have passed the portal you call death, but a realization comes and they understand, their thoughts are of their strongest ties.

"What a commotion of feeling one hears! The same intense feelings exist when out of the old body as when in the physical, and those feelings are just as discernible to spirit sensation as before, only the mode of expression and reception is changed.

"As I was feeling my soul leaving the physical sheath, I heard mysterious chords of rhythmic melody rising and falling like distant waves of the sea. A voice said in thrilling gentleness:

'My child, pass from vision into luminous light, from night to day, from death to life.'

"Then a light beating slowly passed away from about me and to my utter amazement I found myself resting at a place quite free and transcendent with divine light. A deep and gentle sound vibrating through the etherial firmament filled me with joy and happiness, and nothing was perceptible to me except this vibration of the sound. I felt that I must wait till a divine messenger came to guide me into the regions yet unseen. The atmosphere of awe and reverence that swept over me for the moment gradually paled away and, rising as I thought, I walked through the darkness which then encompassed me. As I did this, my other hand was suddenly caught by some one in a warm and eager clasp and I was guided along with an infinitely gentle but commanding touch, which I had no hesitation in obeying. Step by step I walked with a strange sense of happy reliance on my companion and guide. Darkness and distance had no misgivings for me. And as I went onward with my hand yet held in that masterful but tender grasp, my thoughts became, as it were, suddenly cleared into a light of full understanding of the celestial world and its joy. And so I went on and on, caring little how long the journey might be and even eagerly wishing that it might continue, when presently a faint

> light began to peer through darkness, first blue and grey, then white, and then rose. The light, so sublimely luminous, gradually condensed into matter, and in a moment a celestial being of beauty, richly wrapped up in pure white and silken robes, stood before me. After the thrilling sensation, caused by this sudden manifestation, had given a little way for courage and hope, I beheld the same figure transforming into an almost manly and commanding attitude, with radiant face and brilliant eyes now turned towards me. It asked, in a gentle but firm tone, whether I would like to remain there in the ethereal world and enjoy the pleasure stored up for me as a requital for my past life on the earth plane. Overwhelmed with awe and respect, I could give no answer. Seeing me thus puzzled, my guide placed his right hand upon my forehead and a gentle massage filled me with strength and fresh energy.
>
> "I became bold and courageous, looked my visitor in the eyes, and knelt before him. He lifted me up gently and said I could for a time remain in those ethereal regions where all was pleasure and happiness. He said the place I was then in was the destination of those who spend their lives and energy on earth for the sake of their fellow-creatures, people who do great deeds for the uplift of the oppressed and harassed, —the abode of people who showed equal compassion to both men and beasts. This was my welcome, such my second birth. This was my greeting when I crossed the frontiers of the After Life."

We are only tenants in this house of the body for a limited time, and when it becomes unfit for habitation, through disease or accident, we move out, we separate from it, and the material body, that cannot hold its force without nourishment, decays and mingles with the earth from which it was borrowed. So far as I know, no man has ever attempted to describe the final separation of the spirit from the body, in the change called Death. Indeed, such a description from this material plane is impossible. With the ability to talk with those beyond, I have been able to obtain descriptions of the separation of the spirit from this temporary home. Not long ago an eminent judge, about six o'clock one evening, while at work, passed away. At nine o'clock the same night he was brought to me in his spirit body and I talked with him with the same freedom and satisfaction as I had only a few days before. I asked the one who brought him how this came about:

> **"I met a friend this afternoon and he told me that the judge was coming, and suggested that we go down and witness the separation. We did so, and brought him here that he might the more quickly appreciate his condition."**

Among the stenographic notes taken eight years ago, I find the following description of a spirit-passage, given by a spirit who with his company of spirit-workers aids the great change to the afterlife:

> **"But a few hours ago we were called to help in the separation of the spirit from the body. Lying before us was a young woman. When we say 'young, we mean in maturity. Bodily pain and sickness had been hers, and now dissolution was taking place. The one who should have given her words of encouragement and help was on his knees praying to the God of mercy to give her strength to pass through the terrors of death. About her on every side were weeping friends. She knew they were grieving because she was leaving the body and it made the passage darker and harder. The first bodily chill touched the feet. Slowly, little by little, it was creeping upward until it reached the knees. A light began to rise, a clouded substance, gradually increasing in size. Closer approached the loved ones who had gone before. They were waiting and watching and giving her strength, that she should not feel herself alone and that she should not think all was darkness and terror. We saw her face brighten, her lips part in a smile. She saw us close about her. Her hand raised slowly and she whispered, "They are coming. I see them all. They are waiting for me. "The light from the body rose higher, slowly creeping up, just as a white fleecy cloud settles before a storm over the earth. She did not appreciate that a change was coming over her, she only realized that friends were standing near. She did see the weeping ones as it grew brighter. She heard a faint echo, as of music, a song of gladness coming to her in this cloud of change. It took definite form just above her. The brain weakened, the eyes drooped, she slept with the loving voices speaking. The music was not heard by mortals."**

"The spirit was taken out, was held just above the body, with gentle hands, and then she met the loving friends. Her eyelids were lifted, she saw one who had waited for her, whose every thought was in unison with her own. How was it that she, just released from the body, could see all this? Because she had lived a life according to her light and understanding. She will not have to go back to earth and take up a consciousness that would have been compulsory had her life been one of lying and deceit. When she touched the hand of the mother who had gone ahead, she realized that there was a condition between them, but that little by little it would be removed and that she would enter into the home that awaits her.

"She wept, not as you weep, but through happiness, through joy in the fact that she had met the mother-love, that they had come together again where all the conditions of earth are swept aside. She saw herself as she is and as she was. She realized that at times in the earth-life she was human. She regretted and asked her soul to forgive. As she advances farther into this realm of thought, into this new condition, into this perfect life, she will see no darkness, and all shall be well."

By the destruction of matter, life multiplies. Through decay of material, the life force increases. Through separation the spirit is liberated. Released from the confines of an earthly body, it finds greater scope, more opportunities, better advantages, continual progression. This spirit passage is natural. It comes to all living things. Every step on growing grasses crushes life into life, separates it and forces it from its temporary abode, from the material covering it has gathered. Through some seeming destruction vegetable life, like human life, is liberated. The journey of evolution is hastened, and the perfect life is more quickly experienced.

An Awakening

When the journey is done and the night is passed, all must awake and open eyes in another world. What happens and what thoughts speed with them through the brain? I asked a spirit, well known in this life, to describe the awakening. This was his answer:

"It is usually hard for a spirit to get its breath in the different atmosphere; the earth conditions cling to it; this it must shake off and it must then adjust itself to the new surroundings. So the first condition is purely physical, or rather, mental. A spirit feels this change, yet does not understand why it is different. It gasps and struggles. This is soon over and forgotten. Then it is taken to a home it has built—on it's own—and left to realize things a little. Some spirits are in a condition that admit of immediate help and counsel, but others are dazed and must have quiet and time in which to be alone. When a spirit is able to comprehend, its past life comes before it like a panorama. The good thoughts and their results are arranged on the one side; the evil thoughts and their results, on the other. Then begins heaven and hell. The poor soul realizes, perhaps for the first time, how much evil he has wrought, and his spirit is in torment, for he thinks there is no reparation. When this phase of his punishment is over, he is shown how, by influencing thought in earth-life, he may wipe out the consequences of each sin. Then comes peace from the torture of remorse. I am speaking of the average man, with the average conscience. Some there are who have led lives that need very little of this punishment. Others must wallow for a long time in the mire of their own sad sins, —too vile or too timid to find a way out.

"There is another phase. One who has strong earth ties will be held by them, so that spirit-friends cannot get it away at first. The ties may be of different kinds, —family, business, or simply selfish, animal ones; in any such case progression is slower. One who is thoroughly bad, who is surrounded by his own sin, sees nothing else.

"These, as I understand, are earthbound; that is, they cannot sunder the material conditions which made up their lives. In the earth-life, they never lived on the higher planes; they had little, if any, spiritual development, and so across the frontier they practically live on this material plane although in another way. It will take a long time, and some unusual incident, to awaken these to their true condition. Some men are blind to all but material interests, and the spirits of these are blind to all interests except those embraced within their limited plane. One

can no more see beyond this condition than we can see beyond ours. There is no advancement for such men, or for any man, until the desire comes from within. We can catch a glimpse of the next plane and hear voices. So can they, but progression will not be given fully until they are prepared to receive it. It may be said that many, many in this life are today more progressed than some who have gone to the lowest plane of spirituality; for in the change they unconsciously pass directly to the next condition beyond. Those who pass the lower sphere of the earth condition may at first only reach the second plane of the same sphere. They cannot reach the higher planes, because they are not fitted. They must go among those of like character to themselves, in a like condition with themselves. The unclean spirit cannot go into a pure atmosphere, because they would contaminate it. These will find themselves surrounded with the thought matter they have taken with them, to the home they have made, and all the other homes and all the other people they see will have similar conditions and like homes. This may be called the first conscious sphere, the plane of restitution.

"When the soul awakens here and sees about him the wrongs he has committed and those that others have committed, the effect of those wrongs and the condition produced by them, great remorse will come."

Only one who has made the great change, can adequately describe conditions under which people live in the sphere beyond:

"In my weakness I became unconscious of all around; but soon I became conscious of several things. I realized that something that had held me down and fatally gripped me was gone. I was free, and in the place of weakness and pain and sickness, I had a virility and a vigor which I had never known upon the earth plane. I was also aware that I was in new surroundings, most beautiful. Then I became conscious that I was in the midst of a company of fellow souls, whose voices were filled with happiness, all welcoming me, and others whom I had temporarily lost while upon the earth plane. I then knew that some great change had occurred which had taken from me everything that I had desired to get rid of, or some power, had given to me a delightful experience, which I had

often in a measure imagined, but dared scarcely believe that it could be possible.

"Surrounded by an innumerable company, I was quite dazzled with the appearance of some who, it was explained to me, were exalted personages. Then there approached one who seemed to be the chief speaker. He said, before me was the universe, that time was for me no more, that I was henceforth an inhabitant of a new country. You will ask me, —was it all pleasant? Extremely so. How can I illustrate it so that you will understand? Have you ever, after taking a long journey, become extremely tired and weary, and, at last, at the end of much striving and travelling, come to a house of rest? How you sank down upon the downy couch. Oh, the delight of it! With no dreams to disturb your rest, you awoke like a giant refreshed! To me it was something like that; although even that is a weak illustration. But that which brought me greatest happiness was the knowledge that I had gained what I had once believed I had lost. I had health, strength, vitality, friends, and relatives restored to me forevermore.

"I have always been fond of the beautiful. I have spent days, weeks, and months in the picture galleries of Europe, looking at the work of the old masters. Many of them lived hundreds of years before I came upon the earth plane, and yet I seemed to have known them all the days of my life. I have dreamed about them. Da Vinci has always been my companion; Murillo, a choice comrade; for Giotto I had a deep, lasting friendship. I loved the beautiful in all its forms. I loved Nature, —the beautiful lakes of Italy and Switzerland, the glorious mountains, the everlasting hills. My friends in spirit life said to me, 'Come and see the House Beautiful.' Try and understand, if you can, that not only are the landscapes spiritual, but so is the beauty of all that there is on the other side of life. The physical is only the gross imitation of the spiritual. There is no tongue which can describe the beauty of the spiritual realms, wherein are the souls of those who have just entered on their progressive existence, —souls who have striven to do their best according to their light. I say that there is no tongue that can describe the beauties of that land. Take the best that you have, and it is poor in comparison. Then I came next to the spiritual houses, and there I met with more friends, more relatives, and, greater, grander still, with those royal souls who have been my affinities on earth, —been companions, comrades of the brush and palette, and others whom I had deeply reverenced in my soul.

"But I found them much greater, grander, nobler than they ever were in their earth life, and I was privileged to be one of their companions. Still I pressed onward. I came to a Rest House. That will sound peculiar. You will say, how can you have rest houses, if you don't know what it is to be weary? No, there is no weariness like that you have experienced on earth; but there are rest houses, where in the spiritual life we may rest and have delightful intercourse with our friends. In the spiritual rest house, therefore, we entered, and found there relatives and friends. Somewhere not upon the same plane of existence as I was, but they had been permitted to come down to my sphere to meet me, so that in effect I could say, 'He that was dead is alive again, he that was lost for a time is found. And then memory, think of the joy of memory! I had carried personality and memory into the spirit world, and I compared the existence in Rome with that which I was then enjoying. I tell you that it was the expectance of what was still to be which gave me the greatest pleasure and the greatest joy. There is no joy on earth like that which is in Heaven, for it is unalloyed.

"I became conscious that I had to do something, and that I should have to work, and it was a joy. Could I be a messenger? I thought of some on the earth plane I had loved so dearly, and remembered that they were in spiritual darkness. I inquired, "Where is the Heaven of orthodoxy?' 'It does not exist,' was the answer. But my friends were in darkness, and a yearning came that I might go to them and tell them what I knew. I wanted to say, 'Do not be mistaken; there is something better, brighter, grander, nobler for human souls than has been taught you.' I was told that I could return, and became conscious that I could communicate with those still on earth if I found a certain channel, an avenue, an instrument. How could I find it? 'All things are yours,' is the promise. Therefore I must find the way and the instrument. This I did, and you have helped me. That is the work which I am doing, and it gives me increased happiness.

"I was told that there were greater beauties of the spiritual landscape which I had not yet seen, and which I could not yet understand, because the universe is illimitable. There is something overpoweringly grand in the thought that you are not cramped or shut up in a small space of a few millions of miles. No, this universe is vast, and the field is mine to explore. It became mine by right. I had worked for it. Take special note of that. I was to work and earn the right to explore God's dominions, and get happiness from every place, state and condition of my spiritual existence.

"Do you like grand architecture? From what source do you think that the old Greeks got their first designs? Phidias and Praxiteles were, no doubt, the greatest Greek sculptors. There were wonderful architects in those days. When I was upon the earth plane, I made a nine months' tour of Greece, Rome, and Sicily to make a study of the architecture and the ancients. I visited every temple, whether in ruins or in perfect order, and I tell you they are heaps of stones, they are utterly beneath contempt compared with the spiritual architecture of the homes and houses in the spirit world. If you have a spiritual body, there is no reason why you should not have a spiritual house. Get rid of the idea that you are a puff of wind in the life hereafter. Even wind may be solidified, for wind is atmosphere in motion, and it is possible to solidify the atmosphere. Then I came to the inhabitants of that spirit world. I had never previously believed or dreamed that these could exist in such beautiful forms. To most people, beauty of form is a source of joy and comfort. The Greeks and the Romans loved beauty of form, and I know that you do likewise. I saw the most exquisite forms as I progressed, and every day, to use language which you will understand, I met with some that I had previously known upon the earth-plane, and what words can tell you the joy of it? To some of them I had done little acts of kindness. And let me impress upon you that of all the pleasure I have received on the spirit side of life, the most came from those to whom I had previously done some act of kindness. If I had my earth life again, I would spend every hour in doing good, —I would spend my life in doing acts of kindness.

"In our spiritual rest houses we frequently meet, not only with loved ones, but with those whom we reverenced and adore. We make also new acquaintances. We get a knowledge of great and grand souls, and come in contact with them. After a time, I was appointed by an Intelligence to do a certain work. I was to help others to see the light, and I had permission to come back to the earth again. Then my instructor said, 'That which will give you the greatest pleasure, do.' Then I came back.

"I have met with many great and noble characters, who lived upon the earth plane. I am frequently in the companionship of those whom I loved, and I have never yet found cause for offense, and never will. No one has entered into my surroundings who has caused me a moment of sadness. On the earth-plane even your best moments are clouded because someone in your midst was objectionable to you; but each one on the spirit side has gravitated to a certain spiritual level. If he be good, then his spiritual status is good, his affinities will be good, and those who come in immediate contact with him will be good also. There will be no one to offend.

"So vast are the realms or dominions of Nature that in the few years that I have been on the spirit side of life, I have been able to explore but little. When I have been upon the etheric plane for some billions of years I shall perhaps have seen a little of it. But throughout the countless ages of eternity I shall be evolving, developing, getting knowledge and light and wisdom. I shall become in tune with the infinite.

"What there is beyond, I do not yet know. Even on our side of life we are not given more knowledge than we can make use of for the time being. It is all a matter of progression. I have told you that we all have to work. There are no drones. But it is work that is congenial and satisfactory; it is a labor of love. It is appointed by a Higher Intelligence; it is given to you to do; and if you do it, your progress and happiness are assured. Realize that there is no coercion on the spirit side of life, but the spiritual eyes are opened to their responsibility. They see everything at a glance. In the spirit side of life you are not left in any doubt. You have full knowledge that to obey is better than to sacrifice, and to do the will of God is to bring happiness in your progressive existence, throughout eternity. Mothers have had their children taken away by death, and the bereaved ones say, "We have lost our children. You have

> **not lost them. They may have been lost from vision for a while. Perhaps there are some here tonight who laid to rest in cold earth a little form, a sweet child. I do not seek to stir up your feelings, but you remember how the burning tears came to your eyes; you rebelled in your soul when a child was taken away. There was an aching void in your heart and you murmured. That life was only taken and planted in another garden, and when you get on the other side, you will know your child. But not as a babe, for all grow to full spiritual stature, radiant, glorious in immortality, with souls filled with love for you, nevermore to part.**
>
> **"Is it not worth striving for? There is no condemnation to those who are good, those who are living the life, those who are seeking to do that which is right. Let me tell you, that the time is coming when all earth problems, religions, and theology, will pass away. Men are tired of such discussions. They are sick in their soul of being told to trust in another; they cannot fathom the scheme or plan of salvation, but they do know that around them is a world of misery, of unhappiness and shortcomings. It is only the true spiritual philosophy which teaches man to rely upon himself and become his own Savior by being true to himself. There is no religion higher than truth. To serve God he must serve man. That pleases the Father, and continues eternally. We must become servants of each other."**

A Conscious Death

> **"Yes, I know that I am no longer an inhabitant of the earth sphere, that I am numbered among the dead; so because I thoroughly understand the great change through which I have passed, the group of spirit people working with you, and controlling conditions on this side, have asked me to speak to you, and through you to all those in sorrow for their dead. You know, of course, that in speaking I am now using my own voice."**

Out of the silence, out of the darkness, in a room devoted solely to psychic investigation came those words; one whom the world calls dead was speaking. I have never ceased to be startled when a voice first speaks from the invisible world—so unusual, so marvelous, so wonderful, and yet to me, so natural.

"So much, "I said," of the information that we get from the plane where you now live is general in character, won't you be specially specific and tell us, first, something of your occupation and of the conditions immediately preceding your dissolution?"

(This is one of the most astounding experiences ever recorded in a séance-Ed.)

"I came," he replied, "from a long line of soldiers. My ancestors fought in the American Revolution, and were among those who aided in establishing your Republic; possibly I inherited a martial spirit. When the first shot was fired by the Confederates, and Lincoln issued his call for volunteers, I was possessed with a desire to enter the army. I had a wife and two children, to whom as I now know, I owed a far greater duty than to my country, but the speech of people, the danger of the nation, the condition of slavery prevailing in the Southern States, and the preparation for war, incited me. With forced words of good cheer, I left brave wife and little children, enlisted, and became a soldier in the Union.

"I will not take the time to tell you of my life in the army, except to speak of the nights in camp when my thoughts went out to those at home, knowing as I did that funds were slowly diminishing. Ever the idea was dominant that the war would be soon over, then there would be the home coming, and the plans I formed to make compensation for my long absence would come to fruition. But the war did not end as battle after battle was fought with success first on one side, then on the other. I participated in many, seeming to bear a charmed life, for while thousands about me fell, I passed unharmed, and so grew fearless."

"Under what circumstances did you meet your end?" I asked.

"It was at Gettysburg," he replied. "I can see and feel it all over again as my mind concentrates on that tragic event. It was the second day of that great fight. I was then a colonel and commanded a regiment in reserve; in front of us the battle roared. Shot and shell filled the air and fell near us, muskets belched forth their fire, the earth seemed to tremble; wounded in great numbers were carried to the rear, and we knew that countless dead lay where they had fallen. We waited, knowing it was only a matter of hours,

possibly minutes before the order would come to advance. I looked down the line at blanched faces, we all knew that many would not answer the roll call at night. Still we waited. Suddenly out of the smoke galloped an officer from the general's staff. 'Forward,' came the command.

"There was no faltering now that the hour had come. The column moved. Soon shot and shell fell among us, on we went. All was excitement, fear was gone; we had but one desire, and that was to kill; such is the lust of battle. I recall but little more. We reached the front and saw the grey line charging up the hill toward us; then, oblivion. I now know that I was shot."

"Tell me of returning consciousness and what you saw," I said.

"You must remember," the spirit answered, "that these tragic events occurred nearly half a century ago, and that at that time it had not been discovered that there is another life, a plane as material as the one you now inhabit, where life continues. I had no conception of a hereafter, for with all my religious teaching I had no idea of what or where the future life might be; nor was I at all sure there was one; so you can imagine how startled I was to awake as from a deep sleep; bewildered I got to my feet, and looked down and saw my body among many others on the ground. This was startling. I made a great effort to collect my thoughts and recall events. Then I remembered the awful battle; still I did not then realize I had been shot. I was apart from, still I seemed in some way, held to the body and yet separate and apart from the covering I had thought constituted the body.

"I tried to think and realize my situation. I looked about; others of the seeming dead moved, seemed to stir. Then many of us stood up, and like me seemed to emerge from their physical bodies, for their old forms still lay upon the field. I looked at other prostrate bodies, examining many, from each something was gone. Going among them again, I found other bodies inhabited, still living as you would say, though wounded and unconscious.

"Soon I found myself among thousands in a similar mental state. Not one among them knew just what had happened. I did not know

then as I do now, that I always possessed a spirit body composed of material called ether, and that the physical body was only the garment it wore while in the earth life."

"What brought you to the full realization of what had happened?" I asked.

"I am coming to that," he said; "While the passing out of the old body was without pain, it is a terrible thing to drive a strong spirit from a healthy body, tear it from its coverings. It is unnatural, and the sensation following readjustment is awful. In a short time I became easier, but I was still bewildered. It was neither night nor day; about us all was gloom, not a ray of light, nor a star. Something like an atmosphere dark and red enveloped us all, and we waited in fear and silence; we seemed to feel one another's thoughts, or to be more correct, hear one another think. No words were spoken. How long we remained in this state I cannot now tell, for we do not measure time as you do. Soon there was a ray of light that grew brighter each moment, and then a great concourse of men and women with kindly faces came, and with comforting words told us not to fear; that we had made the great change; that death, so-called, only advanced our sphere of life; that we were still living beings, inhabitants now of the first plane beyond the earth; that we would live on forever, and by labor reach a higher mental development; that for us the war was over, we had passed through the valley of death.

"I will not attempt to tell you of the sorrow that came with such a realization, not for myself, for I soon learned that only through death could we progress, and that the personal advantages beyond the physical were greater than those in the physical; it was sorrow for the wife and the babies; their great grief when they learned what had happened, bound me to their condition, and we sorrowed together. I could not progress or find happiness until time had healed their sorrow. If only those in earth life knew that their sadness binds and holds us, stays our progress and development! After coming with the aid of many friends to full consciousness, and being made to move at will, I followed at first the movements of both armies. I saw the route of Lee's army, the final surrender at Appomattox, and I want to tell you of the great effort of this land in which I live put forth, not only to prevent war, but to bring

peace when nations or people are at war, for war has never been right. No taking of human life is ever justifiable.

"This is the first time it has been my personal privilege to get a message through to the world I once inhabited. It has been a great pleasure to tell you something of the sensations during and after the change. There is one experience that I want to relate, for it made a profound impression. One day I saw many people passing into a building having the appearance of a great Temple of Music. I was told I could go in if I desired, —I did. There were assembled, I should judge, five thousand people. They sat with bowed heads in a silence, so absolute that I marveled; turning, I asked one beside me the object of the meeting, and I was told they were concentrating their thoughts, sending out peace vibrations to nations at war. I did not comprehend, but, curious, I waited. Soon above that great company arose a golden cloud that formed and moved as if directed. Having learned that I could go at will, I followed and found the cloudy substance enveloping another battlefield. Again a dark condition with flashes of red, immediately surrounding and above two great armies, for the thoughts of those in battle give out emanations producing such effect. It had substantially the same appearance that prevailed on my awakening. As I watched, the dark condition seemed to change, to dissolve before the peaceful conditions of the light that I had followed, just as mist dissolves before the sun. With the change a better thought filled the minds of those engaged, an inclination to treat more humanly the wounded and the prisoners. This is one of the ways those experienced among us help the mental, as those among you aid the physical; both are equally real.

"Among us are the great who counsel together and work to influence those in authority against war, while others among us, by thought suggestions, help to sustain those poor soldiers forced into battle, either to satisfy the greed, selfishness, and ambition of those in authority, or to defend a nation or the integrity of their country. We know neither the one side nor the other. We see only the suffering of humanity, a mother's mourning, a wife's breaking heart, a child's sobbing. They are all human, and without distinction or class we labor to comfort and help them by mental suggestion. In such work we enter their homes, a great

invisible host, and many a heart has been cheered through our ministrations. Other wars will come, unless the thought of those now in authority changes; then a great work will be required of us, for which we are ready."

"This is exceedingly interesting, but just one more word. How does your earth-life appear, after so many years?" I asked.

"How much do you remember of those first years, when as an infant you gazed upon your world?" the man replied. "So it is with me. I have but an indistinct recollection of the events that made up my earth-life, only a memory remains, still enough to make me regret many lost opportunities. I was not then a thinker, only a drifter; I accepted what was told me without question; the result was that I did not develop my mental faculties. This life offers such splendid advantages, my joy of living in the present is so intense, that I seldom think of the earth-life at all. All the trials, sorrows, and sufferings incident to birth and the few years in your physical world, were necessary, and from my present vantage ground the matter of living a few years more or less, the manner of my going were unimportant; it is all forgotten now in the wonderful reality about me. As soon as I came to understand what death was and to what it led, I immediately commenced to complete my education, and build a home for the wife and children, and I am happy to tell you that again we dwell together, for they are all here in this land of happiness and opportunity."

In the presence of such an experience, listening to an individual speaking from the world beyond, telling of another, an unknown land, where all the so-called dead live, think, move, develop, and progress, the learned should understand and comprehend that three dimensions and five senses do not explain the conditions beyond.

This spirit, describing where she went and what she saw immediately following death, said:

"You wish to know where I went on leaving the earth. Well, there seemed to be a period of unconsciousness; then I awoke and found myself in an entirely different place from any I had known on earth. I was somewhat confused at first; most people are, and find it difficult to realize where they are and what has happened

to them. I was not afraid, however, because I had believed I would be taken care of, and would go on living somewhere. My ideas about the afterlife, however, were very vague, as are those of the majority of people. Psychic work will change all that, however, and people will know better what to expect; instead of fearing and dreading the dissolution of the body, as so many millions do now, it will appear to them as it really is, —just a sleep and an awakening!

"You are wondering, and often have wondered, why I was taken when I seemed to be, and was, so much needed on earth. You have blamed God, and thought it cruel and hard and not by any means as an act of love. This is the result of your limited vision.

"I will give you a description of the place in which I found myself when I awoke after what you call 'death.' It took me some time to realize the beauty of my surroundings, as my eyes were blinded by the sorrow which my going had caused on earth. The grief of my people kept me so sad at first that I was not able to see or think of anything but earthly sorrow. That is why grief for departed friends and relatives is so wrong, and is so harmful, both to those on earth and to those who come over. The longer the grief continues and the more hopeless it is, the more those mourned for are kept to earth. Instead of being able to go straight on when they come over, seeing and realizing the beauty and wonders of their surroundings, and helping others to see them also, they are kept in a state of helpless grief, which renders them incapable of either helping themselves or others. Fortunately, the grief of my people on earth was not of this desperately hopeless variety, and I was enabled in time to rise above it and get on with my work of helping others.

"This is a life of service. Self must be eliminated. That is why folk who have lived unselfish lives on earth get on so well here. They do not need the preliminary training which more selfish spirits need. It is a very long time before some spirits who come over are of any use at all in helping others. This is caused partly by their own selfishness and partly by the selfish grief of their friends and relatives on earth. That is why so many of the messages sent through are a plea to those relatives for a more hopeful outlook.

"All that I have said is necessary that you may better understand what I am about to tell you. When I had been enabled to throw off somewhat the effects of the grief which others felt for my passing, I began to see how beautiful the place I had been brought to was. It was where most spirits go on leaving the earth. They are taken there by other spirits and every effort is made to help them to forget the earth and its cares and worries. This lovely palace is called the 'Palace of Light,' because that is what is most needed by the spirits of human beings when they come over, —more light, to enable them to see and understand many things which have not been clear to them while on earth. Human vision—the earthly kind—is very narrow in most cases. People fail to grasp the wonder and beauty even of the earth, so it is no wonder that they need more light and a considerable amount of training before they can see and realize all the beauty and grandeur to be found over here.

"Everything is so surprisingly beautiful that, once their eyes are opened and the full majesty and splendor of it all begins to dawn on them, they are transformed and become beautiful likewise. Once this transformation is accomplished their training is at an end and they can go on their way rejoicing in all the beauty of their surroundings, helping others to see and realize it, too.

"It is almost impossible for us to help some spirits, as they have no desire to be different or better than they have always been. Prayer by those still on the earth is the only thing which can help them. It will give them a desire for better things. Until there is that desire in their hearts, they will remain much as they were when they were in the flesh. Their spirits still inhabit the earth and they are the evil, or sometimes mischievous, spirits I have told you about before. Prayer is not only a protection against them, but is also their only hope of salvation. Indifference is the greatest sin there is. As long as folk desire to be better, there is some foundation to build on, but if that desire is lacking it is very difficult to do anything with them.

"I really cannot give you an adequate description of the beautiful Palace of Light. It is so marvelous and so stupendous that it would not be possible for any one still on the earth to grasp its significance. It is not just a building, as the word 'Palace' might suggest to your mind. It is a wondrous land of light, where the beauties of Nature, as seen on the earth, are brought to perfection. There we have sea, sky, hills, mountains, valleys, and grassy plains, in all their beauty of form and coloring, but without blemish. There are no barren or desolate places and there is none of man's handiwork to mar all of this loveliness.

"There are forests of noble trees, great rivers, waterfalls, lakes, streams of all sizes, all crystal clear, and lovely meadows carpeted with the most beautiful flowers, over which hover myriads of gorgeous butterflies. There are countless numbers of the most beautiful birds everywhere. Animals of all kinds abound too. Some of them are dainty and graceful, and others are stately and dignified. It is one vast panorama of loveliness, for those who have eyes to see.

"The great pity is that it is so long before some spirits even begin to see it as it really is. Some of these spirits, who have not progressed far enough to see and realize the beauty about them, when communicating with their friends on earth, give them quite wrong and dissimilar impressions of conditions over here.

"You are wondering just what we mean by the term 'progression.' It is the spiritual condition entirely, and has nothing to do with the place the spirits happen to be in. It is the developing and the unfolding of the spiritual nature which is necessary before the spirits concerned can fully appreciate and enjoy the wonderful home prepared for them. Spirits are not obliged to stay in some particular place until they have completed their development. They are all free to go about and see these wonders of which I have been telling you, except that they are not allowed to go and worry the children in their carefree land. Until they develop spiritually, they cannot appreciate all the wonders about them.

"I have not told you anything about the music we get here, except that which the birds make, have I? There is always plenty of beautiful music to listen to. All kinds of instruments are played, and those who desire to do so can play in this great orchestra. Then there is the singing. It is wonderful. Everyone is free to join in this great paean of praise. Those who have not been able to sing as

they like on earth, and have always desired to do better, are able to realize their longing here. It is good to witness their joy over this, when they have progressed sufficiently to hear the singing, and when they are able to join in it, their happiness is complete."

Let it not be inferred that all who have experienced this change have such a delightful experience. The plane one reaches and the character of one's surroundings depend on the refinement of spirituality of the individual. Each will find the condition he has fitted himself for, and they are such as money cannot buy.

Another has this to say:

"I appreciate your kindness in receiving me so kindly. I speak to you tonight about my experiences in the 'spirit world,' as you call it, —I call it the 'higher existence.'

"In describing my passing to the higher, progressive life, I am pleased to say to you that I am giving my own observation, and I do not expect you to accept it as being the testimony of other friends who may have passed over. With what they met, I have nothing to do; I have only to state what I have experienced.

"I may state, concerning my experience on the earth, that I lived for a long period of time, a little over ninety years, and I led, shall I say, a fairly good life. I should like to say concerning the latter days that, though old in years, I was not at all feeble in body or in mind; but as I advanced I felt my powers were failing, and that soon I should be called to leave the scenes of earth for something greater and grander. And so it happened.

"I remember well, on one summer's day, arising in the morning and feeling weak in my body but without pain. It was a weakness, the result of natural decay of the system. And I remember on this occasion that, as the day advanced, I felt more weary. I laid me down upon a couch and fell into a kind of sleep—not a perfect sleep, because I was partially unconscious of persons around about me.

"I awoke somewhere about four o'clock in the afternoon, looked around, and spoke to one or two near me. One was my attendant,

who came and asked if I should like something to drink. I said I should. I lay back and waited, and as I did so I felt a strange but not unpleasant feeling come over me. I can only describe it as a sensuous drowsiness, which seemed to be gaining upon my faculties. The scenes round about me were fading, almost imperceptibly at first, but passing away from me. I was conscious only of that which was just around about me, and then that also seemed to fade away, and my sleep or weakness was merged into sleep which became profound.

"How long that could have continued I do not know, but after a time I again returned to consciousness—these are the only terms I can use to convey to your minds my experiences. Then I realized that I, the Ego, was there just as really as before. I realized that I, the personality, was there, though some change had taken place. I felt as one feels who had dropped something which had burdened him; as a man who had carried a load for a considerable distance, a load that had not been extremely heavy or painful, but still a burden, and I had left it behind somewhere.

"And then, dawning on my spiritual senses, I was conscious that I was in some other state of existence, wherein I was not subject to physical forces as I had experienced them on the earth plane. For instance, the wind did not blow upon me, the sun did not shine, nor did the cold affect me. This I found and experienced with great joy. In place of it I found what you would call, on your mundane sphere, an even temperature, a calm and placid state. I felt that if peace and contentment could be reached, I had reached it. And then I was conscious that round about me there was an innumerable company of people, —they were fellow countrymen.

"As I gained a little more experience, or perhaps, as you would say, as my consciousness deepened, I knew that I was attended by spiritual messengers or attendants. Looking to the one upon my right, I said—if not openly, I said it within myself, because the Ego speaks within itself, because it is the Mind—'This being is perfection.' Divining my thoughts, the guide said to me, 'No, you are being perfected. There is only perfection in the infinite. Him thou shalt know; with Him thou shalt come into contact. This helped me considerably. If my guide, my messenger, who was

to conduct me through this higher existence, was so perfect in mind, so perfect in every way, what then would be the Author of his perfection? I was satisfied."

The Spirit World

"I am fully convinced that the soul is indestructible, and that its activity will continue through eternity. It is like the sun, which to our eyes, seems to set in night; but it has in reality only gone to diffuse its light elsewhere."

—J. von Goethe

Etheric Environment

Desiring a clear comprehension of the etheric spheres outside the physical, and having opportunity to speak with one very learned and advanced in the afterlife, I said: "Describe, if you please, the spheres in which you live, with special reference to the tangibility and materiality." The gentleman answered:

"There are seven concentric rings called spheres. The region nearest the earth is known as the first or rudimental sphere. It is just one step higher in vibration. It really blends with your earth sphere. Growing more intense and increasing in action are six more, distinguished as the spiritual spheres. These are all concentric zones or circles of exceedingly fine matter encompassing the earth like belts or girdles, each separated from the other and regulated by fixed laws. They are not shapeless chimeras or mental projections, but absolute entities, just as tangible as the planets of the solar system or the earth upon which you reside. They have latitude and longitude, and an atmosphere of peculiarly vitalized air. The undulating currents, soft and balmy, are invigorating and pleasurable."

"How does the landscape appear to you?" I asked.

He answered:

"The surface of the zone is diversified. There is a great variety of landscape, some of it most picturesque. We, like you, have lofty mountain ranges, valleys, rivers, lakes, forests, and the internal correspondence of all the vegetable life that exists upon your earth. Trees and shrubbery covered with most beautiful foliage, and flowers of every color and character known to you, and many that you know not, give forth their perfume. The physical economy of each zone differs from every other. New and striking scenes of grandeur are presented to us, increasing in beauty sublimity as we progress."

"Do the seven concentric rings, or spheres, move with the earth as the earth moves?" I asked.

"Although the spheres revolve," he said, **"with the earth on a common axis, forming the same angle with the plane of the ecliptic, and move with it about your sun, they are not dependent upon that sun for either light or heat; they receive not a perceptible ray from that ponderable source."**

"From what source do you receive your light?" I then asked.

"We receive our light emanations," he said, **"wholly from an etheric sun, from which central luminary there comes uninterrupted splendor, baffling description. We have, therefore, no division of time into days, weeks, months, or years, nor alterations of season caused by the earth's annual revolution, for the reason that we have no changing season as you have, caused by the action of the sun on your solar system. We, like you, are constantly progressing from day to day, but our ideas of time and seasons differ widely from yours. With you, it is time. With us, it is eternity. In your sphere your thoughts, necessarily bounded by time and space, are limited, but with us thoughts are extended in proportion as we get rid of those restrictions, and our perception of truth becomes more accurate."**

"How do you use matter, change its form and condition?" I asked.

"Matter," he said, **"with us is only tangible as the mind concentrates upon the subject. Then the force of the mind or thought sends its**

vibrations around the object, holding it in a measurable tangible. Of course, this is something very different from what you call tangibility. Without this mental concentration the vibration pulses indifferently. That is the natural condition of matter in our zone. It requires the thought to change its form and condition. The vibrating action of matter is measured by the space necessary for the volume."

"How can this material condition in which you live be demonstrated?" I asked.

"One cannot prove," he said," **to a child that steam, that pretty fascinating substance, is harmful until the finger is burned; neither can one instill the truth into an older mind until it is not only opened but has the capacity to comprehend. That all is material in different states of vibration is easily grasped by the thinker. It is impossible to prove by your laws, to actually demonstrate the existence of matter in the higher vibrations in which we live so that men may comprehend. When you deal with matter in the physical, you apply physical laws. When you deal in matter spiritual, you apply spiritual laws, practically unknown among men. The best possible evidence is the vision of the clairvoyant together with deductive reasoning, which, as we have said, is really the highest order of proof.**

"Have you ever thought," he said, **"that the result of every physical demonstration reaches the consciousness through the avenue of reason? The mentality in a higher state of development comprehends a fact in Nature without physical proof."**

"Tell us something of your social life, your scientific research, and religious teaching in the plane in which you reside," I asked.

"With regard to the social constitution of the 'spheres,' each is divided into six circles, or societies, in which kindred and congenial spirits are united and subsist together under the law of affinity. Although the members of each society unite as near as may be on the same plane, agreeing in the most prominent moral and intellectual features; yet it will be found on careful analysis, that the varieties of character in each society are

almost infinite, being as numerous as the persons who compose the circle. Each society has teachers from those above, and not infrequently from the higher spheres, whose province is to impart to us the knowledge acquired from their experience in the different departments of science; this, we in turn transmit to those below. Thus by receiving and giving knowledge, our moral and intellectual faculties are expanded to higher conceptions and more exalted views of Nature, the power of which is no less displayed in the constitution of spirit worlds than in the countless resplendent orbs of space. Our scientific researches and investigations are extended to all that pertains to the phenomena of universal truth; to all the wonders of the heavens and of the earth, and to whatever the mind of man is capable of conceiving. All of these researches exercise our faculties and form a considerable part of our enjoyments. The noble and sublime sciences of astronomy, chemistry, and mathematics engage a considerable portion of our attention, and afford us an inexhaustible subject for study and reflection.

"Nevertheless, there are millions of spirits who are not yet sufficiently advanced to take any interest in such pursuits. The mind being untrammeled by the gross material body, and having its mental and intellectual energies and perceptions improved, can by intuition, as it were, more correctly and rapidly perceive and understand the principles and truths on which the sciences are based. In addition to our studies, we have many other sources of intellectual, moral, and heartfelt enjoyment from which we derive the most ineffable pleasures, some of which are social reunions among children and parents where the liveliest emotion and the most tender affections of our nature are excited, and the fondest and most endearing reminiscences are awakened; where spirits meet in union with spirit, and heart beats responsive to heart.

"We have no sectarian or ecclesiastical feuds, no metaphysical dogmas; our religious teachers belong to that class of persons who were noted during their probation on earth for their philanthropy and deeds of moral bravery, who, regardless of the scoffs and sneers of time-serving multitude, dared to promulgate and defend the doctrines of civil and religious liberty. They urge upon us, too, the necessity of cooperation in the reformation and advancement of our more degraded brethren by instructing them in the divine principles of love, wisdom, and benevolence. They instruct them in the soul-inspiring and elevating doctrines of universal and eternal progression, and in the sublime truth that evil is not an indestructible and positive principle, but a negative condition, a mere temporary circumstance of existence; and furthermore, that suffering for sin is not a revengeful and malevolent infliction of God, but a necessary and invariable sequence of violated law.

"They teach also that, according to the divine moral economy, there is no such thing as pardon for sins committed—no immediate mercy—no possible escape from the natural results of crime, no matter where or by whom committed; no healing of a diseased moral constitution by any outward appliances, or ceremonial absurdities; and finally, that the only way to escape sin and its consequences, is by progressing above and beyond it."

"What is spirit, as that term is used?" I asked.

"Spirit," he said, "is the one great power in the Universe. The combination of spirit forces is the great power for good, and through the absence of that force many undesirable conditions develop in your world, — all in the Universe is but an expression of this great force, and if this spirit force were not material, were not a substance, how could it take form and have growth in the physical plane? Those still in your world make a great mistake when they for one moment imagine that our world is not a material one; it is foolish to think of an existence without substance. How can there be a world beyond the physical unless it is material? Without it there could be no afterlife. Strong invisible bands of force hold the great system of spheres in proper place. It is all mind-force, and all force is life, mighty, unchanging, unyielding, and this mind power is increased by every individual life that is developed in your creative sphere. It has become a part of the individual life force of the Universe, and each day it adds something to that force called Good. This addition is made, not at dissolution, but from hour to hour, as the mentality increases."

Such teachings appeal to reason, and I accept them.

Life Among the Spheres

One from the higher life said:

"There is so much to be considered in putting this knowledge of the future life before earth minds. The incredulous and ignorant will only jeer."

"Remember," said one who has been in spirit-life nearly four hundred years, **"the world in which you live is in a very low order of development. In many of the other planets this philosophy of life is universally taught, but you have comparatively only a few minds high enough out of the slough of materialism to comprehend it. In the Fourth Sphere, where I am, that of trial, we are fitted for a higher order of life. Here, any weakness a spirit may still hold becomes doubly alluring and seemingly irresistible. We finally overcome this by throwing it out of our spirit. Sometimes it is a long, hard task. We are made to do anything we do not like to do, or, rather, we must learn to like to do it. Often when we help others, the task is irksome and we long to keep ourselves free for spiritual development, forgetting that each deed for others helps our own growth. In the Sphere of Truth the spirits learn all about the other planets and become wise and uplifted, so that they can enter into perfect harmony with the universe. Of course, this needs special preparation and a high degree of development. There, they are not taught by contact with teachers from the higher spheres—in fact, in my sphere we see no teachers, everything comes through suggestion. Our minds are receptive enough to be taught and guided in that way. Each sphere makes suggestion just a little clearer and easier to grasp than the one before, and so we are fitted for the last, where we are able to throw our individuality into the dominating forces of the universe.**

"The Sphere of Harmony is a preparation for the last great sphere, that of Exaltation, where all the universe becomes one. There, they mingle with all in the universe, and are helped and encouraged by them until they are ready to enter into a glorious communion of spirit. This means becoming an inseparable part of all the great forces of the universe. I have never heard of any spirits coming back to the lower planes from the Seventh, except

through suggestion and influence. But through these, they are very near all spiritual natures. They really constitute the dominating force for good that is in and around everyone. The spirit of good in the universe is not individual, but universal. In the last sphere each spirit keeps his individuality, but each has by then become so great and magnificent that it can mingle with other spirits in harmony, making one grand, wonderful whole. If the spirits in the Plane of Exaltation could by any possible chance become out of harmony, the universe would be obliterated and cease to exist. But this cannot be. I simply say this to show how they govern and dominate everything. You ask if any from your earth have ever reached the Seventh Sphere. I am not sure. Your world is young compared with almost all the others and so there could be comparatively but few.

"Some of the planets do not have as many as seven spheres to perfection. They begin with a higher order. There is not much more that you can grasp, my friend. You have learned the essentials of each sphere, and the minor details are so vast and varied that you would have to write a book on each one. Besides, as I have said, it would be hard to convey the knowledge to material minds. Yet it is simple, and on the same lines as the rest that I have told you."

No voice from the Seventh Sphere ever spoke to human ears. Spirits from this sphere do not return and speak to those on the lower planes. Their work is done through suggestions. In this way they come close to us all, but only the conscience hears.

One from the Fifth Sphere told me a little of the life there and the conditions prevailing. He said:

"I am told that you have never had anyone before from this sphere. Here, we are taught all knowledge and how to use it for our individual good. We are brought face to face with the great problems of life, the reason for all things, and the ultimate result. These are vast questions and are not yet fully comprehended by us, but they must be understood before we can enter into Harmony, where we are taught how to attune ourselves to the universe. There, we will be taken into the life of the worlds, but not until the last sphere are we able to merge our individualities into the creative dominant force. In the Fifth we are taught all there is to know, but in the

Sixth we learn by actual contact, and how to adapt ourselves to all conditions of the universe. We are all working toward perfection, and labor to gain the last great Sphere of Exaltation. My friend, I cannot explain our life to you, because you would not comprehend it at all. We are all tending toward one great harmonious whole, and each day brings us nearer that state of harmony we desire. In these last spheres our home life is almost lost sight of. We are bands of congenial people, of course, but we are separate, individual beings. Man no longer, like the animals, chooses a mate and carries her off to his lair. Here, there is something much higher and better a universal brotherhood and companionship, always growing closer and higher until complete blending is formed. It is hard to put this into words, because it is so vast and wonderful and I doubt if you could grasp the whole beauty and force of it.

"There is life on many planets. Some are more advanced than yours; a few are even newer. Each is striving toward the same end and must reach it through many spheres of spiritual development, just as you will, until all are one. Life on the different planes varies, of course. On some, the people are stronger, both physically and spiritually. Some have a first sphere that corresponds to yours. Others combine into one sphere what we do in three. When a planet is prepared, the life-force of the universe is clothed and individualized. When the soil is ready, the seed is planted. Other planets than the earth teem with life. I have not been to them, but have been taught of them by suggestion and know something of each and what degree of development each has attained. I will not be able to visit them until I gain the Sixth Sphere. I lived in England during the reign of Queen Elizabeth, so you see my progress has been rapid. Fortunately, I was a good man and had no prejudices to start with."

From this I conclude that in the last sphere the soul of man reaches perfection and becomes a part of the Great Spirit that rules the world. Some idea of what this is may be obtained by considering the power of man's mind over matter, in the material sense. By the power of his intellect on this earth-plane man makes matter, in a limited way, subject to his will. This mind through ages of development and change grows in strength and power, becomes pure in thought and uses itself for good. When one possesses all that is to be gained in the lower spiritual spheres he will enter into the last sphere of strength, beauty, power, and splendor. His mind, which has gathered much power in its journey, mingles with all others that have ever lived, and that have reached perfection. This spirit-thought from all the worlds, blending as one, makes the force that is called God—or universal Good.

Here is another description of the spheres received from the beyond:

> **"The Spheres! No tongue can describe them. There are thousands, all rounded into complete worlds, and all the habitations of those who cherish the special idea which rules the sphere. These spheres are not permanent, but the temporary homes of those who pass through them. They are the garners into which are gathered the sheaves of earth, there to rest and gain experience until they become distributed and amalgamated into eternal life. There are spheres of love, where tender natures cling to one another until they are drawn by higher, broader aspirations to broader planes of thought.**
>
> **"There are spheres of every shade of mental light, thought, and knowledge; spheres of special grades of intellect and wisdom. In all and each is a special need of happiness; but, also, in all and each are prevailing impulses to branch out further, to press on, to grow, so that every soul, partaking of the special characteristics of every plane in turn, may glean and gather in at last the good of all, and thus become a perfect spirit.**
>
> **"Worlds in space! Thousands, millions of them; worlds within worlds, the finer permeating the grosser filling up the space of the still more dense until at last you see no finite lines, no end to the infinitely dense. I see the concentrated scheme of the whole solar system with earth, and its zones and belts of spirit spheres, countless in number, various in attribute. Myriads of rare and splendid beings speed through the spaces, piercing the grosser spheres, invisible to all but their own grade of beings.**
>
> **"Myriads of duller, grosser beings live in these spheres, unconscious that they are permeated by radiant worlds, all thronged with glorious life, too fine for the gross to view. Each living creature is surrounded and enclosed by the atmosphere to which it has belonged, which restrains his vision to the special**

sphere in which he dwells, just as you cannot see us in our sphere of life, through your atmosphere. Yet the finer realms of being can view, at will, the grosser, just as I found I could do; I am putting this knowledge into practice in coming to you. In fact, I found the secret of will, which is power.

"In these spheres that so lock and interlace, I saw that the lowest and nearest the earth were dull, coarse, barren spheres, dreary and unlovely, where dark and uninvited beings wander to and from, seeking rest and satisfaction which earth alone could give them. No homes were there, I mean no real homes, where loved ones were reunited. No flowers, no friendly gatherings, no songs of music; the hard cold natures of the wretched dwellers gave out no light, no beauty, no harmony or love, yet all felt impelled and obliged to toil. Toil was the genius of this place; yet whatever labors were performed became instrumental in breaking the clods of hard and wicked natures. Every occupation seemed to come perforce as something that must be done; yet all seemed destined to open up new ideas and new sources of thought, and to impel the helpless laborers to aspire after better things and higher states.

"I saw the flitting lamps of spirit workers, who fill your leaden spheres with their gracious influence; and yet, though often felt, these were unseen by the dull-eyed inhabitants. I do not care to linger on the awful, grand, and wise economy of being; the seal of mortal life is on my lips. The spheres are not all of earth, though countless in number; myriads there are where vicious spirits linger, bound and captive as it were, the ignorant, dull, idle, and criminal, who had not done with earth and who must learn, perhaps for ages, all that belonged to their human duties, before they can pass the threshold and enter upon the life of the upper spheres.

"You cannot look through the radiant realms of upper air and see us; but you can feel the streams of pitying love poured out in tender sympathy, as you stretch your weary arms toward us. Spirit life, glory, peace, and happiness left me for the time, for I felt that it was my duty henceforth to help these unfortunates. This is my present work."

What have I learned of the daily life and occupation of the living dead? One long an inhabitant of the higher plane has said:

"We have schools here for the development of the soul of man, and to teach him his relation to mankind; to instruct him in the wonders of creation, impart to him knowledge of the inhabitants of the numerous worlds in space, to aid man, also, in experimenting in chemistry and all other branches of science, for in this life we can explore the uttermost extent of the universe. We also instruct in political economy and laws governing humanity. We also point out conditions and means whereby to help the unprogressive and helpless portion of mankind."

Another states:

"In the spirit world, as in your world, are numerous libraries. There, men and women grow intellectually. Many books are composed and written in spirit spheres, and the authors endeavor sometimes to impress their words and wisdom upon the brain of some sensitive ones upon the earth sphere. Again, a book written by one in your plane is by mental activity first created in spirit substance. It had to be before it could be clothed in physical substance by you, and we have all those books, as well as those wholly written by spirits, but none are permitted in our libraries that are not founded upon truth. It is interesting to see the vast number of spirit people thronging our libraries, studying the works of the more advanced spirits, similar to what is done in the libraries of earth."

Another said:

"We have hospitals, many of them—mental hospitals, where the insane, weak and mentally deficient are treated and developed, and those who understand that work labor to restore normal conditions, for dissolution does not restore disordered minds or develop mentality.

"There are homes to build, and homes commenced on earth to finish; and they are as different as the homes of your earth. Yours are first fashioned in our ether, then constructed out of earth material by the hand of man. Ours are made out of etheric

material and fashioned and erected by and through mental or, to be more correct, spirit thought. All this, as with you, requires effort. You may hire others to build earth homes, but here each builds his own, and many are very busy doing it.

"You ask me to speak particularly as to the occupation of our people. It is a subject vast in extent, for our labors transcend yours, though our methods are different. While our labor is largely in the mental or spirit field of action, yet you must remember we have fields and vegetation where those versed in such work find occupation. But it is in the more advanced fields of chemistry and philosophy that spirit people seek to enter, and here millions labor to understand and comprehend the laws of Nature, and how to apply them. It is a busy world and no drones are found, except in the earthbound or lowest of the spirit spheres."

Concerning different avocations, this one said:

"I am here in this way to tell you of some of the conditions of our world. Here we have different avocations assigned to us, according to our needs and desires.

"Some engage in teaching and training the intellect of those who need and desire such training.

"Some with great love of children find ample opportunity for the use and enjoyment of this attribute of their natures in the kindergartens for the many thousands of children continually arriving on these shores.

"Some are most happy in endeavoring to assist the friends of earth into higher and better conditions and in counteracting the abnormal influences of undeveloped and misdirected spirits over the minds of mortals.

"So it is that there is work of benevolence and philanthropy for all who are prepared for such work.

"The exercise of active compassion furnishes the same delightful enjoyments to the soul over here as with you, and greater; for here

we more clearly discern the far-reaching consequences of our endeavors to do good to whomsoever is in need of assistance."

Another said:

"Let me speak of the music here, of those harmonious vibrations that touch the soul, that universal appeal that is understood by all races, regardless of the language they speak. The music of your world is crude, indeed, compared to celestial compositions and songs. Here we have harmonious vibrations, expressed in what is called music. It elevates the soul, and we devote much time to its cultivation and to instruments for its expression. It is all vibration. Many are occupied in this work. It is only now and then that our songs and our music are impressed in on earth's sensations.

"We do not devote so much time to spirit matter as you do to physical matter. With you it dominates your thought. With us, matter is secondary, and spirit development dominates. It is so much more vital.

"The coming of infants unborn, babies and children, requires the attention of many. Those women who never in earth life knew the joys of motherhood, find it here and do that work. While some care for these little ones, others teach them.

Again, one said:

"In the lower spheres, when those who are held there realize that the only way to improve their condition is by helping others, and have a genuine desire to help, the way is shown.

"This question of spirit occupation is too great for special treatment. Occupation varies and is as diversified as the thoughts of men. But this you should know: there is work and a place for each new spirit. The pity of their poverty! Few have made any effort to find out what nature requires of them here; few ever gave the subject a single thought. And so they come, one by one, but withal a great crowd every hour, and only now and then we find a spirit that can take up and do good work; the others have to be taught, even as little children are taught the simplest things."

Another said:

> **"Those who have led clean, fine lives, and have enriched the world, come here and, without a break, take up their work and go on."**

I could write a volume on the occupations of those who have preceded us, but enough has been said to impress mankind that the after life is real, and that there we work to develop and adorn the physical, while the spirit hungers and development is stayed.

Again, one describing conditions in the great beyond says:

> **"The realities of the spirit world are beyond description. I might spend hours telling you of it and not reach your minds with any conception of its glory, its greatness, its grandeur. It is so vast in extent, so marvelous, that any attempt to give you more than a faint idea would be futile. Not until you get here and see for yourself can you have any conception of the home of the soul. We have our mission—to try to get knowledge through to the shore line of your earth. We are working our best to enlighten the world and prepare its people for the death change. It is our business to instruct those who need help, the same here as with you. Many thousands of your people cannot even read, and reach us with so limited mental development as to need all our energies in their advancement out of ignorance, wrong education and false religious teachings. Few on your earth have any idea of the changes that take place along the lifeline. As they come, we gather and instruct them as you do in your schools—especially in your night schools, where the ignorant seek enlightenment."**

I am impressed with the fact that very many of those called learned, will realize at the end that they are among those that need teachers, and will find it necessary to attend night school in the spirit world.

Neither the old nor the New Testament makes any suggestion that in the after life there is further advancement to be made or any work to be done. On the contrary, according to its promises, we find rest through death, an eternity without labor. We find that as we are, so shall we ever be, that there is no further opportunity to do, undo, add to, subtract from, or improve; that death ends all growth or progression; that we are weighed and our account is balanced. For argument only, assume this to be correct,

I cannot subscribe to this doctrine. Around and about us Nature is always progressing, always developing, always becoming more beautiful. There is no time, according to natural law, when Nature ceases to progress.

"We are just as much spirit now as we ever shall be."

These words have been often spoken, and I repeat them, that we may fully comprehend their import. If we are spirit in the life to come, we are spirit now, always have been, and ever will be.

At last the knowledge that has long been desired has been revealed, and we find that the future has seven spheres, each containing many planes; they are as follows:

1. Restitution.
2. Preparation.
3. Instruction.
4. Trial and Temptation.
5. Truth.
6. Harmony.
7. Exaltation.

I have written of the conditions in the first sphere as I know them from work done there and general information given me by spirit people; but in taking up the spheres beyond the first, I am now able to give the language of those who live in them and who describe them. One said:

"I know what we all know, —that there are seven spheres. I have just reached the third. Sometimes a spirit can speak from his sphere to the next higher, as you do while in the body, but only in the same way. I mean that there is no mingling together. When a spirit goes from one sphere to another, it is quite unlike death in earth-life.

"He is warned that the change is near and has time to put his mind into a higher plane of thought so that he will be prepared to meet the new life. He says farewell to all his friends. They join in a general thanksgiving and celebration, all congratulating and helping him on his way by strong uplifting thoughts. When the time comes, he is put quietly to sleep, with the thought dominant

in his mind that he is to make the change. When he awakes, he is in his new home in the next higher sphere. He has disappeared from the old. There is no old body to bury and decay. Each change is for a higher and better life, and the home awaiting is more beautiful, as he builds with a surer, wiser hand, or rather, spirit. His home ceases to be among his former friends when this change comes. Thought has fitted him to progress, and when that thought which held him to the lower plane has ceased, the embodiment of the spirit, which is held together by his thought, is visible no longer.

"Each new change is more difficult to explain to you than the one preceding. It is simply a higher life and a busy one in which to develop ourselves along all lines, especially the ones suitable to the individual's taste. In this way, each spirit becomes better fitted to be a teacher and helper. It is a very active, pleasant life, and sometimes seems like a big university town or country, with busy students hurrying from lecture to lecture and class to class. All are congenial and lighthearted there.

"In the lower sphere one sees much suffering among those still earth-bound. They, too, are busy working out past faults and they are often heavy-hearted. Generally speaking, the first sphere is the one where restitution must be made, and where the final wrenching away from earth conditions takes place. The second is one of instruction, a period of study, during which the spirit gains knowledge of self and natural law. The third is one of teaching those in the lower spheres, as I have said. The fourth sphere is one of trial and temptation. The fifth is truth, where error and falsehood are unknown. In the sixth, all is harmony. In the seventh, the spirits reach the plane of exaltation and become one with the Great Spirit that rules the universe.

"There are others, more advanced than I, who can better tell you of the spheres beyond. I have not been to the fourth, and only know of it as you do, by the teaching of those who are there. We are told that the spirits in the sphere of exaltation do not even there lose individuality. They are embodied in all the beauty and good of the universe. I do not know that I can make my meaning clear. Although they keep individuality, they permeate the universe. They have become so great and universal, we sometimes think they go beyond

and must lose their personality, but we have no definite knowledge, and it is generally accepted they do not. It is difficult to understand or appreciate what this last sphere is, the development is so beyond our comprehension. Those in the second sphere do little, except to fit themselves for a broader and better work. Before reaching this condition they have freed their spirit from the burden of wrong done in the body, repaid every debt due mankind, dispelled the darkness of the first sphere. They work with open eyes and clear spiritual vision, and are at peace with all. This must precede the sphere of study and development. I have classes on purity, beauty, and patience, and there are classes on every conceivable subject, —music, chemistry, everything. They are different from those in earth-life, and one has to adopt different ideas. One of our engineers magnetizes your room each time you hear our voices. It is easier for those who have advanced to higher life to reach us than for us to reach you; there are not so many barriers. Yes, we always have places that resemble homes. Thought is not indefinite, and that makes our homes, and while we keep that thought, our homes are permanent. You ask where is that home located? I would say to you that all that is space is peopled with spirits."

This lecture gave to us the sphere of progression. As you see, we were told not only their names, but something of the occupations that are pursued in the higher life.

One in the afterlife gave me a description of the spirit-home of a great, splendid mother, built by the labor of ceaseless love and ceaseless charity, —in the physical as well as in the spirit plane in which she now resides, -one who worked long and earnestly to make women understand the truth so that they might live nearer to the best in nature.

Here is the description as it was given me:

"Before me is the interior of a splendid home, the home made by a spirit, created and built by the thoughts, acts, and works of one who, thirty-two years ago, lived on the material plane. The room opening before me seems like pure white marble with lofty ceilings; around the four sides runs a broad balcony supported by columns gracefully turned; from a point beyond the center is a broad stairway curving outward; at its foot, on each side, are niches filled with beautiful statuary. Going up the stairs now, I find each step a different color, yet all blending into one; on all

sides of this upper gallery are windows through which come soft rays of light. Opening off the sides are rooms; and, as I look, a door opens and a beautiful spirit comes out, taking on, as she enters, the old material condition that she may be recognized. She has reached maturity in years, and has a face of rare gentleness—the beauty of purity—she smiles as we describe her and her home to you. With her is a daughter just reaching womanhood; one that never lived the earth-life but was prematurely born. These two, drawn by the invisible bond of affection, have built this home and made it rich with love.

"Passing down the corridor now, the mother's arm about the daughter, they approach the other end of the building and descend a stairway similar to the first, and go out upon a broad terrace, along walks bordered with flowers, into the garden of happiness. Turning now and looking toward a valley, I see many trees heavy with foliage, and through them I behold the waters of a lake, rich as an emerald in color.

"About the vaulted room which I have described are many others of like material, filled with all that this mother loves. Books that she uses in her work are seen; pictures, created by acts of tenderness, adorn the walls. Musical instruments unlike those of earth await spirit-touch. This is a home where girls, just budding into womanhood, are taught purity—this is a mother's home, and suggests to you the possibility of spiritual surroundings. It was not built in a day, but is the result of labor in the earth and in spheres of progression, where the surroundings are in harmony with spiritual development; the home of a good woman, built by helping others."

I said to one of my friends in the afterlife, at another time: "Tell me of the homes of spirit people," and, in reply, he said:

"That is a most difficult thing to do, because earth people expect to find everything so different, while, in reality, the homes here are practically the same as in earth-life, except that there is in the advanced spheres no discord, no lack of harmony, nothing but light, beauty, music, laughter, blended with earnest, thoughtful study. I am describing the home of a spirit who has grown to know the life principle. There are many poor, struggling, souls

willfully, or ignorantly, looking down instead of upwards into the great possibility of the future, who are living in squalid huts which their deeds and thoughts in earth-life have made for them. Very few have beautiful homes ready for them when they enter spirit-life, for most people live in such ignorance of natural laws that they find insufficient shelter awaiting them, but the wise ones start to build by perfecting their way of thinking and by undoing wrongs on earth, and also, by helping others. No actual physical touch is given these homes, but, as the soul grows in beauty of thought and deed, the home grows to perfection."

"Are these homes as real to you as ours are to us?" I asked.

"They are the abiding places of spirits who gather into them the objects of beauty they love, and their harmonious spirits come and go, as in earth-life. They are as real to them as yours are to you. But we look at things differently; we think them, and the thought is expressed in waves that are visible and real as long as we hold the thought."

Where is the afterlife? Just where do they live? Where are its boundaries?

Let it be remembered that those in the after life have frequently said that every physical thing of this earth was but a poor imitation of what they have there—that all things exist first in the invisible.

Here is what one said on this subject:

"We have often told you, and tell you now, that your earth and all things of your earth have their exact counterparts in the spirit world, just as real, just as tangible, just as substantial, to the inhabitants of this world, as material things and forms are to the inhabitants in mortal form upon your earth."

If this be true, if we have earth and rocks, so do they; if we have shrubs and trees and growing grains and flowers, so do they; if we have houses, schools, great buildings, so do they, if we have oceans, lakes, rivers and flowing streams, so do they; if this earth is peopled, why not theirs? I am told they have also many things that we have not, as they cannot be clothed in earth garments nor function on our planet.

The density of that plane differs from ours, as the density of our atmosphere differs from that of water, in which marine life functions.

We move more rapidly and with greater freedom than the life that exists in the deep; so those in the higher etheric plane move more rapidly and with greater freedom than we do—all because the material conditions become higher in vibration as we ascend the scale of motion, and there is more resistance the lower we descend.

Striving for more detailed description, I asked a spirit in our work one evening:

"Where is the spirit world? What of its substance, and where are its boundaries?"

The spirit answered:

"It is difficult to explain to you who know little of matter, the location and boundaries of the various planes where we live. First let me impress upon you the fact that energy, that is, life, cannot express itself except in substance. The idea that spirit people function without substance and that they and the plane in which they live are unsubstantial, is preposterous and illogical. The gases that compose water, taken separately, are as substantial as when united. Why should it be thought impossible, since matter was created, for Nature to create other material than physical, to create spirit material? There are millions of worlds inhabited by human beings in that space you call the sky. Don't for a moment think that yours is the only world, and that God made the universe for you alone.

"This spirit world is in reality just as much a part of your planet as the earth and the rocks you tread upon. Around and about your globe, and forming a part of it, are separate material, concentric belts or zones, varying in width and vibratory action, and therefore in density, into which all mankind and all planetary life passes, on the happening of that event you call death.

"I only know the boundaries of these planes in which I live and labor. I do not know any more about the boundaries of the planes beyond me than you know of the planes beyond you."

Others have reported of these localities as follows:

"Your earth has belts, but they exist in a cruder condition than those of Jupiter and Saturn. The belts or zones that lie around your earth are designed for the habitation of spirits out of the

body; and as they outgrow the passions of earth and become more refined, they pass to another or higher zone.

"I have discovered, while living here, that there are several magnetic belts encircling your earth, similar in general appearance to the belts the surround the planet Jupiter, and beyond those zones there exists, outside earth's spirit sphere, a vast spirit world traversing the innermost heart of space."

Another said:

"I, too, am permitted to gaze back at earthly scenes; and, for a time, to dwell on earthly memories while bringing to you for your world some experiences and observations of my own, both in mortal existence and the spheres.

"I have observed that there are innumerable states and conditions and diversified experiences in spirit as on earth. We may illustrate by different highways, thus:

"Let one condition be represented by a certain highway, and another condition by another and differing highway, leading through a different country.

"As no two highways of your world lead over the same country and present the same scenery to the traveller, so of the children of earth; no two travel over the same highway or have the same experiences; to each are presented different scenes from those presented to any other.

"One person travelling one road is landed into the spirit world at one point, and one on another road enters spirit life at another point; and a third, on yet another road, enters at a different point from either of the others. And so on the endless procession moves, landing its infinitude of differentiated individualities; and each one has a different idea to relate. Therefore no two relates the same story of the earthly journey.

"But the varied highways of earth continue into eternity, and the traveller on each goes eternally on his own road from the

earth life. And thus all travel on in the spirit world, having different experiences here, as with you; and, on returning to you, we have different experiences and differing descriptions of the spirit world to relate to you, according as each has realized for himself."

I can readily appreciate that spirit people along the Frontier and among the rudimentary spheres cannot tell how many there are beyond, and may not all agree, but here is what another says on the subject:

"There are innumerable spheres in the spirit world. If it were not so, progression would be a myth. Some tell you that there are only seven. That is because they have no knowledge beyond that sphere. I do not mean a place fixed by boundaries, for the spheres or degrees in spirit life are only conditions and are not confined to a limited space; as a soul develops, it naturally arises above its surroundings and consequently experiences a change in its spheres or conditions."

In order to get another impression, I read what I have written to Dr. Hossack, one of the leaders of the spirit group with whom I worked so many years, and for whose statements I have great respect, and in reply he said:

"What appears as space about your earth is composed of-as you know-ether. There are three distinct circles, the outer filled with more radiant vibrations than those within. Beyond these, the spheres, or circles blend with those of other planets. Each circle is very, very many miles in depth, according to your standard of measurement."

I am much impressed with such statements, as they seem natural and appeal to reason. So far as I know, no one has heretofore attempted actually to locate and fix the boundaries of the after life. Two thousand years of Christian teaching have not enabled a reasoning mind to form any definite conclusions as to where that place called heaven is, or concerning the conditions prevailing where the so-called dead reside.

After birth, death is the greatest privilege that comes to mankind. If death did not occur, there would be old age, feebleness, poverty, pain, and suffering forever; with it, splendid life on through the ages, progress, perpetual youth and vigor. Such is the heritage of all who have lived, or who shall live in the ages to come as inhabitants of this plane; such are the benefits coming through death.

"Physically considered, in the final separation of the soul or spirit body from the flesh garment there are no discomforts. As the etheric form goes out through the process called death, pain ceases, and then for a short period comes what is usually called unconsciousness. During the passing of the soul, when the individual leaves the tenement of flesh, when the spirit of man hurried forth from the old housing, there is no sensation. That period of time may be characterized as a sleep; then comes the awakening, the return of sensation, consciousness. Such is the true resurrection, and the possibility of that perfect life, unattainable to an inhabitant of earth. After leaving the earth-plane the immortal has been divested of the physical, and progress is unlimited."

Ever alert to obtain the personal observations of those who have gone on, I said:

"I have been told that the afterlife is intensely real and that with you everything is just as tangible as it was when you lived among us. Tell me something of matter surrounding and composing the plane in which you live."

"The most learned scientist," he replied, **"among the inhabitants of earth has practically no conception of the properties of matter, the substance that makes up the Universe—visible and invisible. I did not when I lived among you, though I made a special study of the subject. That which you see and touch, making up the physical or tangible, having three dimensions, is the lowest or crudest expression of life force, and notwithstanding my long study of the subject, the idea that the physical had permanent etheric or life-form, that which you call space was composed of matter filled with intelligent and comprehensive life in higher vibration never occurred to me; so when I became an inhabitant of the plane where I now reside, I was wholly unprepared to grasp or comprehend the material conditions of the environment in which I found myself."**

"Tell me," I asked, "of your awakening, and how things appeared to you as consciousness was restored."

"Of course, "he replied,**" there was the meeting and greeting of my own who came to welcome me, as naturally as one returning after along journey in the earth-life would be welcomed. Their bodies were not so dense as when they were inhabitants of earth, but they were like my own. Then I was told that my body and the bodies of all those in that life were actually the identical bodies we had in earth life, divested of the flesh covering. I was also told that that condition was a necessary precedent to entering the higher life, and that such bodies in earth life had continuity and, further, that in leaving the old, I had come into a plane where all was etheric, that is matter vibrating in perfect accord with my spirit, technically speaking, the etheric self. To me everything seemed perfectly natural to sense, sight, and touch.**

"Again, let me tell you," he said, **"that the outer flesh garment is not sufficiently sensitive to feel, the etheric body alone has sensation. This I have said as leading up to a clear understanding of what I experienced in meeting the new conditions here. I found little body-change, —I had sensations and vision—and my personal appearance was in no way changed except that my body was less dense, more transparent as it were, but the outline of my form was definite, my mind clear, the appearance of age gone, and I stood a man in the fullness of my mentality—nothing gained or lost mentally.**

"What impressed me most after the meeting with my own was the reality and tangibility of everything and everyone. All those with whom I came in contact had bodies like my own, and I recognized friends and acquaintances readily. Now I will tell you of the one thing that impressed me most on coming here, —that was that matter in its intense refinement, in its higher vibration, was capable of intelligent thinking and direction. Shape and grasp this proposition if you can; I could not in the beginning—nor could I comprehend at once that all in the Universe was life and nothing else. This fact, which we now know, will overturn all the propositions of science.

"In all the orthodox teaching of nearly two thousand years, not one law has been given tending to show how it was possible for

individual life to hold continuity. Theology has claimed it without explaining how or where. This no longer satisfies the human heart or mind, a fact which accounts for the great unrest among your people in every land. For this reason it has been our aim to explain the law through which life is continued, and so simply to state the facts and explain the conditions that all may understand. The key to comprehension is first to realize that your Earth does not contain all the matter of the Universe, that all that you see and touch is but the substance used by life in growth. When one leaves the earth-condition, divests himself of the physical housing, he, through such change, ceases to be mortal. By becoming a resident of the new sphere he is said to take on immortality, but in reality, he has always been immortal.

"You regard the telephone as wonderful, " he said, "wireless telegraphy more wonderful still—but we communicate with each other by simple thought projection. You regard the phonograph as a marvelous instrument, but it is crude beside the instruments in use among us. When you appreciate the truth that we live in a state no less material than your own, you will understand that with our greater age and experience we are much in advance of you, and make and use appliances and instruments that could hardly be explained to mortal mind. At some other time I may be permitted to discuss the subject more fully."

Let me quote again directly from one in the next life who's voice spoke from out of the darkness in our séance room:

"The majority of people are so intent on things material that those of a spiritual nature are either thrust into the background or forgotten altogether. This is a deplorable state of things and one which we earnestly desire to remedy.

"The mere struggle to live and provide themselves and their dependents with what they consider the necessities of life, engage many folks' attention to the exclusion of everything else. They just battle on from day to day because they must, or else become a burden to others. Such endeavor in their case is right and necessary and, if it is carried on in a brave and hopeful spirit, it is greatly to be admired.

"At the same time they would be greatly helped, and their burdens lightened considerably, if they would take time from their incessant struggle after material things to store up for themselves treasures of a spiritual nature.

"Wealth of this kind is of inestimable value and well worth a little trouble to procure. Unlike earthly riches it makes life on the earth easier and pleasanter for its possessor and his associates, and ensures for him a happy and useful time when his earthly life ends and his spiritual existence begins.

"One who has given all or nearly all of his time and thought to material things has so much to learn on arriving here, that it is a comparatively long time before he begins to 'find' himself sufficiently to understand and enjoy the spiritual life. Such a one, if he had given more time and thought to spiritual things during his earth life, could have immediately have claimed his spiritual treasures—which would have been carefully stored up for him until such time as he had need of them—and he would have been helped and his new life made much easier and pleasanter by the possession of these riches. As it is, he has to make his way as a penniless wayfarer, on arriving in a new locality, must set about earning his daily bread in the material world.

"Everyone knows what a handicap the lack of capital is in your world. Well, exactly the same thing applies here. Folks arriving here in the spiritually destitute condition before mentioned have just as hard, if not a harder, struggle to make their way in the spiritual life as anyone who is left without means on earth. People placed in the latter condition may and very often do receive financial help from friends and relatives, or societies which deal with that sort of thing, but there are no charitable institutions here. That is to say, no spirit ever gets something for nothing, or without effort on his part. Though we old spirits can and do help newcomers, we cannot give them spiritual riches—we can only show them how they may acquire them for themselves."

Another spirit says:

> "If newly-arrived spirits have a desire to learn how to make a spiritual living, so to speak, we can instruct them, so that in time they will become independent and will know how to set about the task of amassing wealth of a spiritual nature for themselves.
>
> "Such wealth is not easily acquired, even here, but it is possible for any and every spirit to become possessed of it in time, if he only desires it sufficiently and is willing to work hard to get it. This may sound as if selfishness is encouraged here, but that is not so. Spirits can become possessed of the wealth here spoken of only by loving and unselfish conduct toward others. They must learn to work gladly and without thought of reward before they can hope to enjoy the fruits of their labors.
>
> "There must be literally a 'labor of love,' and when self is utterly forgotten in a desire to help others, great and satisfying will be their reward. No goal on earth is, or even can be, so well worth striving after. For, after all, though it is difficult to make humanity realize it fully, the things of the soul are so much more worthwhile, and infinitely more lasting, than any earthly joys and pleasures can possibly be."

"What is the death change that seems so horrible to the average mind?" I inquired.

> "Death change," one answered, "is simply the liberation of the spirit from the physical body, composing the outer flesh garment, perfectly natural and painless. Every change in Nature is beautiful, and dissolution is no exception to the rule. One simply ceases to be an inhabitant of your world, and in an instant one becomes an inhabitant of the world in which we now live. The second world or plane is just as natural to us as the first, but, of course, we live under different conditions. We pass our daily life as before. Our spirit is just as perfect a human form as it ever was. For your clear understanding of the modus operandi of the death change to this plane we may say that one parts with the physical body only. We lose none of our intelligence; neither is anything added to our understanding."

"What of your daily life?" I asked our spirit visitor one evening:

"Our days are very busy, "he said." **There is no stagnation, but on the contrary, intense activity among everyone, that is, when we have emerged from the earth conditions. There are countless millions of children unborn physically who are plunged into this world of ours, and there are millions of women here who have never known motherhood in earth life, who take and care for them, watch and aid their growth, mentally and physically, and in that manner satisfy the craving of motherhood.**

"The insane pass from the earth-life insane still, and countless numbers of our people are required to care for them and give them proper treatment so that their mentality may be restored to normal. Murderers at war with humanity, hanged or electrocuted on the earth-plane, are liberated in this community and we are obliged to do what the world of men failed to do—control and educate them. Then, again, we have the ignorant and vicious. The atom of Good that has found expression in them must be developed and directed. Few people come into this life with any conception of what or where it is, or of the controlling laws. The ignorance of the masses is pitiful. They enter our portals as helpless as the babe enters yours. So you see dissolution making no mental change, and life being material and continuous, there is just as great need for schools, colleges, and universities as exists with you. In fact, it may be said that everything you have in your earth life is but a poor imitation of what exists here and is largely the result of spirit influence and power."

"What of your homes?" I asked.

"We have houses in which the family relation is continued, where every member-spirit is seeking enlightenment. The law of attraction is the dominant force here. We have a great number of thoughtful men seeking to discover and develop the hidden forces of Nature; we have great lecture halls where those who are learned, discourse upon hidden forces; we have teachers who develop the spirituality, and discourse upon the great force called Good and its function in the universe. It is a busy world where everyone is doing his or her part. We do not have any strife for

money or need for money; so you see the occupation of the great majority of your people is gone. It is only by helping others in this life—that one betters his conditions and enriches himself. This is the law. The only happiness that the inhabitants of earth really get is through being charitable, doing good, and making the world happier. The only wealth that any man carries beyond the grave is what he gives away before he reaches the grave."

"Tell us something of your foods. Do your require nourishment?" I asked.

"Yes," he answered, **"but not in the manner or in the way that you do. Our digestive organs continue their functions, and we require food, but we take the essence while you take the substance. You take food day by day in earth life. The substance is absorbed in the physical garment, but it is the essence of the food that nourishes the spirit body from day to day. The substance is no longer necessary, but the essence is necessary just as it was before. So you see there is very little change in physical necessities."**

"Tell me of your political economy," I asked.

"There is," Dr. Hossack answered, **"no aristocracy in this land of ours, but mind and merit. The law of Nature which is the Supreme force, called Universal Law, has to be obeyed, in order that each sphere may be reached. Every individual remains on the plane for which he is fitted, until he subjects his will to the Universal Law. As he progresses, he learns new laws, but they are fundamentally the same, only they grow more intense and vital, until he becomes a part of that law himself.**

"The political economy of the spheres has reference only to wealth, which being unbounded and free as air and light, can, of course, be appropriated by each and every member of society, according to his or her capacity of reception, the supply being equal to the demand. Hence it will be seen that we have no occasion for gold and silver which perish with the using; but the currency of moral and intellectual worth, coined in the mint of divine Love, and assayed by the standards of purity and truth, is necessary for each one."

"Tell me something of your social life," I said:

"With regard to the social constitution of the spheres," he answered, **"each is divided into six circles or societies in which congenial people live together agreeably according to the law of attraction. Although the individuals composing such society unite as near as may be in thought, agreeing in the most important moral and intellectual features, yet upon careful analysis we find that the varieties of character in each society are almost without number. They are perfectly analogous to the numerous members of the different societies on the earth-plane. Each group has teachers more advanced than the members of the group, and teachers often come from higher spheres. They impart to us the knowledge they have acquired in their progression in the different departments of science, which we, in turn, transmit to those below us, just in the same manner as we are transmitting knowledge to you now. Thus, by receiving and teaching, our intellectual faculties are expanded to higher conceptions and more exalted views of Nature's laws. Our scientific researches are extended to all that pertains to Nature, to the wonders of the heavens and of the earth and to whatever the mentality is capable of conceiving and comprehending. In this manner we get our progression and enjoyment. The sciences of mathematics and astronomy engage our attention. These subjects are inexhaustible. Chemistry is the most interesting of any of our studies, as it would be to you if you only appreciated the fact that all change in Nature is the result of chemical action."**

"You do not mean to say that all of your inhabitants are sufficiently advanced to do that work?"

"No," he answered, **"there are millions of inhabitants of this life who are not sufficiently advanced to take any interest in such studies. As we have passed beyond the rudimentary sphere, our intellectual energy is increased, our perception improved, and we can by intuition, as it were, more correctly and rapidly conceive and understand those principles and truths which are the basis of all scientific work.**

"In addition to our research we have our diversions from which we obtain great pleasure. We come together in social intercourse, just as you do. Families meet and have reunions, just as you do. Not

one particle of love is lost, but rather it is intensified. Everything is intensified to a degree that you cannot imagine. Your pleasure and amusements can in no way compare to those which we are privileged to enjoy."

"What of the religious movement among your people?" I asked.

"In the lowest of the spheres, that is, in the earth-bound spheres sectarian strife and religious movement are just as strenuous among the people as they were before these persons left the physical body. That state of transition is but little removed from the physical, for, while the majority there know they have left the body, others have such an imperfect appreciation of the change, or have led such immoral lives that they are not conscious of the fact. Here the dogmas of orthodoxy are dominant, and the old religious teachings are promulgated, and the priesthood still holds power. One would think that an individual having passed through the portal called death and finding nothing as he had been taught, or as he had believed, would give up the old notions and try to comprehend the economy of the natural law under which he continued to live; but, strange as it may seem, many even then cling to the old beliefs as if in fear, as if to doubt were sacrilege, and in many ways excuse their failure to find what they expected. They go into your churches and mingle with other people, a great invisible host, hear the same old teachings, say the same creeds and continue in the same mental attitude until some condition is brought about them that guides them into the avenue of knowledge, and as time goes on, one by one they break the shackles about their mentalities, and by progression, through individual effort, become inhabitants of the first spirit spheres.

"Everyday matters are no different in our sphere than in your sphere. You do not progress and obtain knowledge and advancement until you break away from the old beliefs and creeds. Neither do those out of the body in that earth-bound condition. You see there is but one law for you and one law for us. All of nature's laws are universal.

"Our laws are meted out on a scale of exact justice. All Nature's laws are exact laws, and from their reward there is no appeal. Punishments are but the natural consequence of violated laws, and are invariably commensurate with the offense, and have reference to the reformation of the offender as well as to the prevention of future crimes."

"What are the results that will come to mankind through communication with your people?" I asked an inhabitant of the afterlife. He answered:

"I will briefly call your attention to a few of the most prominent of the beneficial results which will flow from spiritual intercommunion. It would settle the important question, 'If a man dies, shall he live again?' It will reduce the doctrine of the immortality of the human spirit to certainty, so that the world's knowledge of the fact will not be the result of a blind faith, but a positive philosophy. It will show the relation existing between mind and matter; it will make men thinking and rational beings. It will establish a holy and most delightful intercourse between the inhabitants of the terrestrial world and the departed spirit friends. It will expand and liberalize the mind far beyond your present conceptions. It will fraternize and unite all the members of the human family in an everlasting bond of spiritual union and harmonious brotherhood. It will establish the principle of love to God and your fellows. It will do away with sectarian bigotry. It will show that many of the so-called religious teachings are but impositions on the credulity of mankind."

"I am anxious for a further description of yourselves, your pleasures, your interaction with each other, and it is difficult for us who have only had experience with matter in its physical state in any way to comprehend life in another state," I said.

"We derive much pleasure," was the reply, **"from the exercise of our talents in vocal and instrumental music, which far excels the noblest efforts of musical genius on earth. When we convene to worship God in our temples, whose halls and columns beam with inherent light, our voices are blended together in songs of praise and adoration to the Almighty author of our existence.**

> **"We are moral, intellectual, and sensitive creatures. Instead of being, as you may imagine, more shadowy and unsubstantial entities, we are possessed of definite, tangible, and exquisitely symmetrical forms, with well-rounded and graceful limbs, and yet so light and elastic that we can glide through the atmosphere with almost electrical speed. The forked lightnings may flash, and the thunders roll in awful reverberation along the vault of heaven, and the rain descend in gushing torrents, but we can stand unharmed by your side.**
>
> **"We are, moreover, endowed with all the beauty, loveliness, and vivacity of youth, and are clothed in flowing vestments of effulgent nature suited to the peculiar degree of refinement of our bodies. Our raiment being composed of phosphorescent principles, we have the power of attracting and absorbing or reflecting the rays evolved, according as our condition is more or less developed. This accounts for our being seen by clairvoyants in different degrees of brightness, from a dusky hue to an intensity of brilliant light."**

There were few nights in all the years of my research that Dr. David Hossack did not address us on some subject. He always came with charming courtesy and great cordiality. His voice was low, but he spoke clearly and to the point. No more distinguished or delightful guest ever entered my house. It will be noted that I make no distinction in speaking of those who enter my home. It matters not whether for the moment they function in the spirit or in the physical plane; they are all people and can discuss questions, when proper conditions are provided, with equal freedom. During the period when I obtained these discourses from the beyond, I formed or provided the conditions requisite and necessary, as I have explained elsewhere.

The question of light in the next world has always interested me, and it is one of the subjects upon which I have sought information. I speak of Dr. Hossack, for the reason that he has given me the most satisfactory explanation of any. This was my question to him:

"What is the character of your light, and how does it differ from sunlight?"

The answer:

> **"The light we have is obtained from the action of our minds on the atmosphere. We think light, and there is light. That is why people who come over in evil condition are in the dark; their**

minds are not competent to produce light enough for them to see.

"There is great intensity of light as we go up through the spheres, which comes from the blending of the more spiritual minds.

"Our life is merely the condition of mind which each one has. We create images in thought, and have the reality before us, just as tangible as your houses and buddings are to you. You do not have any conception of the great power and force there is, or may be, in thought. It dominates all conditions and makes us what we are. One who realizes this may control his destiny.

"Thought is a fluid, which becomes substance to us when once it is formed into an expression. It is a vibrating, living thing, and should be recognized as such and controlled accordingly."

Another spirit speaks of light as follows:

"When you speak of the sun in the spirit world, you mistake, for there is no such thing. There is light here, radiated from the atoms. Our light is very different from your sun. Your light is grosser than ours; it is unnatural to us, and therefore, painful to the spirit. Our light is soft, radiant and very brilliant. Your physical eye can never behold it; it is so ethereal, so beautiful, that it blends with sensation."

But why? What natural law produces spirit light? Another's understanding follows:

"There is a great central force, the rays from which gradually lessen in their vibratory action. This force comes from the outside of your world, as you call it, and reaches the lowest ebb in the center of your earth. This central vibratory action is in the highest sphere, and is so intense and vivid that the souls that are in the finest state of development are the only ones who come near its circle. It is the apex of the universe, and that is why there are lesser degrees as it is rayed out through infinite space. These vibrations of light reach the earth and all the other spheres, and the vibratory action of

light on each plant depends on its distance from the seat of this creative or central force.

"Some of the planets are much higher in vibratory action than in your earth, and if you were to go to them, and could still retain the earth conditions surrounding you, as usual you could not see any life because your vibration would be so much lower. The need of this condition is so apparent when once one grasps the immensity of the universe and the harmony of its laws.

"If you were able to see all the conditions and people beyond you, life would be chaos and confusion—each sphere mixing with another—with no regulations or harmony anywhere. As it is, each has its own place in the scheme of progression, and this visible wall of vibratory force is the safety guard to continued rational living.

"This force is life, intense, vibrating, dominant. In conception there is the merest touch to this elemental force; consequently, life is forwarded and the continuation of the species insured. It is something discernible as a part of nature and nature is but an expression of this great force.

"Those souls that progress through each step are slowly, but surely, becoming a part of that great force which is life; life itself is light, and ultimately individuality will be lost in the immensity of that great, harmonious life force and will become, in turn, a tiny part of the new conception in the earth form again. I do not mean that this is reincarnation. An atom only is needed to create life in the lower earth forms, and that is taken from the immense whole. This is the law of the universe. There seem no words to tell you, or to make you understand clearly, the plan and purpose of creation; one must accept it and try to realize that one's own life, seemingly so important to one's self, is in reality such a little thing in the immensity of the universe, and yet just as essential to the whole as one petal of a flower is to the perfect rose. It is a part of the perfect whole, and necessary.

"Make that part that is developed by you clean and wholesome, and the going on will be filled with beauty; it will be but the going

into a new country, among good friends and great advantages, along spiritual and harmonious lines. But to those who live in the dark and do evil and selfish things, the going will be along rough and stormy places and the helping hand hard to find."

We know so little of light. We have always had the sun, but even now know little about it.

The Record of a Night

"Tell me more of the actualities of your daily life," I asked.

"You think," she answered, "That you have vision, but your eyes have never looked upon life itself. You think you have hearing, but your dull ears have never heard one strain of our divine music. You have taste, but your tongues have never touched the essence. You have smell, and the aroma of roses carried by etheric atoms fills the nostrils, but you cannot appreciate the perfumes of this land of ours. You feel the touch of the coarse covering of living form without having any conception of the delight of touching life itself. In this sphere we have opportunities for education, joys, and happiness un-thought of by you in the earth-land, but these are only for those who have come out of the gross material condition in which they were born. We live in homes largely in groups where harmony of thought and action is perfect, but we too have as many grades of people as you do, and in our earth-condition is found degradation as great as that which you know. Here are found the ignorant, the wicked, the immoral, and the vile. Dissolution does not improve or uplift character; that must come from the germ of good in the heart of every living creature.

"Tell those who fear the end, "the voice said," that what they call death is very wonderful and beautiful; that with us, as with you, though you know it not, love is the one great force in the universe; it is the motor that drives the world and causes action. All things are done in and through it, and because of it. Affinity so-called, is the process through which the love-force finds expression. But in this connection let me suggest that love is good, and of God, and walks in the path of honor, never into dishonor. It never brought unhappiness; it is never 'born of lust.'

> **"It has been a joy and a privilege to speak to you tonight, for if any words of mine can help or make happier a single soul, that joy is reflected about me, and I am happier for having made others happy. Such is the law of God, and the secret of the world. Good night."**

The home and environment in the world of spirit are designed in thought, created in spirit matter, which is also mind, and its beauty and grandeur are only limited by the purity and progression of our earth life. They do not give their thought physical expression; they have nothing physical. Those in the other life have limitations, as we have.

I have never been able to make clear in my mind just the process in and by which our thoughts and acts create in the after life the environment that they do. Take the following description:

> **"One passing from the earth plane finds a home which, to his perception, is substantial, objective, familiar and real. It embodies and represents his thoughts, purposes and attainments, the outward expression of his mental, moral and spiritual self. That home is healthful, attractive, artistic and beautiful, if he has provided the requisite conditions. Whatever it is, it is home."**

Mission Work

"God is not the God of the Dead, but of the Living."

-Matthew 22: 32

There is a part of our work equal, if not greater, in importance than any heretofore mentioned. This we term mission work, and we conduct it among earth-bound spirits who are unable in the next sphere to go beyond the first conditions, or who lie dormant in the darkness of their own gathering. Each night, when we are thus engaged, the time is divided by those in charge-a portion is given to our instruction, and at least an equal part is given to helping those who need aid, suggestion, and direction.

It is my experience that nearly all, whether they are educated or uneducated, have little, if any, conception of the condition and state which immediately follows death. Education, as that term is used, does not necessarily aid the primal condition, though it may further one's progress, by enabling him to grasp more quickly the principles which govern progression. One may have learning without spiritual development; one uneducated in the sciences, may have so developed his spirit that he is more advanced than the other when the new day dawns.

There are many who in that new life are helpless, who are like newborn infants in this world of ours, except that they possess all the knowledge gained on the earth-plane, and know the joy that comes of good and the burden that comes of wrong. Though they are like children, and enter consciously, they must be taught to walk, to take sustenance, to labor, to work, and to know the laws that control spirit. For where on this earth can such instruction be obtained? Assuming that one has led a good life and is conscious of his surroundings, he must learn all these lessons from those who have gone before, and there are many eager and ready to help. We labor largely among those who have not awakened, or who fail to understand their condition. Those who lie dormant, who are surrounded by darkness oftentimes cannot be aroused by other spirits any more than human beings can touch the mentality of an idiot within asylum walls. They stay in this condition until Nature restores and strengthens the mind, or until they are brought into the material vibrations made by mortal and spirit working together. When we work, we throw out material vibrations, into which the group brings many, sometimes hundreds, at a time, all in practically the same mental attitude. One spirit is clothed with material, is awakened, is selected to talk. The others there assembled listen to the speech and appreciate all benefits. This chosen one may be heard to gasp as he takes the first breath of our atmosphere. Since voice is produced by the organs of respiration, they must be clothed with material. I do not know all the laws that control this production of sound among spirits; but the production itself is a fact that permits no argument.

Those spirits that greet us on such evenings usually know nothing of the flight of time, or even know that they have separated from the old body. They awaken from a dreamless sleep, as it were, with the old thought dominant, with individuality the same, but with strange surroundings. Imagine, if you can, the varied thoughts that flash through the mind as consciousness comes. Never are two alike, any more than any two persons. When I say that I have talked with a few that have *not had one intelligent thought or seen a ray of light for seventy-five or one hundred years*, and that they speak of the world as it was when they left it, you may at least gain an impression of what it is possible to make for ourselves in the sphere beyond. True, these are unusual cases, but one can create such a condition, and some people have created it. Few have no clouds in the horizon of thought.

The speaker is clothed for a time like us; but the condition that holds the material on the spirit-form is sensitive, and any sudden fright or mental shock will disintegrate the atoms and cause them to fall. Then the spirit loses the power for speech. The first question is often one of inquiry. The spirits are astonished at the strange faces and the new surroundings, and are anxious to know where they are. Few of them even know what has happened. Our first effort is to calm them, and when they are most quiet and reasonable, the thought that was strongest in mind when the change came is expressed and retold. Often that thought was of approaching death, and they tell of the awful fear that filled their hearts and of their seemingly fortunate escape. We then bring them to a discussion of what death is, and make them realize fully that they are alive and in possession of every natural faculty; we teach them by degrees that there is no death, and that the change they so feared is passed. No matter how cautiously this information is imparted it is always followed by a great shock, and often the material clothing then disintegrates. Then, with a cry of fear and alarm, they lose their power of speech. If possible they are restored to a vocal condition, and our efforts are continued. Our work is not finished when they are brought to a conscious state. They must next be taught what spirit is and how it may learn the new laws that will thenceforth govern and control all their thoughts and actions. When one finds that he is out of the body, the thought of those left behind crystallizes, — anxious the inquiry, great the sorrow! Why should not the separation be as hard for him as for those left behind? Then, again, the change may have come before he was ready, when he was needed by friends or family, and many a cry has gone out: "What will they do; how will they live; who will care for them now?"

Those religiously inclined at once want to find the Savior. Many who had been taught that they could be saved only with His help, say they must find Him, and when we tell them that he was only the symbol of a perfect man, and that one has no redeemer but himself, they hesitate to accept our statements. Often only the words of personal friends who have gone before bring conviction. Many give up the idea of a Savior very reluctantly. We next try to bring these spirits to an understanding of what life in the spirit-world is. Those controlling the conditions usually take up the discussion, and spirit talks to spirit. All of us take part in trying to demonstrate and convey to the new-comer ideas of the life he has entered. The spirit-company are able, by laws that have not been explained, to make him see every act and deed that made up the sum total of his former life. As the scenes passed one by one, like a flowing stream, I have heard them shout with joy and shriek with fear. Little can be done except to bring the spirit to a sense of realization, and to point out the avenue called restitution. When the desire to live again the deeds of earth life comes from the heart, others in spirit there show how the acts of selfishness and wrong which created the darkness and which surrounds them may be relieved. But each spirit must carry his own burden; he must go his own way; he must perform his own labor, and no hand may lift the weight from his soul. Each act lived over and lived aright will dispel the darkness that it caused, and so the home and the surroundings will grow lighter and more beautiful. How long the way is, and how unnecessary! If only mankind were taught the truth here! We may sin in ignorance, but this brings sorrow—not so much for the condition it makes for us, as for the misery it causes others. When we appreciate what our wrong-doing has brought to others, and what is denied us for that reason, our grief is great. Remorse is ours, and misery and unhappiness become our close companions. With the knowledge that men have no Savior but themselves, spirits usually assume the responsibility of their own acts readily, and are eager to commence the undoing, through which they shall reach higher planes. Sometimes many spirits in practically the same mental attitude are brought in, and I am asked to take up the discussion of some subject in which all are interested and in which all need knowledge. It seems that my thought and voice vibrate so keenly that their attention is attracted. They become interested and gather close about. I am told that sometimes thousands in a single evening come and listen. When I have interested them and one is, perhaps, talking with me, and many are talking with each other, teachers from other spheres take up the work and carry it on.

This, then, is a suggestion of what our mission work is, and how with the help of an intelligent and powerful group of spirits we labor to aid progression and to dispel the darkness that holds a soul prisoner in the dungeon of despair. But our work is not confined to those in trouble. Others come who have never known that condition. They live among those they love, and work with songs of joy and gladness in their hearts, radiant and happy, climbing the hills of knowledge. These tell me that when the first sphere is passed they know the intensity of life; they are free and understand the joys of freedom. Then they find that popes, bishops, priests, and kings are dead; that the aristocracy of this world has perished; that the personal god whom mankind worshiped, never existed; that truth is a religion that sheds joy on all the spirit spheres. Beyond the plane of restitution they find a world at peace, where honest effort meets its true reward. They find spheres, bright and clear, the married harmony of form and function, where there is no disease of flesh or brain. Then their conception of Nature broadens, happiness unknown before fills every heart, fear is dead, and ignorance and prejudice are left far below.

Among the thousand cases that came into our mission work, some teaching great lessons stand out prominently. There lived in my home city a few years ago a man of great wealth. He had reached the age of four-score and ten, was of unimpeachable character and at the head of some of our largest financial institutions, but he was close in money matters, very close, and saved the pennies as well as the dollars. I knew him intimately, for I had an office for some years in the same building and saw him frequently. He was counted a good citizen, but not much given to relieving distress, — such was the public estimation of his character.

The day came when he passed from the world of men, and was soon forgotten. Five years elapsed, during which period I went on with my work, helping those whom my co-workers brought, regardless of who or what they were, for in the democracy of death, wealth and worldly distinction are lost, and only character survives.

I recall vividly the evening I shall describe, for it taught one of the greatest lessons I have ever had from this source. This night I was not alone with Mrs. French; I had as a guest Louis P. Kirchmeyer, who had psychic sight and could actually see spirit people before they spoke, as could Mrs. French. If a spirit was personally known, either could call him by name, and if I knew him well, I could usually recognize his voice. This condition made identity in such cases beyond question.

Again, this chapel in my home where my work was carried on, with the non-luminous ribbon of light above our heads, indicated that conditions were favorable. There was never a night when we knew who would come or what we should be called upon to do, as much depended on our mental and physical condition, and then atmospheric conditions had to be considered. I seldom asked for any particular individual, — ours was a scientific work, and those who needed help were brought in after the lecture, usually.

> **"It is so cold and dark,"** a voice came out of the darkness. Mr. Kirchmeyer and Mrs. French both psychically saw and recognized the gentleman mentioned above, and told me his name. After he spoke, I recognized his voice, which was somewhat peculiar. I had a high regard for this man, and, considering the lapse of five years since his passing on, was startled by what he said.

"Mr. Wilson, "I said," I am surprised after this lapse of years to hear you make such a statement. Tell me more of your condition."

> **"There is around and about me a wall of money, nothing but money, it shuts out the light. It is so dark, and wherever I go I cannot get away from it, around it or over it,"** he replied.

> **"This man,"** said one of the spirit group who was helping in the work, **"spent his whole life in accumulating money. It dominated his whole thought, it was all he built, and in coming into this life he found only the condition he had created, and, never having developed his spirit, he sheds no light on his pathway."**

Having learned how to help in such cases by suggestion, I said, "Mr. W—, I think you will see light if you will look. What do you see?"

> **"It is coming,"** he said, **"just a ray, but wait, I see a highway leading away in the distance."**

"And what do you see on that highway?" I asked.

> **"Nothing,"** he answered, **"not a living thing."**

"Look again," I replied.

> **"Yes,"** he said, **"I now see sign boards along the sides as far as the eye will reach."**

"And what, if anything, is printed on those sign boards?" I asked.

> **"I can only read on the first one the word 'charity.' What does it mean?"** he asked.

> **"I will tell him what it means,"** the same spirit who had spoken before answered. **"This man never thought of charity, which is the helping of others, either by kindly words or by material aid, so with all his millions of money, he came into this world a spiritual pauper. He has now found the light, will realize his misspent life, and must learn what charity is. When he has practiced it, he can read the second sign. That highway is his to travel; it is long, but it will ultimately lead him to happiness and to a wealth he has never known."**

This experience teaches us that we owe something to our fellow men, and that the more we have the more we owe to those less fortunate

The following incident occurred on another night:

> **"My years have gone swiftly,"** another said, **"since my earth friends said farewell, and I journeyed on. I was glad to make the change for myself, but regretted I could not make those left behind understand that I was not dead and that it was for my good that I stepped out of the tenement of clay and put on the garb of the**

immortals. I realized at once that I was out of the body, but I stayed about the home for some days before I was taken away, when I took up the work of helping those in the lower spheres. I have been familiar with your work for a long time, and am permitted to bring a soul that you can help. When his vocal organs are clothed, he will speak."

"I understand fully," another spirit said, **"that I have left my physical body, and I was relieved when I knew it was not to be done. This is a beautiful world, in which I live, with opportunities beyond your conception. When earth conditions do not bind me, I can attend great lectures, and in temples of music hear celestial song. But I am bound to earth by the sorrow of my father and mother. They brood and weep, and sorrow for me as one dead, and that holds me like bands of steel, so that I can only at times do what other boys do. They don't understand that I am more alive than ever before, but until they give me happier thoughts my progression is stayed and I am as unhappy as they are. And I could be so happy and accomplish so much, if they would let me go. Won't you go and tell them what I have said, and change their thoughts? Tell them that death is life boundless and endless, and our sphere is filled with happiness. Please promise."**

I did promise, and I did go and do what I could, but human nature loves to sorrow for the so-called dead.

I found in the beginning that Mrs. French stood very much in awe of the play of this psychic force. One always fears things which he does not understand, and not understanding the unusual phenomena present, she was often very much afraid. I investigated far enough to find that she was possessed of a vital force unknown to me. She was just as much in the dark regarding it as I, and just as much interested. Accordingly she undertook to joining me in an investigation, to devote her time without money and without price to the mastery of that force in the hope that good might come. Out of that compact came over twenty years of continued work, and experiences which to me seem worthy of record.

In the beginning, spirit speech was faint from the sphere beyond. I was able to get in touch with only a very ordinary class of spirit people, and I often became impatient that those I most desired did not come. I did not then understand as I now do my own limitations, for now I know that instruction was being given me as fast as I could grasp it. When a new fact was stated, the law and the conditions making such facts possible were explained. The first propositions were very simple, but as the years rolled by, we made great progress. We learned how to form the required environment; there was a whisper and then a voice; then the voice took form and individuality. In course of time, those of the group of whom I was accustomed to have speech were easily recognized.

There was one person in particular with whom, from the very first time I worked with Mrs. French, I was desirous of talking. This was my mother who left this life in 1873. Time went on, and she did not come. Finally she requested me to meet with Mrs. French under the necessary conditions on May 26, 1896, saying that she would come and go over many things in which we were mutually interested.

About ten o'clock on the appointed morning the Brown Building in Buffalo, then being repaired, collapsed. The street was full of rumors that many people had been killed. The number was put, I think, at six or seven. Of course, there was no way of ascertaining the truth until the debris could be removed and this would require many days.

Mrs. French and I were scarcely seated that evening when my mother greeted me in her own direct voice, and said with great regret that owing to the accident that morning she must forego the pleasure of our visit until a later time, we would be of great help to those whose lives had been crushed out; they needed assistance. Of course, I readily acquiesced in the suggestion. There was perhaps ten minute of silence; then a voice, choking and coughing, broke the stillness and cried:

> **"My God! the building is falling, the building is falling. This way, this way!"** The situation was tense and startling. I half rose to my feet. Another voice answered in a strange tongue. The words were not distinguishable, but it seemed to me as if someone was responding to the first call, which was followed in a moment by a woman's voice crying out in great fear, **"We will all be killed! help me, help me!"**

This was the beginning of what we term our mission work. There was then, aiding in this work, as I have since learned, a group of seven spirit co-workers who had brought to us these unfortunate people whose spirit-bodies had been crushed out in the fall of this building. After a time I told them what had occurred and brought them to a realization of their situation. Eventually they came to understand that in the fall of that building their spirits had been forced from their physical bodies, and when they came to realize that in the catastrophe they had gone out of earth life, their sorrow was beyond words.

After talking with me, voice to voice, they realized that they had gone through the change called death. Then their friends in the afterlife came, were recognized, and took them and gave them such consolation as was possible under the unfortunate circumstances.

> I asked the leader of the spirit group how it was that the voices when first heard seemed so strained, and speech so broken, why there was so much choking. He replied: **"A person, crushed out of the physical body suddenly finishes, as soon as consciousness and the mental condition are restored, sentences left unuttered when dissolution came; that in the awakening he takes on the identical state in which he passed out."**

After they had gone, Mrs. French said:

"I see behind you a man probably fifty-five or more years old, strong character I should judge, who has been listening to this conversation. He is looking at you with amazement. He does not seem to understand."

I said to her, "Does he know me?"

> She replied, "He answers," **"Yes."**

"Does he give his name?"

"No, not yet."

Of course, being in absolute darkness and not possessing psychic sight or psychic hearing, I could neither see nor hear him, but I asked,

"Did he reside in Buffalo?"

She answered, "No."

I then inquired concerning other localities, and named residents of a city where I had lived for some years, asking, "Was he a resident of that city?"

And Mrs. French replied saying, "He says that he lived there."

Then I repeated the names of many of my acquaintances, trying to identify the individual who was then present, with an idea that I might have speech with him. Finally Mrs. French said, "I see the letters H.G.B."

I quickly recalled the individual described and spoke his name. He had been a leading citizen of a neighboring city. He had been out of the body then about five years. After a little time he moved around apparently to the side of Mrs. French, and a spirit guide who was observing the situation said:

> **"The wrong done in earth-life binds him to the earth condition. While he has left his physical body, he has not left the earth and its environment, and having no knowledge of the great beyond to which he has journeyed, he has never progressed beyond the earth plane where he formerly lived, and he cannot comprehend while in that mental state the change that has come to him."**

It appeared that he had never left his home, and the narrow environment about it, but in a half-awakened, half-conscious state had wandered from one to another until by good fortune he had been told that if he would attend upon our work, he would understand the change that had come into his life. With this unusual experience we said "Good Night" to our group of co-workers, and I walked homeward in deep thought.

What shall be said of our civilization that teaches nothing of the conditions prevailing in the after life?

Thousands upon thousands of spirit people spoke in this mission work and never any two in the same condition or with similar ideas or experiences, for they were different as in this life. Many were awakened apparently after long periods of time; others were in darkness, and could not find the light; others did not realize that they had left the old earth body; others knew they had, but found nothing as they expected. Some had a craving for liquor and a desire to satisfy old appetites; while others came for suggestions and advancement. The procession was endless and the need beyond description.

It was the most important work I ever did, beside which all my professional achievements sink into obscurity and are as nothing.

I was in my home one evening, alone with Mrs. French. A storm had passed and there could be heard the low moaning wind in the great trees outside. It was absolutely dark in the room where we sat facing each other with only a small table between us. The discourse on the scientific aspect of the next state was finished; then came silence and expectancy.

> **"I have wandered for years, searching, searching,"** a voice distressed and low, came out of the darkness; **"and travelled, travelled, travelled; I have found nothing but vegetation, and I am so weary. " Then this benighted spirit apparently realized that I was visible, and**

he seemed to turn towards me, and said; "I don't understand. I am seeking my Savior; I was told He would meet me, but I can't find Him, and I am lost."

I replied: "No man is ever lost."

He replied: **"I will be lost, if I don't find my Savior. I have searched so long!"**

"Did it ever occur to you that you have no Savior but yourself?" I asked.

"That cannot be," he said. **"All my earth life I relied on Him to save me, and I must find Him."**

"Would it not be better to try to save yourself?" I asked..

"No man can be saved except he believe in Christ," he answered.

"We have no Savior but ourselves, and until we understand that fact and help ourselves and others, we don't find a very desirable after life. How do you account for the fact that you have travelled so far, met no people, and seen nothing but vegetation?" I asked.

"I don't know; I don't understand," he answered.

"I know that I understand," another spirit voice answered. **"This man lived a narrow, selfish Christian life, simply relying on the Bible teachings, believing that the Savior would carry his burden and lead him to the great white throne, and when he realized he had passed the portal of death his first thought was to find that Savior that he had been taught to depend upon. This idea became an obsession and he started travelling with only one thought in mind. So intent was he, so centered was his thought, he saw nothing of the people or the wonders of the sphere in which he had advanced. He could not find what he sought, and he could not see or sense what he was not seeking. His journey will not end until he realizes that he is his own Savior."**

"That is a new idea. Who is that man?" he asked.

"A spirit like yourself," I answered.

"Is what he said true?" he asked.

"Has it not occurred to you in all this time, that, if your teaching were true, your Savior would have met you; and has not the fact that you were not so met, caused you to question your belief?" I said in reply.

"It has not before, but let me think. Have I been wrong in my belief? When I came over and tried to find Him, I should have questioned; but I did not. I thought I must search and I have searched so long," he said.

I had learned that when a spirit was really awakened in the condition we had created where the earth and spirit spheres blended together, friends could come and help. I asked: "Don't you want to stop travelling, and see some of your family and friends?"

"I certainly do. If I am wrong and have been wasting my life, I should like to know it," he replied.

"Look," I said.

"It is a growing light. How beautiful! I see great throngs of people," he said. "They are coming toward me, men and women, dead men and women, but they don't look dead. They appear just as they did before, and so do I. There comes a friend who beckons me. May I go?"

"Yes," I answered. "The thought that dominated you is broken and now you are free. Go with those who have come to help you, and they will show you how to help yourself."

He was gone, then silence again, the night wind and the darkness; while in the room tiny non-luminous points of light appeared, and substance like faint clouds in a summer sky floated and visibly formed into indefinite shapes, as the spirit chemist restored conditions to the psychic normal. Again the stress and the expectant speech. We could always feel the effort that was apparently necessary to clothe with ectoplasm a spirit's vocal organs, so that its voice would sound in our atmosphere.

> **"What are you trying to do?"** another voice spoke. **"I have been watching these manipulations with great interest; a gentleman told me to ask and I am curious."**

"This lady and myself, "I replied," come together each week and with spirit aid create a condition where we can talk, voice to voice, with spirit people."

> **"That is positively a most absurd statement. The dead can't talk,"** he said.

"Do you know that to be a fact?" I asked.

> **"No,"** he answered, **"I don't know it to be a fact, but if it were possible, I should have heard of it."**

"Have you ever heard of obtaining messages from departed spirit people?" I asked.

> **"Yes,"** he said, **"I have heard such claims, but never for a moment did I consider it worthy of the slightest consideration."**

"Did you ever really consider what would happen to you in the death change?" I asked.

> **"No, that was a subject I did not care to think about. I have the cares of my business, which are enough,"** he replied.

"Stop and think for a moment; where are you now?" I said.

> **"I don't know; this is not my office and the surroundings are strange. I don't quite comprehend this most unusual situation. Nor do I recognize you or this lady,"** he answered.

"Do you recall your name and recent events?" I asked.

"Certainly," he replied, **"my name is Morris and, as I recall, I had just concluded an important conference; but this is neither my office nor my home. Where am I and how did I get here, and who are you? I have no recollection of meeting you or leaving my place of business."**

"I am Mr. Randall, and you are in my home in Buffalo, and this lady and myself, with the aid of a spirit group, talk at times with those who have left the physical body, just as we are now talking to you," I replied.

"I don't know why you speak to me in that manner. I am not dead," he said.

"Look at your body," I said.

"I am looking at it. I see no change," he answered.

"Look again. Hold your hand to the light," I said.

"My God! What has happened? My whole body is natural but it is transparent. I can see through it. What does this mean!?" he asked.

"Does it not dawn on you what we are trying to convey? Recall your last sensation," I said.

"I am," he replied.

"I was in my office—a feeling of great weakness came over me. I had a sensation of falling, and I don't recall anything more, until I found myself here. Do you intend to convey the suggestion that I am dead? Is that what this talk leads to?"

"There is no death, there are no dead," I answered. "There is only change."

"Can it be," he replied, **"that death comes without knowing it, and that we continue to live in a world similar to that of the earth? It is a most astounding proposition. Have I really ceased to live the earth life?"**

"I should infer from your statements, "I answered," that you passed out of the body suddenly, possibly with a stroke of apoplexy. What is the date?"

"This is January 20th," he replied.

"No," I answered. "It is April, and for three months you have been unconscious."

> **"The suggestion stirs me beyond expression," he said. "Let me think. I was in good bodily health, as I thought, engrossed in business affairs, and the idea that death would come to me never was seriously considered, and now you tell me it has overtaken me, and that I am no more of earth, and that as a spirit I can actually talk to you still in the old life. I want to think it over—I am not fully satisfied. It would seem to me if I was a spirit I would meet other spirit people. Why don't I?"**

"Look about you again," I said. "While we have been talking, possibly you have not noticed what has taken place."

> **"Why it is growing more light, and I can see about me many I thought dead and gone," he said; "and they tell me they have come to help me out of darkness, teach me the laws that control in this sphere of life, and point out the method by which I can develop my spirit, which I have so long neglected. This thought and their presence overwhelms me, and I must have time to realize it all."**

"You have been awakened," I said, "and put in touch with those who will help you. Go with them and all will be well with you."

"Good night," he said. **"I thank you."**

These cases illustrate the condition in which some spirit people find themselves, the method employed in bringing them to a realization of the change that has taken place, and something of the results obtained in this mission work. Volumes could be written from the records obtained, which would further show the urgent need of work of this character.

The Earthbound

There were few nights during the years of scientific investigation that I did not talk with earthbound spirit people, usually with several, and I have learned much of their condition.

"What creates the earthbound condition?" is the first question properly asked. I answer, as I have been answered thousands of times:

"The lives they led, and the conditions they created for themselves, for as a man sows so shall he reap."

The laws of nature, the laws under which we live, are not only fixed and definite, but eternally just.

This is the story told by one:

> **"I was not a good man among men. I was selfish, cruel, took human life, and was, as I now know, killed while committing a crime. When I awoke it was very dark, and, not knowing what had happened, I called in anger, but my companions did not come. My voice echoes back to me again and again, and I began to think I was in a cave. I arose and groped about in the darkness, but I could not find the walls, though I walked for hours. I did not feel hunger or thirst, and days and months passed, while I was ever searching for the walls that threw back the echo of my call. Can you imagine the sensation you would have, to be lost in an open forest with the sun in the sky, to say nothing of being lost in darkness? My sensations and suffering beggar description.**
>
> **"After a very long time I saw a light, and as it approached I saw that it shone or radiated from the form of a man. 'My brother,' the man said, 'you are in spiritual darkness; how can I help you?' He came and, putting forth his hands, would have touched me, but I was speechless and rushed away in fear. Thereafter when I saw a light I would hide, fearing I would be arrested, for at that time I did not know I had left my physical body. I me, a man from whose body radiated, as before became desperate, and the next time a light approached I waited. Coming to, said, "What do you wish?" I replied, 'I want to get out of this prison.' You are not in prison; you are dead.' I cursed him for making such fool statements and he was gone.**

"Again I was alone in darkness. How long this continued I know not, for, there being no day, I could not count time. Again there came one to me and again I demanded that I be released from my prison. He calmly and kindly replied, 'you are not in prison; you are a spirit.' That seemed to me the height of absurdity, for I was very much alive; but I listened and he told me that I had made the change and brought another, an artist, who drew pictures of my youth and the faces of my boyhood friends, and, one by one, sketched those acts and deeds and wrongs that I had done. Then the light faded and they were gone and I was left alone to think.

"When I had fully come to appreciate my condition and to regret the wrong done and the suffering caused by me, there came a desire to do what I could to make reparation. Then came other spirit people to encourage me and suggest what I must do to obtain spiritual growth and, with it, the light. Not one offered to take my burden, or to undo the wrong that I had done; that was for me; they only pointed out the way. I was told there were none to forgive me, except the injured; no Savior but myself.

"Step by step I went forward; hour by hour I made reparation and lived again each wrong and lived it right; and day by day, as you count time, I undid my wrong and added to the right. The way was long, the labor intense, but in it I had found a happiness I had never known before. For I was building my character; the atom of good was striving for its spirituality. Now that is all behind me, and I live in the glorious and effulgent light of the spirit world, laboring among congenial souls. I was seared by the fire of selfishness and wrong. I paid, and paid to the last farthing, the penalty. Now I am at peace with all the spirit world, as it is with me.

"I send this message back to the world of men: 'There is not in the Universe a method by which any one can escape the penalty of wrong.' Had I known this fact, I would have lived among you honestly and been fair with my fellow men. I did not know it, and I have paid in full, as all will pay in full, for ignorance will not excuse.

"It has been a privilege to tell through you of my experience in the earthbound zone of the spirit world. If one man will hesitate

when contemplating a single selfish or wrong act, and turn from it because of better understanding, it will reflect upon me and better my condition."

The following statement as to earthbound conditions is from another spirit:

"The belts or zones that lie close around your earth are designed for the habitation of undeveloped spirits when out of the body; as they outgrow the passions of earth and become more refined, they pass to another or higher zone. Many remain in the first or earth zone for years.

"We of the higher zones try to reach them that they must forgive and forget the wrongs of earth and in that work advance out of the earthbound condition, but many turn a deaf ear to our suggestions and try to revenge the wrong done to them when on earth; all this is intensely human, and this zone, so like the physical, is very real. Those who have progressed, those who in the beginning passed directly through this belt, because of their spirituality, would never come back into that atmosphere, were it not for their love for and desire to help humanity."

In explanation of this condition another spirit said:

"Many on leaving the mortal body are still in earthly conditions, found on the grosser spiritual side you call the lower sphere, where the spiritual senses are not yet awakened to susceptibility or spiritual discernment."

Again, one said:

"I find a great many come from earth life in a very darkened condition; and, of course, they gravitate or are drawn to localities or corresponding conditions. They don't know just where they ought to go or what to do. In fact, many are ignorant of any other than the condition in which they find themselves. Many, too many, are in a condition of slumbering, some in a deep sleep which lasts a long time, and great effort is put forth to awake such spirit people."

This is the experience of another spirit:

> **"I had been in the afterlife a number of years when I was taken into the lowest sphere, and what I saw has lingered in my memory ever since. I was taken by a guide accustomed to work in the earthbound plane. We move, as you know, with the rapidity of thought. My first impression was of a descent in the dark, all about me gloom, and to add to the horror, I could hear voices though I could not see any one. After a time, when as it seemed, I grew accustomed to the darkness, I could see people about me, poor men and women who did not realize they had left the physical body—some shrieking because they could not escape their victims; those they had wronged were not there, — it was their awakening consciousness that brought such vision. The guide spoke gently to them. Some answered with course jests, others with mirthless laughter; but a few came close and listened when he told them of their condition and what must be done to work out of this darkness, which was of their own creation. We have as much trouble in making these poor spirit people understand conditions beyond their sight and touch, as you have with earth people."**

In the beginning when I talked with spirits who did not know they were dead, as that word is commonly used, it staggered my thought.

Let it not be understood that all the living dead are earthbound and held in such a zone of darkness; of all that go, only a few of the many are there held. But let it be remembered that conditions in spirit planes vary as the varying characters of men, and that each reaches that environment for which his earth life has fitted him. There he will live until by growth he has earned a more advanced zone.

The experience of these spirits were unusual, terrible in severity, and possibly extreme, but they are necessary to illustrate what the degenerate and wicked must expect. Others have told of the wonders and delights of the next conditions, as they were enabled to feel and visualize them in the beginning. Where spirit people are, what they see and enjoy, depends on just what their earth life earned. How many know this fact?

A spirit has said:

> **"You have no idea of the nature and extent of punishment which some spirits have to undergo. There is no hell, nor is torture inflicted in the spirit world. Everyone that comes brings the**

punishment with him in his own nature. When a spirit passes from the earth to this world, every trait of his natural habits, principles and passions is delineated on his spirit features. There can be no deception with us.

"You will be placed with those of similar character, whose natures correspond with yours.

"There is no night here, and consequently no day, at least not as I once measured, and as you still measure, time. Time here is measured only by emotions, events and deeds. There are dark places and darker souls, as there are on earth."

So Little Change

How can people be dead and not know it? This was the most difficult proposition ever presented to me. All orthodox teaching has been such that it is difficult for any one to comprehend the natural conditions about them. In my first years of this most interesting research, I talked with many who did not know that they had left the earth-life at all. Why did they not know that they had left the physical body?

Let me give a stenographic account of our work on the evening of May 10, 1897, illustrative of the point referred to and reported by Miss Gertrude Spaulding, now secretary to one of the United States senators from Minnesota.

The spirit controlling our work said:

"Tonight, we must bring into your presence a necessity, bring one who needs help more than you need words of instruction. In this regular work, do not change conditions; if you want to invite strangers, take another night."

A strange voice said:

Q. I am interested to know what you are doing here. I don't want that woman sitting there to take down what I say.

A. She is not here to take down your confession, if you make one. The work we are doing is of sufficient importance to be taken stenographically; that is what the stenographer is here for. Well, sir, how can we serve you?

Q. I don't want you to call me "friend," but as I am here I will present a business proposition. You like money, don't you? I suppose the rest of you like money too. It does a lot of things.

Q. Have you a speculation that you want us to join in?

A. I have a certain block of stock I want to sell.

Q. What kind of stock?

A. Mining stock. It is mining stock.

Q. Is that the most important thing in your mind?

A. That's the most important.

Q. Why do you wish to sell it?

A. I have good reasons, but I don't say very much about it to strangers.

Q. How did you get it?

A. Nevermind that. I have it and want to sell it.

Q. How long have you had that stock for sale?

A. I have had it for about five years. Have not sold it because everybody seems afraid of it.

Q. Now, hasn't it occurred to you that if you have not sold it, there is something about that stock that isn't right?

A. I know all about that stock. Are you afraid of it?

Q. No, I am not afraid of it. You have offered it very cheap, I suppose?

A. Not so very. I don't believe in cheap stocks.

Q. You have travelled?

A. Travelled? Travelled from one end of the earth to the other. I have been to Europe.

Q. Now, does it not seem strange to you that you have travelled so far and not sold your stock?

A. I'll tell you. It is strange to me because everybody that I have offered it to, has turned away after looking at it. People think I am a little "off."

Q. Now, where is your family?

A. You want my wife to sign the papers?

Q. Will she sign?

A. It is not necessary.

Q. Where is she?

A. Home.

Q. Where is home?

A. I will tell you if you want to know. She is in San Jose, California.

Q. You have travelled a good way. Did you ever hear of the city of Buffalo?

A. Yes, who hasn't?

Q. It is a good city, isn't it?

A. Very good, very good.

Q. Now I live in Buffalo. I am in my own home now.

A. You don't mean to say that I am in Buffalo?

Q. You have been brought here for some purpose other than selling mining stock. You have travelled a long way. Now, my friend, where did you get those papers? Be honest with me. Have they not been a burden to you for years?

A. That will do, gentlemen.

Q. Did you get that stock honestly?

The voice of the control interrupted, speaking with great force: **"The man you stole the papers from shot you."**

Q. Who is that? How does he know? How does he know?
The control speaking to us said:

"He was shot while stealing those papers. When we cannot reach spirits of his kind, we find it necessary to bring them into the conditions prevailing here now; we want your help. In this condition their mental activities are quickened, and they are brought out of mental darkness."

I said to the spirit: "If you will come and touch me, possibly you will gather more Strength."

A. You will put handcuffs on me.

Q. You are among friends.

A. I don't trust in friends or strangers.

Q. I want you to listen to what I have to say. You are nearly three thousand miles from San Jose, California. When you were stealing that stock from that other man, you heard the click of a revolver, didn't you?

A. Yes.

Q. Did you hear the explosion?

A. No.

Q. There was one.

A. I should have heard it if there had been.

Q. There was a revolver fired at that time, I am told, and that ball penetrated your body. When that occurred, you passed out of the physical body. You live right on; that life is so like the life here, that you and thousands of others go right on without being conscious of the change; they find conditions so similar, and whatever was in the mind when the change occurred is held sometimes indefinitely. You have been wandering over the face of the earth holding the thought that the stock was in your hands. You are not as you were before you took that stock; a great alteration has taken place, but you are not dead.

A. Am I a ghost?

Q. Let me explain. Every week we sit in a dark room as we are now doing, and understanding the laws that govern speech between the spiritual and physical planes, we are able to talk with people who have passed on, just as we are talking to you tonight. Now, you are in a situation which you fail to comprehend. You must

A. I believe none of that.

Q. Do you understand that there is actually no death?

A. No, I do not.

Q. The majority of people in the physical world do not understand that change at all. One leaves the old, physical body as one leaves an old coat. But the etheric body, the individual self, with its tendencies and desires, goes on and on. Now, don't you think there has been a change with you in some way? Do you want me to demonstrate that to you?

A. I am just like you.

Q. That cannot be, for your body is composed of ether only. I lift my hand to my face. Can you see my face through my hand?

A. No.

Q. Now, lift up your hand. Don't you see there is a difference?

A. Yes, I can see through my hand.

Q. What do you think of that?

A. If you think I am crazy, I had better go.

Q. We are not trying to do you harm.

A. Talk then in reason.

The control interrupted again, saying: **"We will bring a spirit that shall teach you what is reasonable, and he shall prove to you that you too are a spirit."**

Q. Do you know that the man talking to you now, is Stephens, once a citizen of much prominence?

A. He is dead.

Q. He is talking to you. Is he dead if he can talk?

A. You are a queer lot of people.

Q. Possibly, but if you will listen to what he says, if you will earnestly seek the truth, you will find it. Things are not satisfactory with you, are they?

A. Not very.

Q. Now, you would like to get out of your present condition, would you not?

A. I don't like to be called dead.

Q. We will help you all we can. We want you to listen. I tell you again, there is no death.

A. But you said I was a spirit.

Q. Yes, I say that you are now in the afterlife, and that you have an etheric body, almost identical with the old physical.

A. Where are your ministers? Why don't they so teach if it is a fact?

Q. Because the great majority don't know; and the few who do know have not the courage.

A. I will go and ask Father Spencer if this be true?

Q. Do you want to see Father Spencer right here? Is it possible at this time to bring Father Spencer here tonight? I asked the control.

A. I am sending messengers for Father Spencer, who has also passed on since his going," he replied.

Q. Either tonight, or at some other time, you shall talk with Father Spencer, as you are talking now with us.

A. I will wait.

Some years elapsed before this strange spirit came again, and then only to say that he found Father Spencer, and had come to understand the terrible condition which, by a life ill spent, he had made for himself.

From Death's Sleep

"By what right do you presume to compel my presence in this house!?" The room was in absolute darkness; the voice of one called by the world, "dead," trembling with anger broke upon the stillness of the night.

"Do you understand the situation in which you find yourself?" I asked.

"I do not, and will not allow any man to dictate to me," he replied.

"You are not afraid?" I asked.

"Afraid! I am not afraid of God or man, and I will not remain here."

"It might be to your advantage if you would," I answered. "I did not force you to come. You are as much a stranger to me as I am to you."

"Who did force me to come?" he asked.

"I do not know; tell me about it."

"As it comes to me now," he answered, **"an irresistible force seemed to urge me from a dream-like condition. Suddenly I was awake, in your presence, and immediately concluded that in some manner you controlled my conduct. That I cannot permit."**

"You are mistaken there, but does it not occur to you that some great good may come of this meeting?" I inquired.

"I cannot in any way understand your suggestion," the stranger said, "or see how any good can come of an enforced conference. If you did not bring me, who did? I had no desire to come, nor do I wish to remain. This house and its surroundings are unfamiliar to me. With your permission, I will retire."

"Before you go," I said, "I should like to have you know something of the work we are doing, which may account for your coming."

"Well, sir, finding myself in this unfamiliar situation I will not be lacking in courtesy, "he said.

"For many years," I replied, "I have been engaged in psychical research, with this psychic who sits opposite me, trying to obtain a practical solution of that great physical change called death."

"What has that to do with me? I am not dead nor am I interested in the subject," he answered.

'Wait a moment, please. You will be interested when I tell you that I have discovered something of the daily life and environment of the individual after he has ceased to be an inhabitant of the earth-plane."

"You are entirely mistaken in your statements; there is no survival—no continuity of life. Death is the end."

"Are you sure?"

"Absolutely," he replied.

"There is no such thing as life after death," he said," and I don't know, and I don't care," he said.

A spirit once stated to me this statement and I said it to him:

"The justice that meets a naked soul on the threshold of the afterlife is terrible in its completeness." "That is all very well, but what has it to do with me? I am not dead ," he answered.

If you will be patient I will lead up to the personal application.

"I cannot accept a word you say about a life after death. There is no other life—there can be none—a man dies like a dog," said the visitor.

"That is true in a sense, "I said," for the life force and individuality both go on. You cannot destroy an atom of matter, you will admit; so if life-force is matter, that cannot be destroyed."

"This is all very strange talk, but why speak on such a strange subject to me? I am not dead; if I were and there is life beyond the grave, I should not be here talking to you."

"I have talked just as I am talking to you with many who have made that change," I said.

"Do you mean to tell me you have talked to dead people?"

"I did not say that; I said that I have talked to those who have made the change called death. There is, in reality, no death; there are no dead."

"Talk sense," he retorted, **"we have all seen dead people, have seen their bodies buried, and you tell me there are no dead."**

Again I said, "You fail to understand what I have been telling you. We bury the physical bodies but not the spirit bodies; one is just as material as the other."

"I don't comprehend you, and I don't care to continue the discussion. I think I will say goodnight."

"Just a moment and I will demonstrate the fact. Did I not tell you a moment ago that I had talked with many so-called dead?"

"Yes," he answered, **"but I did not take what you said seriously; I made up my mind on that subject long ago."**

"Now to begin the proof—do you know where you are at this moment? Tell me if you know."

"I don't seem to know. This is not my home; the room is strange to me; you are strange too. It is all unreal. Can you explain the situation in which I find myself?"

"Listen to me. This frail little woman, over eighty years old, who sits opposite me, is the most gifted psychic in the world. More than twenty years ago it was discovered that under favorable psychic conditions such as prevail tonight we could have speech with spirit people ."

"It can't be possible," he said.

"The suggestion, "I replied," is so far beyond the experience of man, that I am not surprised at your inability to comprehend the fact. Wait! Having such means of communication, we have not only learned much of the future state, but, acting in conjunction with a group of people in the next life, we have been able to bring many to a state of consciousness after the death change, in quasi-material, quasi-spiritual conditions, such as prevail here to-night; and when we are doing work of this character, many out of the body are brought for help by their friends, as you have been, that they may comprehend their situation."

"But I am not one of these; the suggestion is absurd, I tell you. I am as much alive as you, and my body is quite as substantial as yours," he said.

"Hold up your hand as I do mine, and see if there is any difference between the two ."

> **"Yes,"** he answered, **"there is a difference, I now discover. Yours is opaque, but mine is transparent. I can see right through my hand. Is this hypnotic suggestion?"**

"No," I said, "you are facing new conditions tonight. Do you know that we sit in intense darkness—and cannot see you, although we hear your voice distinctly?"

> **"I know,"** he answered, **"that it is not dark, for I can see you, and if I can see you, you can see me; but never mind that; what is the matter with my body? I think now I have been very ill, and one always looks as I do after long sickness,"** he replied.

"Speaking of illness, what do you recall about your last illness?"

> **"My memory seems hazy, but it is coming back to me. I recall lying on a bed, the physician waiting, my wife and children sobbing. The doctor said, 'He is passing now.' That did give me a start; there were some who would like to see me dead—but I fooled them—for I did not die. If I had died, how could I be here?"**

"What do you know about death?" I said.

> **"I don't know anything about it, and I don't want to."**

"But when that time comes to you, you will be obliged to know, whether you desire to or not," I replied.

> **"Well, I am willing to wait, and I don't want to talk about it. I never did."**

"Suppose I tell you that you have already made that change?"

> **"It would be foolish to tell me such a thing when I am here talking to you."**

"Suppose I now prove it to you? Those in spirit-life cooperate with me in this work and are often able to bring to the stranger those whom he has known in earth-life, and face to face and voice to voice, the proposition proves itself."

> **"I tell you,"** he said, **"there are no dead people, and if there were, I don't want to see them. I have enough trouble with the living without bothering with the dead."**

"Is there no one in the next life with whom you would like to talk to if you could? Remember that your sickness may have ended in death; your body is different, and you know you find yourself in a strange city."

> **"Things have changed, but I don't want to see or talk to dead people."**

"You find life so material, so like the earth life, that I believe no method but actual experience will convince you that you have left the mortal state, and that lesson must be learned. You have been so intent on your conversation, I think that you have not looked around—look, what do you see?"

> **"My God! People, people, people! All strangers, and all looking at me, all with bodies like my own; what strange hallucination is this? Where am I? What am I?"**

"You are no longer an inhabitant of this world but are actually living in the afterlife. Is there no one you know among those you see, who, to your knowledge, are counted among the dead, so-called?" I asked.

> **"Not one, but wait, there comes—John—my old partner. Why does he, of all men, come? He is dead. I helped bury him. I was his executor. Take him and that woman and the boy away. I won't see them, I tell you. They are dead, all dead. They are coming to arrest me. How can they, when they are all dead? Tell me, tell me, tell me quick."**

"What wrong did you do?" I asked

> **"Wrong? Who said I did them any wrong. I was faithful to the trust."**

In answer another spirit spoke.

> **"No, you were not faithful. You stole the money entrusted to you for my wife and my child, and left them to suffer. There never was, and never can be a secret in the world. When you kept from my loved ones that which I left for their support, and let them die in want, I saw, and all your friends in spirit life saw your act and working of your mind."**

> **"No secret in the world? My crime known! The dead alive! Have I, too, left my physical body to find life when I thought to find oblivion? Am I to meet all those I have wronged? I cannot face the future! Darkness is gathering! I am falling! God help me!"**

The voice faltered, struggled for further speech, and was lost. The gross material that clothed his organs of respiration disintegrated, and he spoke no more.

We had participated in one of the most remarkable experiences that it has been the privilege of man to have. We had talked with one who had left the physical body, and witnessed his awakening. This was not a new experience. My records show upwards of 700 nights when this particular character of work had been done.

> I, Thy child forever, play about Thy knees this close of day. Within Thy arms I now shall creep, and learn Thy wisdom while I sleep. Amen.
>
> -"Child's Prayer" by Patience Worth

Child Life Beyond

During my many years of scientific investigation I invited many men and women to witness my work, and among them found a few possessing the psychic force that could be utilized by spirit people in sending messages. I recall that Mrs. S. was told one night that her young daughter, 12 years of age, could do automatic writing if properly instructed. The trial was made. The child sat in an upholstered chair, with pencil and paper, which she magnetized by passing her hand over it for a moment, and then apparently she slept. It was a complete trance condition. After a few trials, her hand would write with great rapidity, and in that manner a conversation could be carried on with spirit people with great satisfaction. In this manner many evidential facts were obtained. There never was the slightest doubt that spirit people controlled her hand.

I have had similar experiences with several others, and there is not a particle of doubt in my mind, and in the minds of others who have witnessed such work, of the genuineness of automatic writing.

I wish to mention Mrs. H., a lady of rare refinement and great spirituality. I aided her development in automatic writing. She is today the most wonderful writer that I know—absolutely reliable. I make this statement after receiving hundreds of messages through her hand. With her, it is spirit suggestion. She gets the messages by dictation, knowing at the moment the word she is writing, but not the communication as a whole until it is read afterwards. This is a most satisfactory method, second only to the direct or independent voice such as I have obtained with the aid of Mrs. Emily S. French.

I mention Mrs. H. and her marvelous powers, for the reason that I am going to append a series of letters from a young boy in the spirit world, written automatically to his sorrowing mother still in earth life.

(Automatic Writing: In the hands of a man or woman spiritually or psychically developed, there are two phases of this method: the first where a person goes into a complete trance, in which case spirit people manipulate the hand and actually write; the second, where the psychic is fully conscious and receives impressions through the subconscious mind and then writes them down.-Ed)

First Letter:

> **"Oh, Mummie, Mummie, don't cry so. It makes me so unhappy, and I can't make you feel my arms around you. If you would only smile and be glad, I'd be quite happy, because, dear little Mummie, I see ever so many lovely people who seem to be waiting to take me some place. They are all smiling, and talking together as they wait for me to be ready to go to them. One just came to me, a darling little girl; she says she is my baby sister, you told me went to heaven; she has the lovliest face—it looks all shiny, as though there was a lamp inside her eyes. Mummie, she wants to take me home with her, but I just can't leave you."**

Second Letter:

"Darling, I held you so tight last night, and it seemed you must have felt me, for you smiled in your sleep and said my name. When I kissed you, because you seemed happier, I went with Marian to see our home. It is a darling cottage, and every room is so interesting. Grandma takes care of us and says the house is one she built when she lived with us; she says she did not know it at the time, but she was just as happy and good and did kind things for people, and each kind thing helped build the cottage. Some people do so much good, they have quite big houses, but they can't be any nicer than Grandma's. Hers is just filled with interesting things. She says she has lived in it and improved her mind. She said at first it was just warm and cozy, because she did not have an intellectual mind; but she has studied, and the rooms are filled with pretty things and books, and all sorts of things. When you are happier, I think I'll have a lovely time and learn a lot. Sister Marian's room is beautiful. She has lived there all her life, since a baby, and everything in the room is so beautiful and sweet."

Third Letter:

"Oh, Mummie dear, why do you grieve so? I am well and could be happy, only your sad face keeps me wanting to be near you and comfort you. I saw Marian do such an interesting thing today. She took me to a tumble-down hut, and let me look in while she went in. There was a man in there, moaning and crying. He kept saying, 'It's so cold and dark, I can't see a thing.' Over and over he said it.

"Marian just went to him and laid her hand on his eyes, which were closed. I could see what she was thinking, without saying a word. It was very strange, yet seemed quite all right. Marian was thinking: 'Dear man, you are just cold and alone, because when you were on earth you never thought of any one but yourself, and were so selfish and cross and horrid; but you were not happy. Don't you want to be happy?

"And the man said: "Yes, I want to be happy, but I can't do anything.

"Then Marian said: 'Oh dear, yes you can. Just think of some one very miserable you'd like to help.

"And the man said: "Why there was my foster brother. I was so mean to him; I'm sorry, —can I help him?

"Because he said, 'I'm sorry, I want to help,' she took her hand from his eyes, and he looked around and could see. The hut that was so dark was beginning to get lighter. He began to look relieved and happier, and begged her to show him what to do and Marian said:

"I'll take you where you can do a great deal for people. That is my business, to help people that way. Her face was wonderful when she said it. I think I have a splendid sister."

Fourth Letter:

"Mummie dear, you have made me so happy, by being cheerful. I know it will be easier all the time for you, because you will come to know that I am not miserable and only unhappy when you grieve. Some way, here in this life, things seem so much more real, and it is so easy to learn things. Grandma says we have to go on learning until we are very wise indeed, because we must try to be perfect, and we can't be that unless our minds are full of good things. I love the music, —the air seems to throb with it some times, and it seems to go so deep inside of you it becomes a part of you, and afterwards you feel as if you had been having a drink of water when very thirsty, so refreshed and washed clean of everything but the nicest thoughts and feelings. There seems to be a good deal for people to do, besides learn things—chiefly, helping others. The very good girls, like Marian, just show people how to begin, and then they themselves have to work and help, and, more than all, have nice thoughts. So many people do not know about it here, and I am sure if they did they would not do lots of mean things they do, because it all counts against you and you have just that much longer to work before you can do all the beautiful things there are. We sing and dance and romp, in our recreation times, and then we listen to very wise people who teach us things. I always wanted to make things up—new machines and inventions—and that is what I am going to study for. When I know how, and have worked out something new and wonderful, I am to find an inventor and be with him a lot. In time I can make him think what I am thinking; then he will make my plans. Won't that be fun?"

Fifth Letter:

"Darling little Mummie, I have not talked to you for quite a long time, because I have been busy, but now that you know so much about me, and are feeling more contented, I can go on living here without worrying over you and trying to comfort you. You see, it's really just as though I was away at school, and at first one is always homesick; but now we can look forward to a vacation time when you will come to me and we shall be together always, and I shall have such heaps of things to tell you and show you. There is no wasted time here; waste means ignorance, and ignorance is almost wicked, because we should progress a littler each day—that is one of our laws. We have to study these laws. I will try and tell you as well as I can some of them. In the first place, we must know what is good, and by knowing that, we know that right follows, and then love and harmony and knowledge and power, and then progress follows as naturally as a flower grows in the sun. You will think this sounds queer from your little boy, that I have changed a lot; but I haven't so much, Mummie, I have just grown to understand the real things in life, what we all have felt inside of us always."

Sixth Letter:

"Dear Mummie, I am learning many things that are necessary in this life, now you are so much happier about me and feel so sure that everything is all right with me. It used to scare me, when I saw any one who had died; or, when I thought of being put in the cemetery, it seemed awful, —so lonely and strange; but now I know how different it is and wish that every boy knew that dying is just like getting a new suit and discarding the old. The real you inside the new suit feels just the same, only we have to learn to think differently about most things. I mean, we must change some of our ideas, but the new ones are much nicer and make living here easier. I wish everyone knew this before he came here and then no one would fear, and everything would be so nice and comfy.

"Marian and I came to you on Christmas morning and kissed your dear face; you must have felt all our love and happiness. We will come to you like that often, and some day you will come and

live with us; then you will learn so many lovely things we cannot some way seem to tell you. There are such nice people always with us, and you will love it just as we do. Grandma says she is happy to have me with her, and to tell you that she, with the help of friends and teachers, will bring me up to manhood and that you will be proud of me when you come.

Your own little boy."

Another spirit described child life as follows:

"I will tell you about the home for little children first of all.

No mother who loses a wee one need grieve, because she thinks the dear mite will have no one to love it and soothe its small fears and worries. You would love to see all the happy wee things we have here, some of whom had a very sad time during their brief sojourn on earth. Not one single baby, out of all the millions which come here, ever lacks mothering. They are surrounded by an atmosphere of love and just grow and blossom, as a result of these happy conditions, like so many rare and beautiful flowers. The place where they are rings with the sound of their happy laughter; there is no pain or sorrow for them here and they have no cause for tears. They romp and play and do all manner of things which delight the heart of a child.

"They are free to enjoy every moment, and they do. There are no quarrels or sulks to mar their happy times together. Their bright faces and sweet presences are a constant delight, especially to those folks who have always loved children. The men and women who were denied children on earth, and had always longed for them, are in their element when they come over and are free to lavish all their love for children on these darlings. The children grow up in time, as they would on earth, but they are free from sin. They can, therefore, go right on helping the spirits of those who spent many years on earth and are not free from the effects of sin. These spirits need help and guidance.

"I will now tell you about the place where the children come to grow up. It is a wonderful place and there are all sorts of lovely

things they can do. The very tiny ones cannot play with the older ones any more than they can on earth. They just need loving arms around them and soft voices to soothe them. They get these always. There are always plenty of 'mother spirits' to look after the wee ones. It is the work they love and are best fitted for. We are all given the work we like best and are most capable of doing.

"As we progress, some of us are able to undertake more and more difficult tasks, and that phrase about 'the joy of being in the doing, not the task that is done,' is very true here. Most of us find a great joy in our work. I will tell you something about the doings of the older children. The toddlers are such darlings and would rejoice any mother's heart. Their faces are so bright and happy and they are so full of life, and bubble over with fun. There are no sad, wistful little faces here—as you often see on earth—caused by lack of love, the sins of their parents, and other things. These fortunate little ones have a delightful time. They run and dance and sing and jump for sheer joy. They paddle in crystal streams and build castles on lovely beaches, where the sand is like pure gold and the water is like myriads of gems.

"There are beautiful grassy places for them to play on, where they can run races and play all the games which children love. There are also exquisite fern groves, where every kind of beautiful fern flourishes, and dainty little streams tinkle gaily along, joining, it seems, in the children's merriment. There are so many beautiful and wonderful and delightful things in this enormous 'children's playground' that you will not have time to write down descriptions of half its beauties."

Rights of Children

A celebrated French writer died in Paris in 1817. She was the daughter of a Minister of Finance under Louis XVI., enjoyed the friendship of Rousseau, Buffon, Gibbon, and other men of letters, and was exiled by Napoleon in 1812. One evening she gave the following talk to a company, which I had invited, on the subject of the early mental training of children and our duties to them:

"There are many things I want to say to you. I was the woman Napoleon feared and hated. I tried many things when on earth and made my brain a brilliant, polished receptacle. I was without a particle of affection or gentleness. I was proud of my wit and cleverness. I have to spend much time here trying to make a few bright flowers bloom in the hard sod, and to tar up the flaming, flaunting ones that had taken deep route there. It would help women very much to understand this philosophy. They are, as a rule, helpless and undeveloped souls. It is pathetic to see the way they follow blindly where they are taught to go, without once considering the wisdom of the teaching. I think this philosophy will teach them self-reliance, and would help them to understand themselves. Their children would profit largely from it and will make splendid new types. I am in earnest on this subject. It is my especial work now to bring understanding to women. I am above all things a worker, and so I find intense joy in thus making my weak sex understand what really great spirits they are. Sometimes I believe it is a mistake to think they are more spiritual than men.

They have not such large vices, as a rule, but their souls are small and petty, and few rise above sordid, every day duties, and see the great, beautiful, wonderful world waiting for them to enjoy.

"Many mothers are selfish and lazy. They either leave their children with servants, or let them grow up self-indulgent, uncontrolled men and women, simply because it is too much trouble to govern and correct. The poor children suffer for this all their earth-lives, and then progress is much harder. If women could be made to understand the great responsibility that rests with every human being, just within herself, they certainly would teach the little faltering feet the way to walk the path of life. Children must learn early to govern themselves, must learn to be generous, and, above all, must learn to think. Stop thinking for your children, you mothers, you stunt them! Teach them they must think in every little thing. Let them decide for themselves when it can possibly be done, and do not make little machines of the poor little souls. If you do, they will grow into larger machines. The brain can be trained from babyhood, and must be so trained to have the best results. Teach the children to see the beautiful in life and to appreciate their souls. Pour into them all the great thoughts of

wise men, simplified for their understanding. Remember that you are responsible for their lives. Indeed, early training can develop a small virtue and kill a vice which might in after years grow large enough to make a man miserable. Never think it too much trouble to work for your child and with it. Your reward will be great and your joy unbounded when you see the splendid spirits of your children. You will remember that you developed them and watched them through childhood with intelligent eyes. Thy will be un-blinded by the dead superstitions of ignorant men. They will be made keen and self-reliant through this new and enlightened philosophy. It sheds a light on all the dark places, and can easily be likened to that modern invention—the searchlight—which clears and brightens all it touches."

Another said:

"Children coming here in infancy are given experiences as nearly those of earth-life as possible, given those experiences that are needed, as it were, to form the soil for the plant to grow. Then they are taken to the Second Sphere, where they remain a long time. They make our best teachers, having nothing to unlearn, and they progress rapidly through all the Spheres. They need some earth-life, but naturally they are more nearly spirit when young, and easily take up the life and conditions here. I do not think early dissolution is unfortunate, unless the parents grieve very much. If they do, they act as a weight on the little spirit and chain it to them. The sweetest sound a good woman knows is the first appealing cry of her helpless child. Each day it grows more dear, and when the little lips respond and the tiny arms are raised, in confident love, the mother's heart grows rich with joy. Can you imagine the anguish of that heart when the child looks coldly into her eager eyes and turns from her aching arms without a sign of love or recognition? This is the anguish of the mother who deliberately destroys her unborn babe. That little embryo life must live, and it is cared for by tender spirits. When that mother enters into the new life, she feels the hungry, unsatisfied love of years beating in her heart, and every year the pain is deeper. She knows her child, but it sees only a stranger at whose door when helpless it had knocked in vain, and it turns away. The awakened mother's heart must endure intense agony

before she can win the love she cast away. It is one of the saddest lessons in spirit life."

Here is what a sojourner in the next plane has said of the little ones:

"Many people have puzzled as to the state and condition of young children in the spirit world, and it is on that subject that I desire to speak, more particularly, to-night. There are millions of young children of all ages passing into the spirit world every year. Some of them are of very tender age, while others know right from wrong. It is an interesting subject to inquire as to what they do in the spirit life. At the outset, I must tell you that there is a divine law in the spirit world, that whosoever passes into that kingdom before he has reached to man's estate upon the earth-plane, shall grow mentally to the stature of a man. You can gather from that, that the youngest child, even the infant that has been taken from you, will grow mentally and spiritually on the other side of life. Clairvoyants and others have often described young children in the spirit-life, who have been recognized by mothers and fathers; they, perhaps years after, have been somewhat astonished to hear of the child looking much older, and they have not been able to account for it. You will understand that the presentation of the spiritual form is in order that those in the flesh may be able to see them through the physical senses, and to note that they appear to be growing toward manhood and womanhood. I am afraid that many people upon your earth-plane today are neglectful of their responsibilities to their children. If God has given you such a flower as a child, it is incumbent upon you by example and precept to train that child in spiritual things, so that ultimately he will be with you in the kingdom of Heaven and will rejoice in the knowledge that you guided him spiritually when an infant. But how careless are many people with their children! They forget that the child is all the time taking grave note, not of what they are saying, but of what they are doing. I assure you that if you are unmindful of your responsibilities toward your children, you will undoubtedly have to pay the penalty when you reach the spirit side of life."

Too little attention has been paid to the going out of children; the world has little knowledge on that subject. No greater blessing can come to the fathers and mothers of every nation and tribe than to know that children with bodies too frail to carry them through the earth-life are not lost in going from among us, but in the other life go right on with their growth and development under the care and guidance of good men and women who for love of humanity do the necessary work, and so enrich themselves.

> **"I want to tell you,"** a teacher in the afterlife said, **"of a little waif that came to us in infancy. We taught and carefully guarded, and schooled her in the pure conditions of our sphere until she approached womanhood, but she had no contrasts, therefore she could not judge of the relative purity and delights of her environment. In order that she should be able to enjoy her home and the glories of the world, it was necessary for her to have a knowledge of earthly conditions. And so I was instructed to conduct this child back to earth from time to time. When this child first returned to earth and was among your people, she could hardly endure even to examine the gross conditions, and could not understand how people could exist in such dark, crude elements. But, as I led her along from one condition to another, over the road she would have gone had she remained on earth for the ordinary allotted period, I said to her: 'Had you lived your time in the body, you would have been in the condition in which you see these people.' I also told her that this one had received a higher training. And we passed along to another place in the earth-life where there were children of the poor and ignorant, as well as the rich and learned. And we tarried until my little charge thoroughly learned the different environments of children on earth, and the great contrast between their homes, daily life, and schooling and those in spirit-life. This child had never known anything but innocence and purity, and she was far removed from the ordinary conditions of the childhood of earth. It was long before she could, in any degree, recognize it as a reality.**
>
> **"And, having learned of the methods of training in the institutions of earth, we pursued our investigations farther along; and, finally we came to where there was a great orthodox church; and there, unseen, we mingled with the congregation. She said: 'This church house is not like ours at all. What is taught here?' Presently the services began. I told her to listen attentively to the minister, for**

here she would get the average experience of the church methods and be able to see wherein a great work, in brave hands, is greatly needed on the spirit side. Then the minister proceeded with his discourse in his regular methodical manner, telling the people all he thought essential to prepare them to enter higher realms of the spirit. But the girl, now grown to nearly womanhood, could not accept the dicta of the minister, for she had up to now been raised in the spirit world and had learned nothing that was in harmony with methods attempted by the church to enlighten the people and prepare them for future realities. Therefore the teachings of the minister seemed to her so gross, so false, so out of line with all she had ever seen, heard, or read of in the land which had always been her home that she hesitated to remain, but I told her that her future work and welfare required that she learned as much as possible of the earth conditions in which your people live, and the kind of preparation such earth conditions make for their inheritance in our life. But the more the young lady heard of the sermon the more she disbelieved it. In fact, it was so much opposed to what she knew of the conditions of this side, and so different from what preparation while on earth for entrance to and enjoyment of spirit life should consist that at my suggestion she resolved to visit those who had just left the earth-plane, schooled under its teaching, and witness the effect of it; we, therefore, journeyed on."

Various Subjects

"To believe that any past generation held the monopoly of truth, or was able to give it final expression, is not only inconsistent with the teachings of history, but is a flat denial of the Holy Spirit, which was promised to guide us progressively into all truth."

-Dr. Cyril Alington

Evolution

Little is known of that constant force known as evolution, or of the great laws that govern the process of advancement. I have eagerly sought information on this subject, have discussed it with many men in the next sphere beyond and have been told among other things:

> **"A most encouraging indication of the progress of the present age is the fact that a few great thinkers and demonstrators of nature's laws have been able to grasp conditions beyond the physical, and are giving such information to mortals, who, because of their environment and duties, have not been able to solve for themselves these great problems.**
>
> **"You ask me to say something concerning evolution, making that gradual, and yet positive, change in the world's condition that has finally resulted in thinking mankind. So be it. Then is not what I have just said a most wonderful and beautiful illustration of the progressive realization of the Master's great purpose—the gradual, yet positive, improvement of matter until an observant and grateful mortal is the final result?**
>
> **"God, as you use the word, is the ALL. That is apparent to every thinking brain. Being, then, that ALL, God cannot be a personality: every bit of matter is a part and parcel of that ALL; every force in nature is an expression of the presence of that ALL; and every thinking brain is a more or less perfect functional part of that ALL.**
>
> **"To a sane and appreciative, active brain, free alike from arrogance and illusion, the proposition that mortal man is made in the perfect image of his Master, God, is the extreme of egotistical blasphemy. Far better is the expression of your countryman, Robert G. Ingersoll, that 'Man has made God in his image.' That part of mortal man that is in any degree like his Master is his thinking brain; otherwise, man is but an expression, in his form and physical functions, of that process of evolution spoken of as environment. All that is great in man is mind, and this greatness increases as he rises to the level of the ideal, the Master Mind.**

"In a previous discussion, I mentioned the fact that we spirit-people do not always agree on many subjects of which we have no actual proof or convincing a proper evidence, and so as regards the early stages of earth and the subsequent changes up to the existence of man, many among us differ; but I am safe in saying that the best informed hold that there has been a constant refining process of earth-matter since the cooling of the evidently original vaporous particles that gradually, by loss of heat, become solidified into rock and water; and that as the chaotic condition gradually assumed separation upon cooling and solidifying, the process of refining gross matter began, and by the action of element upon element, of substance upon substance, the erosion of the primitive rock occurred, with the result of eliminating the fine from the gross; and, by the action of water in causing sedimentary deposits and the raising or lowering of the sedimentary or refined rock, and the consequent re-refining process, chemical action was allowed to come into play, resulting in a continuation of the process whereby gross matter is refined. Necessarily, as the cooling mass must have constantly given off heat, and also absorbed a certain amount of heat by chemical action, there came a period when the earth's crust could support the first life, vegetation. This vegetable life itself is but the chemical product of certain parts of refined matter, resulting from the gradual solidifying of the gaseous vapors fixed in space by the action of some of the planets undergoing a change.

"As regards the earth's actual beginning, there is no authentic knowledge among spirit-people. A theory based upon sound premises may be regarded as a general statement of the truth. From a knowledge of existing conditions, comparative reasoning can, and does, draw correct deductions, and so men of scientific attainments have, by study and investigations, demonstrated much that is not only evidence, but that may be said to be actually demonstrated.

"Among the best informed of the spirit-people the growth of a new planet results from the fixing in space, by the existing stellar system, —owing to that great principle of nature known as the law of gravitation, of some mass of matter revolving wildly through the universe, and the placing of it in a position of harmony with other

masses of matter or planets. So must the earth have been caught when in its state of motion and vaporous matter, conditioned by its flight through space, not by any friction of the particles of its mass against the so-called ether, but because of the unusual disturbance of the particles of the mass among themselves; and also, because of the latent heat imparted to the runaway mass of matter that may be considered the nucleus of your planet. When finally caught and held in its place of career, it came into the lines of force existing from other planetary bodies, by gradual degrees its speed was steadied and, slowly but surely, it fell into the correct and dignified motion that is consistent with the laws governing planets, and it became one of the necessary keystones in the constellations of which it must have been elected a member. And so a new planet is born. Man has since called it earth. All the essentials of the present conditions existed at the very beginning of the earth's creation, have ever been, and are now, stored away in the mass of fugitive matter.

"Evolution is but the action of that great power called by mortal man, God, but which really is the process of refinement and purification of gross matter until the resultant product is living thinking moral man, and then the intellectual man. The next step in that ever-changing ever-progressing evolution, is the endowment of that physical, intellectual man, with what we call spirit.

"As each and every particle of matter depends upon some other particle of matter to allow of that progressive refinement spoken of, so it is throughout the entire chain, the spirit-people are as necessary to physical people as the gas exhaled from the lungs of living animalism is for the growth of vegetation, or as the refined chemical vegetable combinations are to animal life."

The origin of life has been, and ever will be, a great mystery, until such time as we shall, by progression out of the body, come to a greater understanding of life force.

Evolution is not confined to lifeforce, but matter, as we use that term, develops in a corresponding degree. Of this we have material evidence.

A spirit said:

> **"Evolution means progress, higher development. Each vibratory atom must go through each stage of vibration before it can be fitted for the fullest perfection. The story of evolution may be seen in the grain of wheat. It is planted and then develops through each successive stage until it becomes nourishment for man, and thence its development is a part of a soul's progress; and eventually it becomes a part of the life-force, and generates life-force into another grain of wheat, and each new grain that reaches the life-force enriches it and makes more powerful that force, so that, while it completes a perfect circle, yet it is always growing greater and more perfect. Thus evolution is constantly repeating itself on a larger scale each time."**

Wherever there is lifeforce there must be thought. There is intelligent action embodied in every seed that has a living germ.

Materiality of the Universe

> **"Spirit ether fills the universe. It is a compound of two coexistent, co-eternal elements, the one positive, the other negative; one the male, the other the female element. These two primitive elements do exist, and always have existed, in union. Organic life is an aggregation of these primitive, spiritual elements. The law of chemical affinity, of every form of cohesion, of every human desire, of all love and affection, is but a manifestation of the affinity of positive and negative spirit ether asserting itself in organic aggregations of the positive and negative spirit atoms. Sun and systems of worlds are organic evolutions of this eternal life element. Spirit ether fills the universe. Life permeates and is inherent in all things. Nature expresses all there is of creative energy."**

Another inhabitant of the next plane, speaking of matter spiritual and physical, says:

> **"Our world is composed of matter as real and definite as your own, but that matter vibrates at a higher rate, consequently your undeveloped senses can have but little cognizance of it. And, your own sphere being composed of matter at a low rate**

of vibration, it is almost equally as difficult for us to manifest on your plane as it is for you to penetrate ours. Yet we have evolved from your plane, and have all the experience of that evolution, and it is perhaps easier for us to reach back and help you than it is for you to see forward. The principle of cooperation between the two planes is what we desire to establish, for this principle of cooperation is an essential and necessary condition for the development of the consciousness from your low and stagnant vibrations to those that are higher and healthier and more in keeping with the spirit's deepest longing, more in harmony with that process that is working for the ultimate and absolute destiny of the evolving spirit of man."

How little we know, and how much there is yet to learn of that which we call matter or substance in nature; until the mentality grasps in some measure this subject, life beyond cannot be comprehended.

Nature's Laboratory

All the universe is the result of chemical action; this entire earth, and all upon it is one great laboratory wherein nature's forces are ever active, controlled by laws made and kept in operation by the Master Intelligence.

Nature abhors inaction and stagnation; life-force permeates every atom that goes to make up the mass which we call earth. We call the activity and expression of that force, energy. The ceaseless effort of this force to obtain development, coming into touch with other chemical conditions in nature's wonderful retort, is a refining process, working for the advancement of mankind. An interesting discussion on this subject by a spirit is as follows:

"It should appeal to you that each atom, or each element, and each molecular aggregation of sub-atoms, must possess distinct individuality. The scheme of nature, so far as so-called inanimate matter is concerned, is to allow a perfect expression of the individual characteristics of each separate species. The individual expression of those separate kinds of matter, be it in the atom or in that expression of associate atoms that produce separate effects, is to allow the steady and ever-occurring change that matter is constantly undergoing to bring about progressive

conditions. As matter is ever undergoing a process of refinement in the great laboratory, it follows that, inasmuch as the rule must be an all-including one (for no exception is allowed by nature) a period of time must come when the material of which the human brain is fashioned will also be affected by the refining process.

"The time has arrived when this effect on the mortal brain is being observed by men, for the brain of the present day has reached the most sensitive state in the world's history. Being thus attuned by the gradual and ever-active process of refinement of matter, it is quickened in vibratory power, and thus is in more perfect accord with the vibratory activity of the people of the next step in progression, those who live without the clothing of the flesh. It is possible, also, for some few physical beings to be held in mental accord by certain spirit-people. The refined physical brain can adjust itself to the spirit-brain, so that the latter can dictate to the former comprehensive suggestions as to the proper method of procedure to grasp, harness, and control those subtle magnetic forces of fixed, ever-existing, steady, but pulsating, conditions of stress that are the perfect reflex of the ever-active particles of matter.

"It is a well-established fact, that substances of the same kind attract each other and are cohesive in a given mass in so called solid form, by a reduction of temperature. This kind of attraction has no relation to chemical attraction, but is mainly based on the physical characteristics of the substance, made possible by the similarity of the crystallization of the substance. Much has been told and explained to you about this subject of crystallization of substance. It is the true demonstration of the acute individuality of distinct elements and positive (actual) substance. A vegetablism and animalism assert their different species by the process just referred to, so all things in the world of matter likewise assert themselves.

"Different species of the vegetable and animal kingdom, by the fact of distinct crystallization (form), possess the power to give expression to all the fixed and distinct peculiarities that they possess, and to effect others of their kind, or of similar species, and mix and become assimilated with each other in their progressive action, and thus assert that subtle influence which you know as perpetuating life; the one nutrifying the other. Thus, they give expression to that power, which is the deep-seated principle of nature, that you explain as life, and that we know is the spirit. So also it is with matter. It is permeated with Spirit Life, and because of that fact, it is ever-active. If it were not for this fact, that it possesses Spirit or Life, matter could not undergo the ever-occurring changes, all of a progressive character, that it does; it could not change to unite and form substances and, after these new combinations have performed their duties, to break down and form some other substances which also fulfill their functions in the progression of nature's great scheme. Were the atoms dead, spiritless, they would of necessity be non-active, and hence useless for the work of the Master's hand.

"Matter, gross or fine, is but a vehicle for the use of the Spirit, and be it the invisible, theoretical atom of oxygen or of any other so-called element, or be it a perfect physical man, this atom of matter, or these aggregations of atoms used to form man, are but the Master's vehicles to work for, and act as the carrier of, the Spirit. The Spirit of man is the intelligence of man, and nothing more. This Spirit is the highest type that the Master has desired to create on your earth. It is the consummation of the workmanship of that great workshop, your earth; and it is the final result of the activity of all other spirit-forces that matter has for countless ages, as man records time, been manifesting.

"The final product of all of that ceaseless activity of matter is the one result that goes out from your earth as Eternal Life. Every other form of spirit-life is returned to the refinery for the further processes of refinement, until it is fitted for the last act of earth-life, —the creating of a sublime human intelligence, —and then it goes forth into the domain of Spirit, to be further refined and fitted for that purpose of the Master that is not clear to us in the Spirit-World, but, according to reasoning, based on such knowledge as is possessed by some of our most advanced intelligences, to be ultimately a power added to the great Intelligence that rules the universe. But be the further following out of the scheme what it may, of this truth you may be certain: God's use of this earth is to create human intelligence; and further, it is nature's constant

effort to produce the best; and so, true is this, that, if you will but 'read' as you 'run,' you may note that people of your earth possess this knowledge as if by instinct (in reality by spirit suggestion) and they are constantly endeavoring, in their blind, groping way, to prefect themselves. Thus likewise it is with spirit-people.

"Clearly we see, clearly we feel, all that you see and all that you feel. As your sensations are the half-blind groping of a lower organism, sluggish, and dull as to the true facts that underlie real progress; so ours are the quick, clear, and fully-developed faculties for appreciating great truths. This refers only to those spirit-intelligences among us who have been awakened to a complete appreciation of our actual individual spirit-life as when in the flesh, and we have the same distinct personalities.

"Thus, knowing by quick perception, as we do, that only right is right, and that deception cannot succeed; that honesty only is a fact, and that dishonesty is a condition that brings about endless trouble that must be disentangled and made straight and absolutely honest by the causer; and, knowing that nature has established laws which are good, and, if adhered to, beneficial in their results; and which, if broken, must be mended by the breaker, —knowing all these things made possible by our power of rapid perception, (because those tantalizing desires of the flesh have no longer a hold upon us) we are ever and always anxious when we can come in touch with intelligence in the flesh, to give to such persons what we can of the truths that are clear to us."

The Life Mass

There is a query in science as to whether every living thing is capable of thinking, and I am free to say that, in my judgment, wherever there is life, there must be thinking. I care not whether science accepts or rejects the theory; there is the power of intelligent action in every seed that has a living germ. The acorn has sense enough to send its rootlets into the earth, and its trunk and foliage branch up into the air, and select just such elements as will make the oak tree, and reject such as would be proper only for the beech tree. And the grass has the same kind of intelligence in choosing proper nourishment for itself;

and the power of choice must involve the power of thought. Science is on the material and rudimental plane yet, and has much to ascertain.

Speaking of the life mass, one in the next life has said:

> **"The basis of all matter is electricity, the basis of all electricity, for there are many kinds, is ether, —not that ether which is found in the atmosphere, but a subtle ether of which men know little or nothing. The basis of this subtle ether is spirit; therefore, all that there is of whirling planets, of brilliant constellations, suns, moons and satellites, all that there is in the physical Universe is ether clothed, in reality but an expression of spirit. It is the physical in and through which spirit functions, and in that way makes itself manifest to the external sense. When we once realize how infinitely great is the universe, how wondrous, how terrible, yet how beautiful in its simplicity, a feeling not exactly of awe, but of benign thankfulness must rise in our hearts at the knowledge that we are part of that stupendous system.**
>
> **"Until the discovery of lenses and magnifying glasses, man had no idea of the world around him. He could not scan the heavens by night, nor did he know anything of atoms, nor of micro-organisms.**
>
> **"If one is interested in geology—in the various rocks in the strata of the earth—let him take the hardest of these rocks—basalt—and in the basaltic rocks he will find a world of life. If he gets far away in the polar seas at the extremes of the earth, he will find life also. Thousands of fathoms down in the bed of the ocean there is life. In everything throughout the Universe life is found, and the germs of life are no less in the fire mists! The ink of the specks of protoplasm floating in the water. Look at them—examine them with a microscope. Then realize that at last, a long way off it is true, those specks of protoplasm develop into a Shakespeare or a Dante, Thomas Paine, or an Ingersoll. Nature is very wonderful!**
>
> **"The atmosphere that you are breathing tonight contains organisms. You cannot see them with the naked eye, and even the most powerful lenses would fad to disclose some of them to you. There are microbes floating in the atmosphere, some of which produce disease. Most of them are unimportant. But apart from the germs, there are floating throughout this atmosphere,**

life forms which man may never be able to discover with any instrument that he may invent in the future. Near to Mt. Vesuvius there are a few pools or small lakes, which the internal fires round about make very hot. If tonight, I could take one drop from those pools and subject it to a close, rigid scrutiny by means of a more powerful glass than exists, we should find that in one drop of this hot water there is a world. We should find life there evolving and progressing towards perfection. Again, we should find in that drop of water, or it might be in a speck of earth—if we had the knowledge and power, and also the sight of an advanced spirit to disintegrate it—we should find that the speck of matter branches away into electric corpuscles. Searching deeper, we should discover that even the electricity of the corpuscles is made up of a subtle ether, impenetrable, something so rarefied that the sons of men cannot by means discern it. Had we the power and the knowledge that we shall have some day in an advanced spiritual state, we should find in the heart of that subtle ether something of wondrous power and influence—a continuous force which is indeed the Spirit of God.

"Therefore, in the physical we have a universe which at last touches the spiritual. In the infinitely great we have a universe which is controlled, inspired, kept steady, so to speak, and has its foundation, its very existence, in that force called Nature. And the spirit which you yourselves possess, is an emanation from God. This spirit, though manifest in many ways, and through many forms, is eternal. Matter physical is constantly changing, budding up, disintegrating; it is scattered and reformed in the birth, the growth, the life, and the death of worlds innumerable. There is, in reality, no such thing as death. Men enquire from whence comes life? Life came from the Spirit, and when the spirit passes through the subtle ether, and the ether gets into the coarser electricity, it takes physical form—gross matter is then impregnated with life. That life never ceases, because, as I have said, it progresses and develops through the physical and is reabsorbed into the Great Spirit, the Source of all life—light, and power, and wisdom."

Another from the great beyond has said:

"In the whole universe right down to the microscope and beyond, life is found. There is no part of the universe where there is no life, nor where the creatures do not live in companies. It is not good for man, or anything to be alone; consequently all are set in companies, and there has been given to each individual a method and a way of understanding every other one, so that all may be happy in one another's company. Some will say that it is ridiculous to speak of inanimate things in that manner, but it is only ignorance which so asserts; it is inability to realize that the Divine Spirit of God is permeating everything. Walk upon the sands of the sea-shore, examine the tiniest grain; it is impregnated with that Divine Spirit which keeps the whole universe sweet.

"I cannot say much concerning the manner of communication that plants have, but I know from my side of life that they have this power, and do communicate. And the varieties of perfumes, how are they produced, and borne upon the breeze? The present hypothesis is that it is through some chemical atoms. First, the sun impregnated the plant. In the flower are found chemical substances—electrons—which are given off and float on the subtle ether. How do they float? Through vibrations. We have been a long time getting a little knowledge about vibrations, but the processes of Nature are carried on through vibrations. We have thought it most wonderful to set in motion electrical vibrations, and to convey to our friends a message hundreds of miles away. That is but a childish effort, a childish accomplishment in comparison with what goes on daily around us, but of which we are ignorant. Realize first that there is the life of the plant, and there is the life of the animalcule, the life of the insect, the life of the animal, the life of man, and the life of creatures in the uttermost parts of Nature of which most men have no conception. Then we come to the sources of all life, —God. Cannot we understand that from Him flows the entire life of the Universe? When we die, as the expression is, though such a thing does not happen—when a dissolution of the material body and the spirit occurs, what takes place is this: there is a breaking up of a community—you and your body are a community interdependent on each other, —and at death, or dissolution, a colony, a company breaks up—I must for the time being use terms which will be understood—the etheric tenant vacates and goes on to a more glorious sublime plane. Paul said to the Corinthians, 'There is a natural body, and there is a spiritual body.' It is the earthly house of the tabernacle here which dissolves.

"The companies of insects, and of animals, though they make war on each other and may exist on each other, have a language. They know how to communicate, and in a measure they are dependent one upon the other. Is it not amusing to hear some people say that man alone has speech, that is, sound formed into certain word and syllables and sentences through the vocal organs. Let us, for instance, consider the birds. We see them and hear them warble and sing. That is their way of expressing joyousness; but that is not their language. They have a way in which they communicate with each other just as we have. Has the reader ever visited India? In the Burning Ghaut, where the Hindoos and others burn their dead, they carry the bodies up a flight of stairs to a high platform. The wood is already prepared, and the body is placed upon the wood. Look up into the heavens, calm and bright, the sun glaring down, not a speck in the sky. In two or three minutes the place will be black with carrion birds. Can we explain it? Yes, away perched on some high eminence or tree is the sentinel bird; perhaps miles away are his fellows. He speaks to them, the sentinel sounds the signal, and instantly they reply to him, and fill the air. Most people think that the world in which they live is a jumble. I grant that there are things that are abhorrent, which we cannot understand—the mystery of pain and suffering, of evil, for example, but I realize now that out of all that is evil, will finally come good. There is no confusion or jumble in the Divine Order. Everything is in its place, and ultimately it will be seen that in Nature, God has set the solitary in families, that his wondrous power is always recreating matter, and that there is never annihilation.

"There may, however, be change of form. Take, for instance, the coral rocks on the seashore. Little creatures once swam in the ocean in tiny shells; they died in myriads, and the shells in time formed certain rocks. Old forests fall in decay, and the wisest man of the 20th century might have said: 'Show me the wisdom of God in this?' But today the coal farmed from these forests is used to give warmth and light, and all the processes of commerce

are carried on through it. There is no death! Everything gives place to new forms of life."

And this is the fact that we must gather from our teaching: that out of the life contained in the mass, individuality has come; out of the mass of life, through Nature's process of constant change and refinement, every living creature that will inhabit this globe in the ages yet to come must be evolved. The highest form of life that is evolved from the mass is man—and to the highest, all lesser forms contribute. Mankind is the final result of evolutionary action.

Beyond the Atom

We are told that atoms, through their power to change from one form into another, always follow the law of definite proportions; and that, in obedience to that law, they are amenable to the will of the intelligent force. Outside of the operation of this law, they are incapable of being controlled in any known way. This would place them beyond the category of mortal mind and make them, to some extent, superior to it. The atom holds within itself the properties of all forms and material things. It is the central point from which universal creative energy proceeds. It is the basis of all power that manifests form and force. It is indestructible in its nature; its existence is regulated by definite and fixed laws; and the substance into which it enters is held in position, as regards form, by the inherent energy of the atoms composing that form.

The atom, alone, has eternal duration of form, for it alone has the power to enter and dominate all other forms. It has no master except force, and to force alone it is amenable. Whether force precedes it, or is co-existent with it, is not now known; but, probably, the same force which impels the atom upon its course with unerring precision, precedes it in the province of creative evolution. Beyond the atom is an intelligence which has imbued it with these properties and powers.

I once asked a spirit: "What is the force that finds expression in the atom?" He replied:

"It is the individual man, purified and developed to its highest capacity, and blended with other minds in a similar condition. Guided by the knowledge gained through vast intervals of time, and working in perfect harmony with each other, these minds are the controlling power of the universe. I say 'controlling' for they, in

turn, are but instruments of the dominating laws of the universe. They make these laws, to be sure, but, these laws must be of one kind for nature aspires to good. They progress through a condition of intellect bounded by mortality, into a new development until the circle is completed, and a harmonious whole is formed. It is a vast subject to comprehend, and yet, once grasped, it is perfectly clear. What other theory calculated to satisfy rational mind, has ever been put forward, than that the intelligence should ultimately become so effective that, combined with all the rest, it should be the highest force for good? Everyone must feel, and appreciate, that thus only can the inferior order of minds be guided toward their ultimate goal. This is the only philosophy of existence which, when once fully understood, seems true, reasonable, and convincing."

Matter

When we speak, ordinarily, of matter, we refer to sensible substances which offer resistance to the touch and to muscular effort, and which is indestructible and eternal, which reacts against external force, is permanent and preserves its identity under all changes. Again, matter is everything that possesses the properties of gravity and attraction.

On this subject, I am told:

"Spirit is ethereal matter—matter whose home is in ether, which is higher in vibration than the atmosphere in which it formerly existed. Each change into another sphere is a higher, more vitalizing vibration, until the emancipated spirit reaches a sphere of most intense vibration, which holds the power of life. Then it can impregnate matter in a lower material condition, and give it an atom of spirit to develop. The reason that man is continually growing in spiritual thought, is because as this force, this life-giving force, increases, it becomes stronger, and man is being equipped for the development of his spiritual being.

"Matter includes all things that have continued life, —and we know that nothing can die. Ether is the atmosphere of spirit-people. From each man in his natural condition emanates spiritual ether. It is because of this atmosphere that we are able to come close to him, and thereby reach his subconscious mind."

The Subconscious Mind

I asked one far advanced in spirit-life to tell me of the subconscious mind from his point of view, and he said:

> **"The conscious mind is one controlled by yourself. In it are held all the material parts of your thoughts, —I mean those connected with and controlled by, earth things. The subconscious mind is the one controlled by psychic forces entirely. It is the spiritual brain of man. I mean, that it is subject to the laws of vibration, which the other part of the brain is not sensitive enough to catch. It is the subconscious mind that gets suggestion from spirit-people, the connecting link, or battery, that for an instant holds the suggestion, and passes it on, to grow into a thought or impulse. The subconscious mind does not retain suggestion. It is the embryo thought, which takes definite form only as it reaches the conscious mind."**

From this concise statement of fact it is evident that all the strange phenomena, which science has been trying to solve and to which it has given many names, consist, ordinarily, of spirit-people hearing the spoken words or seeing the written message, then finding the person desired and impressing the words or message on the subconscious mind or spiritual brain. When the conscious mind catches the suggestion and makes it a part of the material thought, we have what is called mental telepathy, which, in fact, is except on rare occasions, all accomplished by spirit-people acting upon the subconscious or psychic brain.

Speaking on the subject generally, one in the world beyond said:

> **"It is well, always, to consider that a result is equivalent to the effort put forth. The intensity and constancy of a thought are a positive force. A thought, bearing upon any particular subject, having been thoroughly established in the brain, grows just as a plant grows from the seed. As the development of that seed will be proportionate to the conditions of the sod and the amount of sunshine and moisture, so is it with the growth of thought.**

> **"Thought is planted in the human brain by the next great power beyond mortal man, sown in the form of suggestion, and, as with the seed sown by the master hand of man, so it is with the**

suggestion sown, largely, by the master hand of spirit forces. Some are given birth and grow and fully develop in all their importance and beauty; but many—by far the great majority—fail of birth. Where the latter condition prevails, the human brain must, by a process of purification, be made receptive until it can catch and give birth to the seeds of suggestion sown.

"Progress is the grand object of nature. This word 'progress' is one of mighty import to the material world, and true progress is possible only when those who have advanced to a higher plane help those who are still struggling upward. This applies to all things, material, intellectual, and spiritual. Nature has imposed upon us spirit beings the duty of assisting those mortals in the body by such suggestion as we can impart to them through the subconscious brain; and so, likewise, there are some among us to whom suggestions are imparted by those in the grade immediately above us.

"As on earth there are weeds, as well as useful grain and beautiful flowers, so among your people are there apparently worthless mortals; but who can say when or how the weeds, following the great law of progress, will evolve into useful or beautiful plants; and yet, as simple weeds, may they not serve a great, if hidden purpose? And so with those among you, who according to your judgment, appear worthless, do not forget that the same Master-hand that created them, created you; and that it is better not to criticize, but to endeavor to get an expression of the intent of their condition. Always have charity. If you do not possess it, secure and cultivate it.

"What I have said this beautiful Sunday morning, is a sermon to you, the lesson of which is: Let those thoughts that come as suggestions flashed upon the sensitive plate of your brain, upon your subconscious mind, grow. Cultivate them. As they develop, they gain in strength, and as they become strong in themselves, they can by their own strength, and because of the emanations they throw off, accomplish deeds. Whatever comes to the subconscious mind must be at once grasped and held, if you would make it your own. Then the thought is fashioned and developed to become again a part of the universal stream that flows into the Eternal Mind."

The average so-called man of science seems determined not to accept the spirit hypothesis of psychic phenomena, and offers many other explanations while going through its erroneous process of elimination; but truth existed before, and will be after, this futile struggle is over, and we may be among the last to understand this simple law.

Sir Oliver Lodge, the foremost scientist of the present day, (1908) who acknowledges the existence of an invisible world of spirit people and has proved it to his own satisfaction, says: "The object is to get, not something dignified, but something evidential." It seems to me that when one has proved the existence of a thing, he would like to know something about the thing proved and not try to prove it again. Having long ago proved the existence of the invisible world of spirit-people, I have not sought for an accumulation of evidential facts, but rather for something dignified from the inhabitants of that world. Whether or not such facts have been given me these pages will answer.

Spirit Suggestion

Have spirit-people any influence on our daily thought and action? If so, to what extent and by what process?

One in spirit-life, who has given many lectures, said on the subject:

> **"Come with me through the walks of life, and see the manner of men we can help. It is not the arrogant fool who says in his heart: 'My way is the only way,' nor yet the man who weakly fears to trust his own instinct and vacillates falteringly between the opinions of man; but it is the sane, quiet thinker, who is willing to listen to all arguments and to choose wisely those that appeal alike to his heart and brain. Such we can assist by spirit-suggestion. Without his being conscious of it, we can often guide his thought along right lines, because he is fair-minded.**
>
> **"Suggestion is one of the strong factors in the life force. As you said this morning, all things have their power of suggestion. Does not a low saloon throw out its vile suggestion to all men? Whether this emanation entices or repels, depends upon the man, but its surrounding influence is felt strongly and the suggestion is evil. A beautiful rural scene is helpful with its suggestion of peace and harmonious coloring. And so it is through all phases of life. Hence all should seek the best, and, unconsciously all do aspire to it."**

Power of Suggestion

The inhabitants of this invisible world influence and in some measure control the thought and conduct of every individual. They are more progressive than we, and having no incentive to accumulate money, devote themselves to the acquisition of knowledge. They delve deeply into the forces of Nature, and dealing with matter in greater refinement, make from time to time discoveries, some of which are utilized on the physical plane.

Faraday, who first made practical the force known as electricity, did not cease his investigation with death, but has been a potent factor in its development through suggestion to those who devote their time to the utilization of that force. Raphael did not cease to portray upon canvas his wonderful creations, nor did Michael Angelo lose his ability to chisel marble into forms of beauty when he ceased to inhabit this plane. The years that have elapsed since they went on, have been years of opportunity and progress. Mozart, Beethoven, and all the other musicians who gave us our great compositions, have they gone down into the silent and relentless darkness, or have they continued their work, impressing on others from day to day new music that enriches the world? Milton, Dryden, Pope, Goldsmith, Moore, Wordsworth, Burns, Browning of modern times, Seneca, Pliny the Elder, Plutarch, Epictetus, Tacitus and Cervantes, of an earlier period, were all their wonderful writings and philosophies produced without suggestion from the master minds in the more advanced spheres? I know this one fact, that people in the afterlife are so close, so in touch with our thoughts that it is difficult for any one to say that this or that is the product of his own intellect. Progress owes much to the invisible.

Robert G. Ingersoll, well known to me, in the afterlife, speaking on this subject said:

> **"Let me give the most remarkable illustration of spirit suggestion—the immortal Shakespeare. Neither of his parents could read or write. He grew up in a small village among ignorant people, on the banks of the Avon. There was nothing in the peaceful, quiet landscape on which he looked, nothing in the low hills, the undulating fields, nothing in the lazy flowing stream to excite the imagination. Nothing in his early life calculated to sow the seeds of subtlest and sublimest thought. There was nothing in his education or lack of education to account for what he did. It is**

supposed that he attended school in his home village, but of that there is no proof. He went to London when young, and within a few years became interested in Black Friars Theater, where he was actor, dramatist, and manager. He was never engaged in a business counted reputable in that day. Socially he occupied a position below servants. The law described him as a "sturdy vagabond." He died at 52.

"How such a man could produce the works which he did has been the wonder of all time. Not satisfied that one with such limited advantages could possibly have written the masterpieces of literature, it has been by some contended that Bacon was the author of all Shakespeare's comedies and tragedies.

"It is a fact to be noted that in none of this man's plays is there any mention of his contemporaries. He made reference to no king, queen, poet, author, sailor, soldier, statesman, or priest of his own period. He lived in an age of great deeds, in the time of religious wars, in the days of the armada, the edict of Nantes, the massacre of St. Bartholomew, the victory of Lepanto, the assassination of Henry III of France, and the execution of Mary Stuart; yet he did not mention a single incident of his day and time.

"The brain that conceived "Timon of Athens" was a Greek in the days of Pericles and familiar with the tragedies of that country. The mind that dictated "Julius Caesar" was an inhabitant of the Eternal City when Caesar led his legions in the field. The Author of "Lear" was a Pagan; of "Romeo and Juliet" an Italian who knew the ecstasies of love. The author of those plays must have been a physician for, he shows a knowledge of medicine and the symptoms of disease; a musician, for in "The Two Gentleman of Verona" he uses every musical term known to his contemporaries. He was a lawyer, for he was acquainted with the forms and expressions used by that profession. He was a botanist because he named nearly all known plants. He was an astronomer and a naturalist and wrote intelligently upon the stars and natural science. He was a sailor, or he could not have written "The Tempest." He was a savage and trod the forest's silent depths. He knew all crimes, all regrets, all virtues, and their rewards. He knew the unspoken thoughts, desires, and ways of beasts. He lived all lives. His brain

> **was a sea on which the waves touch all the shores of experience. He was the wonder of his time and of ours.**
>
> **"Was it possible for any man of his education and experience to conceive the things which he did? All the Shakespearean works were, beyond a doubt, the product of his pen, but the conceptions, the plays, the tragedies were the work of many brains, given Shakespeare by spirit suggestion. He was but the sensitive instrument through which a group of learned and distinguished scholars, inhabitants of many lands when in earth-life, gave to posterity the sublime masterpieces of the Bard of Avon."**

The writings of Swedenborg were produced in the same way. Sardeau wrote by spirit suggestion, and as a fact many of the best works of so-called great men have been in part the action of the minds of those beyond our earthly plane, who, working in conjunction with man, do something for the uplift of the human race.

The Attitude of Science

We are apt, with our physical environment, to stand in awe of so-called "men of Science," and expect that all progress, spiritual as well as material, will come through them.

I have never agreed with the method adopted by them to prove the continuity of life. Many attempt to build their structures by tearing down; to establish a fact by a process of elimination; they try to prove a thing is so, by proving it is not so. This method, I am led to believe, is erroneous in dealing with forces beyond the physical plane.

The judgment of spirit-people, with their greater knowledge and experience, is interesting. One now in spirit-life, who has advanced far, made this startling statement which I have hesitated to publish:

> **"All proper respect is due and payable to the man of learning. But when learning, be it the result of book-study, of experimental investigation, or of knowledge imparted from one to another, has the effect of making men self-important, so that they adopt such an attitude towards others as to imply that all wisdom and knowledge repose solely and entirely in themselves, then I say that the so-called men of learning only make themselves ridiculous, and that the institutions which produce savants of**

this type are defective, and antagonistic to real intellectual progress.

"No one has a greater feeling of respect and admiration than I have for men who have, by constant and patient effort, sought to unravel and explain those great laws of the universe, the proper understanding of which tends to help and to advance their fellow-men. We all salute the man who does things; but we also feel contempt for that egotistic group of socialists, to be found in every country, who are always seeking to surround the laws of the universe with a hidden meaning, and to throw a halo around themselves and the cult they seek to organize, by erecting an artificial superstructure of baseless theory upon the facts already explained by the earnest worker, who has by toil and study revealed some hitherto unknown law. The genuine scholar is a plain man of simple ways, somewhat reserved in his expressions and criticisms, because what he knows makes him diffident about speaking in an adverse manner of new propositions which he has not investigated. But the self-satisfied man, who, because of the fact that he, by some chance, has become enrolled among the members of a cult, pretends to know everything and dares to doubt everything, while in reality too shallow for thorough knowledge, is often found among so-called scientists.

"Are there not notes in the scale too high in their vibration for mortal ear? Are there not colors belonging to the rays of the spectrum, too rapid in their vibration to be detected by the mortal eye? Yes, of course. Why 'of course?' Because science has proved it! Nonsense! Let me ask ourselves, what is science? I will tell you what science is. It is the result of the determining of the why and the wherefore, of a few of nature's laws that existed for ages before this word science was invented. Poor mortal man! His opportunities for advancement have been one long succession of trials. First he was obliged to overcome his visible enemies and the fear of the wilderness, then, when he had gained a little confidence, a combination of men arose and ensnared him by fear of the so-called supernatural; and then, when he dared not tell that set of men, 'Begone' so that he might think alone; behold! another set of men arose, who told him that he could think only as they should decide.

"Pray, tell me, what has any man of science, no matter how arrogant his claims may be, accomplished to entitle him to say that he holds the key to all knowledge? For each discoverer of a new scientific principle by which the world is benefited, there are a hundred, who, if they had been guided by 'science' only, would have remained all their lives in intellectual stagnation, but who have, with spirit-assistance, been able to enlarge the boundaries of human knowledge by a proper application of nature's laws. If the word 'science' be confined to knowledge of the laws of the physical world merely, it covers only a small field. The laws of spirit are far more important than the laws of our bodily structure. Man's spiritual future is a grander field of inquiry than the principles of mechanics."

Another said:

"To treat the subject of psychic phenomena by analysis, as you would treat matter, is not within the province of mortals. The soul is the spirit, and can be apprehended by mortals only by the operation of a thinking mind. 'Whence comest thou?' "Wither goest thou?': These are the two great questions for all, and all must some day have the power to answer them. Would not a comprehensive knowledge of these questions be of inestimable benefit to you in your earth-life? Many a great and grievous error might have been avoided, and many who suffer might have been made happy, had it been universally realized that the earth-life is but a preparatory school for a future condition, where progress or retardment of progress is the result of one's own actions.

"It is well that mortals should live the earth-life in accordance with the laws of nature, and not spend too much time in speculative thought as to the why and wherefore of his being; but good being the desire of all, or the necessary condition of all for advancement, a true knowledge of the future state of the spirit is necessary that errors of life may not occur, through your own unguided actions.

"A knowledge of the continued life after passing from earth, can not be determined by weighing, measuring, or comparing as is done with material things; but by an acceptance of truth, manifested by the power of mind. There having been no beginning,

there will be no ending of nature or of natural laws. Is it then to be said that mortal man is to be the sole exception in this eternal order of things? As you are, so shall you be. Your path lies onward; death, as you term it being but a single step, an unimportant change in the journey. Everything moves forward, nothing backward. The ending of mortal existence is but the first change to usefulness. You must not consider that the law that applies to constant improvement, does not apply to the lowest as well as to the highest in life.

"The principle that leads some men of science to hold that the only true laws are those provable by his deepest investigation and research, is a great error. After the limit of investigation has been reached, there are many more questions to be answered that are as yet unanswerable; this being so, you must seek for the answers by a process of philosophic reasoning.

"Great minds require proof of small things, and this is right; but it does not require that great truths should be placed before great minds. Many minds, of more simple attainment, grasp great truths much more easily than do minds which possess the quality of greatness."

Another, who while in this life was a well-known preacher, says:

"I should like to add my mite to your epistle to the 'scientists' and to tell them that the life for which they try to find a scientific, materialistic reason, is as wonderful and as eternal as the universe; they cannot end it by death, any more than they can produce it by artificial means. Life comes from the great force of a mighty blending of souls which permeates all things and all space; life enters in, and is taken by the material atoms, when nature's law, which governs all things, deem the conditions in a productive state. The amount of this great force, which is retained by the being as it develops, depends largely upon the condition of the soil in which it is planted.

"All the talking, thinking and surmising, of all the minds in the world, cannot bring about the birth of a soul; and the great power that can generate a soul may be trusted to look after it justly

and carefully after death. That death is the end, is a belief that a well-balanced mind cannot accept. Life would be but a futile thing, and all effort useless, if the future did not stretch before us endless and unlimited in its possibilities. Believe me, the justice that meets the naked soul, on the threshold of its spirit-life, is terrible in its completeness! If the understanding of this truth could only reach people during earth-life, they would escape much sorrow, —sorrow intensified to a degree greater than earth-dwellers can conceive."

Great was my gratification to receive the following statement, from a man well-known on earth, which I here give word for word:

"Tell your fellow-workers for me that I was working on a material plane all the years of my earth-life; that since I passed out, I have found that the material is but a fleeting thing in the real existence of the soul; that the nearer a man lets himself come to the spiritual, so as to accept suggestion and help from a higher source than the material, the nearer he will come to an understanding of life in its true sense. All these theories about another sense are ridiculous and were begotten in the brains of clever men, who were unable to give up their own petty ideas. They wanted to create, to make the laws that govern the universe; but I tell you that those laws have already been made, —they are fixed and unalterable, and the sooner the mass of mankind realizes this, and comes to a true and definite conception of the simplicity and justice of the laws, the sooner will they live lives fitted to carry them up the next step of progress. They must accept life and its governing forces as they are, at some period; therefore, the sooner the better. I am anxious to be the means of bringing light to some brilliant minds. But they must learn to accept the truth, to put themselves aside, and to realize that as it was in the beginning, it is now, and ever shall be. I am profoundly impressed with this fact: either men of science must grasp these higher laws, or let this new thought fall into other hands."

Men like Alfred Russell Wallace, Sir William Crookes, Sir Oliver Lodge, Camille Flammarion, Dr. Charles Richet and others have had sufficient greatness of mind to break through the limited bonds of physical science, and to tell the world that there are laws in matter, and beyond matter, of which they have evidence and that life continues beyond what is known as dissolution.

This has also been said to me:

> **"If men of science, with all their knowledge and eager quest for the how and wherefore of all things, would only consent to learn a little of something beyond their actual touch! I know some do not deny the existence of life after death, but they spend all their time and effort in proving to their own satisfaction, whether a few insignificant spirits really are whom they claim to be, instead of making their investigation dignified and useful by learning something of that future life, and the best way of getting ready to enter it."**

Vibration

Science can measure the velocity of the wind, of the stars and constellations, and of rays of light; but who shall attempt to measure the velocity of human thought? We cannot demonstrate spirit-forces and the conditions governing them, by the same rules that are applied to physical science. This is simply because there is a difference in the rate of vibration between things material and things spiritual. As long as matter is sensible to touch, science can measure it, analyze its substance, and learn its component parts; but when it reaches a certain vibration, where activity increases beyond their knowledge, the "scientists" are lost in the wilderness which they call "the unknown." This is where the philosophy that we term "metaphysics" commences. We, of this new school of thought, are no more qualified to enter into the domain of physical science than the physical scientists are to come into our domain, and it would be most profitable for each school to confine itself to its own field of usefulness.

Death, so called, is only the changing of vibratory conditions. It has been illustrated to me in this way:

> **"When the body, from disease or long inhabitation, becomes a broken shell, the intense vibration of the spirit breaks through the limiting space to which it has become accustomed, and reaches a plane of higher vibration. The soul-sense dominates all our thoughts and actions; and, consequently, it is held in check**

only by the physical limitations of the body. When, as I say, the body becomes unfit to hold the spirit, the spirit breaks away at the first opportunity, and seeks the sphere best adapted for its expansion. The heavy vibrations of the body, unless quickened by the presence of the keener soul-vibrations, fall back into the still-heavier vibrations of matter, which is earth and vegetation. Nothing remains stationary, and if one part goes onward, the other goes backward. These are the elementary laws that govern change and evolution, and they are the ABC's of spirit-knowledge. As this is becoming more known among those in earth-life, it tends toward their ultimate benefit.

"There are always vibrations depending upon the subjection of molecules that are not so free in expression. I mean they are taken into the life-principle, and given their proper position. They change only to go into the vibration that is gradually made for them. They do not have the sudden release that comes to the soul, but slowly glide from one form into another, all in the same series of vibratory action. The soul's change is usually so sudden as to be a shock; for it is hard for a spirit to accustom itself to the more intense vibration. This is the reason why at a deathbed there is always a gasping for breath. It is not the physical body that is striving to breathe; it is the soul emerging into that higher atmosphere of spirit, unconsciously trying to adjust itself.

"Spirit-material is only earthly matter raised to a higher degree of atomic activity. Chemistry shows that when two elements, having a different degree of atomic motion, come together, there is an attempt at equilibrium, which, being accomplished, produces a new form of matter, and in the spirit-world there is no change of law."

In the progress of matter from the simplest elemental state to the most complex organic compound, there is constantly (a) increase in the mass, (b) decrease in the stability of the molecules. This is well known in physical science, but a new condition is discovered: (c) with all these changes there is an increase in the activity of the properties which continues, not only as long as matter is sensible to touch, but through all the planes of life beyond the physical. There is not one law for the physical and another for the spirit, but one law for both.

Again one said:

"All life is the expression of the overmastering energy of atoms. Vibratory action in the physical world is the ceaseless action and reaction of one force upon another—one undulating wave on another undulating wave. There is never an instant when this action ceases. It is at once the process of elimination, rejection, propulsion, discord and harmony. Nature is apparently relentless. The sweeping storm, the force of the fire and tornado, destroy alike the gnarled oak and the perfectly formed landscape. Mortals with limited physical vision look with horror upon the devastation wrought, but we who have clearer vision see that this is only nature's mode of house cleaning. Out of the chaos, the great law of vibration produces harmony. A universal peace and calmness follow the ravages of the destructive elements. Why should this be so? Because all atoms have been brought together, governed by this law, then as quickly separated: and, after having been hurled apart and crashing here and there, the similar particles fall into harmony once more.

"I am fully conscious that any other statement of this law of vibration must, of necessity, be closely related to the theories of creation. It must fulfill a triple purpose; it must be not only cause and effect but the strange, indefinable, intermediate step that is the growth, as it were, of the real into the unreal. This triple purpose is revealed in the ceaseless action of the positive and negative qualities of every atom. In its power of repulsion and attraction, in its differences and similarities, this law governs the slowly-dissolving elements of every period of the earth's formation from nothingness, nameless ether, into harmony of activity; from this activity into form; from form to organized being; from organized being into other forms of being which again dissolve, and again form, completing a circle back again into nameless, nothings, ether, and the essence of force. When the vibrations grow gradually less, the form begins to be manifested and we have the atom, the molecule, the electric spark, the physical expression of life.

"The freed spirit comprehends the laws of vibratory physical action. To know is to be outside of; hence, not until we have

become disembodied, do we truly know. As disembodied spirits we cannot experience. That belongs to earth-life alone; it is an illusive teacher. Not until we cease experiencing, can we grasp the law that governs. The subconscious mind, governed by this law, grasps it, adds to it, repels and attracts, and moulds itself over and over until, finally, you of earth-life, get a little appreciation of it."

This is a new theory in the philosophy of man. But towards its proper comprehension the thought of the twentieth century will be directed; and, with the mastery of the elementary principle, will come greater appreciation of the future condition of man, in the life beyond the physical.

Facts Well to Know

"Are you ever told by those in the afterlife anything you did not previously know?" I am often asked.

Yes, but future events have never been foretold, for the simple reason that the future is no more known to them than to us. I have been told many things I did not know, and some beyond my comprehension now.

One speaking of the human heart said, **"It is the chief organ of the body. It pumps blood every second to the extremities, to the feet as well as to the brain. Every thought breaks down tissues, every movement produces waste. Let it stop for one moment, and dissolution takes place. It is sending life to every part of the body."**

"We all know," I replied, "that it takes energy to keep anything in motion, and whenever there is motion, there is waste. What then supplies energy that keeps the heart in motion?"

Michael Faraday coming in said:

"You have been told that by the process of decomposition of waste you obtain electricity. This proposition you can demonstrate to be a fact. Now oxygen is one form of electricity; hydrogen is another form of electricity called negative electricity; magnetism is in fact negative electricity.

The tremendous power in Nature's compounds called chemical affinity is due to the union or attempt at union of positive and negative electricity concentrated in the atoms composing the

different so-called elements of the compound. Chemical affinity is the affinity of electricity and magnetism for each other. Electricity and magnetism are both matter in its simplest yet highest or greatest degree of atomic activity. But beyond the electromagnetic is yet a greater degree of eliminated refined atomic activity which is the realm of spirit.

"Electro-magnetism in true equilibrium is etheric, the dwelling place of spirit and the connecting link between spirit and the material compounds in various states of atomic activity. Electricity and magnetism are the male and female elements in the universe. From the oxygen of the air by pulmonic process the blood gets electricity. From the hydrogen of the water by the digestive process the blood gets magnetism. The oxygen of the water is absorbed by the iron of the blood. By the nitrogen of the air partly mixed with the blood at the lungs, and partly by the nitrogen of the food taken into the stomach, the flesh compound is formed.

"Hydrogen and carbon form fatty compounds. One set of blood discs are electric, the other magnetic. The electric discs have an affinity for the magnetic discs when out of equilibrium. But at the lungs they are in equilibrium and hence repel each other to the left auricle, then into the left ventricle, the valves preventing back-flow; this repulsion of the discs to each other must carry the whole crimson mass forward while the equilibrium is maintained to the capillaries.

"The electro-magnetic equilibrium of the two sets of discs is lost in the capillaries and becomes less and less to the right auricle. Of these discs the set nearer the heart because of the inequilibrium, attracts the ones next behind, all the way from the capillaries to the right auricle where, by electric action from the brain in moving the heart to contraction, the equilibrium is again practically established.

"Now the two sets of discs repel each other to the lungs and through the pulmonary capillaries where the equilibrium is more perfected so that the repulsion of the discs carries the blood into the left auricle; thence my muscular action into the left ventricle

and by further muscular action into the aorta. The heart being in equilibrium to arterial blood and positive to venous, attracts."

Knowing as I do that everything in the Universe is composed of matter varying in vibration only, and that the spirit-body is composed of ether, electric, and magnetic in its composition, one evening I inquired of one in the plane beyond the physical, one versed in the action of electricity, how it was that electricity could by its action destroy life, and I recall very distinctly his answer.

"You are aware," he said, "of the voltage used in the various prisons when they put a criminal to death. You are also aware that frequently a current with many times the voltage used in electrocution passes through a body without serious injury. It may startle you to know that any person who has been electrocuted, or who has suffered a lightning shock, or who by accident has received a charge of electricity that has apparently produced death, could be restored to life by proper treatment. The charge of electricity, as applied in our prisons, paralyzes the heart action, all the bodily functions, and the person is apparently dead. But you have probably observed that wherever and whenever a person is put to death under sentence of the law, a post-mortem follows. Death was and is produced by the post-mortem and not by the electric shock. In the beginning, surgeons were anxious to know the effect of the force, and undoubtedly made very careful post-mortems. You would be astounded to know as we know, that post-mortems have lost interest and that frequently they now consist of jabbing a knife into the apparently dead body and passing it on for burial.

"When a person receives an excessive charge of electricity, either by accident or design, and the bodily functions are thereby temporarily paralyzed, if the body were immediately stripped, laid upon the fresh earth and sprayed with water, the electricity would be drawn therefrom, and would pass into the earth. If then, artificial movement of the arms and stimulants were resorted to, the heart action would be resumed, and one apparently dead would get up and walk away.

"Persons die from electric shock because they are not properly treated. When the bodily functions are paralyzed and the electricity is not immediately drawn from the body and the action of the heart is not started by artificial means, death will, of course, ensue in a short time. If the treatment described is administered in time, there is no occasion for dissolution from electric shock. Electricity is life, and life will not destroy life. In this day, where electricity is in such common use, countless lives could be saved if the facts that I am now giving you were known and the treatment applied."

I received this information some years ago and thereafter arranged with one of the wardens of a prison in New Jersey to undertake to resuscitate a convict who was to be electrocuted, but the plan came to the attention of the authorities and was forbidden upon the ground that it was interfering with the due execution of the law.

Again I am asked, "Do you get teachings from the invisible world that are worthwhile?" Let me answer by giving just a few among thousands received:

"Immortality is the first promise of which man is conscious; but, as he acquires that which he considers worldly knowledge, he tries to rid himself of this promise. It stays with him, however, and, no matter how often he may deny the fact, his everyday life keeps before him the claims of immortality. The fields, the fireside, the love, and companionship of his fellow beings all suggest Immortality. The very thought that death ends all, causes him to shudder. Life would, indeed, be a hollow mockery if the earth-life, with its joys and sorrow, its lights and shadows, were the end. Every heart-throb is a protest against such thought. Nature not only promises eternal life, but fulfills that promise, else we would not be here tonight encouraging you to better efforts.

"Ages were required to develop men so they could discuss rather than fight over the matters concerning which they differ, and adjust them in the forum instead of on the battlefield.

"If you live a good life, the day of your death will be a great day; for, it will be a day of liberty; but, if you do not live as you should, the day of death will find you in bondage, bound by fetters of your

own making. The manacles of earth are not nearly so binding as these will be. Follow where the light of spiritual guidance beckons, and do the things you find to do, upon the way. Many tasks will be disagreeable and not to your liking, but they will be the very tasks you will need to perform.

"I feel that it is my duty to help those who try to help themselves. There are many on the spirit side of life who are so densely ignorant that they have no ambition to become better. They continue on in the same old rut in which they were when on earth. Such spirits are of no benefit to the people on earth as they cannot bring useful knowledge to them. If you were able to see and know the conditions of the spirits in the lower spheres and could contrast their condition with that of spirits in the higher spheres, you would understand how important it is that people should be enlightened upon this subject while they are still upon earth.

"Friends, there is one God, the God of Nature; or rather, the God Nature. This God permeates everything and has absolute dominion over all that exists. You are all children of this one God under whose dominion you are here; and you are here, because you could not help yourselves. You had no say as to that part of your destiny; and you will leave the earth-life under the same dominion—Nature—and you cannot change the destiny Nature has marked out for you. Nature's mode of reform is development.

"What is the use of pictures to a person who cannot see, or of descriptions to those who cannot understand? The description of the higher spiritual spheres, even if it were given by one of the highest spirits, would be unintelligible to mortal mind.

"It affords me pleasure and joy unspeakable to know that I am still a man and can disclose in my weak way to some on earth the great fact that life continues, and that mere theories cannot stand out successfully against eternal fact. I was ignorant and weak when I came into this unknown country, and was not prepared to advance, until I learned here what I should have known before.

"What you have gained, what you need, will be yours in the spirit spheres. There is the closest love and quickest sympathy between

the earth-plane and the spirit world, but we cannot make you understand what our lives really are, without becoming exact counter parts of each other. You will each find a different home, suited to you and your work. Your sphere now lies upon the earth-plane, and it is for you to perform the duties allotted to you. You may not be able to give the ignorant learning or the hungry food, but you can inspire their spirits to nobler and better deeds, while someone else, who is able, provides food and shelter. Let them feel that they have your love and sympathy and let them see that, even if the clouds of adversity hang low, your soul is able to ascend to higher spheres. It is good to know that you do not travel the stony path of life alone; to feel that, no matter how rough or dark the way may grow, you can, if you will, stretch forth your hand and feel an answering clasp—a clasp that makes your heart grow braver. The Creator seems so far away to most that, unless they can have the love and help of each other, they feel deserted. It will always be impossible for the finite to grasp the infinite. There are thousands who walk secure in the consciousness of 'leaning on the strong arm of the Lord' when in reality, they are cheered and guided by some unseen friend. It is this spirit that gives to them the feeling of strength that so ably assists them through life. The inhabitants of the spirit world are not bound by dogmas or creeds -that is, those who have been there long enough to get rid of their earth ideas; and they go forth to do good wherever they find opportunity. The main thing is to be honest with yourself, and just to others. Your ideas of good today may not be the same to-morrow. Therefore, do not attempt to lay down a rule for your friends to follow. Let each be a law unto himself; for each must answer for his own actions and not the actions of others.

"It is not what a man does that makes him great, but what he is. Action is merely thought dressed in physical garb. Being must ever precede doing."

On Charity

It is my custom to ask spirit people to give some expression of their views on subjects under consideration, and in reply to an inquiry about charity one said:

"And the greatest of all is charity of thought, without which the utmost gifts of money become as pebbles in the mouths of the hungry. Think of all as you would have all think of you. A thought once born grows to its fullness, not only by the good done to the individual, but by this strength and goodness. It circles around, and after encompassing many in its kind embrace, rebounds to enrich the originator. Cultivate the desire to think kindly of your fellow men.

"Some thought dominates all actions. Those who have evil thoughts are in danger of becoming evil themselves, though they may be unconscious of the fact. The mind flings out a radiance which, to some extent, sheds light on every avenue of life. If that radiance should grow feeble and your life selfish, you would long remain in the twilight, and your outlook would be limited. But, if kindness and true charity dominate your thoughts, the radiance will continue rich and bright till its emanations reach the boundaries of hope, and your soul is illumined by the crowning sun of happiness.

"The best way to judge character is to watch the faces of children who turn toward men. A good man loves them and has patience with them, and they turn to him as naturally as a flower follows the warmth of the sun. A bad man realizes their helplessness, and brutally vents his malignity on their small defenseless heads. Such a man is not to be trusted in any walk of life.

"Again be generous to those to whom nature has limited her gifts, for nature compensates, and the time will come when all shall be equal. The poorly equipped for earth life will more easily acquire the lessons to be learned in the next, for those of patience and humility are learned already. Those who think differently are to be enlightened, not censured or ridiculed, for all who understand this truth of life's progression are entrusted with the great responsibility of teaching all who can understand; and you must get as close as possible to the lives of others, that your words may have weight.

"Let your hearts be fallow ground, plant therein the seeds of love, charity and purity, nourish them daily with the clear water

of tenderness; and you will have a wonderful garden filled with fragrance and white with blossoms, and your life will become a part of the great life principle."

A spirit, well known when in earth life, said one evening to a gentleman who worked with me, and who helped obtain the information now given the public:

"The intense satisfaction that is the constant result of right doing, based on honest purpose, is, in itself, sufficient reward for action. Of all the trite sayings of the Bible, the one that reads, What shall it profit a man, if he shall gain the whole world, and yet lose his own soul?' is one with the greatest meaning.

"Wealth brings many opportunities for good and for evil; in fact, there are more for the latter than for the former, as the besetting sin of mortal man is selfishness and the possession of great riches allows free expression of that greatest of all sources of trouble. The true and full meaning of the word 'selfishness; is in every way opposite to the most beautiful word in your language, 'charity.' Shorn of their meaning, as applied to money, they are the negative and positive of man's character. The fullest opportunity of giving expression to these two opposite words comes with the possession of great wealth. The understanding of the full meaning of these two words is the truest index of a man's character. The ability to make one's life the embodiment of that wonderful word 'charity,' and to understand that other word 'selfishness' so as to avoid it, is the true test of mortal man's ability to control himself.

"Self-control is man's perfect condition. To know charity and practice its meaning; to know selfishness and keep it from you; this is self-control. This state of existence is as near perfection as the earth-tied mortal can hope to get. You have been chosen one among many on your side of life to bring certain great truths to the people of the world. In advance of time, you are to be prepared for the time of your usefulness, and this is one of the moments of laying before you certain truths. To teach the truth, the teacher must be truthful; to induce others to accept pure and honest principles, the teacher must be pure and honest himself; to set certain facts before others, the teacher must be above criticism.

"You may honestly atone for those things that have so far occurred in your life, by making amends to those to whom you are indebted. So far as the errors of your past are concerned, you have well and strongly conquered their chief cause, and you need no longer fear them. You have henceforth no excuse to do otherwise than follow the honorable and ennobling instincts of your nature. Guard well your actions, that they may not be open to criticism from others; and particularly from the one of all others from whom you cannot escape, —your own self. You have been, and you are being, weighed in the balance; and so much is expected of you, that you must not be found wanting.

"Remember that wealth brings the opportunity to give expression to what is best in your nature, and that you will find the only reward for doing good is that intense feeling of satisfaction that can come only as the result of a good deed, unselfishly done. It is well that man should earn his daily bread. It is the intention of nature that every mortal should struggle, for by no other means can he progress in the scale of being. This being so, one so situated that he can live without a proper exertion on his part, is unfortunate. Never forget this principle; the waste of money is not charity, but foolishness. You will find many practical ways to do good and to do it in the right way. A clean tenant demands a clean habitation. A pure heart and a pure mind are the results of your own efforts to keep them.

"Charity is not a formula; it is a thought, clothed with a kind act. Cultivate charity in judging others; try to draw out the latent good in them, rather than to discover the hidden evil. We must do this if we would rise to the full glory of our privilege, to the dignity of true living, to the supreme charity of the world."

The World's Desire

This is an age of greed. We, as a people, have drifted out upon the sea of selfishness, egotistic desire and devouring ambition, and set the main sails to woo the winds of fortune. This is the age of money. Every nation and every people have erected a throne on which wealth sits in state; they have placed upon its brow a crown of gold, and have decreed that the possession of money, with little regard to the manner of acquisition, should be the only qualification for this kingship of modern times. (This was written in 1906, nothing has changed much as I write this in 2012-Ed.)

Man, at the dawn of physical development, is shown this goal, and taught that money is power and the world's desire. He enters the strife and bends his energies, as others do, to grasp the greatest amount of wealth with the least possible effort, matching his cunning against labor, —mind against muscle, —artifice against simplicity, -and directs his thoughts towards wrenching from the hands of honest toil, a portion of its legitimate earnings.

Does wealth ever ask what claim it has on the savings of labor? Why is it adding to its already vast store, while other hands are growing feeble from want, and shadows are falling on poverty stricken homes? Does capital ever contemplate the privation and suffering that must follow close upon the heels of cupidity and deception? Do captains of industry realize that, by directing their ability towards the concealment of base designs under the veil of enterprise, and by the misappropriation of the proceeds of honest toil, they are, according to a higher standard of ethics, guilty of larceny? And that by a law, as fixed as gravitation, the time will come when they, through laboring and suffering, in the life beyond the physical, must make compensation for every dollar acquired unjustly.

The thought that the rich man here may be, and usually is, the pauper in the afterlife, is startling in its possibilities and dreadful to contemplate. A man who has made money his God and worshipped at the shrine of gold, having no other thought, ambition or desire, in earth-life, is poor indeed if his hoard cannot be taken with him, for poor he is in all else, in a world where kind and thoughtful acts are the standard of wealth.

Contemplate the afterlife, where money is not used! The occupation of most people will be gone, they will find themselves disqualified for any other position, ignorant and helpless in a world of activity; then will come appreciation of the lost Atlantis men call opportunity. Upon the pages of memory will be written: wasted energy, false ideals, worthless ambitions, erroneous conceptions, ignorance of the simple laws of nature, —and selfishness will find itself a pauper, in a world of plenty.

In the next life, I am told, the only way to gain advancement is by helping others; in this way only is knowledge gained, for by contributing their efforts to greater good, the Master Intelligence has provided for the individual advancement of spirit-people. Each builds his own stairway to the heights of knowledge, —"all for one and one for all," that is the law of their progress when they have emancipated themselves from earth conditions. Material wealth is only for a day, as time is counted. What the good man does enriches him here, and becomes a part of his own self for all that we call eternity.

Progress

To the average mind that has given no thought to the problem of life after this existence, and to its great possibilities, the suggestion that those out of the body can communicate with us at all, is startling. The fact that any conditions have been made where they can speak in their own voice so as to be heard distinctly in our atmosphere, is beyond their comprehension. That spirit-people control the physical brain and hand to write, is beyond all understanding. The fact that millions of human beings have not heard or spoken to spirit-people, or seen them use the hand of a sensitive to write, does not even tend to prove that I have not had such experiences or that these are not facts. Knowledge is positive; ignorance is negative. I have seen the one and have heard the other again and again, and I know both to be facts; I have had taken down in writing many discussions and lectures on problems that are of vital interest. Let me give the words of a spirit on the subject of progress:

> **"In the great theater of the universe all is harmony that pertains to the management of the play. The one touch of discord exists with players only. Gradually, but steadily, the players acquire a perfect knowledge of their various parts, and, as they learn to conduct themselves so as to allow the play to go on smoothly, the entertainment becomes more agreeable. But much rehearsing is required before a satisfactory exhibition can be given.**
>
> **"That all who wish may enjoy that to which they are entitled is nature's full intent, and gradually mortals are coming to realize that such is the case. An appreciation of universal good for the benefit of mankind at large, can come only when the single and separate individual can clearly understand that he is entitled to those gifts of nature which his senses tell him may be had for the demanding. Until recently it was an almost universal belief that there were special privileges for a certain number of the**

supposed elect of God; but when a few who were barred out of those privileges, fearlessly raised their eyes and studied nature as it is presented on the stage of the universe, and learned that the only true supremacy and greatness lies in the difference of intelligence, and not in any distinction that can be marked by heredity, there came an awakening; and since that day, the scenes on the stage of your world have changed rapidly, and each succeeding on has shown an improvement over its predecessor. And when this appreciation of the only true mark of greatness among mortals has been realized, then and then only, will the chord of harmony be struck, and the play shall be so thrilling that the doors shall be open to the universe at large, and all the different constellations will ring with applause as they see one more evidence of the splendid work of the master mind.

"Knowledge is the key that shall open the door for this great production. Knowledge is the magic key to progress. With knowledge comes confidence; with confidence comes a strengthened desire for more knowledge. When the creeping babe first pulls its body to an erect position by its hands and arms, and finds that it can stand erect on its little feet, confidence in the power of its being is established, and the first forward movement of its feet gives it further knowledge of its power, and, as step by step, its feet carry forward its little body, knowledge of its power begets confidence, and confidence begets the possibility of acquiring further knowledge; and, until something occurs to weaken that condition, the forward and onward movement to acquire more knowledge is continued. As it is with the creeping, toddling child, so it is with the adult; until something occurs to stop that onward movement of gathering knowledge, progress is constant. What, then, is more terrible to contemplate than any system of teaching that can beget, or has begotten fear, the great destroyer of confidence? Like one who sits upon a great height and has an unobstructed view of what is happening on the plains, we, of the spirit-world, can look with unobstructed vision down the long vista of the past, and see the terrible crimes that have been committed against our fellow spirits and earth mortals by those bands of men who dared to intimidate their fellow creatures, and to hold them in subjection by writing and preaching about things of which they were utterly ignorant. Some

> **were mere fanatics; but in the main, they were mean, low, and unscrupulous men whose only thoughts were of personal gain and personal advantage. Awful will be the punishment of such men. Some are now undergoing their punishment in the spirit world, and others are clinging tightly to those whom they have deceived, and, by suggestion, are still doing their harmful work."**

When the intellect ceases to be enslaved, then is the body free. When the knowledge holds full sway, then the intellect is free. Knowledge gives one the power of self-control, and when one has learned self-control, knowledge increases rapidly. And as one acquires knowledge, he gains self-control in like degree.

> **"Let fear and superstition and dread of the future be banished from the minds of men, so that they may see clearly and understand nature perfectly; then will knowledge come to them, imparted by those who have journeyed into the next stage of progress, the spiritual or stage of acute intelligence."**

Emily French (seated), circa 1912

Mr. Edward C. Randall, circa 1904

Mr. Edward C. Randall, circa 1934

Emily Sophia McCoy French, 1871

Former home of Edward C. Randall

Fragments

> "Our object in life should be to accumulate a great number of grand questions to be asked, and resolved in eternity. Now we ask the sage, the genius, the philosopher, the divine, but none can tell; but we will open our queries to other respondents-we will ask angels, redeemed spirits, and God."
>
> –FOSTER

Not withstanding the many years of this research, we were always careful to utilize our strength to the best possible advantage. Little time was spent with tests and personalities, none with frivolities. It was a dignified, scientific work, wherein we sought knowledge to the utmost.

At times there would come concrete and definite statements, with great rapidity and tremendous import. It seemed as if the group of spirit people wanted to say as much as possible in the fewest words. Frequently, I asked slower speech, so that my stenographer might get the statements correctly, and I recall being told that it was impossible at times to slow the message; when conditions were right, they had to send them through or lose the opportunity.

I have gathered from my records short, terse statements from various communications received from those in the after life, some beyond world teaching, that seem worthy of publication. The following are but a few of the thousands, mere fragments of spirit philosophy:

1. "Force wherever found or however expressed is life."

2. "Each plane in spirit existence is partly hidden from the plane below, because the conditions of each change make it best for the soul to fit itself for progression without absolute knowledge of the next step."

3. "When the intellect ceases to be enslaved, the body becomes free."

4. "The supreme need of each man is to reason and to remain, ever after, true to his convictions. Where reason leads, each should follow publicly and openly. This is the highest conception of duty."

5. "Man's conscience is his judgment seat, and reparation for wrong cannot begin too soon. Love for humanity is the basis upon which mankind must stand to gain ultimate good; that to help a sprawling beetle to gain its feet is an act the result of which will follow one through eternity."

6. "Dissolution is simply the throwing aside of the physical garment, the outer covering composed of flesh compounds, whereupon the individual becomes an inhabitant of another sphere of usefulness, differing only in its intensity."

7. "Inhabitants of this material world cannot see the spirit form while in the body, neither can they see it when separated from the body."

8. "All life has intelligence; all intelligence has language; all language, expression."

9. "One who does right and has the courage of his convictions, will find in the after life a radiant happiness, and the censure of this little world will fail to sting."

10. "A thought born in your mind is for good or evil, a thing to be reckoned with again in the after life, when it will confront you face to face, and claim you as its author."

11. "Do you not think that the great intelligence that planned millions of worlds, and made them move with perfect harmony and precision, that peopled them, that fixed and marked each one's course, and lighted its pathway in infinite space, knows what's best?"

12. "At dissolution, each sense is quickened, and all that fills space is visible to the spiritual senses and tangible to spiritual touch and brain. Space must then take form, substance and reality, —a world of thought, boundless and endless."

13. "The rains will come when they are timed. They will replenish the green of the harvest and make it richer. The storms of life may beat upon you, but you will find they only break down the dead branches, and you will be more straight and fair for their passing."

14. "All about this material world there exists actually the psychic or spiritual universe, more active and real than this, peopled with all the countless dead, who, no longer burdened with a physical body, move at will within the boundaries of their sphere, in what appears as space to mortal man."

15. "In the kingdom of the mind there can be no personal dictation; there is no God but universal good; no Savior but oneself; no trinity but matter, force and mind."

16. "Life beyond the grave is the promise that hope has ever whispered to all who have lived."

17. "The sovereignty of the individual must be gained by effort. The weak must be taught; the strongest at some time must bend and obey."

18. "To every mortal who thinks rightly, Nature's laws become natural laws."

19. "Dissolution is a step in evolution, and involves no mental change, adding nothing, subtracting nothing, but simply increasing the opportunities for observation and learning."

20. "Men who deny to others the right of public speech are not qualified for speech themselves."

21. "If you would impress your thought on others, and spread the truth, make that thought the highest expression of truth."

22. "Make yourself attuned to the most harmonious vibrations, so that your impulses will be good, and then obey them. They are apt to be the suggestions of a fellow-soul working out his salvation."

23. "Mind is the aggregate of all thoughts. Mind is the universal thought. As a drop of water signifies but one infinitesimal part of the great ocean, so a thought is but one infinitesimal part of the great ocean of the mind."

24. "Deeds are thoughts grown to maturity, and yet a thought unspoken or unlived, will exist through all the ages, as though expressed."

25. "Everything is governed by law; nothing happens by chance; cause and effect are as potent in the spirit plane as in the earth plane."

26. "There are sounds that our ears have never heard; there is light that our physical eyes can never see; there is an invisible world filled with people that few have ever imagined."

27. "Life would be but a futile thing, and all effort useless, if the future did not stretch before us, endless and unlimited in its possibilities."

28. "The justice that meets the naked soul, on the threshold of its spirit life, is terrible in its completeness."

29. "The tendency of all life, wherever found or however clothed, is to perfect, improve, increase and extend its sphere of usefulness. This is evolution. It is a fact, a law and not a theory, and its possibilities are as boundless as the imagination."

30. "The atom, alone, has eternal duration of form, for it alone has the power to enter and dominate all other forms. It has no master except force, and to force alone it is amenable."

31. "The wealth that all in this physical world should seek, has not the ring of gold; it is gathered by right living and by helping others to live right."

32. "It is far better to have committed an honest error and reaped no profit, than to have great profit and to have honesty gone from your own heart."

33. "Selfishness in the human heart is the cause of all evil; where selfishness dwells, love can not abide. Selfishness and love can not occupy the same place at the same time."

34. "An atom from the great ocean of spirit finds lodgment in a physical organism—and behold, a man!"

35. "Mortal needs spirit suggestion, but spirits indeed of mortal thought have just as great a need."

36. "Life enough is given to rule each day in our kingdom, but not enough 'for tomorrow."

37. "Wisdom is born in the soul of man when he recognizes that natural law governs and accounts for all things."

38. "If a man is clean, he feels clean, and keeping clean inspires him to clean deeds."

39. "Wisdom, power, beneficence, and the peace that passeth all understanding—these come not from above, but from within."

40. "If a man can make himself habitually right in his thought and desire, right in his will and purpose, he must become right in the tissues built up out of the mind's action."

41. "Power is born of desire; no man can earnestly desire to live upon a high plane and yet be compelled to live upon a low plane, since we live in that state of development that we create for ourselves."

42. "Every life is placed exactly where it should be, and is in touch with the environment needed at that hour to unfold itself."

43. "It is thought that builds the body. Thought is food, thought is force—the motor power, by means of which the soul expresses itself in physical form."

44. "Why are old experiences repeated? you ask. Because the tangle of life must be made right, and it must be made right by the individual soul. This is the truth I taught. Only a few are ready for it, and even today only a few enter into my sphere. There are those in earth-life with whom I daily and hourly commune; there are those here who still seek expression through some form of earthly religious belief; few are willing to stand alone and think."

45. "Nature is an open book, with language simple and easy to comprehend; yet man, with all his boasted knowledge, has read but few pages and mastered less. Its lessons are written in rocks, in earth, in minerals and grasses, in grains, in flora, in trees, in bursting bud and growing things, in mountains, in snows and glaciers, in sun and stars, and in all movement and evolution of matter, gross and refined."

46. "Literature, art, all the great work of masters, all the products of the genius of the present and the past, will come to the assistance of those who call. We are here to aid, to comfort, to uplift and to support all who ask for help. Only a few here have a faint glimpse of a life beyond the satisfaction of earth-desires. Like tendrils clinging to a wall or to a decaying tree, through disappointed loves and blasted hopes, they keep tenaciously struggling with the problems of mortal life."

47. "Open your eyes and you shall see the new heaven and the new earth, all invisible to the physical eye, which sees only that which it wants to see, but it sees nothing of the eternal harmony, of which mortals express only a counterpart. Awake to the truth of the joy of being! Awake to the infinite cause of all happiness! Awake to the omni-active energy that surrounds you!"

48. "All beauty is expression in a varied language—not of words, but of pure ideas, hopes and joys. Emotions have a language not yet comprehended, and yet to be given to a listening, waiting, longing world. Be filled with joy! That is the expression of God. If you would impress your thought on others, and spread the truth, make that thought the highest expression of truth! Make your life a continual song of thanksgiving for the good you find, and the good you give to others. Be consistent, looking to the harmony of natural law to guide you, and build your life on the same simple principle. This life means to the true thinkers a wondrous unfolding, beginning with a child's first conscious look, going on and on until the individual is taken into that one great scheme of indivisible good. This is the ultimate end of all."

49. "The universe is teeming with life, —beautiful, abundant life. Open your soul and stretch out as it were with eager hands, and let the spirit of Good enter, and abide. Like dew upon the thirsty, famished flower, it will make a sick soul well. It is the same force that is in the dew, only to the flower it must come in the form of dew, rain or shine; while to mankind it comes as a suggestion, enters into the mind, makes it strong and courageous; for a mind filled with the uplifting principle, which is Good, must be a pure one, one able to lead others to the great book of nature, there to learn to obey its laws—steadily, insistently, working for each blade of grass, each soul of man."

50. "Beware of criticism. It kills naturalness in yourself and others, and the best impulses are suppressed by the frost of self-criticism. Attune yourself to the most harmonious vibrations, so that your impulses will be good, and then obey them. They are apt to be the suggestion of a fellow-soul working out his salvation; and, by letting the impulse hold sway over you, you not only do a good act, but help that struggling soul one step farther on his way."

51. "When the end drew near and I knew my judgment was at hand, my spirit shuddered with horror. I knew I had not lived according to divine good. I had deceived, and, more than that, I had lied and abused the confidence of many who looked up to me. Will I ever be able to complete the restitution necessary? Sometimes my soul sickens under the burden of sorrow and suffering I have caused, and I am afraid. I want, by these teachings I am privileged to give you, to gain much for my own advancement. Perhaps you and I together may grow in greater harmony each day so that much good may come of it. Call me when you will, I will be watching, eager to take up the work."

52. "Beyond the great divide, await all those for whom you mourn; all unsatisfied ambitions, providing they are tending toward progression, you will have the power to gratify by work and application."

53. "There is no such thing as space; what seems so to us, in fact, contains all the elements that produce objects."

54. "Mind, I mean thought, not the habitation of thought, when the earth-life is over, becomes the entire being. It is the only part in man that is of such vibration that it can enter in and progress to spirit-life."

55. "Nature is God, is always good, always smiling, even in her storms nature is but fulfilling her promise of future plenty, as a mother goes through the storm of childbirth that she may replenish the earth."

56. "Nature is natural in all her changes. The God-spirit is breathing through every fold of the rose, every leaf and ear of corn."

57. "All Nature's laws are natural laws. Those things that to mortal minds are mysterious, are called phenomena. But Nature never made anything phenomenal. Things seem so to the undeveloped mentally."

58. "Truth is always an achievement; it becomes such by reversing appearances, turning rest into motion, solids into

fluids, centers into orbits, breaking up enclosing firmament into infinite space."

59. "The appearance of Nature one nearly always finds to be not false, but elusive; and our first interpretation of natural conditions is usually the reverse of the reality. Of course, this must be so; it is the wisdom for creation, and the secret of the world; else knowledge would be immediate and without process."

60. "Time was when every cradle asked us whence, and every coffin whither; this generation, for the first time in history is able to answer these questions."

61. "The eternal dome of thought is high and broad and each should do what he can to change the night of intellectual darkness into perfect day. Every man who discovers a fact adds something to the knowledge of the world."

62. "Back in the past centuries, when the world of spirit had not its present development, there was little original inventive thought. Man built a shelter, killed his food, and fought his enemies, as any animal does. As the spirit-world progressed and became more intelligent; as it obtained greater understanding, and grasped with greater power, the life-forces, in other words, more power of thought and more ability to help mortal development, then, by reason of spirit-suggestion, acting through man's subconscious mind, he began to feel an awakening for something better, and the progress of civilization began."

63. "Gravitation acts upon the physical body, attraction upon the mental state. Gravitation in the physical world, attraction in the spirit world."

64. "One law governs all conditions in the physical as well as in the spirit planes; and whenever we find life-forces, they are clothed with either physical or spiritual material, which is matter in different states of vibration."

65. "Thought is the one thing in the universe formed and fashioned in the human brain; it agitates the ether, and thus permeates all things and all space."

66. "Everything is governed by law, nothing happens by chance; cause and effect are as potent in the spirit plane as in the earth plane."

67. "Savages rubbing sticks to produce fire, looked upon the traveler with suspicion and fear; but when they saw him produce fire with a match, their souls were filled with wonder. Spirit-people look with sorrow upon the people of this generation, for the great majority, in their simplicity, are still rubbing sticks to obtain light."

68. "To the masses, spirit-life is a mystery, death a hopeless problem; while the world of the invisible, just another community all around us, cannot be comprehended by the average mortal mind."

69. "The genuine scholar is a plain man of simple ways, somewhat reserved in his expressions and criticisms, because what he knows makes him diffident about speaking in an adverse manner of new propositions which he has not investigated."

70. "Great minds require proof of small things, and this is right; but it does not require that great truths should be placed before great minds. Many minds, of more simple attainment, grasp great truths much more easily than do minds which possess the quality of greatness."

71. "That death is the end, is a belief that a well-balanced mind cannot accept."

72. "The Master's great purpose is the gradual, yet positive, improvement of matter until an observant and grateful mortal is the final result."

73. "Evolution is but the action of that great power called by mortal man, God, but which really is the process of refinement

and purification of gross matter until the resultant product is living, thinking, mortal man, and then the intellectual man. The next step in that ever-changing, ever-progressing evolution, is the endowment of that physical intellectual man, with what we call spirit."

74. "The atom, alone, has eternal duration of form, for it alone has the power to enter and dominate all other forms. It has no master except force, and to force alone it is amenable."

73. "Beyond the atom is an intelligence which has imbued it with these properties and powers."

76. "What then, is this life, this intellectual force, which is back of the atom and expressed in or through it? What or who controls its movement with perfect precision? Some call it energy, some force; some nature; and others call it God."

77. "Beyond the atom are minds, that have at some time lived in a physical body, working in unison and combining substance that will endow matter with energy which will give expression to life force in the physical."

78. "The conscious mind is controlled by yourself. In it are held all the material part of your thoughts. I mean those connected with and controlled by earth things."

79. "The subconscious mind is the one controlled by psychic forces entirely. It is the spiritual brain of man. I mean, that it is subject to the laws of vibration, which the other part of the brain is not sensitive enough to catch."

80. "It is the subconscious mind that gets suggestion from spirit-people, the connecting link, or battery, that for an instant holds the suggestion, and passes it on, to grow into a thought or an impulse ."

81. "The subconscious mind does not retain suggestion. It is the embryo thought, which takes definite form only as it reaches the conscious mind."

82. "On earth there are weeds, as well as useful grain and beautiful flowers, so among your people are there apparently worthless mortals; but who can say when or how the weeds, following the great law of progress, will evolve into useful or beautiful plants; and yet, as simple weeds, may they not serve a great, if hidden purpose?"

83. "The poorly-equipped for earth life will more easily acquire the lessons to be learned in the next, for those of patience and humility are learned already."

84. "Charity is not a formula; it is a thought, clothed with a kind act."

85. "Wisdom sits in the presence of a theory, but stands in the presence of a fact."

86. "Character is the product of trials, conscience is born of suffering."

87. "Man cannot be saved by proxy; he must be his own Savior, there can be no remission of sin through faith or prayer."

88. "Evil is not an inheritance; it is the result of ignorance of natural law."

89. "Matter is an outer crust, a crystallization of Mind."

90. "The trees and solids of which our earthly furniture is made were once full of sap, which is life. They came out of the invisible by a process of growth. They will disintegrate again, and be worked up into other forms by the permeating Spirit—the restless Energy of the universe that is constantly changing all things."

91. "Different rates of vibration give us different planes of consciousness. On the physical plane, one rate gives us sight, another hearing."

92. "Be true to conscience, which is God's voice."

93. "Another name for vibration is motion."

94. "When I hear music or sounds of any sort, I know that I hear only because sound travels. It moves in waves, just as light does, but the sound waves take a different direction, and are of different lengths than the light waves. Therefore, light and sound are simple energy, or force, moving at a different rate of vibration, and in different directions. All force is motion."

95. "Our progress is through the relative to the absolute, through the finite to the infinite, through weakness to strength, through bondage to freedom, through man to God, through death to life."

96. "When the thought is fully focused by the will on the thing desired, force must be put behind it, else it is like an engine without steam trying to pull a train of cars. Though fully equipped with masterful machinery, it will not budge an inch till the force is applied."

97. "Love is to thought what steam is to the engine."

98. "Thought is a power that must be recognized in the divine economy."

99. "Man has made his own condition; yet the blunders and crimes he has fostered and committed have been ignorantly ascribed to Providence."

100. "Will is an architect; intellect is a builder."

101. "Founders of great enterprises and promoters of philanthropic causes do not lose their interest in this world's affairs, because they have cast off their outer sheaths of personality."

102. "A rational view of life's continuity and a clear statement of what awaits them in the Beyond are among the greatest and most truly answerable demands of the twentieth century."

103. "The seeker for Truth should expect to find it everywhere. Thus alone will he realize the brotherhood of souls, the unity of

religions; for Truth cannot be confined within the limits of a creed, or restricted to the necessities of a few, this is the New Thought."

104. "All things work together towards a high ideal in the kingdom of the spirit."

105. "Living without the light of the New Thought is like having a grand musical instrument in the house without the ability to awaken its magnificent melody."

106. "Every soul is a law unto itself, and would outrage its own sacred birthright, should it accept the criterion of another instead its own."

107. "There should be less worship and more work among men."

108. "A God whom limited intellect could comprehend would not be a God; the intellect would be the greater."

109. "The only religion that will save the world from its sin, and raise it from its degradation, must find its way to the hearts of men through the filtering process of human reason. Science and philosophy will be its handmaids, and eternal laws and immortal truths its gospels."

110. "The imagining faculty, which we all possess, is our creative faculty."

111. "With successful people in all walks of life, thought is concentrated on particular aims; but with the masses of mankind, it is but a wandering vagrant loitering upon the outer wall of circumstances."

112. "The spirit world is the thought world. And as thought lives within the physical man, so the spirit world interpenetrates the material world."

113. "Knowledge is merely a cultivation of that divine spark of wisdom inherent in all."

114. "The goal of yesterday we only reach to be lured to a grander view."

115. "First, the natural, afterward, the possible."

116. "When will the popular mind be taught that there is no age, except as we permit it to affect us? We should put behind us all the thoughts of a life 'here' and a life 'there'; there is but one life, and that is eternal. Then, why reckon upon 'age' at all?"

117. "There is not in the universe a single great problem that man can truthfully say he has mastered, and concerning which nothing remains to be found out."

118. "The law executes perfect justice everywhere and at all times. Universal law is universal justice. Without law, or without justice, the universe could not exist a day."

119. "Those who, through ignorance or prejudice, decry a new discovery, and so prevent fair consideration, are enemies of civilization."

120. "Truth has neither youth nor age; it is, and ever has been, a brother to reason; it does not need the assistance of fame or science; it has never been in the keeping of any particular class of men; it is the heritage of all who live."

121. "I look into the future and see the creeds and dogmas, that for centuries have enslaved the human race, dead and obsolete laws in life's great statute book. I see knowledge take the place of faith and superstitions; I see the awful fear of death banished from every human heart and mankind at peace. I see a world of thinkers, honest and free, teaching the gospel of truth, the religion of nature, and philosophy of meta-psychics, the new science of matter."

122. "Let this fact sink deep into every human heart: the individual thought must at all times be kept clean and pure, for this wondrous and ever-active mind of ours is from day to day throwing the shuttle through the web of life, incessantly weaving the fabric of

condition that will clothe the naked soul on the threshold of the afterlife, and those in the great beyond watch beside the loom."

A Few Last Questions to the Spirits

All life is infinite and of God; this earth is but an incubator, developing and increasing the sum total of life force. Who shall say that ultimately all who live may not become a part of that Infinite Intelligence, and work as one with the force that fashions worlds? I do not know, and those with whom I have been privileged to discuss the question do not know. They do not know what is beyond them any more than we know what is beyond us. They receive and accept teachings from those who are in planes beyond themselves, the same as we do. Discard, if you will, my experiences, treat what I am saying as theory—but does it not seem natural? Does it not appeal to your reason?

"From whence comes all life-force of the Universe?" I asked.

This was the answer:

"There is a great central force, the emanating rays of which are gradually lessening in their vibratory action, reaching the lowest ebb in the center of your earth.

"This central vibratory action is in the highest sphere we know, so intense and so high in vibration that souls who are in the highest state of development are the only ones who come near its circle. It is the apex of the universe, from which the rays lessen as they go out through infinite space to all spheres.

"Some of the other planets are much higher in vibratory action than is your earth, so that if one, retaining earth conditions, were to go to them he could not see any life, because his sensitiveness to vibration is so much lower.

"This condition is apparent when once one has grasped the immensity of the universe and the harmony of its laws. If you were able to see all the conditions and people beyond you, life would appear as chaos and confusion—each sphere mixing with another—no regulations, no harmony anywhere. As it is, each has its own place in the scheme of progression; the invisible wall of vibratory force is a safety guard to continued rational living.

"Those who pass through each stage of the soul's progression are slowly but surely becoming a part of that great force. It is the contention of many here that individuality is lost in the immensity of that great harmonious force, and becomes in turn a tiny part of the new conception in the earth form. It is a part of this force that creates life in earth form, and that part is taken from the infinite whole."

"What determines one's condition, position, and environment in your plane of activity?" I asked.

The answer came:

"Character, and in this regard there are many factors to consider. With you in earth life, wealth and birth have much to do with your position. Education and social status also are factors; one may be selfish and cruel and yet hold place and power, but in dissolution, stripped of gear and gold and all things physical, he comes naked into this world of ours. Before transition one may hide, dissemble, and deceive, but with us character—that is the soul body—is visible, so that as we come in contact with one who has passed the portal, we know at once what he is."

"What law," I asked, "fixes and determines one's status there?"

The reply was:

"The dominant law is one of harmony. It may be said that the law of attraction with us corresponds in principle to your law of gravitation; as your physical body is subject to the latter law, so are you, when separated from its flesh garment, subject to the law of attraction. When one comes here he is irresistibly drawn into that condition and company for which he is fitted by character. So the selfish are together; the immoral and cruel have like companionship; thieves and murderers are among their kind. Also the charitable, the kind, the devout, the spiritual, are drawn to congenial souls, among whom they work in harmonious accord. This is one of the laws, fixed and forever in force."

"What of opportunity for advancement?" I asked.

"That, too, is provided for. A spirit may work out of his environment, no matter what it is, and may climb the heights. Indeed, all must ultimately progress; but the way for some is dark, dreary, and lonely. Only by one's own effort can he advance to higher planes; through work, that is by helping others, the soul of the individual spirit becomes developed, refined, more spiritual. The same law that fixed his status on his arrival will advance him to whatever condition he earns, so that he may constantly be in harmony with his associates.

"Every wrong act in earth life must be lived over here, and lived right, before one can progress. If your world knew this fact, incentive to wrong would be counteracted, so that you would have a better world and a happier people. As you are developing character every hour of your earth life, you see how important it is to build it right."

"Our thoughts, then, build character?" I asked.

"You have so little knowledge of true psychology that it is difficult to explain the process. First of all, you have a mind that functions in and through your etheric brain; it receives impressions and suggestions from our side; it formulates what you know as ideas by catching spirit suggestion, and through observation. It is colored at times, unfortunately, by heredity, selfishness and desire, but it has perfect freedom—limited only by the laws of your society—to express itself, and so to build character.

"You are answerable to the State for violation of the laws of the State, only if you are discovered; but you are answerable to the higher laws for every act and deed without exception, for your world holds no secret from us. I do not mean that a personal God watches you from day to day, but I do know that those who love you and are interested in your development can witness your acts, and do know your very thoughts. When in the death change you come here, your character is visible to all, so that your personality becomes common property."

Another said:

> **"Thought is material as granite, differing only in vibration. It takes not only form, but color; a thought is as real in itself as though it were expressed in the physical, for of necessity the thought itself precedes the physical expression of it. As thought is real and lives forever, you can see the importance of keeping it clean.**
>
> **"One who conceives low, selfish, and beastly thoughts, is even now surrounded by a dark and filthy mental condition, in which foul conditions he will find himself when the flesh garment that hide from your eyes the real self is cast aside. Where else could a wise and beneficent Providence place him? Should such a character mingle with those who are clean and pure?"**

"Explain, if you please, how thought molds one's personality?" I asked.

> **"Let me illustrate if I can. Consider for a moment the brain as a machine, through which passes mental fabric. The results may go far and wide, but the brain is yours, never for one moment to be lost or destroyed. It creates what is called an aura—that is an integral part of your spirit body.**
>
> **"We even now can tell the character, and know the extent of your spiritual development, by the color of the emanations that come from your soul center, and find expression in acts and deeds. Your soul body is a thought body, as all thought is material, so your inner or etheric body is molded, fashioned, and tinted by your thoughts from day to day."**

Our thoughts from day to day, then, are woven like tapestries, in patterns involved and strange, with dreams and fancies interlaced, with harmonies that go from us and return to catch the pulsations of life's great theme, as wondrous as traceries in frost, wrought on grass by winter's subtle art.

"What of memory?" I asked. "Do we retain for all time consciousness of this earth life?"

One answered:

> **"The images that are impressed in one's soul during earth life are so persistently real that it is almost impossible to change them. Thoughts make those images, but few realize that they**

are building something so real and lasting. Here, one lives with these images, until one is able, by effort and strength of purpose, to change them into something more worthwhile.

"The time will come when one must have about him only what is lovely, beautiful and harmonious, for without those conditions, there can be no real progress; then all the old images of deceit, jealousy, and unhappiness must be torn down and destroyed. They are not pleasant things to find in one's home-life here. The home including any of them can never be beautiful or properly built.

"Come to us with as little of the discord of earth life as possible; it will be so much easier to get used to conditions here, and there will be the less to get rid of."

CHAPTER 3

EMILY S. FRENCH SOLVES THE PSYCHIC RIDDLE

The Powers of Emily French are tested in New York City by Dr. Isaac K. Funk, May 29th to June 10th, 1905. Taken from *The Psychic Riddle*, by Isaac K.Funk (Funk & Wagnalls Company, New York & London, 1907)

> "And when they heard of the resurrection of the dead some mocked; and others said, "we will hear thee again of this matter."
>
> -ACTS 17: 32

In the early part of 1905 I received a letter from a prominent lawyer in Buffalo, N.Y.—Mr. E.C. Randall, head of the firm of Randall, Hurley & Porter requesting that I investigate "a remarkable medium" of his acquaintance, by name Emily S. French, through whom come independent voices and for whose honesty he would vouch. Said he, "About fourteen years ago I became acquainted with this woman. I was sure her phenomena were the result of fraud and I determined to expose it. After many sittings and exacting experiments, I became convinced that they were genuine, and finally at the suggestion of the spirit intelligences, I had fitted up a séance-room in my own house in which my wife, the medium, and myself held séance's, and we have done this now for more than a dozen years. I have tested Mrs. French in every way I can think of, and am thoroughly convinced that the phenomena are what they claim to be. The talks are exceedingly instructive and I have had many of them taken down in shorthand. I wish you would do me and others here the favor to investigate thoroughly these manifestations, and I would be very glad to have you visit us and remain as long as you desire at my home for this purpose. Every facility for thorough scientific investigation will be granted you. Rest assured, you will find the phenomena exactly what I tell you they are."

About the same time I received an urgent letter from an editor of one of the leading dailies in the western part of the state, urging "a scientific investigation of some extraordinary psychic phenomena that come through a Mrs. French, and which are perplexing some of our best minds. The phenomena are much out of the ordinary, and the medium is not a public medium who exhibits for pay."

Shortly after this correspondence Mr. A.W. Moore, the secretary of the Rochester Art Club, wrote to me as follows—I quote very fully from his letter as its story is interestingly told:

"My attention was called to Mrs. French's phase of mediumship about twenty years ago, when I was on the editorial staff of the *Union and Advertiser*, Rochester, New York.

"At that time I was not only an unbeliever in spiritual manifestation, but prejudiced against it, believing it nothing but fraud. In reporting of it to the press, I always treated mediumship with ridicule and sarcasm.

"One summer's day I had occasion to visit Hemlock Lake and there met by chance J. Nelson Tubbs, the well known civil engineer, and now inspector of the Erie Canal. Our conversation drifted into Spiritualism which I firmly discountenanced and ridiculed that he asked when, where, and how long had I investigated the subject. I had to confess that I had really investigated the subject very slightly. He pointed out the inconsistency of my condemning mediumship and taking such strong grounds against it without ever having taken the trouble to examine into the subject, and he warned me to be careful in writing about it until I got better posted. Mr. Tubbs then gave me an account of his investigations carried on during a series of years which resulted in his being a firm believer in spirit return. He gave an account of his experiences with various mediums and particularly the phase of manifestation peculiar to Mrs. French, viz.: Independent voices. He advised me to have a talk with Judge Dean Shuart of Rochester, who was for many years judge of the Surrogate Court of Monroe County.

"The fact that two such level-headed men—one an eminent civil engineer and mathematician, demanding 'weight and measure' in his profession, the other, a learned jurist and man of such impeachable character that he had been repeatedly elected to the responsible office of Surrogate Judge-had professed their full belief in spiritism, caused me to reflect deeply. I, therefore, on my return home, sought out Judge Shuart, and that gentleman told me many things that set me to thinking. He spoke of Mrs. French and arranged for me to attend a private séance at the house of a mutual friend.

"I attended a séance as arranged by Judge Stuart. There were present, besides my wife and myself, Mr. and Mrs. Austin (our hosts), and Judge Shuart and one or two others. We met in a small room upstairs and after being seated and taking hold of hands in a circle, the light was extinguished. It was explained to me that it was absolutely necessary that not the slightest trace of light be allowed to enter the room. Judge Shuart asked all present to sing, saying that vibrations were necessary. We, therefore, sang several familiar songs and afterward talked on various subjects, when all at once, a voice, loud and sonorous, high above our heads, exclaimed:

> **"I greet you my friends!"** The suddenness of the voice startled all present into silence, and the speaker continued to talk. After continuing for a while, the voice said: **"Ask any questions you may wish and I will answer them to the best of my ability."** I asked, What is your name?' The answer came, **"I was known as Red Jacket when in the mortal."**

I then asked him to describe conditions in the spirit-world and the passing of the spirit out of the body. In reply, Red Jacket gave a long talk on his own experience. He said at the time of his passing out he was in a very low spiritual condition, due to the excessive use of 'fire-water' which the white man had taught him to indulge in, and also to his intense hatred of the 'pale faces' on account of their having robbed his people of their hunting grounds, etc. He then described some of the ordeals his spirit had to undergo in order to overcome the desire for strong drink which still clung to him, and to turn his hatred of the white man into love.

"I can merely touch upon my experience at this séance. Other voices came, male and female. My impression at the close of the séance was that the whole thing was an imposture, and I determined to find it out somehow. I told Judge Shuart frankly that the voices were made by some living person, and that if he would examine the cellar of the house he would find a pipe leading from thence to the room. The Judge immediately requested me to go with him into the cellar, a damp low-ceilinged place, full of cobwebs, but we saw not the slightest indication of a speaking tube. I then fell back on ventriloquism and accused Mr. Austin of doing the business.

"To all of this Judge Shuart listened kindly and suggested that I follow up my investigations until I had discovered the fraud. 'If there is fraud in Mrs. French's circles,' the Judge said, 'I would like to know it, because my time is too precious to waste by attending these séance's. Continuing, he said, 'I have been sitting with Mrs. French from time to time for the past five years and tested her in every possible way that my mind could suggest, but I have not discovered the slightest trace of fraud. My friend, you will, if you continue your investigations, be compelled to acknowledge that Mrs. French's voices are occasioned by a power beyond the material, and the only conclusion you can arrive at is that they are, as they claim to be, Spiritual.'

"To be brief, I will say I attended another séance at the house of Mr. Austin, with the full conviction that I would be able to detect Mr. Austin as the ventriloquist. But on arriving at the house I found that he had been telegraphed for by his son who was mayor of a town in Colorado. Consequently, the séance took place without the presence of the man I suspected. The voices came as usual and stronger than on the previous occasion. I was placed next to Mrs. French in the circle and took hold of her left hand, her other hand being taken by Judge Shuart. When the voices came Mrs. French placed her mouth on the back of my hand until the spirits ceased talking.

"While Red Jacket delivered an address his voice suddenly seemed to die out like the notes of an organ when the wind fails, and he exclaimed

"Sing!"

When his voice came again he explained that the cause of his voice failing was lack of vibrations, and he entered upon a discourse regarding the wonderful atmospheres, electrical conditions, ethers, and vibratory forces of which mortals were quite ignorant, that formed the conditions that enabled spirits to throw their voices into our atmosphere. At the conclusion of this séance, I was just as skeptical as ever, and still more determined to fathom the mystery of the voices.

"I went again and again to the séance's held by Mrs. French and I took with me one of the chief skeptics in the city, Mr. J. McCall, who denounced the whole proceeding as a fraud, but he failed to point it out. His vehement denunciation of Mrs. French aroused me to protest, and I said, surely before you are so loud in your condemnation you ought to point out where the voices come from. 'The fact is,' I said, 'I am beginning to think that they may be spirit voices, because I have exhausted every device for detecting fraud and failed.' 'Did you ever have Mrs. French give a séance in your own house?' asked McCall. 'No,' said I. 'Then,' replied he, 'if you can get her to produce the voices in your own house you will find, if she accepts your invitation, that the thing won't work.' I asked Mrs. French if she would come to my house. She replied that nothing would give her greater pleasure. A few days afterward, Mr. McCall and his wife were at our house and I suggested that it would be a good opportunity to have Mrs. French over. I walked to her house, a short distance away, and brought her back with me. We sat in my study, and there were present on the occasion Mr. and Mrs. McCall, a nephew of mine just arrived from England, my wife, and myself. We had no sooner turned out the light when Red Jacket said in the loudest tones I had yet heard:

> **"You see Brother Moore, I can come to you even in your own house!"**

He then went on to describe the work he was doing as a missionary spirit. It took him a long time, he said, to outgrow earth conditions and appetites, in order that he might try and undo many things he had done in the flesh. His great anxiety was to come and return good for evil among those whom he called the 'pale faces.' He was happy when he attracted the attention of the white men so that he could teach them something of spiritual law. He said the spirits are working very hard to bring about conditions by which there can be an intercommunication between the two worlds, and the time is coming, said Red Jacket, when materialized spirits would appear upon platforms and address large audiences. The reason that Indian spirits took a large part in spiritual manifestations is because America was their hunting-ground and the red men lived close to Nature and were thus tremendously magnetic.

"Well, in brief, the séance was most wonderful; not only did Red Jacket come with great power, but several other spirits who spoke on different topics.

"The result of this séance was, that Mr. McCall shook hands with me and said, 'Moore, I believe the voices are spiritual!' From that date Mr. McCall became a thorough believer and prominent in spiritualistic circles.

"Since that period I have attended so many of Mrs. French's circles that it would be impossible to give in a letter the many wonderful communications I have had ... I think I can say that I have attended in the neighborhood of one thousand of Mrs. French's séance's in the last twenty years.

"I have learned enough wisdom from the old Seneca Sachem Red Jacket regarding spiritual things to fill a large volume. His sermons are at times full of pathos and beauty, and I have known the circle to be brought to tears by his eloquence. He lays great stress on the necessity of living lives of purity, temperance, and benevolence. He admonishes us especially to be charitable toward those who oppose the spiritual philosophy and cling tenaciously to dogmatic theology. He tells us not to try and convert people, but by our example and words draw them to inquire into that which gives blessings and peace to us.

"I might add many things to this testimony regarding Mrs. French, whom I believe to be a most honorable and trustworthy lady, who would scorn to do a dishonest thing, and would never for one moment give herself over to fraud and deceit. The fact is, she does not have to, as her manifestations are among the most wonderful and instructive to be found in the world today."

Mr. Moore in his correspondence again and again urged that I undertake a serious investigation of the psychic phenomena as manifested through Mrs. French.

Earnest as were these and other urgings, I said no, having so often been led on wild-goose chases in hunting up phenomena of this class and classes similar to it, and besides I long since had made up my mind to accept no phenomena as genuine when the conditions were not wholly under my control, and these, it seemed to me, would not be, especially as they were produced in the dark.

Finally, I was visited in my New York office by a lawyer from Rochester, a man whose integrity and levelheadedness are nowhere questioned and who is a lawyer of state-wide reputation. He came to urge me to the same investigation. He told me that he also had known Mrs. French for many years, and had visited her sittings very many times the past five years; that his partner, now dead, who was also a prominent lawyer and a judge was thoroughly convinced of her honesty, and was convinced that the phenomena were of spirit origin; he declared that he himself was not a Spiritualist, and hence did not wish his name mentioned in connection with the matter, and finally suggested that he should try to induce this aged woman to come to New York for two weeks, and to be wholly under my direction, for the most thorough investigation that I would care to make. He said it would be best, however, for him to send with her a lady friend of his, as Mrs. French was now over seventy years of age and was exceedingly feeble, being afflicted with heart trouble which made it unsafe for her to travel alone. He assured me that she gave no sittings for pay, that she was a refined, well-bred woman, a delicate lady in every sense of the word, and that the friend whom he would send with her as an escort was one that he had known for nearly a quarter of a century, and for whom he would vouch in the strongest possible way. I finally assented, and the conditions agreed upon were as follows:

No one was to come with Mrs. French except the one lady escort.

Both ladies should stop at the home that I designated.

That the sittings should be at such homes as I would make known to them after their arrival in New York, and this house was not to be visited by the medium or her friend except during our sittings, nor by any person representing them.

Both women were to follow my directions absolutely while in New York City.

These terms were cheerfully accepted.

The unconditional acceptance of the requirements made the series of tests a very interesting case.

In the first place, there was nothing doubtful in the history of the medium. The testimony from those who knew her showed that she was most highly respected, that she had in her favor the verdict of the jury of the vicinage where she had lived over three-score years. This rightly counts for much in one's favor. Among those of whom I have since inquired concerning her history are many who have known her for many years, all at least five years, and one, a man who had been acquainted with her for over sixty years. She has come of good stock, and that is also an element that counts; she is a Pierrepont, one of the most noted families of the State of New York; in short she is what the old-fashioned novelists would call high-or lady-bred. Those of whom I have inquired—several of whom are not Spiritualists—are unanimous in telling me that they regard her as person incapable of deception or falsehood.

But, in the acceptance of so uncommon a phenomenon as that of the independent voices, our proof should be of a sort that does not depend at all on the honesty of the medium. People of good reputation, even "Sunday-school men," have been known to lie. Proof that measures up to the standard required must be of a kind that implies an absurdity to suppose the phenomenon is not what is claimed for it. (Astonishing, is it not, that Dr. Funk completely *disregards* the testimony of others. Learned men and women of unimpeachable character who have tested Mrs. French in every known way they could devise and have been convinced beyond question. —Ed.)

Still, it was a satisfaction to have, for testing, a medium with an unblemished reputation, and to have for point two—a séance-room that made trap doors and confederates impossibilities. A close friend of mine, a wealthy businessman in New York, whom I have known for over thirty years, consented to permit me to use a room in his family apartment for this series of séance's. It would be difficult to conceive of a better room for this purpose. The windows of the apartment are so arranged that they all open out about fifty feet above the surface of the ground. It is entered by two doors, one from the hall which leads to the elevator, and the other from the fire-escape. The latter at all of our sittings was locked and chained from the inside, and in addition, a heavy trunk rested against the door. The hall door was also locked from the inside. At several of the series of sittings I kept the key of this door in my pocket during the entire time. The persons at the séance's were this friend whom I will call Mr. Z., his wife and daughter and myself, the medium and her lady escort—these comprised all of the persons who were in the apartment; not a servant, not even an animal pet of any kind was allowed in the apartment during the sittings, except on two occasions—once we invited an outside friend, and once a friend and his wife.

Mrs. Z. had often investigated Spiritualistic phenomena with me during the last twenty years. She is an expert at this kind of detective work. Her daughter also had attended a large number of séance's, and withal is an author of reputation. Both Mrs. and Miss Z. are very skeptical as to the Spiritualistic hypothesis and are, in my judgment, keen investigators and have a lively knowledge of human nature, especially of the woman sort. Mr. Z. himself has been for years a student of psychic matters and has had no little experience with the tricks of mediumistic fakers. I know of no house or family better fitted for the work I here and then undertook.

There is another fact to be noted. After my attention was first called to Mrs. French, I had a friend who is an able expert in psychic matters go from New York to Buffalo to attend some of Mrs. French's séance's and to make report to me. He did so, and his report on the whole was unfavorable, basing his conclusions mainly on the darkness of the séance room, the possibility of the medium producing the voices herself, and also on this other fact, that one of the voices spoke of a physician who was sick at a distance from Buffalo, a fact my friend afterward discovered was known personally to the medium. The opportunities for investigation by this friend were not of the best, and the time was brief and, as he afterward informed me, he was not acquainted "with all the facts that are favorable to Mrs. French." I had the detailed written report of this friend for my guidance in my own much-larger series of sittings. Having the medium in the house of my selection gave me also a great advantage.

I trust my readers will pardon me for digressing at this point a moment in reply to certain critics.

Again and again Spiritualists lose patience with me, one saying very vigorously that I am not a medium and hence cannot be competent to judge of mediumship. The conclusion may be sound, but it is a non-sequitur. I believe that I am better fitted to pass judgment on mediumship than a medium can possibly be, who is always super sensitive and often in a trance. John B. Finch used to say, "I can not lay an egg, but I am a better judge whether an egg is good or bad than all of the hens in the country."

J. R. Francis, the editor of the Progressive Thinker, a Spiritualist paper published in Chicago, has done more—I am sure I am well within bounds in saying it—to free Spiritualism from fraud than any other man in America. Mr. Francis has been pleased in writing recently to declare that he regards me as "an ideal investigator of psychic phenomena," and that he regards my methods as being exact and far-reaching and altogether fair. I think it well to say these things at this point so as to help lead my readers to free their minds as far as possible from all prepossession against my testimony concerning the extraordinary facts I record in the following pages.

The Testing of "Independent Voices" First Sitting, Monday May 29, 1905

Mrs. French and her escort, Mrs. Blank, arrived in New York on Monday evening, May 29, 1905, at about 6 o'clock p.m. At 7:30 they were escorted from the boarding-house by Miss Z. to the apartment which I had selected for the séance's. The room off the parlor had been fitted up by Mr. Z. as a séance room, simply by arranging the one window to the room so as to exclude the outside light. The size of this room is about twelve feet square. We were seated in a semicircle around a small table in the order indicated on the diagram.

It was decided that our series of meetings should be held in the evenings, beginning promptly at 7:30 o'clock and that the sittings were to be strictly private.

I dislike the condition of absolute darkness in the production of psychic phenomena, as it immensely increases the difficulty of making absolute tests. I asked a "control" at one of our earlier meetings the reason why they could not produce their phenomena without darkness. The answer was:

> **"The nature of the phenomena and the physical condition of the medium make any other course impossible. Were the medium in good health we might carefully experiment, but now we cannot. To try would be fatal to the medium. We understand your wishes and the reason for them, but you must believe us when we tell you that you ask what is impossible."**

This, of course, proved nothing, nor did it help us over the difficulty; yet, of course, it is true that light has a certain dynamic power. Every second, millions of light waves strike blows where they are admitted, and there are processes in nature from which it must be excluded. As has often been said, the prenatal child matures in absolute darkness, and light must be excluded from the photographic plate.

Prof. Charles Richet, in his address published in the January (1905) number of the Annals of Psychic Science, says: "Moreover, there is nothing unreasonable in the admission that light may exercise an inhibitory effect upon certain kinds of phenomena. It is often alleged: 'Darkness is required by spirits only because all kinds of trickery are possible in the dark,' but this conclusion is absurd." Richet further holds that if careful precautions are taken "it is rather foolish to consider worthless all experiments made in the dark."

Absolute darkness calls for special care, but it is not a sufficient reason to refuse to investigate.

This evening before we entered the cabinet-room we observed that Mrs. French was exceedingly deaf, so deaf in fact, that it was difficult to make her hear in conversation except the voice was considerably raised, and this even when we were removed from her not more than three feet. This fact became an important one in our tests, and hence afterward I sought for fullest confirmation of her deafness by correspondence with several physicians who have attended her—including Dr. Alvin A. Hubbell, of Buffalo, a specialist in eye and ear diseases recognized as an authority of much weight; especially is his testimony here of special importance as he is not a Spiritualist. The testimony of these various doctors leaves no doubt in my mind as to the genuineness of this serious defect in the hearing of Mrs. French. (see Appendices, the sworn testimonies of Mrs French's physicians concerning her deafness-Ed.)

We waited in darkness about twenty minutes, having joined hands. It will be observed by the diagram that Mrs. Blank was placed between Mr. Z. and myself, he having hold of her left hand, and I having hold of her right hand; and Miss Z. was next to me and Mrs. Z. next to her. Mrs. French sat at the table directly in front of myself, about four feet distant.

(I would like the readers to take careful note of the following points, before Dr. Funk's descriptions of what took place begins:

Mrs. French: 72 years old, extremely feeble and frail, a very sensitive and dangerous heart condition, almost entirely deaf.

Sitting for Dr. Funk with barely any time to have had to rest after the long journey from Buffalo to New York.

Surrounded by people—and their corresponding vibrations—whose intentions are to detect her in fraud, for the sake of "Science."

Mrs. French is sitting right across from Dr. Funk and not moving. —Ed.)

The first voice that came was an exceedingly loud masculine voice which, we were informed by Mrs. Blank, was that of one of the controls, the Indian chief, Red Jacket the inevitable Indian! The voice spoke consecutively about ten minutes on the work the "forces" wished to do at this series of meetings-he and those with him. They were exceedingly anxious, this voice assured us, to make us know, and make those with whom we came in contact know-not believe, but know-that life is continuous.

> **"We live,"** he said, **"as real lives—more real on this side than we did on earth. The laws that govern life are the same here as with you. In fact, everything here is so real that many who come over—die, as you call it—do not know for a long time that they are dead. A great part of the work to be done here is to instruct the dead in the true science of progress. To the circles held by this medium we often bring dazed and earthbound spirits, so as to be able to**

reach their consciousness through earth surroundings. We and they are then brought to the same place and we then can better make them understand their condition, they at these séance's often recognize the voices of those whom in earth-life they knew, and who are in the circle. Many of you people in the flesh think that those who die are done with time and with earth, but it is still time and it is still earth after we pass over. We have not reached the outlines of time nor of the material world. Life on both sides of the grave is part of the same plan and has the same object and is governed largely by the same laws.

"Think not that the spirit world has not a language of its own. We have a language compared with which the earth languages are blundering. It is heart-and-mind language. You have what you call telepathy. Do any of you know what that is? When you find that out you will know somewhat about our language.

"It may be said that the spirit hears what it wishes to hear, and that it makes its own world. Each spirit is a creator. You have faculties that are now only faintly imagined by you. There is reality. The Great Spirit is reality. We cannot explain these things to you. Only the most developed among us know the beginnings of these things. We blunder here as you blunder on the earth, but there is great progress. You must not believe every spirit any more than you believe every man. To some this is a dream world, or rather dream worlds, for there are as many of these worlds almost as there are individuals. But this spirit world is also subject to law. It has its environments and its developments. It has its scientific basis and limitations as you would call it. You must learn to think of this world and of the people in it as real."

The various talks of Red Jacket this evening in all must have covered one hour, bearing largely on the main thought running through the above talk. This kind of talk is not new to those who frequently attend the better class of séance's. If we can believe these "spirits," death is not a barrier, but a highway, like the sea was to the Vikings. But the thoughts expressed had comparatively little interest to me, for I already believed these truths, and some of them seemed to be but an echo from my own mind and might have been gathered by any bright medium through reading my mind. What I wished to know was whether this loud voice was produced by that feeble little woman sitting at the table; or whether the voice was produced through extemporized vocal organs by a foreign intelligence-this latter alternative seemed to me extremely improbable.

The thought expressed by the other voices during this first evening was all of an exalted kind, and they were always ready to answer the questions which we asked.

Some of the voices were bright and one or two even "snappy," but the voices of Red Jacket and Dr. Hossack, another of the principle controls, were exceedingly serious, impressing one that their owners were intelligences of great earnestness.

It was quickly evident that one of two hypotheses must furnish the explanation of these phenomena. Either they were produced through conscious fraud on the part of the medium, a fraud which has been continued now for more than two-score years, or they were produced by foreign intelligences. Let it be remembered that the hand of all in the circle were joined together, except the hands of the medium, I having hold of the right hand of Mrs. Blank and Mr. Z having hold of her left hand. We frequently talked to Mrs. Blank while the voices were talking. Mrs. Blank was in this way practically eliminated from the problem. The voice of Red Jacket appeared to come from a point some four feet above the head of the medium, and about three feet to the left of her as she sat facing the members of the semicircle.

After I had fully fixed the locality in my mind, I asked one after another in the circle to locate the point in the room from which the voice came. This I did without telling my own impression. All located it at about the same spot that I did.

It must be remembered that it is not an easy thing to locate from whence a sound comes in darkness. Those who have never tried it will find it an interesting experiment. At my request, the voice of Red Jacket changed to different parts of the room. This it did always on the side where the medium was sitting. In a reply to a question why he could not come behind those of us who were in the circle and speak, he said:

> **"It is necessary for us to be near the medium, as we draw force from her"**—a possible, but an unfortunate necessity. Had the medium stood on a chair or used a long-jointed megaphone she could herself have made the voice come from the point whence it seemed to come—that is, if possessed of the power to produce the voice.

We sat in the circle about one hour and a half, and as the medium was fatigued by travel, it was suggested by one of the controls that we close the sitting for the evening. Instructions were given us by the controls to have the room on the succeeding nights the same as this night, and to occupy hereafter the same seats. This voice was introduced to us as that of Dr. Hossack, a physician who, we were told, when on earth was a professor in Columbia College, New York City and, who claims to have been the physician who attended Hamilton after the fatal duel with Burr. There seemed a trace of Mrs. French's voice in that of Dr. Hossack, but none of us could discover in the voice of Red Jacket any semblance to the exceptionally feeble voice of Mrs. French. We determined hereafter to watch carefully for this similarity, believing that in it we might get the key to the mystery. Mrs. French is a frail woman of about one hundred and seventeen pounds weight, seventy-two years of age, with a pulse that indicates quite a weak and irregular heart. Immediately after the sitting I felt her pulse, and found it sixty-eight to the minute, missing every third or fourth beat. It is not often that one hears two voices more unlike than that of Red Jacket and Mrs. French.

Second Sitting, Tuesday, May 30, 1905:

Immediately upon the arrival of Mrs. French and Mrs. Blank, we entered the séance room, and were seated as on the first evening. It will be remembered that neither of these two women were permitted to visit the home of Mrs. Z. except at the time of the sittings.

Before the lights were turned out, we all carefully marked the exact location of Mrs. French, and also trained ourselves to locate by the sound, the distance and direction of a voice, observing how, when the head is turned in any one direction, the voice seems to proceed from a point toward the side of the room to which the head is turned. In that way a voice can be made to appear as proceeding from a point near the ceiling or a point near the floor, or to the right hand or left hand, or back of the one speaking.

When Red Jacket's voice came, he directed, upon my suggestion, that the left hand of Mrs. French, and the right hand of Mrs. Z, be joined. This made it more possible for Mrs. Z. to detect any movement of Mrs. French. It should be remembered that Mrs. Z. is not a novice in psychic investigation, and is keenly alert to the tricks of fake mediums. Both Mrs. Z. and her daughter are very skeptical as to the spirit hypothesis, and hence are keen to suspect and detect fraud.

The voice of Red Jacket appeared to be of the same timbre as the night before, and it seemed equally high above the medium's head, about eight feet from the floor, and toward the sliding door between the two parlors. Our various tests again confirmed our partial conviction on the night before-that Mrs. Blank had nothing whatever to do with these voices. This we proved by talking to her and having her talk to us while the voices were speaking. Our tests also eliminated the theory that Mrs. French left her seat or stood up. All of these possibilities had been thoroughly canvassed by us prior to the coming of Mrs. Blank and Mrs. French this evening.

The theory of a megaphone manipulated by one hand of the medium, and the theory of the medium being an accomplished ventriloquist remained. To test these theories, I requested the medium to talk at the same time Red Jacket talked. If this could be done, it would help us also to locate the whereabouts of the medium when her hand was not being held by Mrs. Z. We were told by one of the voices that we must recognize the possibility of failures in this simultaneous talking because of the complexity and difficulty of the phenomena:

> **"You do not fully realize,"** said Dr. Hossack, **"how exceedingly delicate is the organ [medium] we have to work with. She is very frail. Many times we have kept her in her body when even her physicians were sure that she would pass out. She is of very great importance to us as an instrument, and you must not ask us to take undue risks; and yet, on the other hand, we understand perfectly the value of the experiments that you are making, and will do everything in our power to help you make these experiments satisfactory. It is far better for her that she keep quiet while the other voices are talking and are thus drawing upon her strength. We have here a band of medical experts who are watching closely the heart and mind of the medium, and we have also with us a chemical expert and a band of what you would probably call electricians, who are adept in the manufacture and control of the vital currents. It may seem to you an easy matter that the medium should talk simultaneously with us; but I assure you it is an extraordinarily difficult and dangerous thing; and I again assure you that we have come here to do all that is possible to do to satisfy you of the genuineness and the significance of these phenomena."**

"Yes, yes," said the medium. Her "Yes, yes" seemed to be simultaneous with the voice, yet we were not all absolutely certain of this. During the remainder of the evening, a score of times the medium seemed to talk at the same time that did the other voices. Some of us thought yes, others of us were slightly in doubt, believing that there was a fraction of a second between the voices. Mrs. Z., who had Mrs. French's hand, was fairly sure that the voices were simultaneous. To us all it seemed very hard to believe that any human being could have spoken in two different voices so nearly simultaneously and so often, without sometimes using the wrong voice; and also the conviction was constantly growing upon us, that the feeble, quiet, delicately refined voice of Mrs. French could not have produced the strong masculine voice of Red Jacket even though assisted by some mechanism. Another point to be tested was whether the defective hearing of Mrs. French could catch our questions asked of Red Jacket when uttered in low conversational tones. We found that Red Jacket responded to our questions and remarks, no matter how low our tones were. This is a very important factor in the problem of determining the origin of these voices.

As to Dr. Hossack's suggestion that the phenomena is difficult to produce, when we come to think of it, what reason have we to conclude that the spirit world is a simple and easy state of existence? Analogy tells us the contrary. As we progress the problems of life, of thinking, and of acting grow more and more marvelous and difficult. Water seems to us an easy substance to handle, but as we go upward to hydrogen and oxygen, and then back to atoms and electrons, and the combining of these in many ways—well, who cares for all this? We cut the Gordian knot and say "God directs." Why may it not be that there, as here, God works through others these countless marvels, and that among these others are the spirits of the generations that have gone before, and that there as here the doing of things must all be learned in natural ways, and the human faculties developed gradually by exercise, so that there as here all are degrees of perfection and imperfection? This, of course, is only a guess, and yet our unbelief in the immensities of the universe leads us into countless absurdities. Only a few centuries ago, the sun, moon, stars, were believed to be only so many lamps that rose in the east and crossed the sky of the stationary earth to the west, and thus in childlike simplicity, we settled it. Now we seem immensities upon immensities, and complications untold.

The séance lasted this evening two hours, about one hour and a half being taken in talks by some half a dozen different voices. About fifty minutes of this time was taken in a talk of a most serious sort, by Red Jacket, urging the human race to brotherhood and to labor for others, insisting that each one make his life harmonize with truth, and saying that if we did this, we would be well advanced when we entered the other world,

> **"For,"** he declared, **"all real growth springs out of a desire for the welfare of our fellows."**

Ventriloquism or a megaphone still seemed a possible explanation. Mrs. Z., who kept her hand during much of the evening on top of the hand of Mrs. French, declared that she could not detect the slightest tremor of her hand when the loud, voice of Red Jacket was most earnest. Nor could she detect the slightest movement that it would have seemed necessary for her body to have made in manipulating a megaphone. Of course, either of these hypothesis meant conscious fraud of a very depraved sort on the part of the medium whose personality and truthfulness impressed us more and more every time we spoke to her. She seemed an ideally refined, well-born, well-bread, and an ingenuous big-hearted woman.

I urged Mrs. Z. and Miss Z. to study both women very carefully during the day, by calling upon them, giving full play to the intuitive knowledge which women are said to have of womankind. Red Jacket talked very much about himself during the evening. He seemed to understand himself quite well, and it may be, after all, the Irishman wasn't far wrong when he said, "We get the best view of our lives after we are dead." This seemed to be true of Red Jacket's post-mortem of himself.

Third Sitting, Wednesday, May 31,1905:

We added to our circle this evening Miss H., a celebrated author. She sat between Miss Z. and myself. The position of each sitter in the circle was otherwise the same as on the two previous evenings.

When Red Jacket's voice came I told him that the theory of the megaphone or speaking-trumpet would be used by the critical public as a possible explanation, also that ventriloquism would be urged in explanation, and asked him, if he could, to give us some experiments that would exclude both of these hypotheses. His answer was,

"We will do whatever the strength of the medium will permit."

In reply to a question whether he would not tell us his experiences upon his entrance into the other world at death, and also let us know what his present work was in the spirit-world, Red Jacket for fifty-five minutes, as nearly as I could judge by noting the striking of the clock in a nearby room, spoke in his usual loud masculine voice.

My purpose in putting these questions to Red Jacket was to have him make a long speech, believing that such an effort would test greatly the physical endurance of Mrs. French, provided she produced the voice. I have had much experience in judging the carrying capacity of voices, and I have no doubt that the voice of Red Jacket, as we listened to it this evening, would easily have filled a hall with a seating capacity of two thousand people, while Mrs. French's voice, at its loudest, so far as I have heard it, would not fill a parlor twenty feet square. An address in a loud voice, lasting fifty-five minutes, is an exhausting strain upon the average strong man. Immediately after this speaking I felt Mrs. French's pulse, and found that it was as usual, weak and irregular; but not noticeably so beyond what I had found it when she first came into the room.

At the beginning of the séance Mrs. Z. was requested by Red Jacket to put her hands upon both of the hands of Mrs. French. This she did throughout the speaking. Under these conditions the megaphone theory became wholly an impossible one. Mrs. Z. knows well the trick of a medium covering both hands with one, so as to make believe that both hands are being accounted for. She assured us that she covered fully each hand of the medium with her hands. Frequently at this sitting Mrs. French replied in a natural voice, that certainly seemed at times simultaneous with Red Jacket's speaking. During the whole of the talking one of Mrs. Blank's hands was in Mr. Z.'s hand and the other was held by me. The sitting lasted one hour and forty minutes.

Fourth Sitting, Thursday, June 1, 1905:

Red Jacket invited me to sit immediately in front of the little table at which Mrs. French is accustomed to sit, and to place my hands on her two hands. I separated her two hands about twelve inches, so that the one hand of the medium could not possibly be mistaken for two hands, a trick that I have known to have played successfully in a dark circle. I put my hands straight out from my body, so as to have the width of my body between the two hands. I again requested Mrs. French to talk much. Her face could not have been more than twenty-four inches from mine. I could hear her breathe as well as talk. Red Jacket and the other voices talked freely, and Mrs. French frequently spoke, seemingly at the same time. This test probably lasted ten minutes. It made it impossible for me to hold longer the megaphone theory, and it is difficult to see how it was possible to explain the phenomena by ventriloquism.

As nearly as it was possible for me to detect, Mrs. French breathed naturally and talked in her usual low tones, at the same instant that the explosive voice of Red Jacket spoke. Her breath came regular during the sentences of Red Jacket, whether they were long or short.

> **"Sit back!"**

Red Jacket suddenly thundered in an explosive voice that seemed to shake the room. I sat back. He afterward explained that the heart of the medium had begun "to thump," and that there was danger to her if the test continued longer. Just before the command, I was told I would feel the passing of a spirit over my face. I felt a cool breath of air. But this could have been produced by the medium, if she had so desired, for if you blow in the face of another at the distance of fifteen or twenty inches, the air will feel cold.

After I had resumed my seat in the circle there came a strange, laughing voice, very loud, which seemed to come from the neighborhood of the door that led into the hall, or from out in the hall, some six or eight feet distant from the medium. This loud laughing voice was a curious phenomenon, and seemed to startle greatly the medium.

The voice came at our request repeatedly, some ten times in all, each laugh averaging possibly a dozen ha-ha's, and varying from a deep basso to almost a treble. We were told by Red Jacket that

> **"this phenomenon was permitted to show the impossibility of the medium producing these voices through ventriloquism, as it must be manifest to all here that it is wholly beyond any conceivable compass of a female voice, and especially of so weak a voice as that of Mrs. French."**

The location of the voice seemed to change from place to place at our request, sometimes it sounded as if near the floor and then up high near the ceiling, and then about six feet to the left of the medium and then to her right, and then back of her, and then again immediately in front of her. This suggested the art of ventriloquism together with the turning of the head from side to side; but the utter physical weakness of the medium, and her exceptionally feeble voice added to the other tests that we had previously made, seemed almost conclusive—if not altogether so—against this theory.

At times when the laughing voice took place, Mrs. Z., at our request, took hold of both hands of the medium, and Mr. Z. and I held both hands of Mrs. Blank, so that the use of megaphone was again wholly impossible. It is well again to remember that for Mrs. French to have produced the laugh that we heard, requires us to believe that she possesses extraordinarily well developed lungs and vocal powers, while the truth is, her whole physical build is after a most delicate, feeble feminine model. It is as easy to think of a rabbit barking like a bulldog or bellowing like a bull, as to think of one physically made up as is Mrs. French producing such a laugh.

It should be remembered that Mrs. Z. and Miss Z. and I are all seasoned investigators. I myself have been at hundreds of séance's of all kinds. The reader can take it for granted that not one of our company could be stampeded or excited by the novelty or weirdness of this sort of experiences. (How any individual, no matter how scientific or dispassionate, could not be excited by the very proofs of immortality unfolding itself right in front of them is almost beyond comprehension -Ed.)

During the evening there were female voices as well as male voices other than that of Red Jacket's. The phenomena continued until 9:30. The theory of collective hallucination it would be very difficult to apply to this series of phenomena. We did not expect the laughing voice; we had not heard that anything of the kind ever occurred at Mrs. French's sittings. On inquiry I found it had not been heard at the sittings in Buffalo or Rochester. We criticized it one to the other, talked about it, and talked to the spirit's personality, and he responded. We talked in a low voice also to the personality, and were correctly answered. Mrs. French seemed very much amused at the voice, and often laughed in her quiet way, but so loud that we could all hear her laugh, seemingly at the same time that this loud laughter occurred. A transmitted subjective impression is likely to have marks of subjectivity, while this voice had all the marks of objectivity. After listening to it on the other evenings, I have no doubt whatever as to the inapplicability of the collective hallucination theory.

The following question was asked of Dr. Hossack during the evening:

Why cannot everyone be a medium? Why does the spirit-world pass by some of our most excellent people, and chose sometimes unworthy ones for the mediums? This was asked also to test the mental caliber of the personality who talked. The answer was:

> **"Can you tell me why it is that copper is better than gold to carry the telegraphic message, or why it is that one material is better than another to hold the picture on the photographic plate, or why is it that radium is to be found in pitchblende and not in silver or gold? It is, my friend, a natural law, and it is not for us to quarrel with natural laws, but to conform to them. It is only by conforming to them that we can get anything from nature."**

This talk was written down from memory several days afterward and may not be verbally correct, but the thought is. In nearly all other incidents in this series I wrote out the talks the same evening.

Fifth Sitting, Friday, June 2, 1905:

For about forty minutes no voices came. At all of these meetings Mrs. French claims she sees, somewhat over our heads, a string of lights which at first are disconnected, and, when conditions are perfected for the voices to come, the lights join. Tonight she reported the lights are coming very slowly and as being very loath to connect. The weather conditions were reported unfavorable, as it was stormy, and the atmospheric pressure heavy. The voices, however, finally came. Red Jacket delivered a talk of about half an hour in length, a well-sustained and connected talk. His addresses on these occasions are all remarkably free from errors in grammar. Sometimes he will ask for the proper technical word. The following is an outline of his talk as written down the day following by Mr. Z. at my request-it is as unlike as can be to conversations I have had with Mrs. French out of the séance rooms.

> **"Friends, I greet you! I wish to call your attention to some of the conditions used by this medium in making communications possible.**
>
> **"Referring back to many moons ago, or as the Pale Face says, years ago, after my entrance into spirit-life, a number of earnest spirits, anxious to help mortals by imparting more accurate information**

about the conditions of life here and how life on your side affected life here, held meetings in an assembly-hall here called "The Hall of Truth." We decided to search among mortals if we could find any sensitives suitable for the special purposes that we had in view. We found but three, and one of these soon passed over to this side. Later we found that the kind of sensitives we had selected would not answer. We needed a different and higher grade. We made other examinations, testing other mediums. Finally we found the medium we have been using now for so many years.

"You understand the mind works through the brain. But to the mental force is added what may be called the vital force which is more closely connected with the entire nervous system. These forces produce what may be called electro-magnetism. Follow me closely. Now, we have found that there are some mortals born with a double spinal cord. This is very rarely a fact. This second spinal cord generates the force we need for our particular purpose, that is, to produce the vibrations which you call 'voices.' So delicate and important is the force produced by this second spinal cord, that a medicine man stands behind this medium all the time we use this force, and brings a pressure to bear at the end of the cord, near the base of the brain. This explains why this medium says she feels a tapping going on at the base of her brain while we are talking."

The curious explanation of the phenomena by Red Jacket was drawn out to a considerable length, and became very technical.

In answer to a question, Dr. Hossack replied that when he was practicing medicine on earth, he read the report of a case of the finding of a double spinal cord. This was found in dissecting the body of a Scotchman in Berlin, Germany. It was then regarded by the medical authorities as a mere freak, and little attention at that time was paid to it.

Suddenly in the midst of our talk there broke in a voice with a very pronounced Irish brogue. He seemed to pass to the right and then to the left of the medium again and again, and kept up a rattle of quaint remarks for about five minutes. We were afterward told by Dr. Hossack that the object of this interruption was to get us less intense, so as to make it easier for the spirits to use the vital forces of the medium and of the members of the circle. This voice had all the quaint humor with which we associate the typical Irishman. It is quite evident, if these phenomena are what they claim to be, that national and individual characteristics persist beyond the Great Divide.

Of course, the apparent change of location of the voice could be produced by a medium, if tricky, by turning her head as already indicated. The left hand of the medium was held most of the time by the right hand of Mrs. Z. Mrs. Z. reported that the medium seemed to be wholly passive, and more than usually weak— "as weak as a child." I felt the medium's pulse, and it was very weak and very irregular.

Red Jacket's speech is often very picturesque. For example, this evening he was speaking to one in the circle who had just passed through much troubles and was discouraged. He said, **"Your boat has rocked and your oars are fallen out."** Of a public character who was known somewhat for his bitterness of speech, he said,

> **"He shot his words like arrows, and they wounded people. We should give health, not hurt. This is right. Say, friends, it is right."**

During the last sitting or two we have directed our attention more to the thoughts uttered by the voices, and have sought to compare them with the thoughts expressed by Mrs. French when not in the circle, striving to judge of the mental caliber of the medium and mental caliber of the individualities as revealed through these voices. There seems to be as great a difference between the mentality of the medium and the mentality of Red Jacket, Dr. Hossack, and two or three others of the individualities revealed through these strange phenomena, as there is in the voices.

It is well constantly to bear in mind that a quick, accurate ear is rare. A close observer is not a personage we meet every day. An investigator of phenomena of this kind should studiously avoid coming to any conclusions during his series of sitting, for an opinion is sure to bias his physical senses.

And let me just here whisper to the critic, we should all learn to judge leniently the opinions of others, knowing that our own are sometimes in error.

The moral quality of the talks at these séance's is an element that is to be considered. Not once at the sittings this week has there been uttered a word of hate, an unclean word, or even a silly word. In fact experiences at a great majority of the séance's I have attended with different mediums justify the testimony of Frederick Myers that the "spirit" talks are as a whole of an exceptionally exalted character. I find in my notebook this sentence which I jotted down from a prayer of Mrs. Pepper given at one of her meetings in Brooklyn, she supposed to be at that time in a trance:

> **"We thank Thee for that divine and wonderful blessing men call birth, and we thank Thee for that equally divine and still more wonderful blessing which men have misnamed death."**

With dozens of sentences of this kind come from the same individual under various circumstances it becomes increasingly difficult to believe that the soul that utters them is unclean or unspiritual.

Sixth Sitting, Saturday, June 3, 1905:

We made many efforts at the meeting to-night to have talking by the medium at the same time the "voices" spoke. The medium seemed very weak, having had, Mrs. Blank reported, a severe attack of heart trouble during the day, which was treated, she declared, by Dr. Hossack, the spirit doctor, they having a séance in the dark closet in the boarding-house." Mrs. Blank assured us that it is usual in these attacks of faintness and paroxysms of pain "to consult the spirit, Dr. Hossack," and his prescriptions are followed.

The sincerity of both these women, and their innate refinement and nobility of character have steadily become more and more factors in the problem that we have in hand. There has never been the slightest evidence of evasion or deceit. Whatever doubts we have of these ladies in their absence is wholly occasioned by the strangeness of the phenomena, and is dissipated in their presence, so straightforward are they, and simple, and perfectly ladylike in all their manners and talks.

Red jacket tonight gave us a talk on mediumship. Among other things, he said:

> **"Most mediums are mere playthings of their imagination; others, a smaller number, are the dupes of the intelligences, tricky, sometimes sportive, at other times malignant. It is a terribly dangerous mistake to think that there are no evil spirits. There are great hosts of them. They come at times without formal invitation of the medium or of the circle, and control to the hurt of the members of the circle and to the hurt of the medium."**

To revert to Sir William Crooke's vibration theory of the universe: If it is true that we are living in the midst of vibrations from both sides of the grave, then it is not hard to believe that those spirits on the other side who are nearest the earth, that is those who are most earthly, would find it easier to return, and may give us false communications although the medium be altogether honest. Who then is safe? It is well to remember the words of the prophet: "The angel of the Lord encompasseth round about them that revere him, to deliver them." God Almighty is not dead, nor does He sleep. It is quite easy to believe that no mother ever so tenderly cared for her child as He for His children. But remember those words "that revere him"—this attitude of soul may make us recipients of help which otherwise could not possibly reach us.

At our request the laughing voice came again. He spoke for the first time. He said that when he died he was certain his family was glad, for they thought they could get the insurance money that was on his life, and that their grief was hypocritical. He laughed bitterly at their deceit. When he looked at himself in the coffin and saw that he looked so natural he could not believe he was dead. He felt so deeply the wrong done him by his wife and family that he did not speak, and if any spirit talked to him he just laughed. But he said that he now begins to feel that he was wrong in this, and that we must forgive, and,

"now I feel that my heart grows warm again and I now talk."

Then he broke out again into a good-natured laugh, very loud, but free from the bitterness that marked it heretofore. At our request, which we made for test purposes, he laughed again and again, and the medium laughed in a natural, low voice. Mrs. Z. had both hands of the medium in hers on the table, and reported that she could recognize distinctly that the medium was laughing at the same time that the voice laughed. At times her laughing was so loud we could all hear it. The contrast between the two voices was very great—the one loud, vibrant, and even coarsely masculine, so loud that it could have been heard a hundred feet distant; the other feeble, ladylike, that could be heard by us only by close attention, and then not at distance of more than a few feet. Suddenly an explosive laugh, unusually loud, came seemingly immediately from behind the medium. She jumped and cried aloud-we were all startled. The medium faintly called for water. I found that her pulse was beating very feebly, and exceedingly irregular. It seemed for a while that we might have a corpse on our hands and our medium go to the beyond. If this was all acted, it was supreme acting and wholly inconsistent with the reputation of Mrs. French and seemed vastly beyond her physical strength.

After awhile the séance continued. Dr. Hossack's voice assured us that the test was given to show how impossible was the assumption that the medium could produce the voice. And again he assured us that the experiment was extremely dangerous to the medium, and asked that this suffice, because of the medium's condition of extreme weakness, telling us that anxious as they are to satisfy us and satisfy the scientists, they must not risk further injury to the medium, and that as to this danger we must trust their superior experience and judgment.

Mrs. Z. again assured us that in all these laughter séance's, when she held the medium's two hands, she did not feel the slightest vibration from the great lung effort required to produce these vocal explosive noises, but that she could feel the vibrations when Mrs. French either spoke or laughed naturally as she frequently did.

It was decided to give the medium perfect rest on Sunday, and hence no sittings were held until the following Monday.

Seventh Sitting, Monday, June 5, 1905

Before the arrival of the medium and her escort we reviewed our past week's work.

Confederates outside the circle.

Confederates from inside the circle.

Collective hallucination without hypnotic suggestion.

General hallucination through hypnotic suggestion.

Intentional fraud on part of medium through use of megaphone.

False voices through use of various mouth devices.

Ventriloquism.

Unintentional fraud by the medium through trance as by alternating personalities.

Outside intelligences making use of the vocal organs of the medium without the medium being conscious of the fact, or through vocal organs extemporized by the spirits.

The following seems to be a reasonable summing up:

1. Confederates from the outside during this entire series of sittings are absolutely excluded by the conditions.

2. The only possible confederate from the *inside* is Mrs. Blank. Against this theory are:

   a. Mrs. Blank's well-known character.

   b. The fact that she always sits wedged in between Mr. Z and myself, our hands being joined.

   c. Conversation is carried on with her frequently while the voices are speaking.

3.,4. Any one after reading the descriptions given of conditions, and of what has taken place during the past week and who yet can believe the theory of collective hallucination or hypnotism of the entire circle, I am quite sure would be capable of believing anything, and given the proper mental twist toward Spiritualism he would, quite likely, become the most credulous of Spiritualists. The belief or disbelief of persons of this class does not rest on reason or fact, but on preconceived ideas.

5. All in the circle are sure that the megaphone theory has been absolutely excluded by the tests already made.

6.,7. The possibility of the medium either through the trick of ventriloquism or by the use of mouth devices producing the various voices we determined further to test.

8. The possibility of the medium, in trance, speaking in these different voices, and this without intentional fraud, we thought needed further testing.

As to this last theory including that of secondary personalities, the rapidity with which these changes take place and the naturalness of the medium at all times seems to exclude this hypothesis, and yet it deserves further investigation. After many of the sittings I talk with the medium about what has taken place, and she remembers all perfectly, commenting intelligently upon the incidents. Also during the sittings, Mrs. French often comments on what has been said and done, in a perfectly natural way, the same as the rest of us. Frequently I and other members of the circle ask her questions, and her answers are wholly natural. The reader must bear in mind that she is hard of hearing and each evening, frequently, we have occasion to talk to the outside intelligences, and often we do not raise our voices for them to hear us, but talk in our natural tones of voice, and sometimes purposely in lower tones, and are always understood by the intelligences. If we desire Mrs. French to know what we have asked, we are compelled to repeat in much louder tones of voice.

As to intentional fraud of any kind we must bear in mind that there is no money motive for fraud. The medium was paid nothing for her trip to New York on this occasion. If there is deception on her part, there can be no motive for it except that of the gratification of vanity or a sense of power which is effective in many people. Otherwise the motive must be pure cussedness. But a morbid vanity is often a very strong motive in leading people to commit fraud along the mediumistic line, and should not be ignored. All of the appearances are against this theory, but still it should be borne in mind, for human nature is at times exceedingly untrustworthy, hence tests for supernormal powers should be insisted upon along the lines that involve something more than the good faith of the medium.

I asked Red Jacket this evening how he could account for the unfavorable opinion of the friend I sent to Buffalo to investigate this medium, he believing fraud a likely explanation.

> **"What is it,"** said Red Jacket, **"that your friend says took place?"**

"He says at one of these sittings he had with Mrs. French no voices came for a long time, and that when finally a voice did come it explained the delay by saying that the band were helping a doctor at a certain distant prison who was "passing out" [dying]. The next day this friend in talking with a gentleman in Buffalo told him what the voice said. This gentleman remarked that Mrs. French knew all about the case, for she had told him about it prior to that meeting. Now this friend says that this was proof of deception on the part of Mrs. French."

> Red Jacket replied, **"In what way? Is this fair? Mrs. French did not say one word at that time. We spirits did not get our knowledge from her of the sickness of the doctor. We told at that séance simply a fact. We did not give the name of the doctor because some doctors do not like it known that they are sick. Is this the reasoning of science: because Mrs. French knew of this case—saying nothing about it—that therefore she is a cheat? I told you we did not get our information from her, and if we had got if from her mind, how would that have affected her honesty? What we said was true. We do not lie. But your friend is not**

fair, and does a great wrong by these guesses, and guesses are surely not science.

"You say the woman, Miss H., is sick. We did not know until you told us. Sometimes we get this knowledge from the minds of those who are in the circle and sometimes from their words, sometimes from the mind of the medium, and sometimes from the spirit friends of the person who is sick. How is it right to say because we tell something the medium already knows that the medium is not honest? This kind of treatment grieves us when we are trying to do good."

"Now, Red Jacket, "I said," we do not mean to wrong you, nor the medium, but are trying to get the exact facts. My friend does not mean to wrong the medium, but there are a great many cheats in the so-called medium business, and he was trying to get evidence that would shut out all possibility of fraud, even if the medium should desire to commit fraud. The evidence that is to convince the world must be of a nature that will not depend upon the honesty of the medium. You know what I mean."

"Yes, I think I do, and we are trying to give you such evidence, and we tried to give such evidence to your friend, but he did not help us. He was hard to us and to the medium in his thought. The influences that came from him were not helpful. He had no intention to hinder, but he did. Some people give out help, but your friend did not. We will see what we can do for you."

"Would you tell us whether, in speaking, you make any use of the organs of the medium, or whether you organize your own vocal organs?"

Red Jacket: **"We make our own vocal organs. How is it possible for her organs to speak as I speak? Science and common sense should make that clear. How is it possible for her organs to laugh as that laughing voice laughs? You must use your reason as you do in other matters. The medium has come a great distance and she gets nothing for it; but she comes to help you and we come to help you. Now, you must be fair. You have had hold of the medium's hands while I talk, and we talk often at the same time she talks, although this is dangerous to her. This we do to**

give you proof that it is not she who talks, and yet will you say the medium does it?"

"No, Red Jacket, we do not say the medium does it. What we wish is to get proof, not to convince ourselves, who now have met the medium, that she is honest, but proof that will convince those who have never met the medium."

"What do you ask us to do?"

"Would it be possible for the medium to talk if she put both of her hands in one of Mrs. Z.'s hands, and then permit Mrs. Z. to put her other hand over the medium's mouth?"

"Now, this may seem easy to you, and I do not know how to make you understand that any act of suspicion like that increases manifold the difficulty that we have of holding the medium's strength. We cannot try this test tonight. It would not be safe. We will see if whether we can do it tomorrow night. You don't seem to understand that the medium is exceedingly sensitive, and putting her under that kind of test implies that she is a cheat, and this necessarily excites her nerves and affects her heart; but we will do what we can."

Curious that unbelief should hinder the manifestation of psychic powers, but can we be sure it does not? Even the great Master, Christ, insisted upon the condition, *believe.* He could not do any mighty work in Galilee, why? *Because* of the unbelief of the people. Note the words *could not.*

During this evening we had a singing voice which sang very pleasingly, and other new voices spoke.

One voice reproved the thought that the spirits are to blame if in a circle errors are made or communications do not come readily.

This seemed just. I do not find it well in a circle to dispute with the intelligences as it is apt to interfere with the results, just for what reason I am not altogether sure. Quite likely it affects the passivity of the medium. A spirit in another circle explained the imperfection in communication after this manner—

"Mediumship is not like a phonograph that Edison has so wonderfully invented, and that carries a message on it that is

indelibly there, and repeats itself to you again and again. This is not so with the medium. You call up a friend on the telephone, and you ask him a question, and he speaks to you, and you say, "I can not understand a word you are saying." You finally call up "central," and then you may not be able to hear any better. You do not think of blaming your friend, but you blame the medium, that is, the telephone machine and wire. Your friend is all right, but the medium is imperfect."

Eighth Sitting, Tuesday, June 6, 1905

The voices were numerous tonight. The laughing voice again came at our request, and gave us much evidence to prove that it was independent of the medium. This lasted perhaps fifteen minutes. It was a natural human laugh, but the laugh of a physically powerful man. The laughing voice always arouses the risibilities of the medium, and she laughed at it heartily, so that it afforded us a constant opportunity of contrasting the timbre of the two voices. It is as hard to think that the weak delicate voice organs of the medium could produce that laugh as to believe that a lark could imitate the bellowing of a bull. If we heard the barking of a dog in a room in which we were convinced that there was no other living thing than a canary bird, it might puzzle us to account for the phenomenon; but we would not hesitate to say that the canary's vocal organs did not produce that sound.

There was evidently a supreme effort of the intelligences in control to convince us that the medium's vocal organs did not produce these independent voices. But if not the medium's, whose vocal organs did produce these sounds loud enough to fill a large hall? I thought of every possible explanation. The only other persons present were Mr. and Mrs. and Miss Z. and Mrs. Blank, myself, and the medium. As I have already repeated several times, Mrs. Blank was always wedged in between Mr. Z. and myself, and all in the circled had hands joined, and Mrs. Blank was laughing and talking with the rest of us. Then, she is a woman whose history is well known, and she is deeply interested in investigating theses phenomena, as deeply interested as are the rest of us. Had the phenomena taken place in the medium's home or in the house of any friend of hers or of a professed and easily fooled Spiritualist, we might conclude that in some manner a confederate had slipped in, but here a confederate was simply impossible-utterly, absolutely impossible. The performance under the circumstances was a very puzzling demonstration.

Against accepting the spirit hypothesis, spring up to the mind a score of difficulties. Of course, that threadbare one, why should spirits be engaged in a work of this kind? Why not help us to solve some great practical social problem, as a government problem, a great invention? The same old stone wall against which many of us have often before butted our heads. It is evident, if these are spirits, their ways are not our ways. Possibly it is true, as Professor James of Harvard says, they may be under some tremendous inhibitions. At any rate, we do not know enough to dogmatize for or against the spirit hypothesis. Let us keep gathering facts and keep our heads level and our feet within a reasonable distance of the earth, and largely let the research be carried on by experienced investigators.

In answer to questions, the voices talked much about the dwellings, occupations, etc., in the spirit-world, and then told how to live "in the life that now is" in order that our progress in the beyond may be rapid. The burden of the talk was that we should avoid selfishness in its many forms on earth, that we should live lives of self-denial and of service. These talks were of an ennobling character and the philosophy behind them all indicated clear logical thinking of no mean order.

Ninth Sitting, Wednesday, June 7, 1905

This evening Mrs. Z. asked the control whether her father was present.

> **"No,"** was the reply, **"we will send a message for him if you so desire."**
>
> "Yes, do."
>
> "How can you send a message to a distant spirit?"
>
> **"Do you think that you in your world can send messages to a distant one, and we can not? Believe me, the spirit-world is far ahead of your world in the arts and sciences and in all manner of conveniences. Why, my friends, yours is the shadow, and this is the real world."**

Mrs. Z. said she felt a hand on her head. She asked if anyone in the circle had touched her. The medium put both of her hands on Mrs. Z's hands. Red Jacket said,

> **"That was your father who touched you."**

Mrs. Z. said, "Father, are you here?" A voice different from any we had yet heard replied,

> **"Yes, my child, I am so glad to have you hear me and talk to you and know that I talk once more. We know all you think and feel and do, and are helping you every way we can."**

Then the voice indicated certain help to be given to a sick relative at a distance. There are many curious elements in this psychic problem, and that of receiving help from the dead is not the least curious.

I listened attentively to the voice, that claimed to be Mrs. Z.'s father, to see if I could detect any resemblance to the medium's voice, especially as this voice was mild and was within the capacity of her vocal organs and her physical strength. If the medium had so desired she, it is reasonable to believe, under the circumstances, could have produced this voice had she sufficient cunning and deceit, and the much practice necessary.

I, this evening, urged upon the control what I call the water-test, that is, that the medium should hold a measured quantity of liquid in her mouth, and then have the spirit talking to continue. The medium was to take from a measuring-glass which I brought with me two tablespoonfuls of water, colored by a coloring-matter known only to myself, and her hands were to be held and we were to note whether any independent talking took place. If such talking would take place, then a light was to be struck and the water emptied from the medium's mouth into the measuring-glass. This, of course, if carefully done, would be strong proof of the presence of outside intelligences.

We were told that, unfortunately, the medium during the day had had a bad turn with her heart, suffering very much, so that the controls reported to us that it would not be safe to make the test, but that they would be glad to do it at some time later if the medium would rally sufficiently to make sure it wise to take the risk.

I assured Red Jacket that I was very anxious to make the test. To help allay any fear that might be in the mind of the medium I said:

"As to the coloring-matter which I have here, I will drink some water thus colored before the medium takes it, so that she may know that it is safe. I will tell her immediately before the test what is in the water, and I will see that she takes only two tablespoonfuls. Now, if this can be done with both hands of the medium held, and it be made known to scientists, it can not but be regarded as a test having evidential value."

> **"We will do it if we can,"** replied Red Jacket, **"but not tonight—we dare not try it on account of the medium's condition. Even this talk of a test makes her heart beat irregularly. We must talk of something else."**

I was sorry we had not carried on the conversation in a low tone of voice-lower than the medium's ability to hear.

The after-talk was mainly on the mission-work of spirits in helping, as the control claimed, feebly developed souls that come over to the spirit side of life.

There was the usual variety of voices. The medium talked considerably in her natural voice—as before, seemingly at the same time the other voices were speaking.

Tenth Sitting, Thursday, June 8, 1905

The medium was said to be sick and conditions unfavorable.

Eleventh Sitting, Friday, June 9, 1905

Red Jacket spoke eloquently of the wrongs of the Redman, but claiming that notwithstanding these wrongs, a powerful band of his people were seeking to do the Palefaces in this country only good.

> **"We know,"** he said, **"that no other work is worthwhile either to your world or in the spirit-world—nothing but good to others. This is the only way spirits can grow from one state to a higher."**

Red Jacket greatly deplored the terrible war raging between Russia and Japan, as it sent over to the spirit-world so many who were violently forced out of life and hence immature as spirits. He was asked if he had ever seen Washington in spirit-life.

"Oh, yes," he replied, **"many times. I have often been in his home here. He has a beautiful dwelling, and he is a lofty spirit, doing a great work in teaching."**

Red Jacket abruptly asked me, **"What is imagination?"** After my answer, he continued, **"Much of what you call imagination is the result of spirit influence, good or evil. A large proportion of your thoughts and impressions come from above."**

I urged again that we have tests of two voices speaking at the same time. This was done apparently in a number of cases, but only briefly and not absolutely satisfactorily. Again Red Jacket protested against these tests, insisting that such tests compelled "cross-currents" in the medium. He gave an exhibition of the power of his voice in contrast with that of the medium, by suddenly speaking unusually loud. I have seldom heard a more powerful male voice than this exhibition revealed. As quickly as the light was turned up I felt Mrs. French's pulse. It marked forty-eight and was extremely irregular.

Twelfth Sitting, Saturday, June 10, 1905

The medium was weak, seemingly exhausted. Mr. M. and his wife were guests this evening-invited by myself. They sat between Miss Z. and Mrs. Z.; the rest of us sat as on previous evenings.

The voices were of a considerable variety.

This evening we gave the water-test, but nothing satisfactory resulted. The controls suggested that when the medium grew strong another effort would be made. They assured us they fully understood the importance of the test for evidential purposes.

This concluded this remarkable series of sittings in New York.

A Supplemental Sitting at Rochester

Some weeks after Mrs. French and Mrs. Blank returned from New York to their home in Rochester, I arranged for a séance in Rochester. My object was, if possible, to try again the water-test. This arrangement was made through a prominent lawyer in that city, a man well known, but not a Spiritualist. This friend is deeply interested in the investigation of these mysterious phenomena.

We met Mrs. French at a private house of my friend's selecting. I required Mrs. Blank, who was to be present, to coach Mrs. French in holding two tablespoonfuls of water in her mouth and breathing at the same time through her nostrils. We hoped in this way to allay her nervous excitement which in our previous tests in New York was said to have been largely the cause of the fluttering of her heart during the trial. The conditions were wholly under my control the same as they were in New York.

The room was on the second floor, and the keys, after locking the two doors, I placed in my pocket. I bought the matter for coloring the water on my way to the house, and brought with me my own measuring-glass. No one but myself knew the color of the liquid I would use. I took into the séance-room the glass container containing the two tablespoonfuls of water, and then placed in the glass the coloring-matter and permitted the medium to taste it, so as to relieve her mind as to any thought or any fear of it being unpleasant.

The plan to be pursued by us, I outlined as follows:

A candlestick with a candle in it was placed on a table at the side of one of the members of the circle, and when the control gave the word, that gentleman, who is a dentist in Rochester, was to light the candle; then I was to give to the medium the liquid in the presence of all the members of the circle. Holding the glass in my hands, the medium was to take all the liquid in her mouth; I was to place the empty glass on the floor between my feet; the light was then to be extinguished, and immediately thereafter Red Jacket, if possible, was to speak in his natural voice, and then the candle was to be relit, and the colored water was to be ejected from the mouth of the medium into the measuring glass which I was to hold, and we were all to see whether the same amount of liquid had been emptied from the medium's mouth into the glass as was in it at the beginning of the séance, and whether it was of the same color.

The four persons—besides my friend, Mrs. Blank, Mrs. French and myself—who made up the circle were all intimately known to my friend.

The plan of procedure as described above was carried out to the letter, and Red Jacket spoke within a minute after the liquid had been taken into the medium's mouth and the light extinguished. It should be remembered that I held the glass to her mouth before the light was extinguished, and after the voice came the candle was relit and the medium emptied the liquid from her mouth into the measuring-glass which I held in my hand. The liquid emptied into the glass I found to be of the exact amount that I gave her, and was in the judgment of us all the same color.

This test was a perfect one with only a single drawback which did not occur to me, I am sorry to say, until after I left the house. *A very sly, tricky person* (Dr.Funks loophole-Ed.) might have had an empty bottle or glass concealed about her person and, as soon as the light was extinguished, emptied the liquid into this glass and then, after the speaking and before the light was relit, put the liquid back into her mouth. Had one of our number held both of the medium's hands while the room was in darkness, the test would have been complete in every part as far as I can see. This concealed-glass theory is an exceedingly unlikely one under all of the conditions. But it must be regarded as a possible one, and should be guarded against in any future tests. At some future sitting I will try to guard against this unlikely, but possible hypothesis.

Affidavit of A.W. Moore, Secretary of the Rochester Art Club

"I have attended the sittings with Mrs. French of this city from time to time during the past twenty years. I am positively convinced of the genuineness of the manifestations of spirit voices which occur through her mediumship.

"I have, during years, tried, by every device that human ingenuity could suggest, to discover fraud on the part of Mrs. French, but without avail.

"I have known Mrs. French, during some of her séance's, when I happened to sit next to her, to place her mouth on the back of my hand and keep it there while Red Jacket, her principal control was speaking.

"And I have many times heard Mrs. French conversing while Red Jacket's or some other control's voices, have been addressing the circle."

A.W. Moore

Sworn to, before me, this 19th day of April 1906 Mary Jeanette Ballantyne Notary Public

The Return of Dr. Isaac K. Funk

Dr. Isaac J. Funk, a man of much learning, spent forty years in psychic research. He published the result of his investigation and many of his conclusions, but he always lived in awe of the criticism of science. I spent many hours with Dr. Funk going over the details of my own work, and I discussed with him many of the problems with which we had to deal. He was much interested in the investigation that I was making with Mrs. French, and for that reason I arranged for her to go to New York where she spent eleven days with him and his associates. There, under conditions that he desired, she demonstrated the work she was doing with me. The result he published in his *Psychic Riddle*. He was always anxious for proof that the voices which he heard were independent, and he wanted evidence of the identity of those with whom I had speech. These points he regarded as important to prove the continuity of life, and in his work he was unable to satisfy himself concerning them. His method was to attempt to prove a fact by the process of elimination, that is, to prove truths by demonstrating their opposite. He, like all other scientific men, attempted to rear a structure by tearing the structure down. This process has impeded the progress of nearly all psychic investigators, and I often said to him that one should seek what he wanted to find with open and receptive mind, always having in his thoughts that conditions cannot be changed to satisfy any one's particular notion; that we must accept conditions as we find them and make them better, to enable us to gain the end desired. In all of Dr. Funk's published works he left a *loophole* in his conclusions, that he might avoid criticism should he be found in error.

Some time ago the doctor left his physical body, and one night soon after, during one of the last sessions I had with Mrs. French, a man's voice spoke my name. The tone was familiar, but I could not associate the voice with any one whom I had known in the earth-life, although I knew a spirit was speaking.

I replied, "Your voice is familiar, but I do not recognize it."

> He replied, **"I am Dr. Isaac Funk. I have been out of the body but a short time and being interested in your work, I have been permitted to come."**

I then said: "You may be Dr. Funk, as you claim, but we cannot permit you to consume our time unless you establish your identity. This is one of the rules that we adopted sometime since, for the reason that, knowing the person, we can form some judgment as to the value of what he may say. If you are Dr. Funk and desire to continue this conversation, you must establish that fact."

> He quickly responded: **"You are entirely right about that; what you ask is fair. I ought to be able to establish my identity."**

I said: "Certainly, if you are Dr. Funk you can give us some proof of your identity. During your earth life you always made a great point of establishing identity."

> Then he inquired: **"How shall it be done?"**

I answered: "That is not for me to suggest. You know how technical the body of scientific gentlemen to which you belong always is. If you are going to have a test here, we want it to be evidential. If you are going to prove your identity, you must do it without suggestion from me."

> He replied, after a pause: **"Identity was what I invariably wanted satisfactorily proved. I recall a conversation I had with you in my private office at which no one was present but ourselves."**

"Yes, "I suggested," we had many such interviews."

> He then said: **"I refer to one at which I asked you to make a special test at one of your meetings with Mrs. French. I asked that when someone with an independent voice was speaking, you put you hand upon the table and have Mrs. French put her mouth upon your hand; you were then to place your free hand over her head, holding it firmly, and in that situation see if you could hear the independent voice. I wanted such evidence to demonstrate that Mrs. French did not do the talking. No one knew of that conversation but ourselves, and that ought to be proof to you that I am Dr. Funk."**

I replied: "Yes, I do recall that conversation at the time and place. I now recognize your voice, and your proof is satisfactory."

I then put my hand on the table. Mrs. French, at my suggestion, put her mouth upon the back of my hand, I put my free hand over the back of her head, holding it firmly, and then I said:

"Is this what you asked me to do?"

> Dr. Funk replied: **"Yes."**

I immediately said: "Dr. Funk, you do the talking, and we will demonstrate that your voice is independent."

Afterward there was a general talk between Dr. Funk, certain of my group of coworkers upon his side of life, and me, and some plain things were said. I told Dr. Funk that because of his prominence, and as one who had investigated this important subject for many years, he could have been a great force for good; that many people in this world of men were interested in him and his writings and were guided by his conclusions, but that he never published them in full, for which reason his readers could not reach a better conclusion than he did. I told him that he had *failed* at the crucial moment, and had nullified the good he could have done. I added that I regarded this as a great misfortune not only to him, but to the world at large.

> He replied: **"I realize that now more than ever. It is a fact that I was afraid of the criticism of men of science. I now regret very much that I did not fully publish my conclusions. In my own mind there was no doubt."**

> A spirit answered and said to him: **"You were the custodian of much knowledge. Through your investigations you learned many things. By reason of your position you could have done much good. That was your stumbling block, and before you can progress, you must become strong where you were weak."**

CHAPTER 4
EPILOGUE

Rational Deductions

> **Cast aside that which is merely legendary, mythical, or traditional, and dare to walk alone, untrammeled by any bonds and unfettered by dread of any conclusion at which you may arrive. Dare to trust God, and seek for truth. Dare to think soberly, calmly, about revelation. To such a seeker shall come a knowledge of which he little dreams; a comfort which no creed of tradition can afford. He will know of God and His truth as none can know who has not trodden the path of personal investigation.**
>
> —Imperator, "Spirit Teachings," M.A. Oxon

There is not in the universe a single great problem that man can truthfully say he has mastered, that nothing remains to be found out concerning it. The laws that control this world are universal and in force in other spheres as well as in this; they control all solar systems and worlds in space; therefore, a complete comprehension of those laws and their application requires more than mortal life. If this were not so, perfection would be practically immediate and without process, and men would become Gods here and now. The most brilliant men who ever lived, knew but little of natural laws and of the origin and destiny of man. Until now little effort has been made to find them out.

The earth is yet so crude, our senses so dull and our vision so limited, that we fail to realize those emanations and movements of refined matter about us, or the subtle and incessant play of forces around us. From a single ray of light shoot millions of electrons and corpuscles, the basic constituents of matter, smaller than the atom of hydrogen; these, striking blow upon blow, pass by and through us in their incessant warfare with the night, but we feel them not.

We do not realize the quivering and bending of the earth's crust under our feet, caused by changes of temperature or the pressure of atmospheric waves, nor do we hear the fermentations and oxidations of the soil in the changing seasons. We do not even yet know the exact nature of that ether which a recent investigator considers omnipresent and omnipotent. We see the action of gravitation, but we know nothing of the medium through which it operates. We hear the wind soughing among the trees; but we do not hear the roar of sap up trunk and branch, the bursting of the buds as they bombard the air, or the speech of growing trees and flowers and grass among themselves; yet life, where found, has language.

The vibrations from out of the abyss of space would reach our ears if they had more and higher octaves, or if our capacity for catching sound were immeasurably intensified; we do not hear the clang of the planets as they ring down through their orbits, the explosive detonations of the sun, the wild dance and chant of the Nebulae, the comets' note of warning, or the rush of wandering matter of which worlds are made, which must send out impulses and tremblings through the ether to this planet of ours. We are at all times in a great sea of intensely active forces and potentialities governed by a law of which we have little conception.

About us, but invisible to most, a nation, or rather many nations, of spirit-people, "live and move and have their being," more industrious, more active, more intellectual, and more energetic, than we; so intense is their vibration that we do not ordinarily feel their touch, hear their voices, or see their forms; but conditions can be made, and have been made, whereby, not withstanding our limitations, we may have speech with them, and know at least something of how and where they live, and what they are doing.

There is so much in nature that we do not understand, is it any wonder that, having kept our eyes so close to the ground, we have not discovered this spirit world before? We have made conditions in which it became possible for us to know a little of those other people, and, even though many have not had this evidence, that does not derogate from the truth of the discovery, which must forever stand as another fact added to the sum total of human knowledge. The possibility of communication between mortals and those in the world of spirits, has been proven beyond doubt; and it now remains for men of genius to discover new methods, and to bring into this new field of research, the same intelligent action that is applied to the lower sciences, thereby increasing our knowledge of the spirit as they have of the material world.

Those who, through ignorance or prejudice, decry a new discovery, and so prevent fair consideration, are enemies of civilization. The time has come for man to be free and to think alone. Neither the teachings of the so-called dead, nor the conclusions of the living, can change facts or nullify a single natural law. Truth has neither youth nor age; it is, and ever has been, a brother to reason; it does not need the assistance of fame or science; it has never been in the keeping of any particular class of men; it is the heritage of all who live.

From the frontiers of the afterlife, from that belt or zone where spirit people live, they send us cheering messages, they speak in full-toned voice and write, as when they lived among us. And so we come to know the dead have never died.

I see good in every act of kindness, in all the words of tenderness that fall from human lips, and to me the sum of all the good in all the world is God.

Emeline Sophia French-A Tribute

> **There shall be a morning when I shall be removed, and men shall be on with their tasks. The same sun shall lick the paves, and the same shadows fill them. The very winds which now encircle me, shall dance the earth, and I shall be removed. The hand which is the tool of love shall be still, and my tongue no longer left to sing. There shall be a morning when I shall be removed, when men shall behold me singing forth from the script which idly blows apart, or is turned by a listless finger, and they shall hark, and I shall smile in understanding of God's mercy.**
>
> "When the Door Closes" by the spirit, Patience Worth

On June 22, 1912, at her home in Rochester, New York, Emily S. French, the most perfect psychic of modern times, left this world of ours. She had passed on life's highway the stone that marked four score and more, and weary with the burden of good deeds and many years, she crossed the golden bridge from life to life.

On that June day as I stood where all that was mortal of my friend was being put away, memory flashed back to a previous time. I saw the open grave of my mother, I felt again the biting winds, and the chill of another death, a sensation born of ignorance, and I recalled my early resolution to solve the problem of death. Again I stood apart, about me hills and valleys crowned and carpeted with green, winding roads, lakes and streams, trees and shrubs and flowers, and when the casket was lowered, the sun's rays, rich and warm, fell upon it, and birds sang merrily in the trees. With joy in our hearts, we among the many who came to bid Mrs. French God—speed, turned homeward, for this good woman—one among millions—had gone to the next life with absolute knowledge of what conditions were to come. She knew that death was not the end, but the open door.

"Glad," one asks, "that she was gone?" Yes, for it is the most glorious privilege possessed by mankind, after a long and eventful career, when the shadows lengthen, to pass to more intense and comprehensive life.

Mrs. French was born possessed, of what Crookes has termed, "Psychic Force"; from infancy she had unusual abilities. She could not remember a time when she was unable to see people and hear voices which were neither seen nor heard by others; for this reason she was in childhood thought peculiar. There came a period in her young womanhood when, with a pencil in each hand, she could write on different subjects simultaneously, easily conversing at the same time. Automatic writing was not then known or understood, and the suggestion that the beyond was inhabited by people, just as this world is, had not dawned upon our mentality. Afterward there came in her presence under certain conditions, independent voices, that is, a way was found by which the vocal organs of the dead, so-called, could be and were clothed, so that they spoke audibly in our atmosphere, and in this manner came the discovery of another plane inhabited by all the countless dead, where individuality is actually continued—a world as real and tangible as this.

It was my good fortune to meet Mrs. French early, and the compact then formed was faithfully kept to the end. She was as anxious as I was to understand the play of forces in her presence, and without payment she freely gave her time and strength that through her instrumentality good might come, not only to those living here but also to those in the great beyond. The idea of accepting money for such services was abhorrent to her, and she devoted her life to the liberation of the mind, that the mental bonds of superstition might be broken, and that mankind might become better by living more intelligently.

Her work gave the world a new discovery, and her labor opened the door to the Unknown Land. Her love went out to those in sorrow—to the unfortunate, the rich, the poor, and the ignorant, and yet with her great power she was a child, sincere and frank and full of hope as Spring, and she ever borrowed sunshine of tomorrow to make the present glad. She saw into the great beyond where the modes of motion were too rapid for physical sight; she knew the needs of others, and her charities encompassed them, and as the years passed, and the results became more apparent, the censure of this little world failed to sting. Her span of earth's life was exceedingly long. For many years her physical ears failed to catch sounds; she grew refined and delicate as her life force ebbed. Some years before her death she became blind, and all the beauty of the physical world was shut out, but still our wonderful work went on. Toward the end she became weary with well-doing, and met the change with confidence and courage.

Mrs. French passed into the next world gladly, for her psychic sight had already beheld the glories of her new home; she had more friends there than here, and she had often heard the voices of the husband, who gave his life that the Union might be preserved, and of her son who passed just as manhood touched the noon of life. She went not as a stranger into an unknown land, but as one familiar with the way, for just across the border, there waited with outstretched hands and words of welcome *countless thousands* who had been helped through her effort.

The memory of Emily S. French comes like a benediction. Over every cradle Nature bends and smiles, and at this second birth it does the same. She made me her friend by being fair, and so we worked for twenty years and more to learn how to expel the fear of death from the human heart. She grew old as we count time, feeble in body and blind; yet her courage and devotion never waned, and at the end she smiled and met the dawn of everlasting life.

She was an instrument through which a great group worked. In her presence with the necessary conditions the people in the next plane spoke, and never again can it be said, "The dead know not anything."

I cannot give out the knowledge gained through Mrs. French's instrumentality without paying this tribute to her. She was the noblest woman I have known; she was both honest and brave; she enriched herself by aiding others. She helped to stay the tears that fell from furrowed cheeks and looked with pity on ignorance and superstition. She came to know that all wretchedness and pomp lose distinction in the democracy of death and that only character survives. To her in the great beyond where she now resides I send my love. —We shall meet again.

EDWARD C. RANDALL

"To That Mortal Would I Speak"

> "It shall come to pass afterwards that will pour out my spirit upon all flesh; and your sons and your daughters shall prophesy, your old men shall dream dreams, your young men shall see visions; and also upon the servants and upon the handmaids in those days / will pour out my spirit."
>
> -JOEL 2: 28-29

The gentleman who opened the discussion on the "Attitude of Science" was himself, while, in earth life, a great thinker, and has evidently made much progress a chemist in the sphere where he now lives. He is fearless in speech, and has the courage born of knowledge. It is a privilege that I prize greatly to discuss philosophy with him, and many of his discourses have found place in this work. After speaking on the subject above mentioned, I asked permission to use what he had said. With his consent, I give, in his answer, perhaps the most remarkable message that ever came from the spirit-world:

"In so far as you are impressed with the thought that my simple words will enable you to give to the people of earth a clear and honest statement of the facts with reference to the change from one sphere to another sphere of usefulness, everything which is in perfect accord with, and which carries out the intent of that whole, which it so perfectly controls, you are welcome to use. If anything I have said, or may say, can, in any degree, bring to the people of earth an appreciation of the future that awaits them, I am deeply grateful.

"One, older in spirit-life, and far—oh so very far beyond me bids me say:"

"Upward and onward! Always lead the way, for climb ye must, whether ye would or nay! That omnipotent force that has fixed the destiny of all things, has so willed, and, struggle though ye do and will, to follow your self-impulse, and journey to and fro, yet shall your course lay onward and upward. In all that has been, in all there is, and in all you shall know as you journey on, that one intent is the manifest purpose. The one supreme intent ye of earth-life shall not and cannot know, and that is wise and just. But this ye may know, for your very peace and comfort: every change that shall overtake you, is but to prepare you for the next, and further knowledge is but a dream of your own fancy, that springs from the speculative intensity of your desire to know.

"Knowing all, would ye not be that ALL? And knowing all, yet having the wisdom to make use of that knowledge, what blundering fools would ye be! Only as ye shall have wisdom to exercise just and proper care of such things as be, shall ye know the meaning of those things. The servant must ever be able to do intelligently the master's bidding, that he may be worthy of trust; and if he faileth, then must the master bid him begone, and another shall enter into his stewardship until he who hath failed shall be worthy, once more, of his master's trust; and, should he fail scores of times without number, yet shall he be set aside until he hath become his own master; and then only may he be a worthy servant to his master. And so I say unto you, that ye may learn concerning the future, that shall help you in the time that is; but beyond the simple knowledge of the fact that ye shall have answered unto you the great question of Job—asked by every son of woman from all time—'Though I die, shall I live again?' I answer unto you, saying to all in earth-life, Yea! You shall! Let that, then, suffice for I say once more to all men, through you, that no mortal can obtain knowledge of what lies beyond save through the sphere above that wherein he dwells, for all must pass from earth before reaching the spirit-sphere; those in the earth-plane must receive all knowledge of the afterlife from those who have progressed into spirit-life.

"'Upward and onward ye must go; and only by such a ladder, as ye shall have built, can ye mount. So it is well that ye build wisely and with care. Let the rungs be of good deeds, and ye shall mount quickly and joyously to great and splendid heights; but if ye are careless and slothful in the building, and heed not nature's laws, —and they are writ that all may read, —your advancement will be delayed by your failure, for each rotten rung must be replaced; and O ye of earth! If ye could but know the weariness of such undoing and redoing, more heed would ye give as ye rush onward through life.

"And so I say to you this: to know that ye live again, though ye die, is all ye need to know to fit you for the future; and if ye knew too much of that future state that ye shall enter into, it would unfit you for that state in which ye now live. Take ye no heed of the morrow, but see that ye so live, each day, that the morrow may find you prepared. True honesty, like charity, begins in one's own heart. It is far better to have committed an honest error and reaped no profit, than to have great profit and to have honestly gone from your own heart.

"This spirit gives me no name. He says it has been lost so long from his memory that he scarce heeded its going. As you respect a worthy man of much learning and honesty of heart, without regard to his name, so I reverence this other spirit; and I am indebted to you for the privilege of knowing him, as he came to me saying; 'To that mortal would I speak."

APPENDICES

Edward Caleb Randall (1860-1935)
Men of New York — Western Section — 1898

EDWARD C. RANDALL has impressed himself upon the community in which he lives as a man of unusual force and energy. He is a well-known lawyer, and since his admission to the bar thirteen years ago, he has figured as counsel in many important legal controversies. He is still so young that the success already achieved may fairly be regarded as the forerunner of higher achievements.

Mr. Randall was born thirty-six years ago in the town of Ripley, N.Y., and had the usual experience of a country boy seeking a liberal education. He received his preliminary training in the district school and academy of his native place, and was prepared for college under private tuition. He pursued his classical studies at Allegheny College, Meadville, Penn. In 1879 he entered the office of Morris & Lambert at Fredonia, N.Y., and commenced a course of legal study. He subsequently moved to Dunkirk, and completed his preparation for the bar in the office of Holt & Holt. After four years spent in maturing the theory and practice of the law, Mr. Randall was admitted to the bar by the Supreme Court April 3, 1883, at Rochester. He at once opened an office in Dunkirk, and met with unusual success from the start. The professional field there was limited, however, and he decided to seek a larger sphere of labor. Turning over his office and business to Eugene Cary, a local attorney, in the fall of 1884 he moved to Buffalo, in whose future growth and development he had great faith, and formed a partnership with Joseph P. Carr, under the firm name of Carr & Randall. Mr. Carr retired from the profession two years later, and Mr. Randall continued to practice alone for the next ten years. He formed a partnership with Jeremiah J. Hurley on January 1, 1896, becoming senior member of the firm of Randall & Hurley.

Mr. Randall first became prominent in Buffalo for his celebrated defense of Frank Curcio, who was tried for murder in 1887. For five years Mr. Randall was counsel for the receivers of the Tonawanda Valley & Cuba Railroad; and he acted in a similar capacity for the supply creditors of the New York, Lake Erie & Western Railroad, and participated in the reorganization of that company.

In politics Mr. Randall has been an active Republican. A graceful and earnest speaker, he has taken the stump in behalf of his party in the various campaigns of the last twelve years. He has never accepted a nomination for political office, preferring to devote his entire attention to the building up of a legal clientage. Believing in the great destiny in store for Buffalo, he has invested largely and successfully in real estate in that city. He is a loyal citizen, interested in many charities, and an earnest promoter of every measure that tends to the permanent welfare of the Queen City. He is member of the Masonic Order, and is widely known in social circles.

MUNICIPALITY OF BUFFALO HISTORY /1923

EDWARD CALEB RANDALL -After two years in the practice of law in Dunkirk, New York, Mr. Randall located in the city of Buffalo, where he has attained distinction both as a lawyer and businessman. He has acquired not only high professional honor, but of late has organized and financed various industrial enterprises. As a writer and lecturer on psychic subjects, he stands in America's front rank; his books are published and sold around the Globe. He is a son of Nelson Randall, a farmer of Ripley, New York, who later engaged in private banking and became one of the influential men of his town.

Edward C. Randall was born in Ripley, New York, July 19, 1860, and there until 1870 attended the district school. He then became a pupil in a private preparatory school, taught by Alanson Wedge, later entering Allegheny College at Meadville, Pennsylvania. He did not graduate, but left to take up the study of law. He was admitted to the bar at Rochester, New York, April 3, 1883, and for the following two years followed his profession successfully in Dunkirk. In 1885, seeking a broader field, he located in Buffalo and there has continued in active practice during the last thirty-seven years. He has also acquired large business interests. He is now one of the leading men of the industrial world, and is the executive head of various companies in addition to being president of the following corporations: American Super-Power Corporation, Super Power Syndicate, Inc., South Buffalo Terminals, Inc., and Niagara Terminal Buildings Corporation.

A lawyer of learning and ability, and a businessman of successful achievement, Mr. Randall since 1890, has also devoted a great deal of time to scientific psychic research, with the result that he has become one of the leading American authorities. In 1906 he published his first book *Life's Progression*, a work which has had a large sale and has been translated into foreign languages. This was followed, in 1908, by *The Future of Man*, and in 1914 by *Psychic Truths*, published in Australia. *The Dead Have Never Died*, now in its sixth edition, was brought out both in England and America in 1918. His latest work, *Frontiers of the Afterlife*, was published in 1922. In addition to his literary work, Mr. Randall has delivered many lectures in different parts of the United States. In the near future, when business affairs are arranged, he will devote his entire time to lecturing and psychic research. Mr. Randall is a member of Ellicott Club, Buffalo Chamber of Commerce, New York State Bar Association, and Erie County Bar Association.

Mr. Randall married, in Buffalo, New York, October 6, 1897, Maria Louise Howard, a granddaughter of the late General Rufus L. Howard. Mrs. and Mrs. Randall have two daughters, Virginia and Marian, both graduates of Misses Master's School at Dobbs Ferry, New York. The summer homes of the Randall's are "Crown Hill," Eden, New York, and "Ladnar Lodge," in the Canadian wilderness on Blackstone Lake.

BUFFALO NEWS, 1923

Niagara Falls Company Rival Seeking Permit.

Corporation headed by financiers proposes to spend three hundred millions. Plan Two Big Projects. Development at Niagara and on the St. Lawrence to give power to many cities.

Announcement was made yesterday that Henry L. Doherty and A.B. Leach, leading New York utility magnates, had become associated with American Super Power Corporation, with headquarters in Buffalo. Simultaneously, Edward C. Randall of Buffalo, president of the corporation, made it known that this organization plans to make a strenuous fight for the right to develop hydroelectric power at Niagara Falls and on the International reach of the St. Lawrence River.

The American Super Power Corporation has been incorporated in New York State for the purpose of generating and transmitting hydroelectric power in the State of New York ... Mr. Randall, the president, is well known as a power magnate and as an attorney.

The corporation plans to offer to install at the crest of the Horseshoe Falls remedial works to stay the suicide of the cataract if the federal water power commission grants them a license to divert such waters of the Niagara ... Mr. Randall's announcement stated that the A.S.P.C. had purchased Conner's Island in the Niagara River above the falls for an intake and nearly half a mile of river frontage in the lower gorge, where it plans to erect the largest powerhouse on the continent. The whole project, including the transmission lines it is estimated, could cost $88,000,000.

COURIER, APRIL 18, 1926

Quarantine Bars Sister, Friends at Girl's Funeral.

Debutante Who Headed Junior League Activities, Dies of Scarlet Fever and Meningitus—Grave Service Cut Short.

Miss Virginia Randall, twenty-one year old society girl and leader in Junior League Activities, who died Monday at her home, No. 27 Tudor Place, from scarlet fever and spinal meningitis, was buried yesterday afternoon in Forest Lawn cemetery.

The Randall home bore the yellow card of quarantine, barring friends from paying their last respects. Miss Marion Randall, who was presented to society in 1922, at the same time as Virginia, was denied opportunity of seeing her sister for a last time. She remained at Hotel Touraine while funeral arrangements were being made to meet the health law requiring burial within 24 hours following death in such cases.

Edward C. Randall, her father, who is the author of books on Spiritualism, among them *The Dead Have Never Died,* went to the house after hearing of her death. He was permitted to see his daughter. Mrs. Randall had remained with the girl during the illness.

COURIER, APRIL 8, 1904

Attorney Edward C. Randall Before International Progressive Thought League

Attorney Edward C. Randall told a room full of persons at the Iroquois last night all about what becomes of them after death. Mr. Randall is a Spiritualist or psychic philosopher and, as he explained last evening, he is an authority on such things. When stray spirits in the other world don't know just where they are at they can come to Mr. Randall and find out. He has put many of them right acting as their adviser, friend and guide on things spiritual. He and Mrs. French, his medium assistant, have found thousands of spirit wandering around in a sort of spirit daze and have comforted and cheered them and told them who they were and have given them such other information as is good for spirits befuddled by their new surroundings.

It was a meeting of the International Progressive Thought League that Mr. Randall addressed. The progressive thinkers listened to Mr. Randall for an hour and a half and then asked questions for a while. They seemed much interested. The speaker said Buffalo is a great psychic center and then told about the Independent-Voice phenomena; voices of spirits speaking, apart from the medium, without her going into a trance or anything of the sort. Sir William Crookes sent Admiral Moore all the way from England to Buffalo to hear the voices. Admiral Moore heard them and went back to England.

"Dissolution at so-called death is simply separation," said Mr. Randall. "No mental change takes place. No more than we do spirit people know the mysteries of God, life and eternity.

"Many spirits need help and I have, with the aid of Mrs. French, been able to help many, very many. We bring them to a realization of what and where they are. We have awakened thousands of them and we find them able to tell things that happened before they left the body and sentences begun and broken in death are finished when the spirit awakens.

"When we discover one of Nature's laws we marvel at its simplicity. There is nothing in Nature that is supernatural; there is no supernormal, these are but names given to conditions not understood."

Several of the very interesting chapters of Mr. Randall's book are devoted to a description of his methods of work with a medium and the conditions under which that work is carried on, and some of the things he has seen and heard and otherwise experienced not particularly germane to the general theme of his book. "The fact," he urges, "that millions of human beings have not heard or spoken to spirit people, or seen them use the hand of a sensitive to write does not even tend to prove that I have not had such experiences or that these are not facts." These chapters at least give an idea of the experiments which have led the author to speak so positively of his experiences as facts. To him they are established beyond doubt, no matter how they may strike others.

It must always be remembered that spirits are not infallible, and Mr. Randall would not have it understood by his readers that all knowledge comes with the casting off of the physical body. "They" [spirits] he says, "do not agree on many questions any more than we do. They fail to understand many of Nature's laws as mortals do, and are continually laboring to come to a better knowledge of them, just as we do here." But as their limitations are not so great, their outlook is broader, and consequently much that is theory here is fact there.

And so the doctrine of vibration is pursued through many chapters, devoted to thought and mind, to matter, to evolution, to the atom and beyond, there is a spirit explanation of the much-talked-of subconscious mind, a consideration of the influence of spirit people on our daily thought and action through suggestion; and a chapter, which will appeal to the curious, giving a spirit's description of his spirit home. One cannot fail to be interested by it all, even though he doubts or even scoffs.

The Times — February, 1923

Spiritualism Not Religion but a Science says Randall Buffalo Attorney Warns Mediums Not to Try to Make Angels of Their Ghosts

LILY DALE, NEW YORK -"Don't try to make angels of your ghosts," Edward C. Randall, Buffalo attorney, warned the Spiritualists 46th annual assembly in Lily Dale, Sunday.

"The great mistake Spiritualist have made is thinking they have a religion when they had a science," he said. "If the phenomena of Spiritualism had been treated as a matter of fact, Spiritualism would have made greater progress during the past fifty years than it has," he asserted.

Mr. Randall went on to explain that he doesn't think much of religion anyway. At least of religion as it is generally understood.

"We are all handicapped by being born into a religious state," he continued. "I personally was not so handicapped and am thankful that

I was not soaked in orthodoxy. How foolish it is to believe that a single book contains all the knowledge in the world."

Church a Bungling Friend

Mr. Randall said that there was a time when he thought the church was blocking the path of civilization. Now he thinks that the church is not a positive enemy but a kind of bungling friend. "It has not aided civilization as it might," he said.

"But the church has the organization and the buildings, "he reminded his fellow Spiritualists," and we are slowly but surely pushing our way into their pulpits and bringing with us the knowledge they do not possess."

Mr. Randall said that he decided orthodoxy was the bunk one Sunday in Trinity Church, Buffalo. The congregation had risen to recite the creed. In the middle of it he looked out the window, saw the flowers springing and the birds singing and suddenly cut out, murmuring to himself, "I don't believe a word of it."

It was Confucius who formulated the Golden Rule hundreds of years before Christ, Mr. Randall said. And his audience applauded with enthusiasm his statement that "Robert G. Ingersoll did the greatest service to the American people of the last century when he broke the shackles from the human brain."

Mr. Randall seemed to be in agreement on this point. "I am no longer interested in phenomena," he said. "Phenomena teaches you nothing. Any thinking mind knows that nothing can be destroyed; a handful of mud contains the life force that is indestructible, and we know that the life of the human spirit is one that must go on."

Mr. Randall told his audience that his only purpose in speaking was to convince them that there are folks out of the body just as there are folks in it. Most people do not see them for they are blind, he said. They are like blind people walking among flowers and green trees.

Where are they? Well, according to Mr. Randall's belief, there are ethereal zones around the earth which they inhabit. And these places have substance; they are worlds of people and things.

The life belongs to the spirit, which is indestructible, he said. At the moment of conception the ethereal body steps into its earthly garment. And at the time most people call death, it steps out again, very much as one steps out of one's clothes at night. The spirit is there before and after: natural birth occurs as soon as it can stand the light.

Calls Passing Out a Privilege

Mr. Randall rewrote Longfellow's poem, "Crossing the Bar," for his audience, adding a stanza of joy for the soul in being free. "It is a privilege to pass out of this life, he said. "Let us not delay our families by regrets."

Mr. Randall was introduced as the man whom Sir. Oliver Lodge referred to as the leading investigator of scientific phenomena in America. Following the meeting, Fred W. Constantine, president of the assembly said that Mr. Randall is out of step with other Spiritualists in not wishing to consider it a religion. "The religion and philosophy are the heart of Spiritualism," Mr. Constantine said. "The only use of the phenomena is to win new members to the faith."

THE BUFFALO NEWS, APRIL 1904

Psychic Honors for E.C. Randall Heads of National Psychical Research Society Experiment in Buffalo lawyer's Discoveries in Spiritual Phenomena-Believes He has Added to the Discoveries.

Edward C. Randall, the Buffalo lawyer who did much to stir up the Boodle investigation last fall which led to the indictment of seven aldermen, is about to issue a book on psychical researches he has made for a period covering fifteen years. So determined has he been in these investigations and successful in getting results, that he has been honored within the past week of a visit from Dr. Richard Hodgson, of Boston, and Prof. James Hyslop of the same city. These men made a series of experiments at Mr. Randall's home on West Ferry Street and are said to have gone away convinced that Mr. Randall has added considerably to the knowledge of spiritual phenomena.

Mr. Randall, when asked yesterday about his experiments, admitted that Dr. Hodgson and Prof. Hyslop had been here for several days testing the truth of his statements concerning communication he had with spirits.

"My friends are aware," said he,"that I have been paying considerable attention to Spiritualism for years. I went into it first for the purpose of exposing it as a fraud, but soon became convinced that while there were many impostors calling themselves Spiritualists, there is a true Spiritualism. I can now assert that I not only believe, but I know that we can communicate with the spirits of the dead."

Came to Make Tests

"The gentleman mentioned here came to make certain tests of which I can say little. Both of them say they have communicated with spirits. They will accept nothing but evidence based on absolute scientific proof. That is what their society is for. They admit that a great many fakirs are fooling the public and the difficulty is to avoid them and get at the undoubted truth."

COURIER — 1935

Services Held for E.C. Randall Private Funeral Rites Conducted for Lawyer and Businessman.

Private funeral services were conducted at 2:40 o'clock this afternoon in the home for Edward Caleb Randall, lawyer, businessman and leader in psychic research who, died Wednesday after a brief illness in his residence, 27 Tudor Place. Mr. Randall would have been 75 years old July 19.

Bishop Cameron J. Davis of the Episcopal diocese of Western New York officiated at the last rites this afternoon, with burial in Forest Lawn cemetery.

Alert in civic endeavor as in the legal and scientific fields, lecturer and author, Mr. Randall was widely known for various measures he sought to promote for public welfare. Outstanding among these was his proposal some five years ago for a central heating plant, which would furnish steam heat to ail downtown offices at cost.

Such a plan had already proved practicable in Lockport and in certain cities of New Zealand, Mr. Randall told the Common Council at that time. His scheme was received coolly by the city legislators, who asserted it would throw many engineers and other city employees out of work.

Collaborated with Briton

His fame in the field of theosophic research had extended to other countries, and he had collaborated with J. Arthur Findlay, England's foremost expert of psychic research, in his work. Recently Mr. Findlay sent him a copy of the "Unfolding Universe" for approval before publication.

Besides his wife, the former Maria Louise Howard, he is survived by a daughter, Mrs. D. Trenchard Graham, Buffalo.

Looking Back by J. Arthur Findlay (1883-1964)

Noted author of psychic subjects (see Reading List), economics, finance and world religions; Justice of the Peace for the counties of Essex and Ayrshire; recipient of the Order of The British Empire; researched the phenomena of Direct-Voice for many years with the Glasgow medium John C. Sloan.

"Evidence, cumulative evidence, and still more evidence will in the end win the day. With this weapon the walls of ignorance and antagonism are being brought low, and there is no stronger tool available to complete destruction than the evidence of survival of death obtained by the Direct-Independent voice. The Direct-Voice is the highest psychical phenomena yet discovered, and it is the most convincing besides being quite the most wonderful. *All of the discoveries of man fade into insignificance when compared with this great discovery.*

"Edward C. Randall of Buffalo, with whom I stayed when I was in America has, however, been the most fortunate of all the investigators into this great subject, as he experimented for over twenty years with one of the most highly-developed Direct-Voice mediums, Mrs. Emily S. French ... One has only to read his books to realize that his talks went far beyond the mental capacity of the medium, who was a woman of no great learning or education, and handicapped by being deaf and very delicate. Science, philosophy and psychics were discussed between him and those who were men of learning on the other side, a revolutionary aspect of the universe being given which is quite beyond present-day scientific knowledge ... I know of no one who has been privileged to experience the Direct-Voice at its best, who has been able to come to any other conclusion than that the voices come from those who once lived here on earth."

Mrs. Emily S. French (1830-1912)

Alvin A. Hubbell, M.D.
212 Franklin St., Buffalo, NY., an Eye and Ear Specialist:

"Mrs. Emily S. French has been a patient of mine both for her eyes and ears since May 22, 1893. She then had and still has defective hearing in both ears caused by an affection of the internal ear (auditory nerve). There was, also, and still is, defective vision due to affection-slight atrophic changes—of the optic nerves and of the choroid coat of the eye near the optic disk. She also complained of 'nerve' symptoms, shooting pains in the lower extremities, 'cramping' of muscles of the legs, feeling of a tight band around the waist, which, taken in connection with the affections of the auditory and optic nerves, suggested to me the possibility of locomotor ataxia. She had, however, an aversion to doctors and would not consult a good neurologist. While Mrs. French appears to have confidence in me professionally, my skepticism along psychic lines rules me out of her séance's, although she had continued to be very friendly as a patient, whose entire confidence as a specialist I seem to have. There is no doubt that Mrs. French is and has been for years a sick woman."

Volney A. Hoard, M.D.
691 Main Street East, Rochester, N.Y.

"I am a practicing physician, duly licensed as such, and have practiced my profession in the city of Rochester for the past twenty-four years. For seventeen years past I have been the physician to Mrs. Emily S. French. I knew that she was somewhat deaf from my first acquaintance with her. Her deafness has materially increased since that time, and has been specially marked since about seven years ago, at the time of a serious illness. Her deafness at the present time is marked. One sitting three feet distant from her and facing her can not make her hear ordinary conversation, but she does hear at that distance when the voice is raised about fifty percent above the ordinary conversational tone. There is no question in my mind of her entire honesty and integrity, nor is there any question as to her decided deafness. She appears to be a woman whose weight would be 120 pounds, and about seventy-two (72) years of age. I am informed that this day she was actually weighed and that her weight is 117-3/4 pounds. I have this day measured her chest and find the measurement 20-1/2 inches expiration and 30-1/2 inches inspiration. I never knew that Mrs. French claimed to have any powers as a medium and have never witnessed any of her manifestations. I am not a Spiritualist myself and have never had anything to do with its manifestations."

William A. Sutherland
A Prominent Lawyer in Rochester, N.Y.

"I am willing to state that I have known Mrs. French personally for five years past, and she has visited at my house and been entertained by my wife while living; that my wife was very deaf and that I procured an acousticon for my wife, which, however, she was not able to utilize very long, and after her death I presented it to Mrs. French, who has not been very successful with its use. I can certify in the strongest manner my belief in her deafness. I am not a Spiritualist, but I am one of those who are puzzled by these psychic manifestations."

George C. Northrop

Merchant at Lakeville, N.Y., has made the following Affidavit: State of New York, County of Livingston

George C. Northrop, being duly sworn, says: "I am a dealer in coal, grain, flour, etc., at the village of Lakeville in the County of Livingston, N.Y., and have been for many years; I am now 76 years of age; I have known Mrs. Emily S. French, of Rochester N.Y., ever since she was a child; I know that when she was about ten years of age she had scarlet fever and that she has been deaf ever since I have seen her since then on an average of probably three or four times each year, conversing with her. I know that her deafness has been on the increase almost ever since her childhood; I know that somewhere in the neighborhood of six years ago she had a partial stroke of paralysis, since which time her deafness has greatly increased."

(Signed) George C. Northrop

Sworn to before me, this sixth day of July, 1905.

(Signed) Frank S. Roe Justice of the Peace

Officer's Hospital, Libby Prison, Richmond, Virginia

May 22, 1866.

Mrs. James H. French, it becomes my painful duty to address you this letter. Your husband, Lieu't James H. French, Col. of the 100 Mt. Vol's, was wounded in the battle of the 16th of the present month on the south side of the James River, Drury's Bluff. He was wounded in the right leg, & brought to this hospital on the 17th. The surgeon amputated his leg on the 18th, from the shock to his system, he seemed never to recover.

I was an inmate of the hospital at the time and was with him until he died on this day (May 22nd), at about 12 o'clock.

Your husband will be buried here in a lot put apart for the dead of our army. Any information ....

You can address me here, direct to Lieu't A.M. Stark, Q.M., 110th, prisoner of war, Libby Prison in Richmond, Va. My address when at home ....

Yours Truly, (Signed) A.M. Stark

Rochester Local Newspaper

July 24, 1912

Died

FRENCH -in this city. Friday, June 22, 1912. Emily S. widow of James H. French. She is survived by one daughter, Mrs. F.B. Oberst, and four granddaughters, Mrs. W.G. Angell, of Norwalk, O., and the Misses Bessie, Adele and Ruth Oberst.

The funeral will take place from the residence of the daughter, No. 227 Tremont Street, Monday at 4 P.M. Burial private. Buffalo papers please copy.

The Courier, Buffalo, New York

10 January, 1909—reporter unidentified

The other day a friend of mine sneered about the absurdity of the so-called independent voices.

I don't know very far along in spiritology, but I have gotten this far in everything; I no longer ridicule, deny or abuse anything of which I am ignorant. I give everything a good bit of rope. I neither reject nor limit a new theory. A man perspiring over the 26 letters cannot weigh a problem in philosophy. I do not say this thing must be so, nor this thing cannot be so. I can wait. With vital truths a thousand years are as a day. And as for errors they are fleet of foot and take themselves out of the way.

But if I have ever heard anything, I believe I have heard the independent voices.

Through the kindness of a friend who had experimented for many years, I was invited to see an elderly and frail woman, who is regarded by many as the most wonderful medium in the country. She dined with us and she looked very fragile and attractive in her silk gown and fine old lace. She has a little weak voice like a silver thread and she is noticeably deaf. The ordinary conversation did not reach her.

After dinner we went with her up the stairway to a large bare room. There was no furniture except a square table and half a dozen chairs. The walls were red. The one window was covered with a wooden shutter. No ray of light could come through the door. It might have been nine o'clock in the evening and the night was warm with a high wind abroad. Not a good night for a test they said. Too many high vibrations against us. We sat about the table and waited.

My host, a very near, dear friend, was noticeably anxious. He was afraid the conditions were bad and we could get nothing. Within ten minutes a ribbon of light formed over our heads. The medium said, "We shall get the voices." I sat cheerfully waiting in the darkness. I had seen little of mediums or their work, and the thing was of great interest.

Suddenly out of the far upper corner of the room a great bass voice called out, **"Good evening friends!"** I was not frightened, but the power of the voice fairly raised me from the chair. Then followed one of the most remarkable half hours I have ever experienced. On kind of voice followed another. The same voices returned and were easily recognized, as we knew the voices of friends. The owner of the bass voice had a long message to deliver and he delivered it, and to tell the truth it contained information which was and which has since been of great use. An old Methodist circuit rider came, was introduced and delivered a harangue. The polished physician of Alexander Hamilton took his turn, and his conversation and manner of speech were polished and delightful. Indians talked, more than one at a time, and several loud weird voices sang a love song, a war song, and a death song at our request. There was some talking in what they explained was the original Seneca tongue.

When I came out of the room I decided that I had had a remarkable experience. Later at the home of another friend who sat with us that first evening, we spent two evenings with the same medium. My friend, who was amazed at the performance wanted to investigate further. The same results were gotten. Many of the same voices returned and brought fresh news. Even more wonderful was the singing, the speeches, the changing of voices, the deep bass, the mellow tenor, the strident Indian voices, the women's voices, a number of them familiar to the hearers. One noble voice held us bound with words of marvelous eloquence. To one another we whispered, "Only one man ever lived who spoke English like that, Robert G. Ingersoll."

THE COMPLETE WORKS OF EDWARD C. RANDALL

Life's Progression:Research in Metapsychics, Henry B.Brown Company, NewYork 1906.

The Future of Man Meta-psychic, Otto Ulbrich Company Buffalo, New York 1908.

Psychic Truths Told in the Afterlife, 1914. Commonwealth of Australia E.W. Cole, Melbourne Sydney: George Street Rundle Street, Adelaide

The Dead Have Never Died, Alfred A. Knopf New York, N.Y. 1917.

Frontiers of the Afterlife, Alfred A. Knopf New York, N.Y. 1922.

The Living Dead and The Direct Voice, Harbinger of Light Melbourne, Australia August-December, 1926. January-February, 1927.

An Hour in the Afterlife, Psychic Book Shop Buffalo, New York 1931

QUOTABLE QUOTES OF 19TH CENTURY RESEARCHERS

"We cannot but speak the things we have seen and heard."

-ACTS 4: 20

Sir William Crookes (1832-1919), one of the greatest physicists of the last century; discoverer of thallium; X-Ray tube; inventor of the radiometer, after witnessing phenomena through the psychic instrumentality of the American medium Daniel Dunglas Home in 1871:

> "The phenomena I am prepared to attest are so extraordinary and so directly oppose the most firmly rooted articles of scientific belief—amongst others, the ubiquity and invariable action of the force of gravitation-that, even now, on recalling the details of what I witnessed, there is an antagonism in my mind between reason, which pronounces it to be scientifically impossible, and the consciousness that my senses, both of touch and sight—and these corroborated, as they were, by the senses of all who were present—are not lying witnesses when they testify against my preconceptions."

Dr. Charles Richet (1850-1935), founded the study of allergic disorders; awarded the Nobel Prize for Physiology in 1913:

> "The fact that intelligent forces are projected from an organism that can act mechanically, can move object and make sounds, is a phenomena as certainly established as any fact in physics."

Sir Oliver Lodge (1851-1940), world famous physicist; wireless telegraphy; devised a detector for electromagnetic waves. In his report to the English Society of Psychological Research, concerning the phenomena he had witnessed with the Italian medium, Eusapia Palladino, Sir Oliver Wrote:

"However the facts are to be explained, the possibility of the facts I am constrained to admit. There is no further room in my mind for doubt. Any person without invincible prejudice who had the same experience would come to the same conclusion, viz: that things hitherto held impossible do actually occur. The result of my experience is to convince me that certain phenomena usually considered abnormal belong to the order of nature, and as a corollary from this, that these phenomena ought to be investigated and recorded by persons and societies interested in natural knowledge."

Dr. Cesar Lombroso (1836-1909), famous Italian Psychiatrist and Criminologist:

> "I am ashamed and grieved at having opposed with so much tenacity the possibility of the so-called spiritistic facts; I say the facts because I am still opposed to the theory. But the facts exist, and I boast of being a slave to facts. I am a little pebble on the beach, as yet I am uncovered, but I feel that each tide draws me a little closer to the sea."

Sir William Barrett (1845-1926), famous Professor of Physics at the Royal College of Science, Dublin:

> "I do not hesitate to affirm that a careful and dispassionate review of my own experiments, extending over a period of forty years, together with the investigation of the evidence of competent witnesses, compels my belief in Spiritualism, as so defined."

Alfred Russel Wallace (1823-1903), famous naturalist, and co-discoverer, along with Charles Darwin of the principles of evolution. From his book, *Miracles and Modern Spiritualism*, published in 1878:

"I prefer to rest the claims of Spiritualism on its moral uses. I would point to the thousands it has convinced of the reality of another world, to the many it has led to devote their lives to works of philanthropy, to the eloquence and the poetry it has given us, and to the grand doctrines of an ever-progressive future state which it teaches. Those who will examine its literature will acknowledge these facts."

From "A Defense of Modern Spiritualism," published in 1900:

"The subject, of which I have here endeavored to sketch the outlines in a few pages which may perhaps be read when larger volumes would lie unopened, is far too wide and too important for this mode of treatment to do any justice to it. I have been obliged entirely to leave out all mention of the historical proofs of similar phenomena occurring in unbroken succession from the earliest ages to the present day. I could not refer to the numbers of scientific and medical men, who have been convinced of its truth, but have not made public their belief. But I claim to have shown cause for investigation; to have proved that it is not a subject that can any longer be contemptuously sneered at as unworthy of a moment's inquiry. I feel myself so confident of the truth and objective reality of many of the facts, that I would stake the whole question on the opinion of any man of science desirous of arriving at the truth, if he would only devote two or three hours a week for a few months to the examination of the phenomena, before pronouncing an opinion; for I again repeat, not a single individual that I have heard of, has done this without becoming convinced of the reality of these phenomena. I maintain, therefore, finally—that whether we consider the vast number and the high character of its converts, the immense accumulation and the authenticity of its facts, or the noble doctrine of a future state which it has elaborated-the so-called supernatural, as developed in the phenomena of modern Spiritualism, is an experimental science, the study of which must add greatly to our knowledge of man's true nature and highest interests.

"It will be seen that the phenomena of Spiritualism is no mere 'psychological' curiosity, no mere indication of some hitherto unknown 'law of nature'; but that it is a science of vast extent, having the widest, the most important, and the most practical issues, and as such should enlist the sympathies alike of moralists, philosophers, and politicians, and all who have at heart the improvement of society and the permanent elevation of human nature. I would ask all to dwell upon the long series of facts in human history that the phenomena of Spiritualism explains, and on the noble and satisfying theory of a future life that it unfolds."

THE PHENOMENA OF DIRECT-INDEPENDENT VOICE

Suggested Reading List

Bailey, D.E. Thoughts From The Inner Life. Colby & Rich, 1886

Barbanell, Maurice. The Trumpet Shall Sound. Rider & Co. London, 1933.

Bowers, Dr. Edwin F. The Phenomena of the Séance Room. Rider & Co., London, 1930.

Brace, Josephine M. The Descending Light. John Higgins Press, Chicago, 1922.

Bradley, Dennis H. The Wisdom of the Gods. 1925/Towards the Stars. 1928. T. Werner Laurie LTD., London.

Britt, Coleen O. Byron-Station to Station. Dale News, Inc. Lily Dale, New York/ London, 1941.

Chapman, Clive. The Blue Room. Psychic Book Club LTD., London, 1927.

Cook, Mrs.Cecil M. The Voice Triumphant. Alfred A. Knopf Co., New York, 1931.

Conacher, Douglas Chapters From Experience. Frederick Mullen Co. London 1973

Crane, H. Montague. Spirit Voices. Alex Wildey LTD., Christchurch, New Zealand. 1931.

Drouet, Bessie Clark. Station Astral G.P. Putnam's Sons., New York/London, 1932.

Duncan, Rev. V.G. Proof. G.P. Putnam's Sons. New York/London, 1932.

Eddy, Sherwood. You Will Survive After Death. Clark Publishing Company., Evanston, 111. 1950.

Findlay J. Arthur. On the Edge of The Etheric. 1931/Where Two Worlds Meet. 1951/The Way of Life. 1953 (all still in publication) Psychic Press Limited/ The Headquarters Pub. Co. LTD., London

Flint, Leslie. Voices in the Dark. The Bobbs-Merrill Company., Indianapolis/ New York. 1971.

Hack, Gwendolyn Kelly. Modem Psychic Mysteries at Millesimo Castle. Italy. Rider & Company., London. 1929.

Jebb, Robert H. Truth of Life After Death. Aird & Coghill., Glasgow. 1925

Jones, V. Carlton. And The Sound of A Voice. Ebenezer Baylis & Son LTD., Trinity Press. London 1929.

King, John (Dr.) Dawn of the Awakened Mind. James A. McCann Co, New York, 1920

Moore, Vice-Admiral W. Usborne. Glimpses of The Next State. 1911. The Voices. 1913. Watts & Co, London.

Perriman, A.E. Broadcasting From Beyond. Ebenezer Baylis & Son LTD, London 1952.

Pincock, Jenny O'Hara. The Trails of Truth. Austin Pub. Inc., Los Angeles, CA. 1930.

Remmers, John H. Is Death the End?. 1928. The Great Reality. 1967, Ebenezer Baylis & Son LTD. London.

Robertson, F.T. Celestial Voices. H.H. Greaves, London. 1945.

Sewall, Mary Wright. Neither Dead Nor Sleeping. John M. Watkins. London. 1921

The Farewell Address of Edward C. Randall

To be delivered at my funeral by minister or layman, possibly J. Boardman Scovell if the minister refuses.

Let there be just a single prayer, one not read from any book, then the Farewell, and let there be no sorrow in the home when I depart, for I go to join" Ginnie "and" Jack" and all is well.

My Thanatopsis

"Hail, and Farewell for little time. That physical body within the coffin is not me. In the death change as it is called, I emerged from that flesh garment and now stand beside the casket functioning in my own inner Etheric body as in earth life, and this moment have the same form with feature, expression and intellect as before. Nothing gained but opportunity, and nothing lost, not even memory, and I come in this manner in hope of changing the character of funeral services from gloom and sorrow, to thanksgiving and joy for a soul has passed into the reality as planned in the beginning.

"Before my death I became satisfied beyond question that life continues on, that in the democracy of death the rags of wretchedness and the purple robes of power lose distinction, and that personality survives and functions in the same inner body as in Earth Life.

"From the beginning, generation after generation have lived a day on this earth and passed through the death change, as many of the present generation are doing, yet but few in all the ages past have made any efforts to solve the problem or inquired whither they have gone.

"The hope of life beyond was not born of any book or creed. That idea like the sea has ebbed and flowed its waves beating on the shores of time, since men came up out of savagery, all wish for happiness beyond earth life-to meet again the loved and lost. Immortality is a word that Hope has whispered through the ages to all.

"For over forty years I have worked to ascertain the fact and come to know that those who have gone from the physical plane are alive today as when they lived on earth and wore a flesh garment. Death is natural, and comes to every expression and form of life, just a step in life's progression. There is no sorrow at birth, there should be none in this great change and would not be if death advantages were known, and there was less thought of self. The creative intelligence planned both and both are good. Out of the invisible we came and back to that source we go.

"I have also learned that thoughts are things, and from day to day woven like tapestries in patterns involved and strangely interlaced with dreams, hopes and fancies concerning life's great theme, as wondrous as traceries in frost wrought on glass, by winter's subtle art, all visible to those in the afterlife.

"When the gold of evening meets the dusk beneath the Western Skies the tired worker should rest. One cannot live on the earth when the flame lacks oil. When an old tree is visited by rain in spring, when the sun no longer thrills, it is not meant to stand leafless and alone. It is far better to fall where nature will softly cover its outer garment with woven moss and creeping vines, and so with man. No life of any character ever has been destroyed.

"When age creeps on with half-remembered things, over sightless eyes death presses down the lids to rest. As the inner body which alone is alive, throws off the flesh garment in the death change and leaves the world of men, you see it not, no physical sound is made and you cannot hear the words of welcome that greet the newborn soul.

"That something you call death is a great inheritance. When one can scarcely read the blurred and faded pages of the past, enters the open door, sees another world beautiful beyond comparison, hears words of greeting fall from the lips of the living dead, they realize how a great privilege is theirs for then will come from the center of space music of the spheres, for all was planned in the beginning by the God Force for our good, and such should be a time of rejoicing among those left as well as those who have gone before. To challenge the necessity of the death change, is to challenge the wisdom of God.

"When the afternoon grows short like mine, the twilight falls like a benediction at the close of day, and it was time to go. I knew the end was near and I went gladly knowing that those I loved, who had preceded me, and thousands of earthbound souls I had helped in my secret mission work on the other side would welcome and help me, even as I had helped them.

"Earth life is one of the preparations for the reality into which I have entered. A thousand years is but yesterday when it is past, for in that domain there is no time, and knowing something of the plan and purpose of the creative intelligence I was prepared in a measure, and do not I pray, enter the next state with empty hands. The universe is governed by law, and of that law, without bias or preconceived notions I became a student, which led me into the psychic field.

"For a long period of time I have talked voice to voice with the living dead and know something of conditions into which I have entered. No soul is ever lost. On by one in the years that I have lived, those I have loved and who have loved me and nearly all my friends have crossed the great divide, but I have kept in touch with them and know where and how they live, how they labor and serve and continue to progress, and that through such service earn their advancement.

"I would leave as a heritage to this poor world, the idea or thought that the funeral ceremony should be changed from tears and sorrow, to laughter and joy, for the greatest privilege after birth is death, so called, and among earth people should be a period of rejoicing, and would be if those that are left could forget self and their personal loss and think of the advantage a loved one has gained, as they go on to higher progression and greater happiness and opportunity, and I ask you who have gathered her to have no sorrow or regret on my account, but give or send thoughts and love, words of congratulation and good cheer for my work on earth was done, and youth and strength and new courage is now mine to carry on.

"Had Tennyson when he wrote "Crossing the Bar" known that to die and live again was the greatest blessing the God force has provided for mankind he would have made that great poem read:

Sun and Evening Star
As the call comes for me
Let there be no mourning in the home
When I go out to sea

Twilight and Evening Bells And after that the dark Let there be no sorrow In the heart when I embark

Day break and morning light Bring renewed life force to me The dawn of everlasting life, Has come and I am free.

"As you come across the border one by one, I will mingle with your friends and bid you welcome, and possibly in some measure aid in your adjustment and understanding.

I have told but little of the knowledge that I have gained, for the public as well as my friends were not ready to receive it. Perhaps these words from a living dead man may impress you and help you understand the change of conditions, for there is no death, there are no dead, and it is well to know something of the journey's end.

Again, Hail and Farewell for little time, we shall meet again.

And now as an evidence of my sincerity, and to illustrate what a funeral service should be like, I ask you in passing out to join me in a glass of wine, and toast "the living and the living dead."

ABOUT THE AUTHOR

N. Riley Heagerty has been involved in Psychic Research since 1985. After attending Oswego State University in the 1970's, he was a professional musician for almost twenty years. Following the untimely death of his fiance', he dedicated his life to research involving life after death, the past history of Spiritualism and the physical phenomena which occurred in the presence of certain spiritual mediums.

The French Revelation, his first work, is the outcome of this research and deals with the phenomena of Direct-Independent Voice with the medium, Emily S.French. N. Riley Heagerty was, for many years, the American contact of and lead researcher for the Noah's Ark Society, England. Riley's second book, *The Mediumship of the Bangs Sisters,* will be published by White Crow Books in 2015.

Other research and published articles by N.Riley Heagerty can be accessed by any Google search and at his blogsite: the frenchrevelation.wordpress.com and he can be contacted at nrileyh@hotmail.com

Paperbacks also available from White Crow Books

Elsa Barker—*Letters from a Living Dead Man*
ISBN 978-1-907355-83-7

Elsa Barker—*War Letters from the Living Dead Man*
ISBN 978-1-907355-85-1

Elsa Barker—*Last Letters from the Living Dead Man*
ISBN 978-1-907355-87-5

Richard Maurice Bucke—*Cosmic Consciousness*
ISBN 978-1-907355-10-3

Arthur Conan Doyle—*The Edge of the Unknown*
ISBN 978-1-907355-14-1

Arthur Conan Doyle—*The New Revelation*
ISBN 978-1-907355-12-7

Arthur Conan Doyle—*The Vital Message*
ISBN 978-1-907355-13-4

Arthur Conan Doyle with Simon Parke—*Conversations with Arthur Conan Doyle*
ISBN 978-1-907355-80-6

Meister Eckhart with Simon Parke—*Conversations with Meister Eckhart*
ISBN 978-1-907355-18-9

D. D. Home—*Incidents in my Life Part 1*
ISBN 978-1-907355-15-8

Mme. Dunglas Home; edited, with an Introduction, by Sir Arthur Conan Doyle—*D. D. Home: His Life and Mission*
ISBN 978-1-907355-16-5

Edward C. Randall—*Frontiers of the Afterlife*
ISBN 978-1-907355-30-1

Rebecca Ruter Springer—*Intra Muros: My Dream of Heaven*
ISBN 978-1-907355-11-0

Leo Tolstoy, edited by Simon Parke—*Forbidden Words*
ISBN 978-1-907355-00-4

Leo Tolstoy—*A Confession*
ISBN 978-1-907355-24-0

Leo Tolstoy—*The Gospel in Brief*
ISBN 978-1-907355-22-6

Leo Tolstoy—*The Kingdom of God is Within You*
ISBN 978-1-907355-27-1

Leo Tolstoy—*My Religion: What I Believe*
ISBN 978-1-907355-23-3

Leo Tolstoy—*On Life*
ISBN 978-1-907355-91-2

Leo Tolstoy—*Twenty-three Tales*
ISBN 978-1-907355-29-5

Leo Tolstoy—*What is Religion and other writings*
ISBN 978-1-907355-28-8

Leo Tolstoy—*Work While Ye Have the Light*
ISBN 978-1-907355-26-4

Leo Tolstoy—*The Death of Ivan Ilyich*
ISBN 978-1-907661-10-5

Leo Tolstoy—*Resurrection*
ISBN 978-1-907661-09-9

Leo Tolstoy with Simon Parke—*Conversations with Tolstoy*
ISBN 978-1-907355-25-7

Howard Williams with an Introduction by Leo Tolstoy—*The Ethics of Diet: An Anthology of Vegetarian Thought*
ISBN 978-1-907355-21-9

Vincent Van Gogh with Simon Parke—*Conversations with Van Gogh*
ISBN 978-1-907355-95-0

Wolfgang Amadeus Mozart with Simon Parke—*Conversations with Mozart*
ISBN 978-1-907661-38-9

Jesus of Nazareth with Simon Parke—
Conversations with Jesus of Nazareth
ISBN 978-1-907661-41-9

Thomas à Kempis with Simon Parke—*The Imitation of Christ*
ISBN 978-1-907661-58-7

Julian of Norwich with Simon Parke—*Revelations of Divine Love*
ISBN 978-1-907661-88-4

Allan Kardec—*The Spirits Book*
ISBN 978-1-907355-98-1

Allan Kardec—*The Book on Mediums*
ISBN 978-1-907661-75-4

Emanuel Swedenborg—*Heaven and Hell*
ISBN 978-1-907661-55-6

P.D. Ouspensky—*Tertium Organum: The Third Canon of Thought*
ISBN 978-1-907661-47-1

Dwight Goddard—*A Buddhist Bible*
ISBN 978-1-907661-44-0

Michael Tymn—*The Afterlife Revealed*
ISBN 978-1-970661-90-7

Michael Tymn—*Transcending the Titanic: Beyond Death's Door*
ISBN 978-1-908733-02-3

Guy L. Playfair—*If This Be Magic*
ISBN 978-1-907661-84-6

Guy L. Playfair—*The Flying Cow*
ISBN 978-1-907661-94-5

Guy L. Playfair —*This House is Haunted*
ISBN 978-1-907661-78-5

Carl Wickland, M.D.—
Thirty Years Among the Dead
ISBN 978-1-907661-72-3

John E. Mack—*Passport to the Cosmos*
ISBN 978-1-907661-81-5

Peter & Elizabeth Fenwick—
The Truth in the Light
ISBN 978-1-908733-08-5

Erlendur Haraldsson—
Modern Miracles
ISBN 978-1-908733-25-2

Erlendur Haraldsson—
At the Hour of Death
ISBN 978-1-908733-27-6

Erlendur Haraldsson—
The Departed Among the Living
ISBN 978-1-908733-29-0

Brian Inglis—*Science and Parascience*
ISBN 978-1-908733-18-4

Brian Inglis—*Natural and Supernatural: A History of the Paranormal*
ISBN 978-1-908733-20-7

Ernest Holmes—*The Science of Mind*
ISBN 978-1-908733-10-8

Victor & Wendy Zammit —*A Lawyer Presents the Evidence For the Afterlife*
ISBN 978-1-908733-22-1

Casper S. Yost—*Patience Worth: A Psychic Mystery*
ISBN 978-1-908733-06-1

William Usborne Moore—
Glimpses of the Next State
ISBN 978-1-907661-01-3

William Usborne Moore—
The Voices
ISBN 978-1-908733-04-7

John W. White—
The Highest State of Consciousness
ISBN 978-1-908733-31-3

Stafford Betty—
The Imprisoned Splendor
ISBN 978-1-907661-98-3

Paul Pearsall, Ph.D. —
Super Joy
ISBN 978-1-908733-16-0

All titles available as eBooks, and selected titles available in Hardback and Audiobook formats from www.whitecrowbooks.com

www.ingramcontent.com/pod-product-compliance
Lightning Source LLC
Chambersburg PA
CBHW031943080426
42735CB00007B/237
9781910121467

PAUL
SEXTON

HER SOUL BLED OUT

A POST MODERN POETRY NOVEL

BLACK NICKEL PUBLISHING
DALLAS, TX 2009

n

Her Soul Bled Out: A Post Modern Poetry Novel by Paul Sexto

Black Nickel Publishing
Po box 860-337
Plano, TX 75086

ACKNOWLEDGEMENTS

The Author would like to thank all of the people that made this book possible.

D.Anson Brody, Project Manager,

Roderick Richardson, Devorah Titunik, Jack T. Marlowe, Janice Brewer -Early Draft Edits

Crystal Dozier, Final Editor

Cover art from photo by Johnny O.

ISBN 978-0-578-01453-1

http://www.myspace.com/paulsextonpoet

For Lexy

Table of Contents (Poetry)

HER SOUL BLED OUT

A POST MODERN POETRY NOVEL

hummingbird

I was outside on the patio
doing bench press
surrounded by flowers and
bushes and trees.

I'd finished a set
then sat up to rest for a moment.

Directly in front of me was a
Hummingbird.
I could see it clearly.
It's frantic wings
darting from place to place
flower to flower
taking what it needs to survive.

It seemed like time stopped
as I, and this beautiful thing
existed together in
a frozen moment.

It was beautiful.

The kind of beauty that
lingers
forever.

Then,
suddenly, it was gone.

I went back to my bench,
but I was different than before.

It reminded me
of you.

Her Soul Bled Out

10/03/07

There is something wrong, she said.
This can't be all there is,
all we are alive for, she said.
Sometimes I just want to give it up,
not go on,
Other times I feel like
I'm giving in,
losing the important part of myself,
my soul, bit by bit, at the edges
giving it up to the day by day.
It's painful, this existence as an artist,
with this need.

No one ever really understands me.
My boyfriend doesn't get me.
He thinks I'm wasting my time with music.
He feels threatened by my true self.
You know, it's weird to realize
that you are with someone
that you've never actually had
a decent conversation with.
A conversation about something real
like you and I are having right now.

Even places I go around other musicians,
no one really gets me.
It's like I let my soul bleed out
into the air too much, expose too much.
It's weird to even find someone that gets this,
that gets me.

It all seemed so understandable,
so familiar.

I listened to her sing and play her guitar
a second time.
I had listened the first time
and loved her voice.
Long, slow soulful notes
bleeding out melancholy into the room.
But the second time

I heard her words.
They were all her own words,
and they were about the exact things that
we had been talking about.
I got it, I got her.
I started to cry a little.
It felt like I feel. Like me.
I really, really, got it.

Her voice was like warm, smooth honey
poured over a pale, yellow moon.
beautiful beyond reckoning.
Like the birth of something real.
What she was singing
and saying was real.

I loved it, I loved it, I loved it.
She looked over and saw my face,
small tears and all while she was playing
and smiled at me. A lot.

After, she said, it's an incredible thing
when someone gets you,
gets what you do, but you know that
you've been doing it for a long time.
That's why you do it.
Yeah, I said, it sure is something.

I pleaded with her to do some of my shows.
We hugged goodbye softly, and I left.

I could love a great artist like that.
I could really love a great artist like that.
Because in all the world
nothing, I repeat nothing
deserves true real love and understanding
more than a great artist like that,
and like me

sometimes

10/07/07 Sunday

I met a new friend this week. She plays and sings and writes songs. An awesome talent with an amazing voice and presence. Overwhelming really. She's very gung-ho about working with me and promoting, performing, all of it. You will hear more, very soon. She inspired something, some vibe I think.

10/09/07 Tuesday

The Sacred Way. The wind blows surprisingly positive today. It's the bliss of following the sacred path. YES, my world is in chaos. The people that come and go and stomp upon the poor poet's heart and exist in timeframes exceeding the speed of reason, they still explode, they explode leaving tattered shadows. It's never ending it is. But I walk a sacred path, I do! The path of the artist. You either get it, or you don't. Fallen angels, beautiful devils. Machiavellian misfits...

I got to take my new singer friend Lexy to the Mic in Fort Worth last night. I was already in Fort Worth when she called, but told her I wasn't, turned around and drove miles back. Picked up her and her sister at a coffee shop. There was a really positive vibe. I needed it. Everyone was real. I was real. Lexy was incredible. What a find! What a talent! Yet, she seems so, perhaps... misunderstood? In the sacred path. All the thoughts and struggles and fears and needs that all we artists have, that both uplift and destroy us. Such a joy to hear my words I think, about the culture, the angst, about Art, and being an artist, the creative force within, the muse , the manifestation, the struggle against Corpocracy, the existential, Sunyata, the grind, on love and life and truth. OH! So grand to talk of such things to someone to whom either, as most of my poets friends are already living so immersed in such things all the time it is no new deal, or as with other companions it doesn't matter because they are sadly of the world, or at least they think that they are, choose to be. Even the ones that aren't or shouldn't be. At any rate, no more joy than to share the whispered words of the sacred path, the Shaman path, that of the poet, of the creator. What a way to escape from ones self. To rise above. I feel more my true self in sharing these things than I have in a while. Less mired in the mundane-ities of the day by day, and more in connection with self of my true face. In other words, bliss. Heh!. When I mentioned to Josh the other day about her, the things she says, how excited she is to meet like minds. He laughed, said we ought to have initiation rites at times like these. Black robes and candles. Some profane rituals. Heh. True, it is a rite of blood, this sacred path. The artist's path.

10/11/07 Thursday

Early this morning, my mom saw a listing in the paper for poetry in Mansfield. We actually met the lady hosting it once in FW, not the best get along I'd say. Wasn't sure it was her, but I hadn't been out, so I called Lexy, who happens to live down there. Told her about it. Message, she called back later when I was in the gym. (weird, sometimes you meet people who ACTUALLY return phone calls!) said yep. We made a plan to meet out there. KIDS!!!! I tell ya! We, she and I, we OWNED IT!! Wow! There were some nice interesting cool folks, but she and I were like top professionals! It was incredible. My new friend is very talented. Incredible talent, voice, style, just a huge, huge fan of her work. I was really on it myself. Did three sets of 2 poems, especially the set where I had 2 memorized... wow.. I had them eating out of the Palm (psalm?) of my hand. It was an awesome feeling... really good. I told Lexy later, how she and I had really both pulled it off. It's weird that she is nowhere NEAR as confident or even as egotistical as she should be with her talent. She was like "Really?" I said " Hey, when it was all over, who was EVERYONE talking to, chatting up, getting website and email info from, complimenting. All that... yeah.... ME...and YOU. She smiled real big. It was cool. Plus she is one hell of a networker! She was really talking people up. Talking about her new gig, the Sunday event, all the gigs...wow....how awesome to have someone who talks that shit up as good as me. I can't wait to mix her up more with my poets Saturday and Sunday night.......great, great, great!

10/21/07 Sunday

What a grand time we are having !!! It feels like one of those moments when the open mic scene is really grooving. It makes me eat my bliss. When there's enough stuff happening, there's something for everyone. I love all the voices, I NEED all the voices. Not only to survive, but to thrive. I'm blessed sometimes, despite the painful indignities we poet Shaman must endure, the ridiculous inequities. We're sometimes blessed with the grooviness. The grooviness of the voices. Hell, yeah! Last night was great. Lexy's new gig is really nice. A coffeehouse on a Saturday night, a nice large space at that, it makes for a different vibe than some of the other stuff . I can bring my boys on the two Saturdays that they're here. They were happy. They BOTH read. Nan was magnificent. He owns his space. He even sat and wrote something new for the second round. Everyone was blown away. Lexy said that he was like a smaller version of me. She did a marvelous job! WOW! What can I say about this new friend. She is overwhelmingly talented and passionate about her art. We have had such long all night in-depth conversations about life, suffering, art, meaning, value, all of it. I find myself inspired and renewed. What a **serendipitous meeting of human artistic souls!**

Windshield Wipers

10/18/07

I thought my windshield wipers, in the fog,
sounded like a distant thunder.

I thought that I kept seeing flashes of light
out of the corners of my eyes
while in the cubicle.

I thought I heard the far off sound of a dog
injured and howling,
while in the shower.

I thought that a woman in the street
was saying that she wanted to make love to me
but not with her voice
only ***with her eyes and her smile****.*
I thought that the faces of notorious men
gazed upon me with recognition
from black and white photos on a wall.

I thought that a woman I loved was done with me,
then she rang me on the telephone
and spoke about nothing in particular.

I thought that my bank account was overdrawn
but I only needed 4 cents
and I had until 8pm to make it in.

I thought that art was everything
and that there was nothing else.

Then I thought that art had abandoned me
and that there was absolutely nothing anywhere.

Then I thought that no woman would ever love me
again.

Then I thought that all women would love me
if only I could learn to love myself again.
Then I realized that women are incapable of love,
and that loving one's self is redundant if breathing,
and that art can never abandon anyone.

It's not like a mythic god or a false notion.
It is simply everything.
and that there is absolutely nothing anywhere,
anyway.

I thought that ***tornados were touching down***
out the window.

I thought that the winter would repeat itself again*.*
I thought that people's faces looked like demon rats.

I thought that monotone voices were **whispering**
secret thing*s in my ear,*
educational voices
serious voices
and they spoke to me
of women and love
of art and truth
of Sumer and Babylon
of poverty and disconnection
of penis and vagina
of sacrifice and fire
of dead philosophers and poets
of transitional quantum dimensional planes.
of Spiritus Mundi Synchronicity

I thought that the voices would never end
and they didn't.
It all kept doing what it was doing
even more
than before.

The way I moved through a scene

10/24/07

I was sitting at a table in the Sunshine Bar, it was loud, very loud. I was more than a little drunk, having just co-hosted our big crazy drunken monthly Fun City open mic, across the street at the Good Times Bar. My poets were milling about. In fact there were wall to wall people I knew there that night. Some very well, some a little. Some I liked, some not so much. I was thinking about it all; the last heartbreak across the way and to the left, the next one close by on the right, but it will be quick and like a band aid, from here on out. Never be drawn out and painful again, I think.

To my left, up by the bar, I see one of my best drinking buddies, Shane. He'd been at my show and we'd seen him earlier at dinner, talking over noodles about recording a demo. Some loud drunk dude was cursing the female bartender, one of Shane's friends. He told the guy not to speak to her like that, to get up and leave. The dude told Shane to "**shut the fuck up.**" I saw his eyes glance my direction as he repeated his request. I stood up. They were four steps away. I took three. Before I reached them, the dude stood up and sucker punched Shane in the mouth. Say what you will about Shane, he's not perfect, but he's not violent. In fact, he gets quite stressed when my co-host buddy Josh shows his rowdy drunk violent side. I can't count how many times Shane has been there for me, drunk in a mud puddle, crying out my broke up heart over a dame. This is the guy that's there. So as one can imagine, not so thrilled with the sucker punch. I reach the dude a second later, grab his shoulder. He spins around, and the dumb motherfucker has the audacity to swing on me! Seriously, no kidding. Perhaps he didn't really have time to get a good look first. I was in close so his pussy right hook barely made it half way up before I got a hold of him, brushed his blow aside and pushed him down onto the rail with my hands around his throat. Someone was saying something, and grabbing at my arm, to the right. As I was listening Josh got up close, said the dude was gasping out the words "help me, help me, help me," I suppose barely able to breath with me throttling him. So he went ahead and sucker punched him a couple times. I grabbed the dude up, pushed him towards the door. The bar manager came and took him from me, probably a good thing considering I was drunk as hell and probably would have smacked the dumb mother fucker around a bit outside. They tossed him, and wouldn't let all my screaming buddies out as the dude ran like hell for his car, I assume, suddenly quite aware that he had picked the way wrong guy to punch on the way wrong night.

Shortly after, everyone piled outside, said all the goodbyes, got in cars and drove away. When we got back to my place the girls stepped in to piss before driving home. While Lexy's sister Tonya was in the john, rattling fan sound in the background, I looked Lexy in the eyes and said; "Hey, I hope you don't think ill of me, seriously I'm really not like that, OK? I'm not violent and I don't usually go smacking dudes around, it's a pretty rare occurrence actually." She took my hands and looked me in the eyes and smiled and says "No, it's not like that, I totally get it! You were taking up for your friend, you care about your friend, I get that. It was quite chivalrous. It's OK, better, in fact it makes me feel safe, like whenever we're together, I know that you'll protect me." This lights me up. This one, she always knows just exactly the absolutely perfect things to say, every time, she always has just the right words in just the right way. It's astonishing, it borders on_unbelievable. The mood now is all smiles as she gives me a nice long hug goodbye. I even pull her sister in and we all laugh together as we hug.

Then it's done, Time to sleep and wake and sober up. Walk into the world of gray and light that destroys shadow. It's nothing, really, these nights. The art of it all is spoken out loud and then disappears forever. The buddies are there until they are dead and gone. The drunk assholes that want a fight are never any kind of real challenge anymore. They are less than nothing. And the women, no matter where they sit, ones who never said enough or ones who say exactly the right thing, it doesn't really matter in the end. Because they will never love me, they never will because they never do, and even when they do sometimes, it's only a flicker. A fallen shadow sliding away, and all that there is really, are nights like this, and the smiles and laughter at the end of it all.

Hot Black Tar on Her Heart

10/28/07

She said
that it felt like
I had poured
hot black tar
over her heart,
and she cried.

This turned my breath heavy
and made the air swirl
with a squeezing regret.

Dear Girl,
I hope you know
that I would never tar
your heart so.
I didn't mean it.

I hope you know
That if I ever need to push you away
It would be out of mature self-preservation,
but with the greatest affection.

I hope you know
that all apologies are sincere
that I do not in any way find you naive
or lacking in wisdom,
quite the opposite,
your truth and wisdom and insight
are a beacon
in my dark night.

Let's wipe clean that hot black tar
off your gentle heart
and dry these tears.

I am here.

HALLOWEEN

"What happened last night?" She asked. "I was worried when you didn't show up to Mochalux, are you ok? Anything I can do to help?" "Yeah, I guess so." I responded. "So what is it?" "Are you upset about something?" "Yeah, it's us Lexy, I can't do this anymore, it's fucking me up. I'm an honorable man, you know I would never try to hit on somebody's girlfriend. I thought we could be friends, but we can't. We've developed this intense emotional affair. Nothing dishonorable, but Craig knows it, how close we have become. That's why he hates me, was shitty to me. That's bad enough, spending all night with you, every night, taking you home at 4am to him. But now this Anson guy is suddenly here and he doesn't have my sense of honor. Hanging all over you in front of me. It's unbearable. It makes me so fucking jealous, and you're not even mine to be jealous of, you're Craig's. But he's not here, not in front of me, but this Anson guy is. If this is the way it's going to be, I can't do it. We need to get some space, be not as close." There was a long moment of silence. "I.... I gotta go, call you later." She hung up. I got out of the car, walked into the gym, did a half-decent workout.

A few hours later, I was home lying in bed when she called. " Are you ok?" I asked. "Not really, I've been crying, I went and took the dog for a run to try to run out this energy, but it didn't work. Craig came in and saw me crying, asked what was up. I couldn't tell him. Just yesterday when we were talking about breaking up, I was ready, had no emotion, was cold. It is time. I couldn't tell him that I was crying over you. That you pushing me away made me cry, but he didn't." "I'm sorry I made you cry," I said, "I didn't mean to." She said, "When you said those words to me, It felt like you poured hot black melted tar on my heart. I couldn't move, couldn't breathe, my heart was in slow motion, it was terrible. Why are you doing this?" "Listen, Lexy," I said "It's not that I don't care about you, it's that I care too much. Seriously, I've been so lonely for a long time, so sad. If you had come to my closest female friends a month ago, Janice, Grace, Opal, with some magic ability, what does Paul need to be happy? Design the perfect woman, the way she thinks and believes and speaks and feels and behaves, they would have 100 percent created you. You are my perfect woman. You appeared for me like destiny at the exact right time in the exact right way. Only, the gods are cruel, you're not available. We have already created this intense connection and even though I feel no love for Craig, he is a fellow man, and I feel guilty about having an emotional affair with his woman. I guess I justified it because you keep talking about breaking up soon anyway. But this thing you're doing with Anson, him hitting on you and hanging on you, it's too much for me. It shows me how strong my feelings already are, and you're not even mine. Regardless of what the future might or might not bring, lets not do this. I know me, I know what's going to happen. I'm going to fall desperately in love with you and act like a fool, Let's just skip it please, get some distance, just be friends, ride separately, we'll still see each other and if it's meant to be, we'll grow close slowly regardless of what happens, OK?" We talked for well over an hour more, many things were said. By the end it wasn't really clear what we were doing. She liked things the way they were.

Three days later it was Halloween, she drove to my house. We went to the music open mic in Dallas across the street from the Mad Swirl. The one that had been cancelled on the first Wednesday when we met, and moved to Halloween night. My old buddy Tim Miranda met us up there on his Harley. We drank some expensive freaken beer. However, I covered half of it with a 50 dollar prize she won for sexiest costume. She was dressed like a slutty devil or something. It was hot. She was the sexiest dame in the bar. Hell, she may have been the sexiest dame on the planet. On stage she played a new song. My buddy Tim leaned over and said, "Hey, that's for that Anson dude." "I know" I said. **It made me literally physically ill to hear it. A churning anger inside. I hated it, I really fucking hated it!** "I'm about done with this shit" I told Tim. "Don't be like that." he said, "you give up too easy, you can overcome that guy, I've seen you, just be a man." "Fuck it," I said. "I don't want to overcome shit anymore, I don't care how perfect for me she is, If I have to overcome some fucking dude, it will always be some fucking dude, it'll be never ending, I need love, not struggle." "It's always struggle my friend." Tim said "That's unavoidable, you just have to decide is she's worth it."

A little later, she said, "I talked to Anson about the flirting thing, you were right it's not fair to Craig, I told him we had to stop." "That's not what I said," I said. "I don't really give a shit about Craig, I was talking about me. "She looked at me for a moment, then said "Well, either way it's over, I'll just have to deal with the thing with me and him**." She was so pretty I wanted to kiss her really hard. She was so self-involved I wanted to kick her goddam ass**. A little while later, before we left, she disappeared for a while, Anson was nowhere in sight as well. Tim shook his head at me said ' You better step up brother before it's too late." then rode off on his bike. She appeared, we left.

My buddy Shane was celebrating his Halloween birthday at the nearby Goth club called The Church. We went and found him. It was insane, a Goth club on Halloween. A girl with nothing but electrical tape on her nipples practically molested me while Lex was in the bathroom. She said "mmmm, baby I'll be back to see you when I change my shoes!" I have no idea what that meant. We found Shane, in his orange space suit. We sat with him for a while. Some cheesy ass fucker came over, sat and started getting in the middle of my conversation with Alexcie. Shane had recently read *'The Game,'* a book about manipulating women to fuck them. One of my good friends Julie, that I was working an open mic with, had suggested it. She had discovered her children's father was teaching classes on infidelity, charming. Shane said he was only reading it to protect us from scammers hitting on our women. Drunk as hell he came over and told the dude "Hey! My friend is talking to a lady, you need to step the fuck off, OK?" The dude split and Shane took his chair. He and I had previously spoken about Lexy's impending breakup with Craig and her needing a place to stay. Shane had a house with a spare room I sometimes used when I had drunk female friend overnighters. We talked about it and he offered her the room for a while if she needed it. She said "Look, I'm not going to fuck you for a place to stay if that's what you're thinking." Shane laughed and said "I totally wasn't thinking that!" "Then why would you offer to help me?" she asked. "Because Paul is one of my best friends and you and he are close. He cares a lot about you and I would do this to help him out." She looked at me and I said "Seriously, Shane is an honorable guy, I wouldn't have asked him about it if I didn't trust you being in his house."

When we got back to my place, where her car was, we sat and talked in the street for long time like we always do. About anything and everything. It got really late and Craig kept calling. She gave me a really sweet tight beautiful hug, something she does better than anyone I've ever known, before driving off. As I watched her drive off, I thought "man, I'm screwed." We're not going to get any distance. Craig is still pissed off. She will be at Shane's house. It's not over with this Anson guy, that goddamn song tells me that. And worst of all, I am already head over heels hopelessly in love with her. This is not a good idea, not a good idea at all. This is going to hurt.

Spiritus Veritas

11/01/2007

I just want something real,
he said
I just want something real,
he said.

This common experience.
This shared suffering.
This birth into tragedy that has shaped us so.
Demented us so.
Made us artists.
Let our spirits soar.
I just want the real experience now.
The authentic.
I suffer for it.
I await it.
I yearn for it.
This is the truth I toss about in
meandering lines.
We are in a space outside the tribe.
We are the neurotic episode.
We are heaven's offerings unto the dirt.

I don't want the ones who hide from it
wearing the hiding like a mask.
I don't want the ones who fester in it
wearing the festering like a mask.

Let us transcend it.
Let us overcome it.
Let us be all at once above it.
Let us enlighten ourselves with the healing of it.
Let our spirits sing.
Let our words be divine.
Let us be more and more and more
than the mere circumstance of it.

Faith! Faith! Faith! Faith!
Faith! Faith! Faith! Faith!
Goodbye to being, hello becoming.

I just want something real,

he said.
I just want something real,
he said.

I'm not sure what I want
she said.
Something altogether different.
I think.
Come and be
real with me.

White Lace Skirt

11/07/07

There was this girl
and she wore a soft white
lace skirt.

And the way it
fell upon
the dark skin
of her soft brown legs,
made me think of snowfall
on predawn mountaintops.
It made me think of
cotton cumulus cloud forms
mixed with dark thunder ones.

And when she stood up
or sat down
or walked by,
the way the silky
garment slid around against
her warm living blood pulsing flesh,
made me think of
Summer breeze,
diving kites with flickering tails.
A pond with swans
upon it.
It made me think of
Polar icecaps
and volcano lava.

It made me think of star-filled nights
slipping away sand castles
orange Autumn leaves
spiraling groundward.
Spring rain.
Daffodils
yellow lightning
city streets
Christmas trees
waterfalls
goldfish
the Rings of Saturn

a spinning wheel
whispers
wild applause and
a million, million
other things.
It was just white lace cloth
on dark flesh.
A skirt, a pair of legs,
The various movements of being alive.
But for a moment,
it seemed as if everything
that ever was
or ever could be
was right there
in front of me.

And I think
It was.

FATAL FLAW

11/08/07 - with music co-written with Michael Miranda.

Here I am, here I am, right here in front of you
Here I am, here I am, right here in front of you
I am the one, not like anyone,
right here in front of you
not an echo, not a shadow, not an encore
no repeat performance
If only you, could see me here, see it through
right here in front of you.
I could be your somebody.
I could be your somebody.
I could be your somebody.

You've given up, you've given in
come to believe nobody's out there.
But it's not true, we're not alone
I am here, I am here, I am here
I'm the one that you've been waiting for.
I'm the one that you've been waiting for.
Faith would move you past your fatal flaw,
your fatal flaw
Faith would move you past your fatal flaw,
your fatal flaw

I change your direction
I'm your reflection, at home in your affections
it's that connection,
It is me, it is me, it is me.
If only you would believe.
I'm the one that you've been waiting for.
I'm the one that you've been waiting for.
Faith would move you past your fatal flaw,
your fatal flaw
Faith would move you past your fatal flaw,
your fatal flaw

In an instant, what you see in me
If you would believe in me
What you could be, what you feel
we would surely be, we would surely be.
I'm the one that you've been waiting for.
I'm the one that you've been waiting for.

Faith would move you past your fatal flaw,
your fatal flaw
Faith would move you past your fatal flaw,
your fatal flaw

I'd lick my wounds and come alive,
be reborn against the sky
begin again, be your best friend,
your final end.
live again inside of you.
finally knowing there is something true

I'm the one that you've been waiting for.
I'm the one that you've been waiting for.
Faith would move you past your fatal flaw,
your fatal flaw
Faith would move you past your fatal flaw,
your fatal flaw.

Right here in front of you
Right here in front of you

11/10/07 Saturday

Morn job... Blech! It's two of my kids birthday party today! Nan and Ari. Neighbor kid, niece, Lexy's two nephews.. Fun fun fun. Clean up, take the kids home, then to OUR Open Mic! An awesome evening! God I love OUR stuff together!

11/18/07 Sunday

Damn!! Lexy and I were up LATE doing that intense thing we do. Talking about anything and everything. Ideas that go to the very core of existence, of the human soul, suffering and joy, life and non-life. All of our experiences and ideas. The best times always seem to happen at 4 AM, why is that?!? I haven't enjoyed anyone or anything as much as I am enjoying Lexy and our gigs together right now, in a long time, If ever!

11/20/07 Tuesday

Morn job!!! BORING!... nap? Stuff with kids?... not sure....see if Lexy needs anything. BOY we had a grand night last night, so much powerful energy... Panther...8.0...Shine.. ALL these weird positive energies ALL NIGHT, and the dear... damn... damn...we spent the wee hours talking it AGAIN! I'm so crazy, she's not mine! Even knowing that heartbreak is mere inches away, somehow still able to have this glorious time, this glorious feeling of connectedness... of not despair GODS GODS GODS!! If only this would last forever, WE would last forever! Today?...I dunno... we'll see.. play it by ear I suppose.....

11/24/07 Saturday

Cartoons... My kids are supposed to have a play date with Lexy's nephews... I think the boys enjoy spending time with each other as much as I do with her, it's the best! Then OUR OPEN MIC tonight! Should be great. Despite the thing... stuff is pretty grand!

IT WAS ONE NIGHT: NOVEMBER

It was one night in November. Exactly a month after we met, at the same mic, when she tells me they had broken up. I'd always been honest with her from the start about what she does to me. We were so close, I could feel our energy perfectly in synch. We were walking the sidewalk back into the bar after the break where everyone smokes and drinks trunk whiskey. We were holding hands. It was the most beautiful feeling. I felt alive and in love. Everyone was asking about us. I looked into her eyes and she said "Are you about to kiss me?" For some inexplicable reason, I said "no" and that was that. Shortly after, we had her at Shane's. She knew I loved her but she never gave me a chance, not even a consideration, then again I never really asked her to, never tried. I was scared of my own emotions, to scared to make even the effort I would have made with a dozen other women I didn't love so desperately. Her offhanded rejection of me, unlike any I had experienced, was an excruciating blow. She fell unexpectedly into a deep depression over the ex-boyfriend. I fell into deep depression over her

I was trying to be there for her, trying not to think of myself. Of course there was the bass player, Anson. He was around sometimes, but mostly when I wasn't. It seemed like it might be him instead of me. It was undoubtedly the most painful thing I've ever known. The first fight we ever had was about him. It bothered her that he was hanging around a girl named Amy. That bothering her bothered me. We were driving down the highway on the night we lost our Sunday gig. We loved that gig. It seems like some of the light went out of the scene, and out of us, that night.

Chess with My Son

11/11/07

"You were playing chess with my son last night." I said, with the first tears this whole thing would bring me, in my eyes. "Should I not have?" He looks puzzled and a little nervous. "No, it's not that," I say, "It's just that's how my poet mind works, in images with emotional resonance. Now that I have this image of you playing chess with my son It would be difficult to kick your ass." "Do you want to?" He asked. "No, it's not that, I like you, we are similar in many respects, it's just that we've been cast in this role as rivals, it feels uncontrollable. I tried to get some distance when you came around, but it hurt her and I couldn't. With everything she's going through, I've become the one that's there for her, really involved, day to day, emotionally, taking care of her, feeding her, listening to her, hell, gassing her car. I'm all in." "I like you to!" He said, I don't want that either, I feel really bad here, like I'm messing up whatever this guy I really like is trying to do. "Seriously man, I'm not trying to do anything," I said "I know, it seems weird. Any dude would have an agenda, some angle; I am really, really trying hard not to be like that. I'm trying to be unselfish and just be there for someone I'm really loving, without selfish motives in the equation for now. We got close way too quick and now I've become *'helping her through the breakup guy,'* which is OK. But it already looks like you are going to be *'rebound guy.'* Which, shit happens, I've looked like a fool before, not this bad, it's just that as crazy as it sounds in such a short time, I already really love her, almost instantly, I've never met anyone like her, where we get each other on these levels. I have this code of honor, it's everything to me. I know I shouldn't have gotten so close to someone that was with someone else, but I made excuses, justifications, now I can't walk away. I can see this road, especially seeing how she is with you, but I can't stop. I'm doing everything for her now, taking care of her, emotionally, listening, feeding her, drinks, all of it." He told me about a mentor that he'd been talking to about the situation. A psychologist. He had told him that there were certain kinds of girls that need to keep three or more men under their influence, maybe don't even realize it, or why, but that it is a very poisonous dynamic spiritually. The bartender at the bar we were standing in front of, my friend Julie, had been telling me the same thing.

"What should we do?" he asked. "Look man; let me be clear, I am not trying to tell you what to do. I don't control people; as much as I'd like to here, it goes against everything I am. But, I do control myself. I have a code of honor I try to live by. What I'm asking for is honor in return. That's all. If it turns out to be you and not me, with all this time, emotion and energy invested, it's only fair that I know, before if possible, so that I can, in an honorable fashion, walk away. Get some distance. Retain some dignity. Not be the fool, the patsy. Like I say, right now, no agenda, just trying to be unselfish, be there for someone I love and see what happens naturally, seriously. It's just hard when you're around. "We agreed. We shook hands on It. He liked the unselfish put it out of our minds for now, thing. Plus, he said he really needed to think about some of that stuff this mentor had said, how that related to his religious values. We shook hands, I cried my first tears over her as he walked back inside to see who was on stage. I'd had someone else calling people up to the mic, while we'd been outside speaking.

Just then my phone rang, it was Lexy. She hadn't ridden with me because of a work meeting that ran late. She was frantic. She'd never driven to this part of Dallas without me and was lost and almost out of gas. I talked her in, street by street, until she arrived. She was less dolled up than usual but just as beautiful. There was this photographer who took some pictures of us. I loved those pictures because they were of one of the very last days before she said that she didn't see me as worthy of her. When I still had my dignity with her. We did the rest of the show. Sundays, while they lasted at that bar, were always awesome. We stayed late talking to Julie. I was supposed to head over with Lexy to 7-11, to put some gas in her tank. Anson tried to slip out the door. He was serious about the words of the mentor, needed space. But Lexy saw him on the way out and went to hug him goodbye. The hug lasted over ninety seconds. Ninety excruciating motherfucking close held seconds. I couldn't turn away. I wanted to leave then and there. I wanted to fucking scream and break shit. I hated it, I hated that I was in this fucked up dynamic with someone that was like this to me. Treated me like some half assed man servant. Like Anson's mentor had said, spiritual poison. But then again what dame had I ever known that wasn't some type of spiritual poison? She needed me right now, and I loved her. Motherfucking sucker that I am. Even sitting there in the excruciating pain of watching her hug him, like I was an after thought piece of shit, I still fucking loved her. I'm sure there is some kind of Chess metaphor here, but I was never any good at chess, or women, or any game. Much of anything really, except writing some poems

Your Beauty

11/13/07

Your beauty,
Your beauty,
Your beauty
Is not a common beauty

Your beauty, Your beauty
Is so much more than beauty of eye
of face of form
although this cannot be denied
Is undeniable
This type you know is
a dime a dozen or so.
pretty empty shells
desire pre packages
stacked on shelves.
don't let them fool you
It's not uncommon
Not like you.

Your beauty,
Your beauty
Your beauty Is more than this

Your beauty is the beauty
of spirit
of heart
of mind
of point of view
Your beauty is the beauty
of character
of voice
of guts
of intellect
of humor
of perseverance

Your beauty is the beauty
of conviction
of originality
of style
of grace

of truth

Your beauty,
Your beauty,
Your beauty
Is all that makes up you
It gets me through
It's something new
It's all of you

Your beauty,
Your beauty,
Your beauty
is not dime a dozen, it's
rather one in a million
or maybe a billion
a billion billion billion.

Your beauty,
Your beauty,
Your beauty
Your beauty.
I like it.

This is What NOT Despair Feels Like

11/14/07

You write a poem called "**This is what despair feel like**"
It's about the stabbing pain of nothing at all happening.
You read it for the very first time, red light, dim room,
and then something happens. a face bursts from the darkness.
It's a woman, she is drawn in by your words and you
are drawn in by her words.
She opens up right there in front of you and even though
you are scared and don't want to, you open up too.
Soon you come to realize that this person,
this small female person, opposite from you in some ways,
is more exactly like you inside in the ways that really matter
than anyone you'd ever encountered.
She thinks like you, feels like you, knows things like you.
Yearns and struggles and suffers and desires more, like you.
There is an seemingly impossible emotional, spiritual,
intellectual resonance.
a synchronicity that heals the spirit and sooths the soul.
Pretty soon you know what **NOT** despair feels like.
It returns all phone calls.
It talks with you openly for long periods if you really need it.
It doesn't accuse you of over thinking things.
It's sweetly comfortable around your children.
It truly appreciates you as an artist.
It shares your views on most things, while
challenging you on others and it never accuses you
of being just too much. It feels very nice.
NOT Despair feels very nice.
Not alone, not misconstrued, not mistreated, not misunderstood
It feels nice.
Something happens that makes you need to push her away
but she won't let you, and then you become even closer.
Hours upon hours talking way deep into the night
every possible secret shared, every weakness fearlessly revealed.
You begin to act and speak as one, inside jokes
half-sentences where you both know exactly what it means
with a look or a single word.

You both love with a focused passion the same things,
the same places, the same art, and you become partners
and what you are both doing becomes so much stronger
so much more, in the context of your partnership
in the context of this uncanny synchronicity.

She is in your heart now.
There is laughter and tears, challenging debates
Drunken, wild times and serious, supportive times
You're both moving through it as before
but it's different, because now you have a best friend.
So many nights surrounded by circles of awesome creative people
as quite a few buy into your shared energy.
As the 2 of you share something magnificent and infectious
with so many others.
Your shared passion for what you are creating
and your shared yearning for something real.

It's a marvelous partnership.
So many of your friends comment
on how uncanny you seem together.
On how different you have become now.
Now that you know what **NOT** despair feels like.
Whenever she's not around, during the day
or on the rare evening you're not together, you find that
you are always thinking about her.
Some little thing she said, laughing about some joke,
thinking about the way her voice sounds,
worried about her current emotional state,
considering some point she made.
Just generally thinking about her getting warm fuzzy feelings.
Wondering if she needs anything at all, because that's how you are
when you care about someone, you always want to do stuff for them.
Hell, even on those few nights when she is feeling the female
and she gets a little moody or pushy,
you don't care at all, it doesn't bother you.
You welcome it, you eat it up,
in fact you feel pretty sure
that you could take that in all the time any time
every day forever and ever and never get tired of it,
never get tired of her, at least that's how it feels.
THIS is what **NOT** despair feels like.
It feels **nice.**

But, you can feel despair waiting as always
at the frayed edges of time and mind.
Like tiny knives at the back of the neck,
and she, **despite your love** and contributions
still knows despair as well. It's not enough, you are not enough.
She has fatal flaws and you have fatal flaws
and they will somehow meet and create an impermanence
and despair will return.

You can feel it coming even now, like a distant ringing.
Despair is **danger**ous, creeping from behind on tiny **mouse** feet.
But there seems to be nothing you can do but wait.
Wait for the mousetrap to spring, with its **crushing** blow.
So you cherish **every single solitary moment**, because sadly
Very, very, very sadly
That's all that there is,
all that there ever is.

You KNOW what **despair** feels like.
and NOW you know what NOT despair feels like.
You can't help but *wonder what the point is.*
Is there any real meaning to either anyway?
Or is it all just faded days and wishes flying by?

My Clueless Dear
11/17/07

I understand you (she said)
you know I do.
We're just alike
We think alike.
We are the same, just the same.
That's why I'm alone, just like you.
I hear the same things you do from people,
about the way I think and see the world.
No one gets me either,
well except for you, you get me
like I get you.
So, I understand what it is to be alone.
To be always waiting for that one person
to come along
that will really get you, inspire you
accept you completely as you are.
We're both looking for that
so I get it. I totally get it.
Seriously what are 2 people like
you and I supposed to do?

She was looking at me from my right
her head tilted left, nodding a bit
with a charming earnest expression, slight smile
her mouth curving up a bit in that
oh so pretty way that it does, deep primal
wide eyes that seem to reflect the nature
of all that there is, or at least all I
could ever want.

I believed what she was saying.
That she understood it,
and that she was at a complete loss
for an answer to our dilemma.

It was astounding to me, almost beyond
comprehension,
that such a brilliant and insightful female,
one worthy of such praise, admiration
and respect, and other such grandiosities,
could actually be so utterly and completely
clueless.

AM I Really?

11/17/2007

Am I really? Am I? Really? Really?
Am I really who I am
Am I? Am I Really? Really?
DO I mean the things I say?
Do I? Really? Really?
Is my love undying?
Is it? Is it? Really? Really?
Am I for real? Really? Really?
You tell me,
AM I just another shallow liar
another empty temporary resting place,
another percentage
another not quite Mr. Right,
a home that is not a home
a downgradable friend
an interchangeable man
a replaceable half-man
another story for a year from now
too much of a chance
somehow less sincere than the others
not pretty enough, not young enough
not shallow enough, not disposable enough
not meaningless fun along the way
to nothing because you can't see
What's really real, enough?
AM I not good enough? Really? Really?
Not smart enough?
Not unique enough?
Not exciting enough?
Not admirable enough?
Not impressive enough?
Not creative enough?
Not compatible enough?
Am I really not enough?
REALLY? REALLY? OR, Am I too much?
to serious, to real, to unrealistic,
to emotional, to neurotic, to easy, to thinking,
to accommodating, too nice, too giving, to nurturing
Just too much? AM I just too much?
Am I? Am I? Really? Really?
Am I for real? Am I? Really**?** Really?

suspended

11/20/07

ever feel suspended
in the air,
mid heartbreak?

I remain silent
when I don't want to be
silent.

I want to scream PLEASE!
please,
please,
please
don't.

This fear of loss in my gut
doubling me over.

I'm not ready

I'm **so**
not ready
to lose her.

The Thanksgiving Shakes
11/22/07

My hands shake
My soul shakes
I awake to the sounds of my oldest son
having printed out my song for you
and he is singing the words
over and over and over again
"here I am, here I am, right here in front of you,
here I am, here I am, right here in front of you,
faith would move you past your fatal flaw, your fatal flaw."
and he is playing the guitar, such as it is
he is playing the guitar to be like you
he says that he is inspired by you
and I understand that.

I awake
my hands shake
my heart aches
tears are flowing like a dirty death river
all over my terrible face.
I drank and drank to forget about the pain I feel
living in my fear of losing you.
But it didn't do the trick,
you still drove me home.
You were still as kind as ever to me.
As good as always to me.
I thought I might go ahead and drink enough
to be an asshole,
and that this might hasten things along
It's worked before, hasn't it?
But not with you,
because when you tell me to behave
I cannot help but comply
regardless of how drunk I am.

I'm awake
my body shakes
caught in mid-air suspended heartbreak
with these thoughts of losing you.
I can't stop the tears, goddammit
hands shaking, goddamn shots of whiskey.
Balled up, baffled up, curled up, crying shaking

you will be the greatest loss yet, I fear.
A soul, a mirror of my own,
one who thinks and feels exactly like me,
my motherfucking soul mate.
You will be the greatest loss yet, I fear.
More than my last, great, indifferent love.
More than my darling ex-wife.
More than my beloved dead homies.
When you, my beautiful, yearning, tortured mirror
choose to cast me off,
that will surely cement the whole thing,
won't it?
Even the long-craved she, just like me,
cannot abide in me.
No one can.

I'm awake, and everything possible aches and aches.
It is the inverse this morning
the opposite of yesterday.
When I awoke, sober but tired from lack of sleep,
you having been the one who drank so much
so far from me,
killing my guts with the possibility
of someone causing you some awful harm.
But we were lucky,
a fine and kind gentleman brought you to me
to protect you, to care for you, as I always do.
Vomiting in the street, all full of regret and pain,
sleeping contorted in an uncomfortable chair
where my daughter asked
"*Who sleeps in a chair like that*?"
"*Silly people*" I said
Before she threw her arms round you, exclaiming
"*good morning sunshine*!"
As the suffering dropped from your face
in the shining light of her face, I get that.
I put you to bed to sleep it off, while I'm off to work
attempting to chastise you, but barely able to
in light of your amazingly beautiful, sleepy face.
I say, "*Me? Not so happy,*"
you say "*Me neither*"
We embrace, you scruff my hair
and say "*I Love you,*"
with that emphasis on my name at the end of the sentence,

something only a poet could truly appreciate,
the way words fall naturally and all.

I'm awake, I'm shaking, I feel the shadow of it all
It's Thanksgiving, but I don't feel thankful.
I feel scared and alone and like I'm about to die.
I'm shaking and shaking at thoughts of losing you.
My Soulmate, my motherfucking soulmate,
because I'm no longer man enough to figure shit out.
My sons are still strumming the guitar in awe of you.
They are still singing the words of the song that I wrote for you.
I can barely stand it,
I feel like the new hair is bleeding
from my scalp too little too late.
I pick up the phone and dial you.
knowing that you'll be slightly annoyed because it's too early
but I call anyway, because I need it,
I fucking need it.
It rings more times than usual;
you pick up groggy "*WHAT?*"
"*Sorry*", I say, "*rough morning,*
say something kind and I'll hang up"
"*I LOVE YOU, I'll call later*" We hang up.
But you don't really, not fully, not completely,
and I just don't know what to, how to be, how to feel
tortured mannequin, beaten beast, harlequin frozen mask.
Two peas in a pod, a fractured, abused, mixed-up pod.

Awake, awake, awake. It's Thanksgiving,
but I don't feel thankful.
I feel hung over like a tragic orange harvest moon.
I feel like the decline of Western Civilization
I feel like Greek Tragedy, like bad mojo
like the machine of almosting
always the motherfucking machine of almosting.
Caught up in the Spiritus Mundi slow trickle
of dying soft entropy flowers and black tar sunshine.
I told you last night that I wish I hadn't met you
but I lied, I lied, I lied, I fucking lied
You're the brilliant shining one, even if you don't know it
it's me I wish I'd never met
it's me I wish I'd never met up with
and had to endure
with my silly old soul.

you chase them away

11/23/07

I said;
"Why did you drink so much
that night when I wasn't around?"

She said;
"I think that when I'm with you
I feel good enough that
I don't need to drink that much
I'm not drowning any demons
because we're already ok when we're
together, and we don't need that."

Now,
if you are not a bit of an alcoholic,
or something of a melancholy poet
you may not understand this, but
That was one of the nicest things
anyone has ever said
to me,

fucked up
or not.

LOST IN YOU

(Non-Public Poem number one)
11/26/07

In my cubicle, I'm squeezed in like with a shoe horn
angles of mind slanting up at both sides.
I'm lost in you.

Taken down all the black and white photos
of men that had previously stared at me
in poems.
Now there is only one photo.
You, playing, on the night we met.
The exact face I fell in love with
even before the hours upon hours.
with only the lyrics, long, mournful notes
and talk of the struggle.
There is only one photo of you
because I am lost in you.
You are in everything I do
internally and externally.
In my space
In my heart
In my life
In my time
In my art
In my endeavors.
In every word I write, it seems.
I've never really known such a love
a love for such a woman
a beautiful, overwhelming woman
who I respect, enjoy, listen to and desire
in every single possible way,
my very best friend.
all I want is you.
I think of nothing else but my desire
to be with you in every way
every day as long as I can.
Forever, if you would let me.

I just don't know what to do.
Your words tell me that I am not enough.
You push me slowly out of your heart.
Each sentence a bleeding hammer blow.

But I love you so much
I can barely hold back tears of separation
Alone in the car, in the cubicle
looking at your photo on the wall.

What should I do?
Walk away to avoid the pain?
Or just continue to love my best friend
with all my heart as long as I can.

A CERTAIN BEAUTY

(non-Public Poem Number Two.)
11/26/07

There is a certain beauty to you, and while always beautiful
this particular beauty manifests mostly when you speak.
Serious, melancholy, social commentary, laughter,
it doesn't matter..
It's the beauty of coming alive.
It has to do with your soft eyes
and the way that they transfix, almost hypnotize
in their repetitive reflexive widening and narrowing
to accentuate various emotional assertions.
Your mouth, perhaps the simple shape of it or
it's that the love of watching you sing spills over
into other more private moments, but your mouth
it commands my attention, so perfect, female, soft.
Always drawn in when you speak to me.
The world itself, falling away.
Just your mouth, and your eyes and me
floating in the air..
Your eyes seem to see right inside
see my greatest weaknesses
and strengths as well I hope.
Your real words, they have affected me.
The heart and mind and thoughts and spirit and guts.
bleed out for me and into me.
It is this beauty, this true real beauty
somewhat cruel in it's accidental flame perhaps.
This beauty you possess, of the face
and all that pours out
is unlike anything I have seen.
it baffles me and captures me and holds on to me
I can't look away I can't stop wanting more I can't stop.
I don't want to stop,
I want more of this certain beauty

WHAT I WANT

Non-Public Poem Three
11/26/07

It's not just that I want you to share with me your
sublimely superbly beautiful desirable physical form,
I DO. I want to show you beyond a shadow the epiphany inducing
life altering heights of pure erotic spiritual dirty orgasmic bliss
that I crave desperately to gift you with repeatedly,
with skilled passionate intensity
until you are weeping in soul shaken disbelief.
Hell yes. But not just that.
It's not just that I want to be your best friend.
Being your best friend is one of the best things that
has ever happened to me. True understanding, true partnership,
true deep sharing of everything. Hopes and dreams,
weaknesses and fears, all of it. A perfectly symmetrical
working best friendship, socially and artistically supportive
emotionally, intellectually, spiritually, supportive.
The very best all around friendships either of us have every
experienced.
I wish it could last forever, but seriously, it's not JUST that.
What I want is to make a difference
by being something completely different.
Not the compartmentalized best friend or lover, but all of that and
more.
I want to wake beside you each day with an embrace and a kind
word.
I want you to truly feel for once what it feels like
to be treated with dignity and truth and honor.
I want you to share my life with my children, who adore you
as much as you are comfortable with and experience the joy of what
that brings.
I want to be your lifeline, your redemption, your proof.
I want you to be valued and cared about and listened to,
to be respected and cherished and loved and befriended
unconditionally.
I want you to understand that a man can be,
that I can be, all of these things and more, all at once.
I want you to have power and influence over my life and activities
and decisions, and to trust you to use it wisely and compassionately.
I want us to both follow our bliss together, supporting one another
along the way to fulfilling creative artistic success.
I want you to find the strength to undertake the spiritual journey
of fighting your demons and finding the growth you need,

which is sometimes a solitary battle,
but to know that even in that solitude
I would be behind you, or at your side, holding your hand.
I want you and I to know, finally, true partnership.
I want you to give me the chance, to de-compartmentalize,
rather than different men being categorized
worthy of different types of love. To be the everyman,
To be everything, best friend and lover, boyfriend and partner.
What I want is a real chance to make a difference
A chance, before time slips away,
to be something altogether different
for you and for me.

11/28/07 Saturday

Then I made this new best friend. She had a boyfriend, but they were on the outs. She wanted to spend all this time with me doing all the exact things I really love. It's been the best couple months I've had in forever, even with the celibacy thing. We've shared every possible secret, experienced every emotion, every idea. I've rarely been as close to anyone in my life. Last time I felt this close to another human being, I married her. BUT here's the difference. With Thais, we had a LOT in common, good stuff, but the sex blinded a lot of differences. Even the ones I could see. The differences killed an eight year relationship in the end. We were never just alike. She NEVER really got me. I have NEVER EVER in my life known anyone like me, not really. Not that feels, sees, experiences, processes, like me. I've known a lot of poets, some are pretty close. Enough to be family. I love them all, but always felt alone, even among them. Even among the women, all the women, always alone. Even with the wife after the first couple years, alone. But Lexy? Exactly like me, not alone. I've never in my life experienced this not aloneness. This reflection of soul, spirit, intellect, art, creative drive. She's the best friend I've ever had. No one gets this, believes me, it's intense. Remember when I would say that all I ever wanted was someone like me, someone who really truly gets me? Well this is her. These last couple weeks since her break up, she's been a wreck. I've been there every moment. All the emotions. She is now in my place. Artistically, emotionally, financially, the parallels are uncanny. All of my own demons, the ones I've been drinking down, are now resurfaced. I'm not sure what to do with all this. This soulmate, we are best friends. It seems as though we should be together, but it doesn't look like it's going to happen. In fact she seems resentful and moody towards me and my feelings. The one person there for her and taking care of her. I'm not sure really if she is just fundamentally incapable of dating or being involved with her actual best friend or if she just sees the two things so differently and hasn't the actual life experience and wisdom to know they are the same. Possibly a pattern. Or maybe I'm just too fucked up in a dozen ways and not good enough for her. Also quite possible. She's already slipping away. I feel like pretty soon I'll lose not only the once in a lifetime chance to be with someone just like me, that truly gets me, what I've always searched for, but also lose the best friend I've ever had.. Gods! opening myself here before you, praying you alter our views.

Intellectual Whore

11/07

Couldn't have been more than a couple months before I met her that I'd discovered the website about Intellectual Whores. To bottom line it, it's about women that use men. These intellectual pimps use a man for everything he's worth even though they may have no intention of dating him or sleeping with him. They put him in a non-man category. Use him for intellectual and creative stimulation, money, time, social influence, whatever he's got. Usually because knowingly or unknowingly they can't reconcile their own need to date or fuck morons, douche bags, or whatever brand of idiot they find themselves attached to. Whatever guy that gets the pussy but isn't good enough to satisfy all the other deeper needs. It was a real eye-opener. I stumbled across it posted on the Goth club posting board. Ironically, by Holly, a delightful woman for whom I had strong feelings, for a good while. She and I had never quite made the connection and I'd gone crazy with meaningless dames and trying to reconnect to past ones, through most of 2007 as a result of trying to deal. The site helped me get past her a little. Not because I was ever her whore, but because I realized her real authentic interest in me would always be only high middle on her ladder. Meaning that some douche bag could always come along and be above me. It actually happened. Hell, it started out that way. It was awful and painful. I had my druid poet do some spells to help me over it. It did dawn on me that I had been an intellectual whore twice before. Recently, with Brittany, my dark souled tattooed poet girl, but only a little, and only for a few months. And with Melissa, who I'd spent time with just before meeting my ex-wife many years earlier. My Sweetchild Madness that ended in in-patent treatment. It was a terribly humiliating realization and I vowed never again to be an intellectual whore.

When I first met Lexy in October, when we would talk all the time all night in the car. She was with Craig who she claimed from the beginning never to have had a decent connection with. Especially an intellectual one. I would absolutely have approached her COMPLETELY differently had she been single. She would say in every conversation how alike we were. There were always percentages and one or two guys from the past that were up in my percentage of alikeness range. I discovered that one was a guy she always had the big thing for but never wanted a relationship with her. Someone that would cause me never ending jealousy. The other was Reese. Reese had been her **"best friend"** like me for a while, less than a year I think. She was really hurt by the way he had blown her off a couple years earlier when she had first gotten with Craig. She couldn't understand how someone that supposedly valued her so, could blow her off like that. I remember laughing saying, "What is there to understand?" He had feelings for you, he was your Intellectual Whore, and it hurt him when you hooked up with some (what you considered) good looking moron. He couldn't deal, so backed off." I explained to her then the Ladder Theory/Intellectual Whore website. About Holly and Brittany and Melissa. She had this huge aversion to the idea, not even accepting that such a thing was real. I was vehement that it was real, and that I was in no way ever going to be that. That I needed respect as a man and nothing less, period. Walter, the guy at the job I discussed such things with daily, felt sure I was heading towards whoredom. That all the signs were there. That she needed a new whore to get her out of her boyfriend, just like she had one that led her in. I thought maybe, but it seemed like so much more, and I had to play it out see what I could do. What I could overcome and win at now armed with this new knowledge. She seemed like the answer to my prayers. The result of the Druid spells. As long as I NEVER let myself BECOME the whore, never go along with anything remotely whore-ish. Stood my ground, stayed strong, I would never be the whore, and would have this chance at real love. The only chance I'd had for a perfect match in so long, maybe ever. I couldn't let it go just out of fear of becoming an Intellectual Whore. My poet buddy Roderick and I sat and talked about it at Hooters one night, I justified it by saying that I was going to give it a certain amount of time and see how it played out.

I only met Reese once. It was late November, not even two months in. She wanted me to come to the gig that she went to with Anson on Tuesdays. I hated Tuesdays! I'd lie in bed all night unable to sleep imagining her being fucked! God, I hated Tuesdays! We get there and she tells me that she had gotten a call from Reese, first time in a long time. I figure he must have heard through the grapevine that Craig was gone, still felt his feelings, and was looking to size up the situation. He arrived and seemed like a nice enough guy. Shaved bald like I had been when she and I first met. In fact in a very surface dynamic way, not unlike me. It made sense. He wasn't an artist though. More of a capitalist and I could envision him during her pre-artist lifestyle time as cool party guy partner. I did my Nihilist counter-culture posturing bit as Lexy explained to him her new Bohemian artist values and lifestyle. His eyes said that he was a socially aware clever guy. The kind of guy, like me, that could size shit up, be aware of dynamics. He got me. He got Anson. He smoked a lot. He decided his best bet was to show how awesome he was now without her. What dude hasn't done this when around some ex? After the acceptance that is. Harder still to do around a former intellectual pimp, because they won't show it, even if they do give a shit. He zoned in on two girls at the table next to us, hit em pretty hard, buying drinks, charming them, not bad really. Tried to call me over to get involved in it, I couldn't. The look in his eyes told me I should. I was at that table when Lexy went on stage. It was not her night, not her crowd, not the place for bleeding it out. It was all rather shallow. I thought maybe that she was looking at me at that table with Reese and those girls, and didn't want me there, but if I wasn't imagining it, she didn't say anything.

A little later I asked Reese to let me buy him a shot. Lexy was near at the bar being bought drinks by some creepy pervert. The same guy apparently responsible for the just before Thanksgiving fiasco. Reese and I ordered a shot. I told him that I really liked him and that I felt a bond of some sort, that we should hang sometime. I knew we never would. I lifted my glass and said "To Lexy!" he surprise smiled and lifted his glass. Before we hit though, I leaned in and whispered, "And the suffering that comes with loving her!" His face told me everything. Shock, then a big smile and a shake of the head. "Amen brother!" he said "Amen!" The next shot was on him. I spent a lot of time trying to convince myself that I was more than the next Reese. It took a lot to ignore all the dynamics I had seen that night. Walter took every opportunity to tell me what a spineless whore in denial I was. I always answered him with, "Maybe you're right, but I'm not sure, it seems like there is so much more to us than that." He would laugh and call me a fool. As far as Reese, I never saw him again. I don't know if her ever called her or if that was just some closure that he had desperately needed. I just know that I never saw him again.

She, Reflected Beside Me

12/01/07

The way she looked reflected in the glass
my back to her.

Green ahead orange behind
neon lights and coffeehouse sounds,
my head the
predominant image on the left
rather serious in countenance
aged and rascally.

Her shape,
her form, image held slightly right and parallel
different light, different clarity.
The shape of her bare shoulders, hair falling.
Soft, like the gentle music she
continuously siren calls crashing me.
Her melancholy beauty reflected there
beside my own dark depths,
in a window frame on a winter night, more
beautiful to me than anything humanly possible
as the sky, falling, calls me in close
dropping beautiful, dark symmetry ringlets.
I love her neon green
I love her dark reflected.
I love her hair and shoulders and the
shape of her mouth from the left.

I think that I would do absolutely anything for her,
to cleanse her of this throbbing pain.
all of me to make her stay,
to make her all ok.
but I am merely reflected continuously beside her
an image, a trick of sorts.
The actual distance being somewhat more
than what it appears.
She doesn't pull me all the way in.

Not Too Late

12/01/07

Not too late yet I think. Although It's late it's late it's always late.
She was darker tonight than I'd ever seen her, really.
I get it, I felt it and it occurred to me that she doesn't quite have my light,
hasn't quite got it yet, can't see herself the way that I see her.
I know what it is like to be suspended. to fall from grace
to be a non factor a non entity to have nothing, to lose everything.
Swimming in impermanence
Swimming and a sea of desperate nowhere despair, I'm there.
but this light of who I am carries me through
This knowing beyond knowing that I am something special
and she is something special, something very special too.
She doesn't quite get it though, not yet, maybe soon.

"God is sending me a message, but I'm not seeing it," she said
I'm supposed to be hearing something that I'm not hearing"
(I know, I'm right here and you're not listening baby.)
I keep talking, convinced that I am a universal gift to her
The thing the voice told me that first night.
Only she has stopped listening to me now
I pushed the wrong buttons with my own brokenness.
Even the hugs have grown more distant, Not everyone's, just mine.
It is as if she wants me to run away and fulfill expectation
But I can't seem to. I have no power left,
I've given it all away to her.
But she's not getting it, not getting it right
It's the light she needs, the confidence
Not in the world, but in the true inner need
What she has is as special as what I have.
She is the shining one, even if she doesn't know it yet.
I'm just the symbol for endurance
I love her and I would give her everything if I could,
but I've been denied before so very often.
I love her, she is my rejection and my reflection
I need to show her some light.
God is trying to tell her something,
There is a message in here somewhere
I am the message. Truth, love, honor, endurance.
The voice spoke to me that first night,
but as usual I've made mistakes.
All for the dream my friend, you and I.

It's late,
I would do absolutely anything to cleanse her of this pain,
It's late,
It s not to late though, because I never give up
I never give up I never give up
That's my thing, I suppose the never giving up
It all makes sense for a second here,
the beautiful memories
the dancing, the phone calls, the melancholy laughter
I find unexpected strength in it all tonight.
It's late, But it's not too late for us,
not really not really not really
It's not to late yet, maybe it never is.

December Second, Irony and Almosts

It was December first. Three years earlier on that date the wife had moved out taking the children away behind some strange red brick wall. The next day I went out with my buddy TJ to a high class strip joint where he dropped a wad and I picked up drinking again, a habit I never again put down. I spent a month in Denver with another old buddy, thought about staying gone, but couldn't stand the thought of losing my children, came back on Christmas Eve. It's hard to remember December first of 2005, I was likely working the door at the bar. In 2006 I was already in the cubicle part time, hanging out pretty regularly with a young tattooed poet girl. I'm sure both were dark days. But here it was, already 2007. I was with Lexy, our usual Saturday night open mic, drinks somewhere, not my usual watering holes, because she wasn't comfortable there and liked to be in control of such things. Her mood was dark, darker than I'd seen her. She had gotten increasingly moody towards me of late. Me who had once been a more difficult loss than the empty unsupportive boyfriend. But now, the last few weeks, his loss seemed to overshadow everything we did. It seemed unending. I was given the brunt of the mood swings, taken for granted and given precious little love, emotional or otherwise. By being way too available and supportive I had made myself into something far less.

I dropped her off at Shane's place and drove away feeling more lost, frustrated and rejected than I had in a good while. I'd tried to get support from her about the December first thing, but it wasn't there, not that night. I started making phone calls while driving home, looking for some kind words, even though it was very late. I talked to a couple people, then a certain dame that I had dated for a couple months early in 2006 called me back. Her name was Chastity. She was real sweetheart. We had gotten on famously, but didn't last because we had almost nothing in common. Socially, beliefs, interest, just very different. She was as I say though, a real sweetheart. The abrupt way she had broken it off had hurt more than the actual break off. We didn't speak for several months. Then talked and had a date, sort of an anniversary thing, in March of 2007. We joked about making it yearly, but it actually turned into weekly for a bit, Sunday afternoons. Until I missed one for some reason, sick I think, and broke the streak. I think I saw her maybe once or twice after, but it had been a few months. I liked being with her because we knew where we stood. We knew that we didn't have the commonality to be together but we were both terribly fond of one another, really enjoyed the other's company, and could find the occasional solace in each other arms. It was nice. It was comfortable. I, in actuality, as much as I love women, hate dating, hate it. Hate being with someone new, going through that process of getting to know someone new, emotionally, socially, intellectually, physically. So the occasional old times sake was a real value. She called back and we chatted, told her how I was feeling about the December first thing. She was sweet and supportive. Said I should come see her at her new place in a small town about an hour south.

The next day on Sunday, in the late afternoon I got a 12 pack and headed south. She had been in the mid-cities dropping off her kids and we got this clever phone tag thing going. What exits we were passing, laughing and joking all the way. I was ahead of her and finally pulled over, let her pass and followed. We got to her cozy new house, started in on the beer. We had some of the best conversation we'd ever had. Stuff about our lives and pasts. What we had been doing lately. It wasn't just about me looking for the hookup, we were enjoying the company a lot. As if my recent experiences had changed me a bit. She shot a video of me doing some strange Rap song in kind of this William Shatner voice. We got a drunk on Michelob Lime, went in the kitchen and put on aprons and straw hats. Cooked homemade tortillas on the stove. Laughed and laughed side by side on the couch, taking photos and saying silly things. I couldn't help think of the irony. How this beautiful fun woman could have a good time with me, would be with me, see me as a man, and appreciate me, but ultimately we couldn't be together because we had no real common ground. While Lexy, my soulmate, I'd spent every moment with the last couple months, I had more in common with in my heart and soul and beliefs, than anyone I ever imagined possible, wouldn't or somehow couldn't. How that was slowly killing me inside. Being with her every day, loving her, but not being fully appreciated by her. How when she and I had first met there had been so much laughter, but by December second, the shadow of our situations; him, her, us, and all of it, had made everything dark. I looked into the eyes of the beautiful woman I was with. One I had been with many times before. One who, hands down, was the most comfortable intimacy that I knew, familiar, awesome. I thought about kissing her, make it happen, get the party started. I leaned in started to, but stopped. Put my arms around her and held her a bit instead. She pulled back, looked into my eyes, puzzled, could tell something was off. She asked "What is it?", I told her "I'm not sure." But, she knew me well. She smiled and shook her head, said "It's that best friend girl from your Myspace, you're in love with her!" "I, well, it's complicated." I said. "We're not together, I'm not cheating or anything. She's my best friend and we're together all the time, everyday. There are these feelings, this dynamic, it was great, but now it's gotten not so great. She's become kind of demanding and bossy and takes me for granted, but it's just because she is going through a lot. A breakup, nowhere to live, really she's awesome! I'm just trying to be there for her, you know." At that exact moment my phone rang. Actually, the seventh or eighth time since I'd been there. I'd been ignoring it. All the calls had been Lexy or Shane. This was the first time in a long time I hadn't spoken with her by that late in the day. Chastity said "Answer it! Talk to her!" So I did. The conversation was uncomfortable. She wanted to know where I'd been all day, why I hadn't been answering the phone. Said that they'd been trying to call me. I told her that I was depressed about the December first thing, knew she wasn't in a good place, so I had called up some old friends to hang out with to get my mind off of it. She was annoyed, rather short and bossy. She said that we needed to go to the plasma center the next day to sell, and that there were a couple things I needed to do for our gigs that I hadn't taken care of. I said "Ok, ok, I'll do that, no problem, see you tomorrow, I love you." and got off the phone. Chastity looking baffled, said "You have never at least eaten that girl's pussy? Nothing?" "No," I said, sounding defeated. "I find that hard to believe, I know how you are." she said. " What's up with that?" "It's complicated" I said again. She laughed and said "Hell, she talks to you like that, runs you around, without giving up any pussy? Neat trick, I've got to learn that one!" We both laughed, a lot. I admitted that it was pretty funny. We threw down more beer. She got up and started walking to the bedroom "C'mon," she said. " I don't think I can," I said. "You're kidding?" "I wish I was," I mumbled flatly. " Ok, c'mon then, we'll be good, let's just sleep it off, you can't drive all the way back drunk!" "I'll be ok," I said. Gathered up my stuff, hugged her, a tiny peck on the mouth, thanked her for the food and the laughs and drove away.

I cried while driving all the way home. I cried about the wife that had left me three years earlier and the kids I had dropped off the night before. I cried about the beautiful woman who was sweet to me that I had nothing in common with. But mostly, I cried about the one I had everything in common with. More connected in deep real ways than I'd ever been with the wife. I cried because I was losing any hope that we would ever find our groove and be together. That she would never get past the grief she was in, and her demons, look up, see her best friend loving her and realize that this was what it was really all about. Allowing herself, and me, to finally be happy again.

The next day the cubicle was unbearable. I texted that I wanted to go to the plasma center Tuesday instead. That I would handle any expenses after the night's show. I couldn't take the day. Feelings of regret and sadness, but mostly of guilt. That I had somehow betrayed a heart that didn't want me anyway. Was dishonest to the love inside me. Tears kept leaking from my eyes. I finally went into the private bathroom, locked the door and fell to the floor in tears and anguish. I called Lexy, said "Look, I know that you are not in the place that I am in, you're grieving him, and no matter how our dynamic is and feels and appears to everyone who knows us, you don't want me, not now, don't think you really love me and believe that you have never loved anyone in the way that I love you and probably never will. I hope it changes soon, I get all that. But I'm going crazy here, I didn't do anything but in my heart I feel guilty like I did, I need to tell you something, but I need to not talk about it. Because anything you say either way will just make it worse and I really didn't do anything wrong anyway." I told her the whole thing about being frustrated with her, calling Chastity, went to see her, wanted to hookup, but didn't. Because I couldn't not love her even for a moment. Even there with the most familiar comfortable person from my recent past. That I was fucked in everyway imaginable, except the good way. There was a long pause, she didn't sound upset one bit. She said "You really are different from everyone else, aren't you?" Kind of laughing she said, "You know I love you, come pick me up at 6:30, try to relax." Hung up the phone. I got up off the bathroom floor, went back to the cubicle, finished the day, got home, took a nap and wrote a poem. I picked her up just like she said and we went to the Fort Worth gig. The story wasn't over. No, it was a long way from over.

I can feel you loving me less

12/02/07 a country song, I think

I can feel you loving me less, while I love you more.
I can feel you loving me less, while I love you more.
Your embrace has grown colder, but only for me.
Where once I was special, lit up your eyes
Now I'm just someone you love from the side.
I miss the warm deep closeness and your long soft beautiful sigh.

I can feel you loving me less, while I love you more.
I can feel you loving me less, while I love you more.
I was the one, who made it ok
kept you from darkness, kept demons at bay
but now I can feel you slipping away.
You feel more alone and grow darker each day.
No one to hold you, no one is there
No one in your corner but I love you more and more.

I can feel you loving me less, while I love you more.
I can feel you loving me less, while I love you more
The gods have abandoned you,
what is the message that you can not see
everyone a disappointment, all things impermanent
yet I am always here at your side, barely recognized.
I've run from so many, for so much less
but with you I just don't want to go
You've opened me up in one thousand ways
but now, like furniture, scapegoat-ed, maybe I'm not sure.
Slipping away slowly, an already acceptable loss
another story of loss.

I can feel you loving me less, while I love you more
I can feel you loving me less, while I love you more.
You said I was so much like you, that my words inspired you
That my honor impressed you, That my truth uplifted you
That my presence comforted you, That my intellect challenged you
That I could protect you, That I was your very best friend
That you felt a part of all that I do.
May I remind you, that all of this could still be true.
And that I need you too, need all that you do.
Your words are comforting, Your voice is soothing
Your presence is warming, Your genius enlightening
Your talent consuming. Your laughter exciting

The depth of your soul, so much like mine.
I need you too, I need all parts of you
I want you there, I so badly want you there.

It feels like so long since you held my hand
since you scuffed my hair, or told me you loved me
or held me so close, god, I want you there
I want you there.
I can feel you loving me less, while I love you more
I can feel you loving me less, while I love you more.

Do you mind me asking?

12/03/07

Crystal, a well known female poet turned to me in a moment when no one was near and said; "Do you mind me being nosey for a sec?" I laughed a bit. "You know me," I replied "I've got nothing too hide." So she asked; "Are you two together at all?" Pointing to the seat where my very closest associate had been sitting a moment earlier. "Alas, no," I sighed." "Really?" she asked, "I don't understand that you seem perfect for one another, there seems to be beautiful balance to your relationship!" "Oh, there is", I told her, "I know this sounds crazy because I haven't known her long, but I feel like she is the best friend I've ever had. There is a resonance like I've never known." She smiled, "I can see that. So how's she feel?" "Oh, I'm her best friend too, pretty sure." "Cool, so what's the problem?" "Well, I suppose that she's just not in that place where she realizes what a big deal a best friend truly is, what that really means, she still separates men into categories like a teenage girl would." She frowned a little; "Yeah, I learned that lesson from my first marriage, that's why I have the husband I have now." I half laughed; "Yeah, I remember your story, I guess she hasn't had some of the experiences that we have." She took my hand; "I'm guessing from recent poems that you're having a hard time?" I smiled; "Eh, some days, yeah, then others it's just really great to have this awesome person in my life." She nodded knowingly; "Well, I want you to know that I've been thinking about the both of you, and praying for you. You're both such amazing people. As people and as artists, you know how I feel about your work and she is incredible, believe me I grew up I a family of artists an musicians, I don't impress easy, I think she is truly something amazing, just like you. I always love to see both of you, and I love to see you together. Just keep the faith and whatever is meant to be will be." Then she gave me a hug. I love these people, these fellow artists that I am lucky enough to know. Sometimes they are all that I have to get me through.

The Hatred of Demons and Tuesdays, Especially Tuesdays.

12/05/07

Objects floating in morning time-space
seem hollow, empty
lacking in substance like echo.
Canned peaches in the fridge.
Grandfather clock mid-chime.
Bricks, waist level along the wall
running together down the hall.
A semi-beat off rhythm,
all seem quantum molested by
a hatred of Tuesdays.
Fitful broken sleep punctuated by
irregular anxiety heartbeat and
bad, bad dream imaginings.
What dreams may,
manifest fears from dementia.
Drowning in duplicity,
dread desire, delusion, derision.
Inhale suddenly upon waking.
I find in my mind's eye
pictures of you;
bent and broken, scattered askew
disheveled, done in, disaster-ed
damaged, demented, defeated
bedeviled by demons
shackled by history and thoughts of history.
Push me down away like wet carpet bad animal
Push me into a well, a wall, a diving wale.
Pick me out, pull me in then
slide me off like handcuffs.
Like the orange yellow moon of your soul.
Like lit matchbook childhood innocence,
sweetheart. My heart. Dearest heart.
In far away night skies low bright stars form
memories of my own childhood
alone in the darkness
visions unseen, you'll never see me.
I hate Tuesdays.

Giving Up, Take What Remains

12/06/07

The Mad Swirl Open Mic had just ended. Many aspects a bit fuzzy due to Merlot, Whiskey, Vodka, Beer, and such. Lexy was driving my car home, it was darling. I said "I feel bad making you drive. She said, "what are you talking about? How many times have you driven me?" I went on about something or another, she yelled "Don't argue with me!" reached over and smacked me in the head. A habit she has picked up of late. As I say, darling and rather endearing for one with my twisted preferences. Except for the way she doesn't love me back quite enough and all, I'd be pretty thrilled. We dropped off Roderick our drunk poet associate, then headed south toward Shane's house. Oddly, he called, said; "Hey, I'm gonna have one of your beer in the fridge, come in and drink a few when you get here, so I did. By and by it was nearly 5 am by the time I got home in bed.

Of course the cubicle cares not for such things. The day was likely the most excruciating ever in that small square space. Only the constant company of the fellows at my side makes it even somewhat bearable at times. The day was long and torturous. I kept slipping into what can only be described as some type of existential coma. At one point with only an hour or two left to go, left side wise guy, Walter, turns to me and says, "Man you look utterly defeated, like the women have completely beaten you down!" (laughing) "I suppose that's true my friend," I responded, "I pretty much give up on the whole thing. Trying to be decent, and find something real, it's always this fucking almosting that kills my heart." He laughed some more, then suggested that I should call every woman I know, and throw in the towel, tell them that I give up. We joked about it and somehow the idea evolved into a single mass text message sent to every female in my cell phone. So I wrote it, and sent it, leaving out ONLY my sister, I even asked him in my half lucid state if I should include the ex-wife, He said this sounded like a good idea, so I did. Here is what the message read;

"DEAR LADIES, I AM GIVING UP, TAKE WHAT REMAINS"

It didn't take long for reactions to pour in. Although my dearest Lexy did not respond. Likely she knew me well enough to instantly recognize my poetic hyperbole. Two different females took the pronouncement as a sort of post-modern suicide note and were quite upset. One threatened to call 911. I think I must seem pretty much on the fucking edge lately, for this to happen. Most of the other responses where merely puzzled messages asking what this meant, understandable I suppose, men hardly ever give up, or at least when they do, they likely don't poetically pontificate such things. It's usually more of a quiet defeat, a voiceless surrender. But I suppose I never go gentle into the night. There were several text messages, several voice mails, it was all very overwhelming, this sudden interest. There was one who obviously didn't have my number saved, she asked "Who is this?" That was about right. Another said, "I Like your happy poems better, don't feel blue!" Interesting. One who still resides in the corner of the heart, wanted an explanation. I called and reassured her. The most interesting of all was one who called and said that I shouldn't give up, that she had just shaved her pussy clean last night and it was feeling great. She suggested that me eating it out would make it all better She said that she was wet right now just thinking about it. This kind of talk went on for a real long time, very descriptive. It became unbearably uncomfortable in my cubicle and I felt like I was literally going to pass out right then and there, but it was time to leave, so I did. And YES what it did sound terribly appealing, it makes me wonder if it is even possible for a man to give up at all, maybe that's what she was trying to tell me in her own way. And no, I probably won't go see her, because of these emotional attachments I have, that's just how I am, I have to be real, I have to be decent. I don't seem to have a choice in the matter, giving up doesn't seem like an option for me, although I sometimes wish it was.

I crawled home, into bed and slept hard. My dreams were dirty and nasty and vivid and excruciating and yes they were all about Lexy, even while pushing me away she draws me deeper in still, It's pure fucking madness, but as I say giving up doesn't really seem to be an option. So I dreamt about her, and the dreams were impossibly wonderful. In them she was very happy and so was I. Very different from the last few weeks, I was dreaming about her still, alone in the dark when she called and asked me to take her out for a beer. She said it was OK if I didn't want to, but I said, "I cherish every single moment that we have together while it is here, I'm always here for you one hundred percent, I'll be over to pick you up after a while."

From Hero To Zero

12/08/07

You've turned everything completely around in such a short time. Where once I was a hero, a guiding light, an inspiration, a like mind, a kindred soul, one of the best most real interactions you've had, your very best friend. Somehow, trying to be the one who is there for you made me instead taken for granted and the object of your rejections and negative feelings. In just a couple short weeks, hero to zero. I dreamed we would be together, that your love would continue to grow, the way it was while you were still with him. While it was still safe for you to actually feel. I dreamed every day and night of lying at your side. You left him, then the hole opened wide. The same hole that you are able to see in others, filling it up with others. Why am I getting the push? Have I offended you, bored you, bothered you? Or is it just that the hole is so wide now, it is sucking everything positive away? Me, the hero that you no longer love. Perhaps I let myself be so close with no boundaries that I automatically suffer the fallout of whatever you feel? .

I do know I love you, a connection I've never felt. Has it really turned so quickly then? My only crime to dream, to love you more, never asking for anything but time. I loved you at the start. Your biggest fan, supporter, partner, friend, soulmate. For a while you were happier than ever, having everything. Me out in the world supporting what you love. Him at home supporting the rest, the physical, the material, the safety. Sure you were happy, who wouldn't be, but how can such a thing last? He couldn't take it, he knew in his heart that he could never accept you for who you are and that he couldn't share you. Now that safe world broken up, you push me away.

I'm not good enough, I may never be your ideal of a man, rather a boy man. You want both, the empty boy man, and the deep fulfilling best friend. You dream of one that can be both, but it's not me, I'm almost nothing now, your embrace grown cold, but not for others. Sorry if it spoils your two men happiness memories, but I'm a man too. I always was and I have always loved you even when it was impossible to have you I loved you enough to be your best friend. Even rejected I was still your best friend. When you needed help, and love and patience. Someone to watch out for you, be there and help support your art, spirit, intellect and emotions. To love your beautiful freaking soul. I was your best friend. Never asking for more, mostly happy to be at your side, whatever scraps you give me. Taken for granted. Not long ago you didn't know unconditional love. Not because I do a few things for you. That's NOT what I mean, find a roof, buy a few things, take you around, all that, I'D GLADLY do these a million times over, a joy to be good to one you love. What I mean is my heart. You take my love and friendship for granted. That I will be there no matter what. I know it's my own fault I have told you this and I have told you that I can take whatever you have. I just didn't think it would be the negativity for me. From hero to scapegoat in such a short time. It's fucking me up. My love for you is unconditional. I AM there for you. Still, it would be nice to still have some kind of me and you left If we are ever able to make it through.

<u>Text Conversation between 2 artists</u>
12/09/08

A: Black Tar Sunshine
what now, what cost would I gamble.
Deal me in.

P: Does that mean, time for me to go then?

A: **It's a state of mind,**
I love an idea at this point,
you love a person.
neither can bow out.
Regret would be our only comfort
and we would be made perfect in it.

P: What great nothing I must be my beloved so easily taken off my hands. Oh, but for one more hour one more day, one more moment. Curse the gods, I am undone, empty, defeated.

A: **Your withdraw halts me brother friend, what is your solution, what would you have me do?**
I am open to what you say.

P:* *Do not know, my tears are like iron knives
in this unkind season. I wished only to empty myself of me,
be only here for her, but in this moment I am feeling me again.

A: **Are you OK?**
I don't want to lose you either.
I feel closer to you now, not that you know me as well as some but that we are more the same
I don't want to lose her, or you either.

P: Let us speak again later
I find I am unable to compose myself
I am overwhelmed by tears and sadness
Perhaps some of her recent darkness has rubbed off on me.
I feel completely lost, I need to compose myself
and finish what remains of the day.

A: **Later then my friend**

P: Yes, later.

I'm Sorry, Sorry Like Roses Time and Fear

12/09/08

I'm sorry for that time I hurt you so,
weeks ago.
Hurt you so much that you remember it still,
Some water doesn't flow
under this bridge so easily it seems though
I've been hurt too
once or twice, by you,
but I let it go, I let it go
because I love you so.

What I need you to hear right now,
Is that I am sorry.
Truly deeply profoundly unreservedly sorry.
I couldn't be more sorry.
Every bit of everything inside me is unabashedly
uncompromisingly, unwaveringly, unashamedly, sorry.
I apologize.
I apologize with the veracity of ancient stone text.
I apologize with the burning power of a rocket ship.
I apologize with the cool sweet desire
of a Summer breeze.
If there was but one single waning moment left;
one single solitary singing thought to be thought
in all of creation at the very end of time itself.
But one universal truth cosmically entropy pressed compacted
into but a single moment of existence
yet to be expressed.
It would be me
apologizing to you,
for hurting your beautiful soft gentle wonderful
wispy feelings.
I know you are tough on the outside,
and you can take it
by everything inside me in every single way
reminds me
that when it comes to me, and to me and you
you deserve in every way nothing more than
complete and total kindness,
generosity, compassion love and respect.
So please, forgive this awful flawed fool, I also am
merely human and I need to be loved, flaws and all.

I didn't mean to mock you,
or betray your trust in confided secrets
through careless, oafish, thoughtless speech.
I was wrong.
Bad TV wrong.
Corrupt politics wrong.
A friends early death wrong.
The suffering that comes from true real love wrong.
Understand then, that when I misspoke in that
careless, thoughtless moment
That wasn't to hurt you, never to hurt you
That was only about me.
My own fears and insecurities
My own desire to be more than I am or can be.
My own terrible weaknesses and flaws.
My own longing deep never wavering weeping desire
to be, for me and only me to be
everything, everything, everything more
much, much more, haunting my every waking thought and breath
desire to be
for me to be
for me and only me to be
that which caused my moments frustration.
That about which I painfully misspoke.
Do you understand me?
You must know I would never intentionally
hurt or mock, it was merely my weakness wishing
to be something more than this
something much, much more than this
There has got to be something more than this.
Please forgive me,
I am sorry,
for what it is worth.

If I could offer you all the roses
of all the earth
they wouldn't be enough.

I Loved Her Before and After

12/11/07

I loved her before I'd ever met her,
when I would sit all alone and pray to meet her,
the way she thinks and feels and speaks and creates.
I loved her even then, before I even knew that she was real.
I loved her the first time I heard her voice, and it called to me
melancholy and mournful, a reflection of my own lost soul.
I loved her the first time I heard her words, they
hooked my spirit, and captured my heart.
I loved her the first time I spoke with her, and
we instantly understood everything the other said.
She got it, the whole thing about art and bliss and truth.
She wanted it too.
I loved her when I took her to our first shows together.
I loved her when we would perform, and we both
were the ones who captured the room,
and everyone would talk us up, and we were almost
mystically in synch, in our promotional and social endeavors.
I loved her in those late night hours upon hours
covering every topic imaginable, when she would say
that I was more like her than almost anyone before,
maybe equal to one or two.
I loved her on the drunken crazy nights.
I loved her on the mellow intelligent nights.
I loved all the work we did together, perfect partners.
I loved all the fun we had together, very best friends.
I loved her when she would tell me sad tales of her past.
I loved her when I would tell her sad tales of my past.
I loved her when I would tell her secrets
and was scared that she would judge me, but she didn't.
I loved her when I would show my flaws, the ones that
makes others push me away, and I'd expect it, but she didn't.
She would say "No, it's Ok, I get you, we're the same."
I loved her when I was sad and she made me happy.
I loved her when she was sad and I made her happy.
I loved her most of all when I tried to push her away
but she wouldn't let me, because she needed me.
I loved her when she needed me.
I loved her when she would embrace me at the end of each night.
I loved her when she would meet my other friends,
and she was charming and delightful and intelligent
and witty and we would have a grand time laughing all night long.
I loved her when she would hold my hand, and I'd feel like

my heart was going to explode, like it was literally
going to burst from pure joy just being near her.
I loved her when so many people time and again would ask
if we were together, and I would say, "No, it's complicated
she is still with someone else, but she has become my best friend
and we are just close like that, It's weird. I love her though."
I loved her when she hurt my feelings.
I loved her when things were rough, when
she really needed her best friend, and I was there and maybe she
wasn't always as nice as someone could be but
I LOVED her when she wasn't as nice as someone could be.
I just fucking loved her.
I loved her in her good times.
I loved her in her bad times.
I loved her when she felt like she had nobody and nothing,
but she had me, and I was there and she had everything I could
give.
I loved her every single time when she was with my children
and I would fantasize about them all sitting around her
in her lap, adoring her, and she would be reading them a book
or something and I would dream of how we would look
all sleeping together in one big beautiful pile, her in my arms.
I loved her. I loved her. I loved her.
I loved her when she rejected me.
I loved her when I felt lost and alone.
I loved her when I felt confused and like I was going to die
because I was afraid to lose her, because it had to happen
but I didn't want to lose my best friend.
I loved her when she was dark and gloomy.
I loved her when she was brilliant and inspiring.
I love her when she was funny and silly.
I loved her when she was insightful and full of amazing wisdom.
I loved her when she loved me and said so and
I loved her when she didn't love me back, and her
actions let me know.
I just loved her.
I just loved her and loved her and loved her
and I wanted her in ways that I can't recall wanting someone before
not just regular ways, not just animal ways
but in deep true powerful I can't fucking believe this person is real
ways.
I just loved her and loved her and loved her.
I loved her when it was easy to love her.
I loved her when it was hard to love her.

I just loved her.
And sometime soon, when she is gone, when she has left me
maybe into the arms of another
maybe she will leave town and be far away
or maybe she won't even make it, sometimes it feels like
with this struggle, she might not even make it,
like she won't even live to see it all said and done.
But no matter where she goes, or how she is gone from me,
from my side, from the warming, encouraging, supporting
protecting, caring, embrace of my love.
I will love her.
I will love her in my heart.
I will love her always
far or near, dead or alive, with me or without me,
I will love her unconditionally and without fear.
I will love her., I will love her., I will love her.
I loved her before, and I will love her after
always did, always, always will.

St. Paul, of A-Town

12/11/07

He was lying on the floor.
a very great musician, but
one of the weakest drinkers I've known.
We were talking about the night
that I had first gained some respect for him.
Something that is always earned with me,
and never freely given.
She had been very bad that night
drunk and vomitey.
Any number of things could have happened,
any number of advantages taken,
by several others or by him.
But he didn't, he took her safely to me.
(*rescuing her from the predators*)

The way he drunkenly said the words;
"***and I took her back to Paul.***"
seemed to have a touch of envy in them.
Which I found somewhat baffling.

As if somehow being the asexual protector saint
is something a man should envy or aspire to.
Sure, I may have something he might never have
but he may end up with something I may never have.
An idea that eats my soul like a fucking cancer.
Don't get me wrong,
her love, friendship, and appreciation,
knowing that I am in her heart
is likely the best thing I have going on
in my life these days.
Hands down.
you see, it's just that

Sainthood,
on a cold dark Winter night
still feels an awful lot like
loneliness.

FUCK A BUNCH OF THAT SHIT

12/12/07

He was playing THE GAME. Or maybe one of a dozen other similar Internet bullshit scam artist scenario systems that pretty much represent every single motherfucking thing I despise about living, working and loving in this piece of shit post-modern culture. He spotted Alexcie at the bar and went in. Calculated, steps one, two, three, a chapter in a book to cover each move, each scenario, each reaction. I suppose that she IS as she claims, " too smart for such bullshit." BUT, we were broke like American politics, like a sad poet, so she let him buy a beer. The game was on.

He came to the table with 2 more beer, one for me and one for a Tim Thompson. In seconds I caught his scam. It was the eye contact, the calculated speech patterns, kiss ass behaviorisms. The way he would put his hands on her for a specific amount of seconds when speaking, then put them on me from across the table as well. The worst part for me is the knowledge that he had instantly pegged me as the chump. The sucker he could easily overcome through empty flattery. Through buying too many drinks so I would become disconcerted. I've seen all this before. Heard it from buddies who read the bullshit. Browsed it on the Internet. I fucking HATE being pegged as the CHUMP. I fucking hate it. I fucking hate it. I fucking hate bullshit and I fucking hate bull-shitters. LET ME SAY IT AGAIN, I FUCKING HATE IT! I gotta tell you, there was fury swelling in my heart. But I kept letting the bastard get me drunker and drunker, all the while thinking, "He'll be sorry." You see, this dark soul-ed poet bad ass mother fucker isn't really the type to get more disconcerted, passive and easy to manipulate when really drunk. Not so much. And yeah, I know there is a chapter that covers that, how to make me look like the drunken asshole. I've been there, had that happen about a year before at the Swirl, with Brittany, but guess what motherfucking cocksucker? This poet doesn't give a rat's fucking ass. I stopped caring about that shit at least a year ago. I let it fucking be what it needs to be, fuck the consequences, that's how I fucking roll, get it?

Lexy has already walked away and he is focusing on me, talking me up, kissing my ass, telling me I'm a genius. All the while, trying to have this philosophic debate abut how my notions of truth and art and meaning are quaint and outdated. That success in life is measured by what you get, who you get, and how much you get, no matter how you get it. He asks me to read him a poem, so I tell him to come to the car. I open the trunk to get the book, and read him my latest Lexy love poem. He tells me how awesome I am, but that old ideas like this will only cause me defeat and suffering. He says "What would you rather do, honestly, create this great art and live true to your principles, or give up on all that shit and have a nice comfortable place with cool stuff and lots of babes?" I say "Are you fucking kidding me?!? I'm a poet, I want art and truth and meaning, fuck a bunch of that bullshit. I couldn't care less about a bunch of empty dames. All I need is one woman with truth and guts and beauty, something real." I put the book back, making sure to move Black Justice a bit. He asks "What is that, a bat?" I take it out and show it to him, with a few stories about where it has been before. Played it up pretty big. Made sure to keep eye contact.

Inside the bar, he offers to buy me a shot, not giving it up, still looking to chump me out. I say "I'm not sure, let me ask Lexy if I should." She says "OK, but just one." Then he starts in. "Did you just ask a woman for PERMISSION to drink a shot?" I say, "It's not like that, we have an understanding, we watch out for each other. Sometimes I get a bit out of hand, it's for my own benefit." He say's "Let me ask you a question, you're in love with her, right?" I say "That's none of your goddamn business," He says, "OK, you are, but here is the deal, you'll never be with her, because she already knows you care, you're too nice, it's too late. You can never be real like that with a woman. Women are not capable of understanding real. They have to be manipulated into what you need them to do, when it comes to women, you got to have game, and if you don't have game you got nothing. You're a loser."

I respond; "First off, you represent everything I despise in the world. You are Capitalism and Corpocracy. You are profit above value. You are pure pragmatism, manipulation, greed, the ends justify the means. The worst of everything post-modern humanity has to offer. It makes me sick. You know what? You are probably right about me, I am a loser, but it's the poet in me, I can't be anything other than real, and I don't want to be, and you're probably right, she will never be with me, hell, it might well be for the reasons you say. I know that I am too much for most, I don't hold back enough and even this one who is the most motherfucking real goddamn woman I have ever come across, probably can't handle me. But, I still know in the end that I was nothing but real to her. Nothing but genuine and honest and true. I would never want anything from anyone in any way that I had to get through dishonesty or manipulation, fuck a bunch of that shit." He shook his head like I was some crazy old fool spouting nonsense and got up and walked away.

Soon, he was back over near Lex again, playing the game. She was trying to ignore him. After a bit, I walked over and pulled him aside. I shook his hand, looked in his eyes, and said, "Hey dude, I really appreciate the drinks and the conversation. Sure, we totally disagree, but I certainly appreciate the open exchange of ideas, I actually really like you, (I'd been holding on to his hand firmly, the entire time.) "It's a shame, cause I'm actually going to feel really bad when I fuck your shit up." "What do you mean?" he asked. " What I mean," I said, "is that my life has been exploding with some pretty insane emotions of late, and frankly, I'm about on the razor's edge of some self-destructive, I don't give motherfucking shit, asshole behavior. It's highly possible that with all the drinks you've been throwing at me, and if you keep fucking with me, you are going to be unlucky enough to be my "*fuck some shit up*" trigger and I'll have to bleed your fucking ass and hurt you pretty bad, DAMN! I must be drunk, because I'm already seeing it in my head, you know, you fucking bleeding and shit, FUCK, that can't be a good sign (LAUGHING)....Anyways, I'm just saying that I really like you and all, and that I'm going to feel really bad when it's all said and done."

He stood silent, my hand still holding his, looking directly into my eyes. I could see him calculating it all out, searching for the correct chapter in some book. Was I for real? Had he fed me too many drinks? He was trying to cipher it, look for the next control words, the next manipulation, the next buttons to push, but came up with nothing. "OK then, I understand." He said. "Awesome" I said, releasing his hand and giving him a friendly smack on the back. And even though I was walking away, as Lexy reminded me the next day, he had penetrated me somehow, gotten in, left a bad taste in my soul. Seriously, FUCK A BUNCH OF THAT SHIT. Next time, it's hit first, ask questions later.

Ragamuffin Bloodletting

12/12/07

My very life's blood was flowing from my arm and into a machine. Separating liquid plasma into a plastic bottle and pumping red blood cells back into veins. This is what the poor do sometimes, just to make it through the week. It's rough, and all the people that do it are a bit rough around the edges, if you know what I mean.

I was groggy as hell having been up most of the night before, drinking. It was hard to focus, but you have to keep your eyes open. I just kept staring at this ragamuffin slip of a girl in the bed across from me. Her clothing was tattered, strings frayed and hanging, no makeup, hair pulled back. An expression of some lost waif character from a Dickens novel. I memorized every line in her face and neck, stared intensely with longing at every shape and curve of her form. Her shoulders, her arms, her legs, the way they all collided. An accidental beauty lounging listlessly there in perfect broken symmetry, lost soul familiarity. Her skin, a perfect subtle swirling dark light shade mystic rhythm. Not unlike the light and life in her eyes. She was overwhelmingly beautiful. Tiny tears like blood droplets trickled from me in half lucidity. She turned a little, her eyes caught mine. I mouthed the words, "I love you." She grinned, shaking her head, rolling her eyes a bit.

The blood letter, a friendly fellow, stopped and asked her "Are you two together?" A smile as large as her whole sad, lost, lovely face came upon her. She paused, 1....2....3...4.... then carefully said, "That's my best friend." He unhooked her from the mechanism, she was done. She arose like resurrection, soul still intact for now, walked directly to me and said, "I'm going out to take a piss, I'll be reading in the lobby when you're done," I smiled and said, "You look like a ragamuffin darling, a beautiful, wonderful ragamuffin." She made an overly expressive face and laughed "Seriously? You know what my life is like, you're right here with me!" Then she picked up the umbrella and said "I'm taking the umbrella, sorry, I know it goes with your eyes and all." Scrunching up her flirty pretty face and laughing a bit, while turning to walk away.

The gentleman flesh penetrate-er walked to me and said, "So, that's your best friend, huh?" "Yeah, pretty much," I replied." "Dude, she's kinda beautiful!" " Yeah, pretty much" I replied. "What are you going to do with that?" he asked. "It's one day at time brother." I replied, half-shrugging my shoulders. He laughed "Whoo!" and wondered off. I laid my head back down for a bit. See, my sweet lost little ragamuffin had walked away, but the blood was still bleeding out of me.

<u>December 13, 2007 - Thursday</u>

Well, that was the worst thing ever. lost.

<u>One stray word</u>

12/ 07

We always get too drunk there. on that night each month, at the Good times bar.

I was freaking out to begin with, because she had said that she didn't want me to pick her up. It was something weird about her voice. I thought, maybe some dude. I talked to Anson, he said it sounded like that to him.

Before the show I was waiting and talking to this poet girl and throwing back drinks like a motherfucker. She was telling me not to stress, but I was stressing. I figured this was it, it had to be some dude or maybe she was looking to fucking hookup or something, hell, I dunno, but she was dressed to the nines when she arrived.

The show went fine, there was no dude, I have no idea what the energy, or the voice or the not riding was about. Everything was fine, It was over, we were promoting. One of our buddies had brought a bunch of his hip young bozos to our show.

I was by the bar talking to Anson. He said, "Look at her, her body language, why does she have to do that? She says it's just promoting, but you don't have to sell art with sex like that. It's like she's hitting on those young morons. It's fucked up" I'd been trying not to even think about it, drinking it down, but he was pointing it out. It wasn't even a big deal, but he was pointing it out so I said, "fucking motherfuckers."

Josh walked by and said, "Who? Lets kick their ass!" He was fucking drunk, I was fucking drunk. I said, "Those guys talking to Lexy." without missing a blink, he went right on over and started talking shit to them. We should have stopped him, but we were stunned. Anson turned to me looking surprised and said "Holy Shit, he's really doing it! What should we do?" "I don't know," I said, frozen in my tracks.

Lexy pulled Josh aside, then he started crying. Something he does sometimes when he drinks to much. He was pointing at me, implicating me, Holy shit.

I thought I'd play it off, drunken foolery I went over and said "Hey, we're going to the Shine, across the street, do you want me to get you some French Fries?" I don't know why I asked about French Fries, it was all I could think of.

She seemed OK for a moment, I though it was cool. Then she was saying something about those dudes and Josh and I could have gotten by if I'd been less drunk, more calm, but I heard Anson's words about how she was acting with those bozos and I said something about her hitting on 18 year olds or something and that was it, she started in on me, then she said "I'm done with you." I freaked.

I walked to the Shine and fell down in the middle of the floor. I was looking for Shane but found this guy Billy instead I fell on the ground outside and started
crying. A gay guy tried to hit on me. I walked back over to the Good Times bar, went in and tried to talk to her but she wouldn't fucking listen.

I was outside with Anson. It felt like everything in my entire life, all the pain, all he suffering I'd ever experienced was pumping through me. I punched myself repeatedly in the face. I smashed my head repeatedly against the brick wall. I fell down and smashed my head against my car severely damaging the front quarter section on it. Anson stood in mute horror unsure of what to do.

Josh came, and we argued in front of the building. Everyone came out, everyone was yelling something. Lexy came out and I tried to talk to her but she wouldn't. She wouldn't even fucking goddamn talk to me. I begged Josh to tell her that it wasn't my fault but he wouldn't. He was all worried about his hurt feelings and he wouldn't.

I walked back over to the Shine. Everyone followed. We were arguing out back, I was furious. I kicked over the picnic table and screamed as loud as I could. Josh and I were about to throw down in a big way. Suddenly, we were both pushed to the ground, it was Rod. It looked like he almost had tears in his eyes. He said " Y'all are two of my best friends and I'm not gonna let you fight like this!"

Just then the bartender came out. He took one look at my bloody face and one look at Josh, and said, "Goddamn it Josh! Look what you did! you fucked up one of your best friends!" Everybody calmed and Josh looked stunned, he said, "Hey man! He did that to himself!" Every eye silently looked at me. I said "yeah... I did. I was really upset. The woman I love won't even talk to me because of him!"

The bartender shook his head and said "You guys are fucked up, you all need to go home." Somebody drove me home.

It Can't Rain 4 Ever

12/14/07

The words, they sounded like death. "I'm done with you." There was a **tornado**. No one would calm and help make it right. Smashing of the face against brick wall and car, banging of the head. Everything had gone from picture perfect to a cluster fuck mess in mere moments. A stray ill-thought drunken word is all it took. They left me there on the couch with those words ringing in my ears, a terrible buzzing singing sound. She had been the first to get into my head so much and even though it was all **fatal flawed**, she knew me better, more honestly, and more real than maybe any other before. It felt just like the last one to say those words. I wanted to die.

I left messages, spoke with people, couldn't sleep. It got worse, a long night of the soul like few others. There was only sleepy half-lucidity. From 4-6 am I sat with a large kitchen knife trying to muster the will to cut out the heart that is always so terrible to the poor fellow who houses it. I noticed that the pendulum of the grandfather clock was swinging in an exaggeratedly slow motion. I remember other times long past when time would slow, in the very worst moments. At 7 am I sat up and stared motionless at the silent wall, then wept like a madman for a good bit. At 8am I put on my boots and realized that I was still wearing all my clothing from the night, even the leather jacket. I drove to the gas station, purchased 10 dollars in gas and a six pack of Coors Light, her favorite beer. I returned home, bringing in her CD. I played the first song, about drinking beer as I opened one. I drank the beer and my swollen head felt a little better. I cried during every song really loud, sure that she wouldn't call. I looked at myself in the mirror and called myself terrible things. After the CD played twice all the way through I turned it off. I checked email, returned a few, and sat back on the couch. At 10:00am I put in the Bukowski tape and cracked open another beer. Started making phone calls and sending text. I texted her and said that I was empty without her and that I was sorry for letting her down. I spoke with Brittany, a poet girl that I was once close to who texts me when she is sad. She said that I shouldn't drink so much. I left a message for the ex-wife, the last one to be done with me like that. I told her that I wasn't doing so good and to call me. I spoke to one of my favorite dames that I'd dated a while back, Chastity. She told me a story of how crazy drunk she had been a few nights earlier, we laughed. I spoke to a close female friend Grace, that I hadn't spoken to in a while. She was the most comforting. She said "Don't worry, she'll call, I've seen you two together she'll call for sure." She also said that I shouldn't drink so much. I left messages for a few others. The boss called and yelled at me for not being at work. I'd forgotten. At 12 pm Thais, my ex-wife called back. We spoke for the first time in real open ways in 3 years. I told her about Lexy, and how she was done with me. How she had been the last one to say those same words to me. I told her how it had made me feel all those years ago. She was nice about it. She said that she didn't hate me. That she regretted a lot of the things that she had said. She said that she was really sorry that it all had worked out the way it did, something of an apology, at least the closest I'd ever had. We talked for a good while, when we were done. I sat in quiet amazement for a bit, downed another beer, then put back on Lexy's CD. All of her songs sounded even more melancholy. Again I cried really loud at every one. This time the most at the one that is a prayer for change. I was still sure that she wasn't going to call. I Blogged a one word Blog that said "lost". I tried to sleep for few hours, but never really could. I did change out of the same clothes, though. It wasn't until 7 pm that Alexcie finally called. She said "Shut up and listen to me!" I listened very carefully, everything she said seemed right. I cried and told her how sorry I was, and about talking to the ex-wife. She said, "Well, maybe something good comes from everything." She told me several things I needed to work on. I told her that she could count on me, promised that I would do better. She said "OK, that's behind us. We have a lot of work to do with our projects, lets focus on that." We talked for a while and I felt better, like maybe I could keep going a little bit longer. At 8 pm I drank another beer and ate for the first time, realizing while chewing, how much my face hurt. Shane, Josh, and Rod all called to see if I was OK. I told them that I was making it through. Around 8:30 pm she texted and said "I love you, we'll be OK, It can't rain forever." I took a really deep breath for the first time all day. I noticed that the Grandfather Clock seemed to be swinging normally now. I realized that I hadn't slept in a really long time. It suddenly seemed as if I could. I faded out on the same couch that I'd been on all day.

12/16/07- Sunday

Been here with the kids by myself all weekend... by myself most of the week...taking the kids back a little early hopefully.....Lexy and I are going to the office Xmas party supposed to start at 7 at this bowling alley not to far from Shane's house..... NOTE: It was the weirdest thing!! At the party, they were doing a raffle. They got to the top gift at the end, a digital camera. Lexy looked at me and said "This is for you, I can feel it!" They called someone else's name. I said, "whatever", she said "No, wait for it." The person they called wasn't there. They had to redraw, and GODDAMN if they didn't call my name and I won the camera. Holy shit. Now in addition to the list of freaky amazing things about this broad we must add precognitive psychic powers!! No... maybe that's not it. Not precognition but some kind of black magic voodoo reality control shit! Daaaaaang. Well...that would explain the spell she has cast over me. Heh. Heh.

The Dungeon

12/07

We had driven to Dallas for a show, arrived early. We were sitting in the coffeehouse in the Southside building. The same building as the open mic where we had met. A giant ass old building converted to retail space on the bottom, the bar, this coffeehouse, a restaurant or two. Mostly art galleries I think, but all the upper floors were these ridiculously high dollar loft living spaces that had come into vogue with the regentrification efforts all over the city. We were sitting at a long wooden table sipping lattes or some such. We weren't talking much. She was a bit moody that night, perhaps the period. So, I'm kind of tapping my fingers and looking off into space, her directly next to me on my left looking the other direction, reading something. To my right is the opening where you can see the stairs that lead up to the street. A couple walks in, typical for the building, Yuppie types. Their eyes scan the room, and stop on me with something like a look of recognition. They start walking over. I figure they must have seen me perform around here and were coming to say howdy. They walk over to my right, and the gentleman says; "So you guys are here for the dungeon?" "What?" I say. He responds, "The dungeon? You guys are here for the BDSM dungeon?" "HUH?" I say this time. "Torture, role play, sex, the meeting?" I laugh. "Uh, no that's the first I've heard of this, a torture role play sex meeting here?" "Sorry," he says, "I just figured, I mean you just look like, well you look like you two would be here for the meeting." " Did you hear that hunny?" I tap Lex. " He think we look like we're here for a torture sex meeting!" "Yeah, I heard," she says. The couple wonders off looking uncomfortable then exits via the same doorway. A few moments later another couple wonders in, same scanning around look. Also finding Lex and I, walking over. This couple is a little different. He looks like he should be dressed as Obi-Wan at a Sci-Fi convention. She, younger and hotter like she might sometimes wear the Princess Leia gold bikini at home. I peg him for a computer nerd, programmer, networking, something that pays well enough to reel in a hot younger babe without much spirit. She looks bored. He looks excited. smiles, asks me quite jovially "Hey! Are you two here for the dungeon?" I laugh " "Sadly no," I reply. "OH! How disappointing!" he says, glancing towards Lexy. "Yes quite." I say, shaking my head. "How does one get invited to such a thing?" I query. "Well, it's an online group," he says, "but I'll ask if there's room for more when we find the dungeon master." he says with an oddly straight face. They wonder out as well. "Darling, look," I say, "Everyone seems to think we look like an S&M sex couple this evening!" She laughs a little. "That girl looked like she should be in the Princess leia gold bikini" she responds, "HA! I was thinking the same thing," I laugh. Lexy then launches into her nerd at a convention lusting over the girl dressed as Princess Leia imitation, it's one of the bits she does occasionally, it's pretty funny. Just then a single mid-forties gentlemen walks over. Could easily be one of the lame asses that hangs around the patio at the local Goth club whipping young half nude girls lightly on Sunday nights before waking up early Monday for his geek squad job. Before he says anything I say, "Dude, if you're going to ask me about the sex dungeon, I don't know anything about it, people have been asking us all night!" He says "Oh, that's surprising, you two look like you'd be here for the meeting. Actually, I'm the dungeon master." Hands me a card actually advertising BDSM products. " We're up in room 917, you guys should come check it out, you look like a cool couple." I laugh. I ask, " So what exactly do you do in such an environment, in case I can talk her into checking it out," I wink at him. "Oh various torture, we have equipment, role play, scenario, animal play." "What?" I stopped him. "You mean like you're fucking a chick and she barks like a dog or something?" "Well, it's a little more complicated than that," he says, "Animal play can put one in touch with primal aspects of sexuality." "Hell yeah," I say, " I'd love to fuck a chick barking like a dog, that sounds awesome!" I shake his hand. "OK, we'll drop by, 917!" He looks directly at Lex with this cheesy pervo grin, like he can't wait to see what her tiny little ass looks like under that tiny ass black skirt she's wearing. She ignores him. "Wow! Waddaya think?" I say half laughing. She turns and gives me a look one would only expect from a large black woman on the Morey Povitch show chiding a dawg like player. She says "Seriously! I'm not going to some nerd sex dungeon, and I'm sure as hell not barking like a dog. And if you even ask me, I'm gonna punch you in the face." "Oh, you're no fun!" I say. "No, I'm not." She responds. "OK, but I know plenty of dames that I hang out with all the time, all over the place, and no one ever thinks I look like a bondage sex couple with them. All I'm saying is that it must be you, you must have that vibe." I laugh. "Shut up." she says, returning to reading something. The rest of the night is decidedly less interesting. Well, except for the folk singer couple on stage that sang the song about how marvelous their lives and jobs were, and that they were over paid and felt guilty for accepting vacation time. That upset Lexy a lot more. It was quite the juxtaposition. She kept talking about it, trying to decide if they were being genuine or ironic. But I couldn't stop looking at her short black skirt, her smooth beautiful legs, black shear hose, and imagining the sounds of a barking dog.

That is one hardcore broad.

12/07

Seriously,
the kind of broad that will kick you in the nuts
then make you apologize
for making her that mad
to begin with.

That's hardcore.
Shit.

And all you were doing was this little Bukowski bit.
the one about the smog people
and the inflation people.
I mean, you were doing the voice, the inflection
she should have known it was a bit.

"Young sir"
"I will pay for this ladies burger!"
"my behavior has been unacceptable"
"In fact charge me double!"
"No triple!"
"Actually! Charge me a thousand dollars!!"
"A thousand dollars, and a hundred dollar tip!"

It was hilarious
but you forgot about her extreme germ phobia.
what with wiping every beer glass 17 times
with a napkin clockwise, then counterclockwise
and having to leave eating establishments
on more than one occasion
you shouldn't have

But a kick in the nuts!!
In front of everyone at the Whataburger?

Damn!
that's hardcore
especially considering how hilarious
the bit actually was.

Just Another Poem

12/22/07

She was lying curled up in a chair at a party
it was quite late.
One of the regular bar dudes walked by and said
"Damn man, there are no chicks at this party
well, there's this one (pointing) and she's beautiful."

I was drunk as hell, I replied
"Dude, you don't even know the half of it,
all that means nothing.
No matter how beautiful she may seem
on the outside, this dame,
is 10 times more beautiful on the inside,
where it really counts.
Depth and heart and mind and
and talent, soul and guts!
Way beyond what you see before you."

The guy said "Damn dude" and walked away.
My good buddy Andy, nearby, said
 "Damn! I want to fuck you right now!
I'm not sure but she may have smiled just a teensy bit
her eyes were mostly closed.

Seriously though, I know she fixes up nice.
I get it, I see it, and sometimes I get caught up in it too
a little bit.
But, I don't think even she realizes how little
that all actually matters, in the sum of who she really is.
It just seems like a big deal
because she does the thing, fixes it all up
and pretty much everywhere we go
any lame ass douchebag dipshit
with a pulse, a hard on, and half a brain cell
wants to get into her space.
It's lame, its disconcerting, it goes a long way toward
bastardizing the sublime nature of her,
of her very presence.
As if just anyone, any schmo, is even close to capable
of getting something so profoundly poetic as
walking, living-breathing, art.

My favorite, is when we go to the plasma center,
hell, I do it when I don't even really need the money.
There's no pretence. no makeup,
just a natural wonderful human face. Hair unkempt,
Old tattered clothing,
like some lost dejected Bohemian beauty.
like she's working through something big.
Now that's something to see, that's something special,
that's my girl lying there,
blood flowing from her veins into a machine.
She'll look over and say something to me like
"Well, it either this, or my soul?" Awesome.
Or maybe she'll repeat one of a dozen or so
comedic bits that I come up with when I'm drinking.
Like; "America, It's not Bosnia"
She's always listening to and repeating my little bits.
As if what I say is actually being heard and remembered,
as if I somehow matter or something.
Then they become these inside jokes
that only we can really share and laugh at.
Lighten the mood no matter where we're at.
As if somehow it's she and I, kind of on one side
and the rest of the world on the other.

Yeah, that's what I like
my little in-joke, no pretense ragamuffin
with the biting wit, laughing, or moody
deep and thoughtful, explaining some big idea she has,
or sharing insight into the nature of the world,
stories and experiences about it all.
Or telling me what I need to do
yeah, telling me what to do,
this brilliant slip of a girl, that's something.

That I think, is when she is truly the most beautiful.
Well, that and when she is singin out the melancholy,
bleeding out her soul in front of an audience.
but that is an entirely different poem
altogether.

TONIGHT,THE WORLD, THE GIRL

12/23/07

Tonight, tonight, she
will indulge the beast, maybe a little
maybe all the way, but it claws at her,
makes her harder than she really is.
Broken little girl. Shattered soul.
Lost, lost sweet soft, work of art.
Never having known true real love,
she doesn't know any different.

Tonight, tonight, he
is far away shining exploding desperate poet.
His grief like black tar teardrops.
He, dimmed like an eclipse the
darkening of the sun in blackest of skies. Flickering hero.
Lost man spiritus machine almost everything nothing.
With every inhale he pictures her,
his lost dark soul indulgence.
With every exhale he spits out grief.
Grief at a life misspent.
Grief at an inability.
Images of his pulling away girl,
his final work of art, his sharp and splendid stabbing love.
Elsewhere.

Tonight, tonight
He loves her more than every shade of love allowable.
His dreams of devotion to her unknowable.
Tonight, she won't embrace him anymore.
She won't create and recreate herself for him anymore.
She pulls away, not wanting his love and
even the beautiful gold green purple lovely friendship
they once swam in will be smoke float goodbye faded.
She takes it all away.
She is scared of him, and she doesn't want him.
She decries her poet; she denies her poet;
and his words like acid honey raindrops
are lost in bygone time,
because she doesn't hear them.
She chooses dark clouds
hard painful memory wind and thunder instead.
She pushes him away. She pushes him away.

She doesn't embrace him anymore, she embraces
anyone and everyone, but she doesn't embrace him anymore.
As if somehow he is so surface and shallow and silly
that his love only goes that deep.
Rather than the singing, pleading, deaf ears depths that it is.
She is scared to show him the love in her heart
Scared to indulge him, to encourage him, to satiate him,
because she doesn't want him.
She is already far away and gone
even though she's right there.

Tonight, tonight, she
grieves only at the loss of another whom
she settled for to begin with anyway.
Tonight, she begins the process of
seeking out another barely acceptable loss.
Time and loss, broken hearted memories
of her deep dark tall walled room awful, awful, awfuls
cleaving at her through time like a shattering ax.
Tonight, this is the world we live in.
Tonight, this is the world we must endure.
Dreaming poets like lingering lungfish.
Real good men like post-mortem lumps of coal.
Darling, beautiful, mournful works of art like
cracked glass figurines.
Wishing, longing, gentle, amazing-souled beauties
with beautiful, beautiful eyes wide open but
completely unable to see what's right before them.
This is the world we must endure.
Where bad people with bad hearts and bad intentions
do bad things with fists and words
and thoughts and hearts and body parts.
That cleave time and echo, echo, echo, in requiem.
This is the world we must endure.
Where good and beautiful broken artists
need and crave and long for and desire
only that which they can possibly give to one another;
but rather die a thousand, thousand deaths,
unable to connect their hearts together
and be the love inside them
tonight.

IT WAS ONE NIGHT; DECEMBER

It was one night in December when we had our third fight. Christmas night in fact. On Christmas eve she had been suicidal and said that I was selfish for wanting her alive for my own feelings and not respecting her desire not to be. We all got drunk and slept there at Shane's. I spent hours writing her a several page letter she probably never read. It was about how much I loved her, would do anything for her, and why it wasn't selfish to not want her to kill herself. Christmas morning, she went to her family's, I went to mine and took Anson with me. That night we were all sitting around Shane's house making up an idea to sell DARK POET X- mas and other cards for all occasions. Josh, Shane, Anson and I came up with some pretty hilarious shit. She came home. She wanted to go to the bar. Anson refused to go. Told me her energy was weird and didn't feel comfortable. I drove her there and all our friends came. I was so fucking into her I was kissing a few of my buddies just to impress her. Like some weird gay clown jumping through hoops. Then I leaned down at her side, no one was near, I looked her in the eyes and said "Kiss me." I could feel our energy, like I frequently could, and it seemed like she might. She said "It might change us." I said "After all we have been through, if you never even kiss me once, how will you know, how will you ever be sure what you feel?" There was this moment that lasted forever in my mind. I could feel our energy, all my hopes and dreams, like if she would move this one tiny inch, we were so close, she would feel it, and wouldn't be afraid of my love. It wouldn't be too much for her, wouldn't scare her away. She would feel it in one kiss and we would be together forever! But, the moment was broken by one of my pals. A dude I'd been putting on the gay ass clown show with for her. A dude that used to let me make out with his girlfriend when we were drunk. He said, "We should all three make out" He couldn't have known that it was the very first time in all that time, I had asked to kiss her. He leaned towards her, I'm not sure if she leaned, but I thought she might, and pushed him away by the neck. The moment was forever destroyed. She was angry at me. Said she wouldn't ride home with me, caused a scene. Shane came in and I asked him not to give her a ride no matter what, that I needed time alone to be able to talk to her down. Within two seconds of speaking with her he caved, and I knew that he would never have my back again. I drove to Shane's house like a madman, and talked to Anson, he had been right. Two days later she called and we made up, but the moment never came up again, not like that. The biggest regret I have ever known, that moment without that kiss. A regret that burns my soul more than any terrible loss, a loss not of something I had, but of something I should have had. It's the worst kind of loss there is.

A Love of We

12/28/07

It was the weirdest thing for someone like me;
The poet aging oddly and finding no solace in
the things of the world, with
an obsession for words that has collected
madness at the edges, and loss
like a residue that obscures vision and feeling.
I always notice words, big and small words.
As I sometimes say, words are everything.
They're the beginning and the end of every single story.
With her, I remember one particular word among many
that would catch my attention every single time.
It would make my heart go soft and
my resolve melt each and every time.
It was the word **WE;**
and she used it often, **WE**, a **W** and an **E,**
a very small word. It
doesn't seem to have much meaning out of context,
but in, it speaks eternal truths of the heart.

For instance:
"What do **WE** have going tomorrow?"
Or "**WE** will drop by a few different parties"
Or "What do **WE** have for Wednesday"
Or "Who are **WE** riding with to the show"
Used in the assumptive here it says something.
Something about familiarity, closeness, obligation, I think.

Then there is:
"**WE**'re not like everybody else, **WE**'re different"
Or, "I understand you, **WE**'re the same."
Or "**WE** see the world differently"
Kind of a descriptive designation, a ranking,
them-and-us grouping.

Of course there are many other usages,
Such as:
"**WE** host shows together"
"**WE** are best friends"
"**WE** see each other every day"
"**WE** are great partners"
These are all descriptive, they identify a truth.

and lastly there are the deeper **WE**'s
like:
"**WE** need to watch your drinking."
"**WE** take care of each other."
"**WE** need to work on that issue."
"**WE**'ll find a way to get through this together."
"**WE**'ll figure everything out somehow."
"**WE** are always there for each other."
Yeah, 2 letters, 2 little letters. One small word.
Words you see, have so much more
than mere meaning. They have feeling,
they say everything that there is to say.

She, was my little **WE** girl. It was always **WE**,
and when you have had the experiences I've had
in the last several years.
A little **WE** goes a long way.
I've had way to little **WE** for way to long.
Look, don't get me wrong,
I know I never had all of her,
or even close to all of her.
It only took me a few weeks to figure out
something was amiss.
Right at a month, when I got that
I wouldn't likely ever have what I craved.
Another week, to get that it was probably
going to hurt a lot before it was over
and that this was nothing new for her.
See, a shattered beautiful soul like that.
With all that heart and depth and broken love,
doesn't ever give everything to anyone
not ever, ever.
No one hundred percent.
It's always about degrees, and categories
and roles to be played to get through it all.
I'd gotten my designation, accepted it
as much as I was capable of.
Maybe I should have walked away earlier,
It's just that this **WE** thing, it was pretty fulfilling
for a while, even the partial, even a divided part
of someone you find so beautiful and compatible a soul
can be something, can mean something special for a while.
Can be something powerful and meaningful for a while.
It's a kind of love really, in my estimation

just as valid and as real as any other flawed kind
this flawed world has to offer.

Thing is, even knowing all that
living through it with the knowing.
Still, today, on this day,
walking though this cold and unkind world,
(something she would understand)
feeling for the first time in a good while
like a **ME,** and not like a **WE**...
Well, I must admit to you,
it's still pretty damn sad.

And I can't help but wonder while typing this
If **WE** are actually sad,
or if it's just **ME**.

No strength

12/29/07

My best and most true friend I fear that
if we are to gain whatever level of separation that we need.
That upon which we both agreed,
it will have to be you with the strength instead of me.
For when it comes to you my dear
I have only weakness and no resolve.
Even as one who would not be my lover
I have loved you so much more than any other.
Just your presence by my side
makes me feel more alive.
your smile, your words your depth, your mind,
your thoughts, your heart the songs of your soul,
This is where I thrive.

Because I miss you already so,
you may find me, calling, begging, pleading, weeping,
for your company.
For it to be like it was. You and I, always side by side.

I don't think these tears
are going to wash this away anytime soon,
this absence of you
This lessening of us.
Even though I pray there will always be some kind of us.
This lessening, in the context of the depth of
my real love for you
feels like such loss.
Each day without you feels sad and so much less.

If anyone will have strength It is you.
I have none
when the best friend I have ever known is concerned
only love
and now a sadness.
inside.

12/31/07 Monday

Damn! The end of 2007! What a fucking year, not my fav. A LOT of misdirection, waited energy, too much drinking, not enough resolve, what a year. Lessons learned? Mmmm...maybe. Maybe times like these are a necessity, are a part of it. Maybe new things, the growth and understanding that comes only from certain kinds of suffering, are just around the corner. I do so love many of the people I got to spend non productive time with this year, and although the art fell apart early in the year, the last several months of the year were some of the best ever in memory, in life, as far as the art goes. There are certain periods I remember back to that were the biggest, boldest and best as far as the work I'm producing, the synergy of the people around me, the energy of the scene and what it brings out, manifests, all of it. To be sure these last several months have been one of those times. Will it create something bigger? Or more nothing? I don't know, pray for me if you can, and for my closest associates. That we keep our creative hearts intact one more year, without death of the soul or actual death. That we keep it real, and that 2008 has something better, more real, and more positively productive. That something really happens in the year to come. For this poet and the band of rag tag artists that he seems to always surround himself with and love. As far as tonight, New Years eve, well there are four party possibilities that I know of. Two of which I've hit in the last few years. One with bar people, I dunno, I'll likely end the year like I've spent the last few months, following Lexy wherever she takes me. I don't know what near future times have in store for us. If we will be able to stay close or not. I hope, but with us it always seems like the strongest pull I've ever known with this sad sad slipping away mixed right on in. Who knows, but I want to spend this night with her, no matter what she is doing or where. A family party I think mostly. Although we may travel around as well. I DO love her so, she is the best friend I've ever had, even if we never ever find each others hearts, Gods I wish that we could. I pray that this next year 2008 will hold better things for she and I. That we are both able to find the spiritual, material, artistic balance that we both so desperately crave. Together would be awesome, but if not, I pray we both find it somehow, apart. Pray for a meaningful, positive year to come.

Resoulution; Sadness and Love

01/01/08

I get it all a little bit more now
my sweetest broken dear.
Having seen the father
and the dynamic that surrounds the father,
standing toe to toe with the father,
refusing literally,
to bow down to the father.

I see it all a little more clearly now
my sad, beautiful darling.
At the bar for last call,
the whole scene still stinging,
starting to act out the act.
Watching the periphery for my reaction.
But I don't this time.
I swallow it, sitting alone in non-reactive silence.
Unable to hear even friendly voices.
Eating anger and frustration like an Atom Bomb.
Cognitive cancer like soul-burning acid.
Deep heaving hollow breath after deep empty breath
until you lose momentum.
Even my buddy is surprised as you fall into despair
with nowhere to channel this thing.

I feel it more clearly now I think
my dark soul mate reflection.
Standing in the street, you over your steering wheel
won't even get out of the car.
We button up our coats and simply wait.
I see it in your tears, in the shaking frailty
of your beautiful, sad limbs.
In your momentarily speechless affliction
when I hold you, briefly,
feeling the emptiness, it hurts
like a terrible, empty burning away.
Both of us.

I love you even more, my very best friend
as we do it differently.
No reactions, no acting out on either side.
Only open, honest speech to one another.

Another beer or four to drown the demons.
Another toast to what we will face together.
I love you with encouraging words that
I didn't even know were inside me anymore.
I love you with these words until even I
surprise myself with my resolve and
start to feel better about all that I face,
in the face of strength mustered for you.
We talk it and we talk it and we talk it
which is what we do best, what created us,
until enough of it has faded.
There are jokes and stories, light laughter
and you can sleep at least, and that's something.
I take my buddy home
and I drive home,
calling you one more time to tell you I care.

I think I know you and love you and feel you
a little more clearly now,
a little more resolutely now.
I think I understand myself a little better now.
Feeling my own open, broken and needing heart
in the first moments of a brand new year.
We are together
and the sunlight begins to shine and
it’s all new, even as it’s all old.

I think I love you even more, you
wonderful, broken, melancholy, beautiful soul.
It's a brand new year and
I resolve to love you
and to be the very best friend to you
and to myself
and to all the struggling burning souls
that we know
Finding my real true balance again
through compassion and love and creation
in the year to come.

Why I Pissed All Over That Last Poem

01/02/08

I'd written this poem on the first day of a new year. It was all about an emotional experience the night before on New Years eve. The poem was gutsy and real and powerful and insightful. It was profound and revealing and deep. And although it was about this struggle, I felt it ended in a very positive place. The lines were sharp, the flow smooth, it had symmetry to it. Even the shape of it was appealing the way most of my favorite poems look to me. A few very good poets had commented it online, saying how powerful a piece it was, I was really feeling it.

Next day, I'm at work. I print it up planning to read it that very night at the big monthly open mic. I decide to show it to the two fellows who sit in the cubicles to the right and left of me, as I sometimes do. To my surprise, they say I shouldn't read it. They say that I shouldn't read it! They say " Look, it's obvious by the phone conversation you were having in hushed tones an hour ago that Lexy is already upset with you. Why do you want to make it worse?" I'm taken aback, "what do you mean?" He says, Don't get me wrong, it's a powerful piece. It's just too much. Your going to do what you always do and just make shit worse. Why do you do this? Why don't you ever hold some shit back man. It's just too much, too revealing. Pretty soon she's going to get sick of your shit. Seriously, don't read this tonight. Why do you do this to yourself?" "It's just what I do," I say, "I can't help it, it's a kind of compulsion!"

Then they suggest maybe my New Years resolution should be to write happier poems. Maybe find happier people to be around. Stop fucking shit up, getting drunk, acting like a fool. One even suggests that this spiritual void in my writing might best be filled with, yes, you guessed it, the love of Jesus.

I'm out the door, holding the poem in my hand. I stop in the men's room before hitting the elevator. One of the corporate elite is washing his hands. I balance the poem in between the metal pipe and the wall. Unzip, and start pissing, while staring at the words. Then suddenly I stop, hold back the urine stream, grab the poem, and toss it into the urinal. Then I piss all over the goddamn thing. Soaking wet and vitamin pack yellow. I piss the fuck all over it. Guts and feelings, insight, sharp and beautiful and everything. Thinking about how I should piss on every motherfucking poem I've ever written. Every single fucking one. I should piss on the beautiful muses. I should piss on my truest closest friends. I should piss on all the other poets. I should piss on everyone listening to my bullshit neuroticisms at the open mics, telling me how profound and moving I am. I should piss on every goddamn one of them. But mostly I should piss on my stupid ridiculous self. On my stupid over active brain that's "all crazy in there." On my stupid emotional heart that won't fucking stop with all the goddamn emotion no matter how much beer and liquor I try to fucking kill it with. I should just piss on myself and my useless art and truth and need for something more. I should just stop afflicting anyone near me that loves me, anyone I'm close to, with my insane neurotic, anachronistic, painful, over revealing writings. I should fucking stop and stay away from anyone. Especially anyone I really love. Find a real job. Find Jesus. Give up on love and meaning and absolutely anything and just fucking STOP! Because I hate me. I hate having to be the way I am. I hate writing poems and living this life like this. Because it fucking hurts.

I leave the pissed on papers there for someone else to clean up. I take the elevator down and it seems so fucking slow. I think about her in the parking lot while walking to the car. Tears are streaming down my face. Some fake blond secretary with a joker's laugh and expensive shoes looks at me like I'm a fucking mental patient. I get in the car, and somehow impossibly, her song is on the CD player.

"The efforts required drains my life quite out of control, my motives have all succumbed to mold. Along with all my most valued thoughts anything worth having is that all it costs to be? In this place I'd rather not be at all... now I'm here bringing nothing more to you than an honest quest for truth. As my words reawake what vicious years depleted telling me in such soft whispers that was all you needed"

I drive home, alone in the car. Alone in the car, a fact that completely impacts me at that moment. The first thing I do is reprint the poem because I will read it eventually. Not that night, but I will read it. Because I don't seem to have any choice at all, but to piss all over myself.

Dramatis Personæ

01/05/08

I tried to contain my love for you
as though being viewed through
a white paint tattered framed window
in an old wooden home.
I needed you, I needed you, I did.
And it wasn't just the beautiful you.
The one that made me feel more alive;
innocent damsel in white lace.
I needed the one that would fuck me up.
One I could resonate and love so much.
Finally unable to turn my gaze away from, seeing
my own true face reflected at the bottom of it.
I needed the other you, only hinted at;
whore of Babylon in digital lacy black.
A rescue of sorts, you, secreted away
embedded and captive with an almost
non-entity, barely noticed until
a void was all it took to break you down.
Then it was my turn.
See, I'd made an uneasy alliance with the shadows
long ago,
a peace of sorts,
allowing darkness free reign in it's time,
for all things a season.
Old school Elysian
Mystery School shit.
Except that I'd become stuck.
Existing in-between spring times, your permanent November.
I needed a sanguine song bird Persephone
to descend with me.
Who wouldn't, what hero soul wouldn't
want to strike a deal with gods
to raise you from your underworld captivity.
But sadly no dark nymph ever returns the love of
any misguided martyr complex savior poet,
Bleeding out Golgotha alone in it.
On dark nights of long knives
hungry with smoke and smokey mirror whispers.
Having just first handed the Rex Complexes.
A state of mid-heartbreak downgrade.
pushing me away,

polar icecap alone, fears my own.
It occurred to me then what had inadvertently transpired.
Stuck in twilight between darkness and light, one might
need pursue sad love into darkest nether depths,
complete the journey, be reborn, come alive.
But no martyred poet ever saves anyone else.
Darkness, in it's familiarity, becomes itself.
I became a spiritual extension of you,
to share in non-redemptive self-loathing
pulled down into demon dark abiding.
How could I be loved by one desperately craving light.
I think I want to love you more than that.
I want to love you outside pre-assigned archetype roles.
I want to love you in ways that pulling you up,
holding your white lace form above a precipice just isn't enough.
I want to love you without condition.
I want to love you outside confines of
any tattered window frame.
I want to love you finally understanding these guts,
these grand esoteric symbol plays within.
I want to love you enough NOT to destroy myself
for the sake of you.
More than the mere circumstance of it.
I want to love you enough to rise above it.
To love you enough to find my own way back into the light
and show it to you,
see if you can do anything with it.
See what you make of it.
Real true spirit to soul love
hero journey love. unconfined fearless love.
A love powerful enough to do something different,
first.

Dragon Night

01/06/08

There was this guy that came to the open mic. A bit odd. Recently divorced, a recent mental patient, a young guy, early twenties, an odd presence about him, nice enough I thought. He followed us across town where my female, um, well let's just call her my time/thought/feelings and emotions human, Lexy, wanted to see some band that she enjoying. But me and the guy, and Shane's girlfriend, that we were watching out for while he was out of town, didn't want to pay the cover. So we walked across the street to this tiny bar that I'd never even seen, but happens to be directly next door to one of our weekly open mics. Okay? Make sense?

The three of us are sitting and chatting over a pitcher of beer. The guy is telling us his entire life story. Shane's girl is mostly disinterested, text-ing her pals. He's talking grand ideas of romance, love, marriage and loss. Too many all too familiar things. He says something about Lexy, then is visibly surprised to learn that we are not a couple. He says; " Are you serious? I can't believe that! I'm really good with reading people, I would swear all evening that the two of you are a couple! The way you interact seems clear, wow!" I say; " Yeah, I've actually heard that a hundred times, I'm used to it. But no, we are partners and best friends. We do everything together, but we're not together." He says; "Listen, I'm going to tell you something. I grew up with a single mother and a single grandmother. I know women and how they behave, their body language, how they feel and what they do. I can read her easy. She loves you. It's obvious in every way that she interacts with you. She's just scared for some reason. Or she doesn't think that she deserves to be loved as much as you love her. I've seen a lot of women with hurt inside that are scared and push away someone that they really love or that really loves them. It's some kind of defense. They don't even know they are doing it, maybe, but she fucking loves you. I can see it." Right then Lexy walks in. Her show over, on a huge high from the music. She made a few jokes or some bit, her usual thing. Then walks off to the bar or the restroom or something. The guy leans into me and says, "Look man, I'm serious, don't ever give up on her no matter what. She was made for you, you are perfect. I don't like to use the word destiny because it seems to imply no choice, but you two just feel like destiny, like you were created here in this time and place for each other. It's like the old romance stories. You have this presence like you are this knight in shining armor and she is your fairy princess. Your damsel, and you have to fight through these trials to get to her. You have to slay a dragon or two to win her hand. But in this world all of her dragons are inside her heart and head, in her soul. Those are your battles. But she's worth it. You need to be strong and patient and never give up. She needs your strength, don't give up! What a tragedy that would be. It's as if the two of you were made for one another and life wouldn't even be worth living if you don't find your destiny together. You'll never find another like her and she doesn't realize it yet, but she will never ever find another like you, either."

Shortly after, he talks her up while I'm sit and listen. Then we're eating some late night taco's, she leans over and tells me that he had made her uncomfortable. Not in an upset way, but that he had really hit the nail on the head with this impromptu psycho analyzing thing. That people are always doing that to her but are usually way off base. But this guy had really gotten some stuff, and it was weird. She was eating a taco, her knee resting against mine a little. I'm watching the way her facial expressions over exaggerate when she speaks passionately or with intense emotion. It's the oddest thing. It's very unusual. I smile a little. She's talking about the music, and I remember thinking that she is absolutely perfect. A little insane perhaps. Well, more than a little. But that he was right, she is absolutely perfect. She seemed perfect to me in that moment.

We say goodbye to the dude. He says he'll come out again soon. I'm really not ready to stop looking at this perfect mad dame and drinking in her every word the way I do. It feeds me somehow. Shane's girl is asking me to take her to the mall to see an old pal who is an overnight security guard, which seems crazy, but honestly in that mode I'd do anything to get just a little more face time with my soul mate and keep our flow of energy going a bit longer. I agree to the venture. We drive over and find the guy. She gets out and chats him up, catching up and such. Which leaves me in the car with my favorite person. It's us in our zone, like on our best longest nights. We talk and talk and talk. I swear to you that I could listen to this person's silly cognitive fire and never ever get tired of her. Then just like that it's 4:30 am. We need to get some water because we've talked ourselves silly. I take the girls back way across town to Shane's house. He is one hell of a buddy, helping Lexy with a place to stay when she had none. A brief hug and they are gone. I'm driving home, It's nearly morning. It's days like this that can make a man crazy and wild or bring him that much closer to the joy he needs to survive. But we never know do we? We just catch whatever sleep we can and move on to the next day's fight. In the end we will either defeat the dragons, or they will defeat us. What else is there?

Please, Please Do Something

01/07/08

My god, do something with me
My god, do something for me
My god, take me somewhere, anywhere
but this nowhere in between somewhere and here.
Make me into something
Make me do something
Take me and make me and use me and make me feel
needed, useful, purposeful, loved, meaningful, beautiful
wonderful, absolutely vital, indispensable.
My god, make some use of me, please
Love me, make love to me
tell me what I need to do, to be, what I want to be
to have it all.
Give me a chance
Give me a reason
Give me a break
Give me my soul back, give me my soul back, give me my soul.
I want it, I need it
I spill apart for the very sake of it.
Every breathing, waking, thinking, suffering moment.
Every burning moment
Every Atom Bomb moment
Every slipping away slipping away slipping away
moment.

With all of it just out of reach
Eyes close, eyes closed. eyes closed
face all lit up with orange yellow street light.
The perfect love for me
The perfect art for me
The perfect friends for me
The perfects times for me
The perfect razor sharp love, love, love, love, love
for me, I want to scream
always, always, always just out of reach

My god, my god, my god,
make me into what she needs
take from me whatever I don't need
make me into what I need to be
take me where I need to be

My god my god my god my god
Make something happen
Make anything happen
Do something for me
Do something with me
Make it all real, make me feel real,
again.

beautiful mad head fuck

01/09/08

She is beautiful, crazy mad fucking beautiful. When I say that I'm not talking about her tight little ass, or all the other bullshit that draws so many men to her. No, I'm talking about the million fucking things that only I can see. I'm talking about this voice and this spirit and this passion. This endless mad passion that never ends. It spits itself out into the world and I drink it in. It's these thoughts, feelings, longings and never ending words. It's this mad wild cognitive field that is finally something close to a match for my own. I crave it like blood and air and truth.

We have this energy that creates this synergy, this mad creative flow. Pretty much everyone I know that sees us says it's something to see, some kind of mad, terrible, beautiful, life exploding show. She is more alive than anyone although she doesn't feel it. She is always going and it makes my head spin. I get so caught up I go nuts. I get crazy, or jealous, or scared it will end, or insanely drunk and cry big wet tears in public, or become a crazy mad fool, or get this look in my eyes that she considers unreasonable but it's just the overwhelming nature of it. Of her.

Then she gets upset or frustrated with me and pushes me away. Motherfucker how I suffer when it's like that. It's all dark and the energy is broken. Then something happens, some tiny thing perhaps, and she lets me back in again. Best of best again, all is forgiven, like bliss, like sunshine, like heaven. She would do it too, she would be my very best friend forever if I let her. I can see it in her eyes. She would love me and take care of me and watch out for me and put up with all of my bullshit and never ever fucking leave me alone. She would be the best friend I've ever known, if I could do it. Get past her bullshit men issues, her broken views. Her demons that bite and scratch and claw. But who can do that? Who can live with demons like that? Share a love like that? She knows that. She assumes my love is conditional and situational like everyone else. But its not, it's not! It's just that it is all so fucking intense. She won't be with me. She won't let me fully love her!

She talks of death and says I'm selfish for wanting her alive for my own reasons. That can't be selfish, can it? I barely know how to think or feel or what the hell I'm doing. I know I love her. I love every motherfucking moment of it. I love the joy, the truth, the suffering, the closeness, even the pushing away, even the fear. It's all so real, the great stuff is real, the terrible stuff is real, I've never felt more real, I've never felt more fucking alive! it feels like classic drama, like true fucking art. It's a crazy mad beautiful head fuck, but I love it, I fucking love it. Which means at this point it must be me that has gone completely fucking insane.

For Lexy

01/10/08

My love for her is like some mad exploding stream of emotions. It flows on and on in thought and feeling and spirit. It is incomprehensible I suppose to some, who have not known such love. Meaningful only to those capable of fully loving and understanding what love is, like me.

An example, a typical day; were eating dinner. She reaches up, scratches her nose and I notice the back of her hand. First I feel excited. I think of how beautiful her hands are, especially the backs of them. They are in at least my top five of my absolute favorite of her physical features. Along with her mouth, the small of her back, shoulders, the flesh at the sides of her torso and her nipples in a tight tee shirt. But that's a different story, that's more of a blood rushing enthralling excitement, and less of this mystical feeling, like the hands. Those hands! I think about her lifting a glass with them. Taking a drink. How they look when she plays guitar. All the minute details. Holding a piece of fruit, maybe an apple or an orange. Then I wonder if I've ever actually even seen her eating an apple or an orange or if I've just thought about her hands so many times that I've just imagined that image. Just like all the other images, the deeply embedded alone at night ones. I think about the feel of her hands accidentally brushing against me messing with a CD in the car while I am driving, conflagrating me, taking my breath away for a brief but endless moment. Or when she is handing me something and I take just this extra microsecond to linger on her hand. Just a tiny fraction of a second stretched out in my mind.

I think about closer times when she would touch me ever so slightly, hold my hand in her hand for brief periods. In the car, talking, at the coffeehouse, walking on a Dallas sidewalk. I think of her hands placed upon on my chest while speaking, giving me instructions, telling me something to do. On my shoulder or forearms, My GOD! Those hands! I'm looking at those wonderful, beautiful hands, but what is it? What makes them special? Sure, they're unique, different, strong for her size, but surely there is no magic in them? Where does this overwhelming feeling come from? I follow wrist to elbow up to shoulder, neck, face (My god what a wonderful face!) All lovely and nice, but physical attractiveness is not magic, it doesn't feel this sublime, this otherworldly, it isn't this love, it just isn't.

Suddenly I get it. I think about her voice. The way her eyes look when she speaks. The entire cognitive tornado that she is. It’s then I realize that this is where I love her, inside somewhere. In her heart, mind, soul, spirit. I love her humor, compassion and sadness. Her joy, heartache, hope, intellect, desire, anger, pain, fear and need, her ideas, her flaws. The way she thinks and feels. The way she expresses herself in big giant ways in art and grand ideas. In small everyday ways, in a million tiny things she says. I love when she is speaking so intensely and becomes frustrated she just screams out this silly sound, waving her hands around like a loon. As if her physical form somehow can't contain all that is inside her. I really really love that. I love her laughter. Her laugh is the best laugh I have ever known, and when she laughs while I laugh, I am loving her with my laugh. When she laughs at something that isn't really funny but dark cynical and covering some real internal pain. I love her even more. Because I love her so much, I want to love her through absolutely any pain she has, and show her through word and deed that there is something and someone better.

I want to walk beside her in anything that she faces. To support her in creativity and feelings and all needs. Show her that I can be understanding and flexible and love her and be with her while encouraging her to be everything she longs for, while being loved by me. I want to hold her and put my hands in her hair and kiss her on the face and neck and mouth and absolutely everywhere. With passion and desire and respect and dedication and truth and real love.

I want to hold her and never let go and be at her side through anything she faces never alone for all of her days. What I love is her. The real her. Her heart, talent, mind, body, soul. Both strengths and weaknesses, the whole thing. Only somehow in that moment, it all seems to be there in her hands. It's not the hands, it's all of her inside there waiting If only she would just give me her hands, those beautiful hands.

There it is racing through my mind all at once. All that really happened was that she scratched her nose, but I see those hands and it's all right there. Me, with all this inside my exploding mind. I sit dumbfounded and transfixed, unable to express the depth and truth of it all. She looks at me and says "What?" But I can't possibly put all this into words. Not there in that moment, this thing about her hands and her soul, and how I much I love her and need her, and would die for her. It's all too much. So instead I say " I was just thinking how pretty you look today." Because that's the simplest, mildest thing I can think of to say. She responds " Whatever! " I say "NO, seriously! I mean it, you're very pretty!" Again she says " Whatever!," Rolls her eyes a little bit, and that's it. That is the nature of my love. The whole of it. I sit back, breathe, and melt back into myself. Stuff it all down, smile, and continue on as usual with my best friend. Who, it seems, will never ever understand what she does to me just by being who she is. She consumes me. She consumes me like time, and longing and fire.

As I say, incomprehensible to some, who have not known such love. Meaningful perhaps, only to those capable of fully loving and understanding what it is, like me.

Regarding Conversation Over Lunch.

01/10/08

Hey,
you're beautiful.

oh,
I'm not just talking about
 your hair
unkempt
at lunch.
Although admittedly
that fills me with
joy.

I'm talking about your
ridiculously hardcore soul.
Frustrating,
somewhat disconcerting, and
beautiful.

damn.
you have a
beautiful
soul.

I can't stop
feeling it.

A question of revelation

01/11/08

It's always that way with us, I wonder why? I'd just walked in, bringing your dinner, some small spark started a conversation. Only with us its never small talk. It's always depth, philosophy, or some kind of revelation. You're always laying out casual tales of terrible tragic past events, just for me. On this night you threw a few new bits out. Two separate stories. Anson looked at me with astonishment. He says that you're less revealing around him. He sometimes says how jealous he is of me. That you give me this unusually open trusting part. That and the way you always tell me you love me. I'm way more jealous of him though. Not as much since he expressed actual feeling towards you and you pushed him into a buddy role, Which I knew would happen. Of course it's possible that you and he have fucked and lied. I think that sometimes. But this revealing thing seems to be specifically aimed at me. Why is this? Why do you want me to know everything terrible that has ever happened to you? This endless story of things that have effected you and made you what you are. All the beautiful wonderful parts, and all the nearly impossible to handle parts. Is it because you want me to feel this deep compassion for you? This tragic love? Is it on some level that you know that the more I feel this the harder it is for me to ever push you away even if it hurts, and you need me? The same reason I'm the one who gets the ongoing suicide talk. As one friend suggested, it keeps me near and available all the time? You know I have this savior complex, are you somehow using that to keep me near? Or is it possible you believe that I might actually save you? You say that no one can save another, ever save you. Do you want me to try? Do you wish that? You know that's what I do. I dig in and get at the root of the human condition. That's my poet role. Get in there and understand every detail, every motivation. You know me, you know my years of experience in confessional art, Buddhist meditation, cognitive awareness psychology, therapy, treatment, 12 step groups, books read and absorbed, you know me. You know yourself. You know you need some of what I've had, but you always say that you aren't strong enough to face it. Or that you know you should, but who has the time when simple basic survival dominates every day. You know you have a journey, but you are scared and you aren't sure what to do, how to even begin. Is that it? Am I your Guru? Your therapist? your sponsor? Or is it something else, are you opening up to me, giving me your worst, telling me all the worst stuff so easily because you love me? Trust me? Because you really want me to love you but don't know how to love back? You say that you have never been in love with anyone in your life. How would someone like you handle that feeling? Would it be fucked up like this? All full of misdirection, slow revelation, self-sabotage and fear? Why are you like this to me? Why push me away and pull me back in? Why do you treat me so special and then tell me I'm not special? Why do you need me so much, but never ever really give me a chance to be with you? Why does every single decent person around us see something really unusual and special. True love, tragedy, beautiful madness, they all see something unusual and extraordinary. What am I to you? Hero? Best friend? Saint? Protector? Teacher? Student? Eventual lover? Therapist? Savior? Am I here to show you something? To save you? To lose you? To be with you forever? To love you then let you go? Your motivations and actions are mysterious, maybe even to you. You're always saying that you need a sign. That you prayed and prayed to your god, to the universe, for aid, for help, for guidance. You can't understand why nothing has been forthcoming, I feel sure that it has. That it's me. I am somehow sent here for you. What do I do? How do I save you? How do I love you? How do I show you the path and can that path possibly be one that walks beside my own? Could I be that blessed? Could you be the answer to my prayers as well? Are you already? I love you so much.

VORTEX

01/12/08

It's this vortex of despair, of untime, of untruth
It's the song forwarded through in the car all evening
because it finally became emotionally too much to bear,
too torturous. Too painful to hear.
It's the dishonesty of parents.
It's the dishonesty of children.
It's the casual detachment of words on a voice mail.
It's Champagne and I wish you the best, I wish you the best.
It's three nights alone in my house where she just won't come.
It's questions on surveys about soul mates,
which is different than attraction, or emotion, or even love.
It's about a connection of the soul, all the more rare, the more rare
your actual soul.
I said that I'd only ever known three.
The first institutionalized me, and is now a lesbian.
The second took 8 years of my life, and now married another.
The third tragedy has not been completely written. Yet.

It's about Moo Goo Gai Pan.
It's him answering the door sock footed for the third time.
It's casual familiarity.
It's body language and scant clothing.
It's moist hair and moist eyes.
It's time itself slipping away and everything exploding in the mind all
at once.
It's I hate you and I'm not sorry for hurting you.
It's that Pearl Jam song she would always sing to me.
It's we're just alike, we're just alike, we're just alike.
It's her tiny body crying against me at night.
It's small hard nipples, in a white shirt.
It's small hard nipples and lotion rubbed on them.
It's fuck me and impregnate me one last time before I go.
It's the roommate fucking her in the next room.
It's the way he would cry about his father and his dead wife.
It's the way **her** father made her hard
It's the way **her** father made her hard.
It's the way **her** father made her hard.
It's the way that **my** father made me soft.
It's the way that **my** mother made me hate.
Stuffed away in a drawer.
It's all of our stupid, fucking never ending, painful secrets.

It's the edges of a smile.
It's art and pain and cries for help and threats of death.
It's small hard nipples that are like never ending secrets.
It's no one and nothing and nowhere.
It's she and I finding one another finally and
her choosing another over me.
It's this death of hope, this finality of untruth.
It's sandals and unkempt hair and expensive lunches.
It's the death of Bill right over there.
It's the window ledge at the madhouse.
It's the red brick wall.
It's my son saying I'd always hoped that someday
we would all be together again, but now I know that we won't.
It's soul mates, it's soul mates, it's soul mates, its soul mates.
my goddamn fascination with soul mates.
It's the dishonesty that comes with it all.
Emotional dishonesty.
Spiritual dishonesty.
Sexual dishonesty.
Every single soulmate is a mother, with a terrible book of secrets.
Every best friend is a mother, every wife is a mother.
Every mother, is a terrible, selfish, soul-destroying creature.
Like their mothers destroyed them.
Like their fathers destroyed them.
Like my capacity for too much love is destroying me.

It's catchy little tunes in a comfortable bedroom setting.
It's suburban white boy tunes when I've never been unselfish
enough to wish anyone the best, not really, or maybe just too
honest.
It's when she came to see me in the mental hospital and said
"This is my fault, I know I'm a bad person, I can't help myself"
It's that I'd never noticed the similarities between them before
tonight. Only with the other one, the wife, but I liked that,
I liked it so much I craved it like a never ending desert thirst.
It's hammers, and skirts and breakfast tables and other images from
songs that they sing to me as I attempt to decode all of existence.
It's standing by the elevator in the courthouse with her back to me
chatting some inane bullshit about how our son wants a puppy.
As she signs away our life together with the same artistic flair
as designing our first chapbook cover together, her nude silhouette.
It's my children singing her songs on Thanksgiving morning.
Its all the 4am's that made him so upset, strangely, perfectly
innocent, except for in my heart, which he must have known,

because he is a man, and not a woman, capable of living in such falsity.
It's about bus stop teardrops and bloody snowflakes.
It's about the Celestine Prophesy.
It's about altering views and wanting more and those goddamn demons.
It's about over and over again in the car soaking up every tortured note.
It's always, always, always about thinking some dude is a friend, that any man is capable of anything honest or real, or honorable, except me.
It's about being loved, but never loved enough.
It's about finally, finally, finally, finally, finding another soul mate again after giving up, after seeking so much less, after degrading myself in barrooms, and parking lots, and bathrooms, and strange houses.
After giving bits and pieces of myself to absolutely anyone and everyone just to feel something, just to feel alive, just to destroy myself more slowly instead of all at once.
It's about the way she trusts me, and looks to me, and needs me and loves me but chose another over me, chose another over me, chose another over me.
It's the way her hands look in a certain light.
It's the way the small of her back looks for brief moments.
It's the way the emptiness inside her needs to be filled and I am the only one with enough heart and soul and guts and love to do it because I'm motherfucking superhuman that way.
But she won't, she won't, she won't, she won't, she won't let me
It's not about having something and somewhere to put it,
or some bullshit
It's about soul mates, about fucking soul mates, her and only her
It's about a complete spiritual inability to connect with any other female, even a little, even
at all, since that day on October 3rd.
It's sock feet and casual dishonesty.
It's hard nipple truth.
It's a posture and casual fluidity that makes me insane
that makes me mad with sadness and loss and gets me lost
in this vortex, this spinning killing timescape in the head alone vortex.

It's this phone call.
"Are you OK? Why did you take off like that?"
"Are you sick? Are you depressed? Are you upset? Is it the ex-wife?"

Yes, Yes, Yes, Yes, YES, It's all of that, it's these last three years of numbing emptiness. Of un fulfilling self-destructive indecisive emptiness.
It's everyone goes, everyone betrays, everyone dies, everyone lies.
It's finally finally finding one person, one human being in this fucking cruel godless universe that I feel truly connected to that I truly overwhelmingly FEEL And being one sentence away from losing her One unspoken sentence away from disconnection.
One unspoken sentence away from a pain too great for me to publicly cope with. It's non-returned text messages and a night of painful sleeplessness. It's this unshakeable image of aloneness again alone in the car, alone in my heart, alone all the time.
It's this image of me on a Polar Icecap, a giant never ending featureless sheet of ice, in gray twilight. Splayed out like some bleeding Christ.
This is the image that twists my guts when I'm losing her losing even the small portion of her that fucked up "all crazy in there" me is allowed to experience, to enjoy, to love.

It's not OK. It's not even a little bit ok. It's spinning.
It's this vortex of untime, of untruth, of sadness and awful despair. and it's spinning and tearing and eating away
until there is almost nothing left.

FEARs

Averting the
eyes was an
impossibility,
while she stared
at herself in a
full length
mirror,
straightening
her hair, the
small of her
back exposed.
The entire
texture of her
flesh making
itself aware of
itself in the
collective
consciousness.
She asked about
fears, I told her
I have none. She
said I was lucky,
she had many
that had been
installed.
Her memory
is the one I fear
will
never leave me.
Even after she
has,
fears,
and all

I'm going inside and inside and in and

01/13/08

I wish I could stop thinking about the ex-wife being remarried. It's opening up all these doorways. Lifetimes of feelings. My performance last night of my most recent insanity was overwhelming, and NO, she didn't bring it up or talk about it. We've been playing the empty space between us game ever since Christmas. Where once there was this god-awful honesty, now there is this slight "no talk zone" at the edges. It hurts, feels like fading. That space is there, we are roller coaster-ing it now. At the open mic I got the thing again. A woman we met the third time we performed together. She pulled me aside and for the five thousandth time I heard "Are you two together? " ARGH! "No," I said, she has different ideas about what she wants in a man. She sees me as her best friend, she's mine, but I want the other because I know it's right." She says, "WOW! I would have thought you were together. It seems so obvious you guys make the perfect couple, so great together! It would be beautiful!" I hear it from different people almost weekly now it seems. She says; "I've been around, divorced a few times, what greater joy than to be with your best friend, marry your best friend!" Yeah, I know, I hear that too, I get it, I'm there. She's just never been through it. It's not me, and by the time it's someone like me, it'll be too late for me." Then she says; " Don't give up, be her best friend, be there, be as wonderful to her as you can. It makes a difference in the end. I'll be praying for you." Damn, we seem to be in a lot of prayers now. Later, we stop by see her family for a few, then across town to hang with some poets. A serious all night-er. We were sweet, laughing, in our zone. Suddenly she was shitty to me, lashed out at me, hurt my feelings. I got quiet. She called me out in front of everyone. We got mad at each other, everyone was weirded out. Christmas memory, I suppose. She left the room. I followed and apologized. I said "Look, let's not do this, I love you OK? I'm sorry if I was too sensitive. Let's just not make this night like this." I was thinking about that growing empty silent space and how it could all be gone soon. I didn't want it yet. Just one more great night, right? We somehow did it, moved along. Then we sang together. She played a new song about her childhood, and I fucking cried. It was as dark and as real as the stuff I've been writing. She played my favorite song and we sang it together. It was one of my best moments ever. Then we wrote a song together. Her, Kat and I. It was freaking beautiful. "*In the cold in the cold in the cold, it doesn't have to be that way, .maybe it has to be that way.*" It was amazing. Then we dropped Rod home. It was five, we hit Pitt Grill. It was the same stuff over and over again. Her and the men. Her and her ex. Her ex, my ex, the same reasons over and over in my head the same differences the same old fatal flaws. Why she will never love me. Sitting in those moments like that it hurts not being a JESUS, or at least not looking like one. Being too real, too much, too me. I take her back. The goodbye is casual at best, brief, the least affectionate of hugs. Her dreaming still of the empty ex I think. I stop down the street, text her the nite nite love message we always ended every night with a few weeks back, before Christmas. Three nights in a row, no response. What am I doing? All this energy, all this love, all this power. Taking her everywhere, feeding her at the break of dawn, doing the roller coaster argument thing like a great love, but I AM NO GREAT LOVE. I am empty and alone. As alone as she complains about being. Stupid, stupid dame. She'll call later. I've lost touch in all the small ways with every single person but her. God, this is gonna fucking hurt. It means so much to have someone who you can call at moments notice. Like FRIDAY at work, sick as a dog with this freaking flu. I had to get the kids then run to work a delivery shift. A LONG painful day! I called her at noon. She didn't want to wake up and bring medicine, but she did. Drove it up to the office. It saved me. She's always there, every single motherfucking day. Lunch, the plasma center, open mics, on the phone, a beer or two, late at night, projects, calming me, SERIOUSLY!! can I afford to lose this person?!?! Even though she makes me fucking nuts! Even though this thing hurts so badly? Can I afford to lose this!?!?? Who the fuck has what I have? Is jealous as hell, wishing they had a best friend like me?? I want so badly to kick her ass sometimes. though. I'm totally fucking crying my eyes out.

Shut up

01/14/08

We were in the small bar below the Monday night open mic. There were at least a dozen of us poets, many of the old school variety I had first encountered over a decade ago. Lexy was directly across from me. I was a little moody and she was doing all the talking. As usual, everyone was listening. She was talking about art, and life and value. How she couldn't do the regular life anymore, she would rather die. She had dedicated her life to art, to music, and it was either that or death. Ron Boyer was at her right, he kept throwing out all these ways that he makes a little cash here and there. He had survived through music and art alone without a chump job for many years now. Many of his methods weren't much more than panhandling, which he actually did quite well at playing on the streets of Fort Worth, and he wasn't opposed to playing covers to get the people's attention. Lexy didn't think this was her style. Everyone was telling her that she shouldn't be suicidal, that it wasn't worth dying over. She said "Look, don't get me wrong, it's not that I want to die, I love life. I love the faces of children. I live for music. I enjoy interacting with people, it's just that I'm running out of options. I hope that I make it with my music. My needs are very little, I just need a roof and enough food to get by, I'm not greedy. It's just that if I can't get it, then other people have to help me and I become a burden. I've been a burden before, to family, I don't want to live that way, I can't do it. I'm a burden now, people are taking care of me now. I don't want to live like that. If I can't make it with music, I won't live as a burden." I'd had enough. I stood up and loudly pounded my fist on the table, several beers bottles tumbling over, every one looked up at me. I proclaimed, " Stop it god damn it! You are not a burden! You are wonderful and beautiful and not a burden to me, not ever! No matter what! You'll never be a burden to me! I love you! OK!" I turned and walked to the bar to order a couple more. She got up and walked to a corner beside the brick wall. I walked over to where she was. She gave me the weirdest looking up sideways grin. Punched me in the shoulder and said "Shut up!" I responded, "You shut up, I fucking love you." She put her arm around my shoulder and hugged me a little and smiled, shaking her head. I handed her a beer. We tapped our bottles, then once on the table for our dead homies, then drank more.

Overly Sentimental crap

01/15/08

Gods, it kills me when you yell at me like that. I wouldn't care except that I really do care, a lot, too much I'm sure. Sorry I was being a baby though, I shouldn't have cried like that, and we were having such a grand day with awesome dinner conversation and all. I wasn't sure what was really triggering that level of emotion in me, until I drove away. The same thing that was triggering it in you I suppose, MEMORY.

You were upset because I had not taken down a photo of us, from a particular day. To you the day reminds you of something really bad. Your breakup, a hard time, something with a lot of emotion behind it. I didn't realize it, but it was the same for me. Yes, you were going through a hard time, but I was really there for you and really loving you, more than you knew. Still do now, just as much, hell, even more. It's just that then we hadn't had the same challenges we have now faced.

Before the Thanksgiving shakes poem where I was sure that eventually I'd lose you. Before you made it clear I was just some asexual buddy. Even though we have had some really great close times since then, that feeling has never really gone away. No matter how much I love you, want you, work together with you, am your truest best friend, It won't stop you from being gone one way or the other sometime soon.

I guess that picture was from before that feeling. When I thought maybe we could be something special, or at least something forever. It was when you still held me close when we said goodbye. It was before either of us had ever raised our voice at the other. Something I still wish I had never ever done. It was when I still thought maybe, just maybe I could be enough for you. I didn't feel shitty and like something not good enough then.

Wow, I know that's a hell of a lot for a simple picture, thousand words and all. Of course it's not the picture, it's the feelings I haven't fully coped with. like the feelings of pictures of that day invoked something totally different for you. Your loss of him. For me it represented a time, before my loss of you, or at least my dream of you, of something real.

I'm glad to be your best friend. Like you said drunk at that bar the other night "I will cherish it and enjoy it as long as it lasts." It's just on some real level I know that what we have gone through together will always mean something a little more to me than to you. You have spent most of our time together trying to get over him or trying to figure out how to just be the real you. While I have spent that same time just loving you and wanting to be the best me for you. It's the best thing I've got, and I'm pretty damn sure that you will never fully understand exactly how much I have loved you.

Things You Say

1/16/08

You say that you are alone
but I'm with you in every way that matters
in my heart, and would be in every way possible
if you would only let me, give me a chance.

You say that you are alone, but
you haven't been alone since October 3rd
not in any way you HAD to be.
You say that you only attract these
"21 year old boys and old psychos," but
That's not what you want,
you need more experience, not just sexually,
but in life, intellect, ideas, art.
Here I am, your best friend,
sharing all of those things with you every day,
but not good enough to love??
I figure I must be one of the old psychos then.
but you say "no, we are really just alike,
you're different, just like me, the same."
Are you just ignoring my love then?

You say no one is in your corner, but
you stopped, grabbed my hand for a moment,
and said "I mean you are, in many ways."
Which was nice, but wrong.
I am in all ways, or should be, if you would let me
for as long as you live, if you would let me.

You say that you are sexually frustrated
Three times a day?!? damn. Yet
here I am, loving you and dedicated to you
and perfectly capable, skilled in a few things
your best most trusted friend.
that you've never even given the slightest chance.

You say that you are alone, but
that's only because everything I have
doesn't seem to be enough.

You and I

01/19/08

It has been said
that you
are not enough.

It has been said
that I
am too much.

Quite a funny pair.
We laugh about it sometimes.

Other times not so much.

Sounds like a perfect match
I'd say.

If only.
If only.
If only.

maybe if you
were just a little tiny bit more
and I
was just a little tiny bit less.

I'll always
always love you
though.

Always.

SOUL RELEASE
01/20/08

I release you my most beloved, my most true
most adored, most everything, I release you.
I release you from me
From my insecurities, My obsessions
My sadness, my attachment, my need. I release you.
My greatest, truest, closest, best

I release me.
I release me from your categories your patterns your fatal this and that. Your fear. Your obscured view. I release me.

The beauty of the poet. The beauty of the poem,
Is the walking through, the epiphany
The enlightenments, or at least the mini ones.
The Satori. Writing the big real gut level dig in poems
It's like the magic breath of god almighty his or her self.
No one or nothing gets it or lives it like the poet.
We poets OWN truth.

It's clear you now have issue with me.
Your words express lack of stimulation from me.
Your lack of words express lack of love for me.
You weak embrace is worth a thousand words
the words I hear so clearly while watching
as you embrace others now.

You should find them
The younger, the types, the next, you know.
Whatever you are missing not finding in me.
Although, I cannot imagine another living human being
that will love you as I have loved you in true and real
open and honest, accepting, non-conditional ways.
Although, I cannot imagine another living human being
that will befriend you as I have befriended you.
With compassion and caring and patience and concern.
With enjoyment, and dedication and learning and respect.
Although I cannot imagine another living human being
that will be as one with you as I have been.
Artistically, philosophically, emotionally, socially, business wise.
I seriously cannot imagine a better me for you than me
but if there is, find them

You are released from me and the pattern
we have inadvertently created in recent days.
I want more and better from you and from myself
or at the very least, LEAST, I need as much as we had before
When you first became my absolutely everything,
and for good reason too.
Let me be absolutely clear here,
because we know communication can be difficult

and blurry and problematic at best.
This is not goodbye, or me pushing you away
I am not, one hundred percent not, upset with you
or angry with you, nor are my feelings
lessened in any way.
Quite the opposite, I'm feeling a moment of clarity.
I just need you to figure it out
If that means you walk away from me, that's what it means
I hope not. But recent days aren't ok with me,
and I want to love you enough to not live in what is not ok.
Which is more than I have ever loved anyone else before in my life.

You are without a shadow of a doubt
In my mind, my absolutely favorite person alive
My favorite person I have ever met in my life.
I love you with a real truth more than I have ever loved before.
You are the best friend I have ever had.
I am your biggest fan. My arms are wide wide open to accept you
any time you come to me with something more.
Tomorrow, next week, next month, next year
I will drop anything, anyone, anywhere, to be at your side.
But what I won't do is continue with the exact same pattern
we have had these past few weeks. I release you from that.
If I don't stimulate you, entertain you, support you
If I hold nothing but darkness for you
and you cannot see the light that I am struggling to reignite
than find something, or someone more.

I'm still here though, one hundred percent in any and every way
If you decide otherwise. With nothing but compassion, friendship
support, acceptance, companionship, and the biggest love you can
imagine If you decide otherwise.

I openly honestly release you from me while hoping that you stay or
at least come back.

Tears Upon Samsara

01/25/08

The Buddha image, porcelain white and 8 feet tall
in the deep and dim light, seems less like an image
and more like an actual perfectly still Buddha,
eyes saying "haven't you gotten this yet?"

I was vomiting a little bit in the coffeehouse bathroom.
I'd been on this quest for quite some time
to make this real dig deep gut level confessional art.
It's only objective being to shine such an obscene
un-obscured light upon a slice of the human condition
that it makes the audience uncomfortable in their own
skin.
It was getting there and the emotional toll was heavy.
Hence, the vomiting.
On the wall, in dry erase marker, someone had written
"attachment is the cause of all suffering"
Ironic I thought, while cleaning my face.
The next week the words had disappeared.

The Dharma teacher, now a trusted friend
used lines from one of my recent poems to illustrate a
point about the nature of being and existence.
What are we?
What is this thing existing always in a state of flux
becoming something else in each new moment?
What are we if not our attachment?

Home, writing, holding on to meditative detachment
for a few hours, until just before sleep.
Plugging in the cell phone,
I notice the name of a woman I love with a consuming
ferocity. A missed call from earlier,
whereabouts unknown.
I got her voicemail.
I think long and hard about every single detail of her.
Everything inside and outside of her.
Then began to weep myself to sleep.
My tears are not regular tears,
they are porcelain white, like little dim lit Buddha eyes.
Each drop a Lotus flower descending in spiral.
Each drop a link in a chain of causality that

perpetuates things like love, art, desire, and need.
Each drop a melancholy rain upon Samsara.
My round and round and round.
Never empty, never still.
In love with the very movement of the universe itself.
With myself.
With her.

We Met At A Poetry Reading

01/25/08

PART 1 : Our 3rd Date Was the Buddhist Temple (Thais)

Our third date was the Buddhist Temple. Our first, kind of, was the first night we met. You had talked to me when I got off stage for the Poetry Slam at the end of the day at a street festival. Lightning had split the sky when I read, you complemented me and bought a Chapbook. I wrote my number in it and said that we should go out sometime. A while later you said "When?" and I said "How bout right now baby?" We walked around, our cars were side by side, and we spent the entire night making out till sunrise. On our second date we met at restaurant in Oak Cliff near your sister's house, near where we would later live. I came with red roses and they seemed purple under the blue neon sign from next door. We made out in the car for several hours again. Our third date was the Buddhist Temple. I remember you being particularly drawn to the paintings on the wall depicting the life of the Buddha. You explained your fascination for imagery and feel. Every bit the visual artist even in your spiritual leanings. We ate at Denny's and made out in the car again. I mentioned to you my skill, and love for Cunnilingus. I remember your voice cracking when you said "Really? " Funny, thinking back how little actual experience and skill I had with that then compared with now. Soon you called. I was sick but you came to my apartment anyway. We spent the entire night together for the first time. My LOVE for you was like this glowing hot ball of energy in my heart. It burned and burned and grew and engulfed me creating a light that covered my entire body. I knew that you were my soul mate. I remember the song that was playing the first time I told you " I love you" at the coffeehouse where I hosted the Sunday night open mic. The same coffee house I later proposed to you at on stage during the reading. The light of my love for you sustained me and took me to new levels of understanding of everything that there is. I thought it would be in me forever, but it wasn't. Years, kids, responsibilities and jobs that I really hated but had to work to support our family, changed our energy. Like many women, you have this thing where someone starts out great in your mind and heart, but then you slowly pick them apart. See, in life, shit happens. But unlike myself and many men that I know who simply learn to forgive and forget, you never do. Each incident would lower me ever so slightly in your eyes and heart. You would downgrade me little by little.

Eventually the light which had started as this burning ball in my heart and covered my entire body swimming in and out of my soul, was stripped and warped and dimmed, like a dying star or a fading fire burning out. Each downgrade like a hammer blow until you saw in me nothing anymore of value. The really unfunny part was that neither did I. Our children though, well that's something. No one that meets them and sees how special they are, how unusually bright and creative and compassionate and insightful, the children of two artists, ever doubts that there must have been a special love there once, to create three such amazing people.

PART 2 : Another Beautiful Woman is the Last Thing I Need. (Lexy)

I walked in to one of my favorite monthly open mics. The host, Johnny O, a hell of a guy, always glad to see me, gave me a hug., put me on the list, then smiled and pointed at you. He said "Hey man, there's this cute guitar player chick you should hit on. I threw my hands up and said; "Dude, another beautiful woman is the LAST thing I need!" I'd had this rather sad but giant infatuation for a bar girl that mostly ignored me. I loved how different from me she was, how positive and fun. The emotion from it had sent me on this crazy fucked up hedonistic summer that I was just recovering from. It had been a good month or more, letting go, and finding some inner peace. Then I heard you sing and it fucked me up bad. It was like your energy reached out and ensnared me by mixing with my own. It was pretty overwhelming almost instantly. But I was still determined not to do it. I told one of my associates, Josh, to talk you up and invite you to perform at our other shows. He did. But then on break, drinking whiskey on the sidewalk, I kept noticing your face. It was like metaphysical gravity or something. So beautiful and smiling in my direction. Inside, I was standing by the bar and you started speaking to me. Instantly I knew there was something powerful and so did you. Everything we said, everything we believed, everything we felt, the instant bond, the common energy was unbelievable. Your songs made me feel like I was on fire. The fire of your fire burning up my insides.

Then, it was one open mic after another, night after night and even though you were already with someone else, (I met him the third time we went to a show, he was very rude to me) I knew without a shadow of a doubt that you were my soulmate. Not that I ever tried to hook up or anything. After all, I'm a man of honor and wouldn't ever do that. It's just that you were so very perfect for me in every way, I thought " what could it hurt? Talk to you, befriend you, let our shared energy be what it is, enjoy it all for what it is " Even though it was blocked like that. God, we spent so many hours talking late into the night in that car. Just talking about everything. Art, life, our pasts and the world. No one had come even close to opening me up like this in years, not since Thais. It was the most exciting thing I had experienced in years. We were so in synch, everyone near saw it, t how alike we are, our views, our humor, our ideas on art and life and meaning. It was amazing, you were the greatest match, the most perfect soul mate possible. You told me over and over that I was your best friend and I thought, that you must be my best friend too, because I'd never felt an energy like this before, this resonance, this soul similarity. So I let myself become your best friend and depend on you, even though I knew full well it could be trouble. Your relationship with your man had been troubled and it got worse the more time you spent with me. Talking and being on the unique artistic high that we shared. He could feel our high in you. It was one month later at the same open mic, when you told me you had broken up with him, we seemed so close that night, the closest emotionally. Holding hands, talking, I wanted you so bad it hurt, it made my head spin, but it wasn't what happened. No matter how much I had wished and prayed for it every day. Weeks later, you needed a place to stay and I got you one. My LOVE for you was like this glowing hot ball of energy in my heart. It burned and burned and grew but I could not express it. Because you never even gave me the slightest chance. Not even a little, not even the least bit of consideration it seemed. I remember that first shoot down beat down with a crystal clarity, and the second. It was confusing and overwhelming. You had already put me in this category as your buddy, nothing more. Yet you didn't treat me anything like a buddy, no we had something way beyond that between us. The beat downs made were a painful emotional contradiction. I could have tried to walk away, but goddamn it you ARE my soulmate. I do love you more than anyone, and you are the best friend I've ever had. I just couldn't make any sense of it all. It hurt, but walking away from this thing, this incredible thing, made no sense either. It was so much, so strong, so meaningful, that even if I could only have small part of you, I would take what I could and savor it while I could. It feels like we have lived an entire lifetime in so short a time! We even joke about it. However, like many women, you have this thing where someone starts out great in your mind and heart, but then you slowly pick them apart, see, in life shit happens, but unlike myself and many men that I know who simply learn to forgive and forget, you never do. Each incident would lower me ever so slightly in your eyes and heart. You would downgrade me little by little. Now, where once you expressed love for me, even if only "best friend" love, you remain silent, or say "OK " when I say it. You have this really fucked up thing where you end each night now with this half-assed side hug thing as opposed to the close affectionate warm hugs you once shared. The kind I still have to watch you give to others. It's insulting, shitty, and painful. YET STILL this best friend relationship feels more like a lover relationship, dynamic wise, than anything I have ever known. DOZENS of people express astonishment that we are not a couple, not a week goes by that I don't hear it. Not because we are close, there are lots of close people that don't look like couples. Because of the exact nature of our dynamic. You feel like my wife. I know this, I've been married. We watch out for each other, know what the other is thinking, we check with each other on everything, you're not shy in pointing out my flaws, telling me what to do, all kinds of familiarities that honestly would be perfectly fine with me if we were together, but we're not. All my attempts at flirtations were met with a stinging mocking. It didn't really feel so good, and I know enough, I've been around enough to know what the downgrading process feels like, I know it well. I wonder if you even see me as your "best friend" anymore, in your heart.

PART 3: Whatever Form of Self Torture You Need, I'm There (a meeting of lines)

I was practicing walking meditation in the Buddhist temple, and so many things were flying through my mind. It hit me, this is my fault, being this machine of almost-ing. Was it only two weeks since that night I got a voice mail while delivering Chinese food for Shane? Where Thais said, "I got remarried a few weeks back, the children asked me not to tell you until after the holidays, but I don't see why you would care." The only thing I could think of to do was call you. I was driving. I had no idea what or how to feel. It was like a haymaker to the soul. You said, "Whatever you are feeling now, you have a right to feel it, just feel it, be in the feelings, we'll talk about it later." It was the perfect thing to say. In fact, despite our many disagreements, you had amazed me on so many occasions with the perfect thing to say. I got off, went to bring you food, stopped for some beer and saw a cheap bottle of champagne. Picked it up with tip money. You opened the door, saw it and said, "baby, whatever form of self-torture you need, you know I'm always here for you, pop the cork!" It was beautiful and it was perfect just like you, it helped me through. But now, here I am wondering if we have indulged too much in the self-torture, both of us. Ruining the beautiful initial nature of us. I had written this beautiful poem in our first weeks, about spiritual healing together, my desire to heal with you, and to be with you. About this soul thing, being and becoming. I knew you were a soul mate for me instantly and your soul loved me, and your heart loved me, but your head told you that I wasn't good enough. Not even for the journey up together. I realized then, that you were right. See, just like last time, the universe manifested a soul mate for me, out of my hopes and prayers and desires and needs. It was you, and if you had met me, and I had been what I was back when I first met her I feel sure that you would have loved me all the way. The confidence, spiritual balance, emotional equanimity, physical fitness, inner strength and light. Several things you have said to me recently, criticisms about my darkness, my flaws, my weaknesses, they hit me hard. I understand it. It's a cruel joke. The universe manifested my soul mate, but I'm not ready, not even close. I had three years, three freaking years to realign myself. Recreate myself once again, mentally, intellectually, spiritually, physically, into the man I once was. Before my marriage beat me down into nothing. I had three years, and I squandered it with drink, self pity, guilt, depression, all that bullshit. Instead of having faith, walking the path again and getting ready for the real soulmate. I lost whatever little remained of me after my marriage in the void. Now you are here, and we can both clearly see that I'm not good enough. Now you are pulling away, you will soon be doing other stuff with other people, other men. As much as I would like to believe that we will stay close. The next brilliant artist will come along, if he hasn't already, and that will be that. I go back to that same Buddhist temple tonight and all this is in my head walking around looking at the paintings depicting the life of the Buddha, thinking about how long they must have been hanging there. Looking at them with her, then looking at them with you 11 years later. My LOVE for you is like this glowing hot ball of energy in my heart. It burns and burns but I have no idea what to do with it. It is burning me alive with nowhere to go. Even while you are slipping slowly away. I walk the temple again, and think that this is it. This is all that there is, I have to keep walking it over and over again. I CAN'T BELIEVE THAT IT WON'T BE YOU! You are absolutely perfect for me, more perfect than she ever was. But it's probably too late, Isn't it? Women never forgive once the downgrade has occurred. Or if they do, I've never seen it happen. What can I do, cry and scream and push the feelings down? I've done all that before, I can't do it anymore! All I can do is try to walk through it this time, not drink it down, not stuff it, just feel it, survive it, and live anyway. Get back on the path again, the best I can. Be ready, become the man I'm supposed to be again. I know the children are disappointed, they love you more than anyone I have ever seen them around. They worship you, your music, your smile, your kindness, everything about you. They have each told me that they wish that we were together. My daughter asked " don't you love Lexy enough?" I said, " Of course I do, but love isn't everything in this world, there are lots of factors that go into it, just like with me and your mom." She actually said to me in a telephone conversation, how sad it was, how much better it would be for the children, to see me with love in my life again. Ironically, I never would have been speaking to her at all, had it not been for your influence. Me, listening openly to your views on that and being affected, feeling my love for you and wanting to heal old wounds, to be better. It's hard to get past the fantasy that maybe you'll still be around, that you will see me transform, but who ever has that kind of kindness from the gods? These same awful gods? Not me. I suppose it's possible that another perfect soul mate awaits out there. Doesn't seem likely though. I mean it's like playing the percentages, you only get so many chances. Not likely, but what else to do? The worst possible thing would be to never become whole again, always be the wreck she left me in while she moved on along, and never be good enough for you or anyone else. I have to at least try.

Lame broad razor blade words tears

01/27/08

The words were razor blades. I tried to be mature, tried to be level headed. But in all honesty, hiding my emotions has never been my strong point, even drop dead sober. It was an unusual week. I spent three days inside myself. Went to temple, wrote a lot, heavy gym time. I was making a decision to process long overdue emotions, really be in them, type and lift and feel. A real human experience. Anyone can decide not to drink for a week or a month. The point is not to fill it with TV, or jacking off, or over eating, or something else to distract the mind. I seriously don't think that Lexy and I had gone that long, maybe three days, without actually speaking, since the day we met. It wasn't like I was ignoring her, I sent her a text telling her that I love her each day. She called me on Wednesday, I was on the way to temple. I tried her back, left a voice mail. I was just feeling that things were emotional and weird and drunken and I thought I should think it through a bit. The sobriety almost lasted. We were at the reading, Opal said there was a weird uncomfortable vibe. I thought it was probably just the days apart. I noticed she took Jack and Devorah outside separately to speak. Very odd, but she is always doing odd shit. The mic was small but cool. My old buddy Tim's dad showed with his roommate. I actually talked Jack into joining us after the reading for once. Lex was very happy about that. She said, "Hey, I'm riding with you and you can drop me back off, OK?" Of course I said "ok" because I ALWAYS say "OK" to her. I just do. I thought we might be working up one of those stupid pointless arguments that we have. I figured I'll just be extra pleasant, so I was. The bar was nice. I didn't drink but got her a few. She sat beside me and we laughed and joked. We were in full US mode. It was cool. Then Pitt Grill for 5. Getting to be a habit.

We're heading back down South Collins almost back to the car when she says, "Hey, I don't know an easy way to say this. I know you're going to be upset. I thought about not telling you until the last minute, but with the way we've been weird the last few days, I think I should so that we can be our regular selves again for while. I'm leaving for Colorado on February 15th. I don't know for sure if I'm coming back, it all depends. I don't really have anywhere to come back to. My sister is having surgery and she needs me for at least three months. It seems like a sign. Like the right thing to do. Get my head together." I said " I understand, I see, well if that's the right thing." I was trying really hard to say just the right thing, to be supportive, as I have always tried to be, but my emotions got the best of me. I began to weep uncontrollably. I seriously can't believe that the one person I've let into my life, that I have let all boundaries down with, that I spend pretty much all my time with, that I love with all my heart, that is probably, despite some weirdness and the occasional disagreement, the best motherfucking friend I've ever had in my life, the ONE person I've really let all the way in since my divorce, is fucking leaving, is going. Maybe for three months, maybe forever. I tried to be supportive but the sadness just fucking overwhelmed me. Even with this strong sober week behind me. One thing just kept going through my skull. February 16th - February 16th - February16th. I kept thinking, " That's the day I become alone again." Really pretty unbearable, you know. In the parking lot she holds me while I cry. Her arms feel so nice, nothing perverted, just comforting. We've been having issues, so it's been a while. She was getting out, I can't tell you what the look on my face was, but it must have been screwy, because she looked at me and said " OH PAUL! " and hugged me again slow and hard. She got in her car, was going to leave. I got back out and gave her a copy of the last story. She hadn't read it. I was about to drive off when she said " HEY! Just got a message, some people are drinking at Shane's house, wanna come?" I said "if you want me to" She said, "Of course I do! Come, I want to make sure you're OK, I'm worried about you." We walked in. Shane and five other guys were there. He immediately pulled me into the other room, said, "So, she told you? "Seems like everyone knew except me, big ol fucking over emotional me. I cried in his arms for a while, too. But I DIDN'T want to hear his advice or consoling words or whatever, just didn't. The guys suggested it wasn't good time for sobriety. The first shot was Tuaca, then beer... then enough of a bottle of something brown from a bottle, that everyone seemed a little freaked out. There was a cool time, she played and sang and Shane recorded it. The entire room was transfixed by her haunting, sad, beautiful voice. I knew the words to half the songs and she made me sing along with tears streaming down my cheeks in front of everyone. Then we were all in the kitchen. I drank some more and fell on the floor. I was looking up at her, said, "It doesn't matter, I won't miss you, you're lame anyway, who cares, you're stupid. Who would miss you? Seriously, what's so great about beautiful, intelligent, compassionate, funny, talented, chicks anyway? That's lame, who needs that? Seriously, what's the big deal about having someone in your life every day that listens to all your shit, and believes what you believe, and does everything with you, and understands you, and cares about you, and is there for you and is your fucking best friend, that's lame, what's the big deal about that? Who cares about that? Not me that's for sure!" But who could take me seriously? It was slurry and with all those never ending tears on my stupid face. Like the ones I drove home with at 8 AM, like the ones I woke up with, like the ones on my face right now. goddamn fucking broad. Goddamn it. Fucking goddamn it. Fuck.

I talked to her a while ago from the gym. Sent her a text while I was lifting. It said :"I so so so love you my best friend ever." she called right back. We are starting a new open mic at the Bar of Soap tonight. We were supposed to have this gig together, but I guess I have to handle it alone now. I remember back when I first met her, she once referred to herself while helping me host, as my "lovely assistant." Jeeezus I fucking loved that, I gotta get cleaned up, go pick her up. She was hinting about being hungry, mentioned Subway. I think I'll drop by there on the way and get her a sandwich. Of course I know exactly how she likes it. Yeah. Goddamn broad. Fuck. FUCK!

ALTER MY VIEWS- By Alexcie (My favorite)

This way of life, has gotten quite expensive. I have lost touch with all my senses. I....... oh........ oh My attempt at anything worthy so lame the efforts required drains my life quite out of control my motives have all succumbed to mold. Along with all my most valued thoughts anything worth having is that all it costs? to be, in this place I'd rather not be at all...oh.. Now I'm here bringing nothing more to you......than an honest quest for truth. As your words reawake, what vicious years depleted, telling me in such soft whispers that was all you needed I'm so dazed now in this vital surrender, please teach me to remember, the wonderful things you're telling me I am. because I can't quite say I understand, I'm opening my self out before you, and praying you'll alter my views. Praying you'll alter my views, praying you'll alter my views. From this relentless vacancy there seems no escape not to mention humiliation and shame of fruitless pursuits and the self-abuse in my desperate attempt to distract myself from this sick state of mind, ironically called life still I...can't recall when it ever felt-that-way-at-all oh.........oh... Now I'm here bringing nothing more to you, than an honest quest for truth. As your words reawake what vicious years depleted telling me in such soft whispers, that was all you needed, I'm so dazed now in this vital surrender, please teach me to remember, the wonderful things you're telling me I am. Because I can't quite say I understand. I'm opening myself out before you and praying you'll alter my views. Praying you'll alter my views Praying you'll alter my views. Thick are the clouds in my mind Stagnant the waters I wade Stifling is the air I breath And deep the anger nourished by defeat The very monster feeding my drive And nursing this sick state of mind That prompts the change I so desperately seek Despite the fears that shackle my feet. Still I'm here bringing nothing more to you, Than an honest quest for truth.

You Away From Me

01/27/08

I did it- I did it
even though you said stop it
with that kind of sad look
when I told you what I was doing.

I took enough glances
while driving
to perfectly memorize
your face.
Sweet sweet face.

Now, soon,
when you are gone from me
and I am all alone
all alone- all alone- all alone.

At least I will have the memory
of your face
Sweet sweet face.

To keep me company
and make me smile.

Me Away From You

01/27/08

When you are far away
in a different place
nowhere near your
very best friend.

And you are hungry
you imagine that
It would be nice
If someone just showed up at the door
with your favorite sandwich
exactly the way you like it
without having to be told
exactly at the precise moment
that you are thinking about
how much you would really
like a sandwich.

You'll stare at the door
but no one will knock
the bell will not ring
It will be perfectly silent
and you will go hungry.

Not like today.

When that happens
in that moment
will you pause
feel an empty void.
smile, a bittersweet smile,
and think of me?

Love is
in the tiny details.

Do you think
you will miss mine?

Parting Thought
01/28/08

I've decided that
I need to be really
really
super nice
to you
until you leave town.
Because if I don't
then once you are gone
I'll be sitting around
all alone
crying
and missing you
and regretting it.
While
this way
once you are gone,
I'll be sitting around
all alone
crying
and missing you
but without the
regret.

A Question For Ron Boyer

01/29/08

I was on the coffeehouse mic barely holding back the tears,
reading about my most beloved Alexcie, who had profoundly
affected my life, being about to leave me for Colorado.
I could feel the poets in the room feeling what I was feeling.
why I love the poets so.
Then my sweet beautiful dear sang her haunting melancholy
Then Ron Boyer was up.
He's been doing it longer than most of us. In fact
he was one of the first I'd ever seen all those years ago.
He addressed me, saying; "What is it about Colorado that
takes our most loved friends away?
I've had that day too, and I just relived it when you read."
I knew who he was talking about,
and I knew by the look in his eyes
he really did know how low I was feeling.
The next day crying in the cubicle
a question occurred to me, for Ron Boyer,
this was it;

Ron, you've been at this a couple decades longer than me
living the life, the poets life aging outside and on the edge
of the culture seeking only truth and Art
Living and breathing with poets,
artists, players, creators, livers,
Let me ask you, is this how it is for aging poets?
Nothing to show for a life of struggle
but a big pile of poems
and a big pile of memories?.
Is this how it is for we who live as poets?
Must they always leave us?
Won't they ever love us enough to stay?
Or are we just here to be what we are,
give what we have to give, before they go away?
Is this it? They come into our lives
we love them with all our big poetic hearts can love
then they leave us?
with poems, with memories
with children scattered everywhere?
With regrets and wishes and lonely nights?
Can’t they ever stay forever?
Do they ever love us enough?

Are we ever, ever enough?
Are aging poets ever not alone?
Or in the end is all we’re really left with is all these poems?

Tell me Ron,
unless you think I'm not strong enough yet.
In which case, lie to me and let me have that,
just a little bit longer.

After days back in the zone of goodbye bliss

01/31/08

Sabotage much?

I have
NO
APOLOGIES
LEFT
for this.

Silent place.
Brick wall.

Biggest
shame
of all.

I am, only what I am, I suppose

01/31/08

What you call the brick wall
I call the silent spaces at the edges of us.
I've never really lived a don't ask don't tell. Well,
in the big decline that time, but only in a huge philosophic sense
This is different. It's like a tiny poison
seeping into something otherwise terribly beautiful.
It's why I had to spend several days away
from the person I love even though I absolutely didn't want to.
Before the news of the big goodbye.
It's why I give everything of myself
and consider 12-Step meetings. Seriously consider.
It's the downgrade from "I love you" to "OK." In response.
It's the sudden side hug switchover.
It's the non-returned text messages.
It's why I'm there to raise your voice at.
It's why I'm there to have my flaws pointed out sometimes publicly.
It's why I'm there to get involved in pointless heated arguments
with,
and then apologize and make it right.
It's why I'm there take your frustrations out on
when the day is blue and you need someone.
It's why I'm there to take for granted and
continuously lose and regain interest in.
All things you do, and have done, with a boyfriend.
With me. That kind of investment.
Don't get me wrong, I can take it, I don't mind it at all,
I actually make a damn good boyfriend.
But as you sometimes remind me, I am not your boyfriend.
More, I think sometimes, an in-between substitute, and not the first.
(Something I swore to you I would never be at the start)
As far as my feelings; My true, honest, something real feelings.
As best friend. As artist partner. As biggest fan.
As spiritual soul journey partner.
As I want to love you forever and be with you,
It's all already out there.
You've heard my thousand words.
My thousand damn fine poems.
My thousand everyday open-hearted actions
that should have long ago proved myself beyond
your scrutiny, in my sincerity, if not, it's not about me,
at least not that part.

All I ever had was honesty and honor.
Even if I have mistakenly let my dignity slip away at times.
With drink and all.
I have no apologies left for this.
Plenty of love, friendship, compassion, caring.
But no apologies, not for this.
Everything else, sure, but not for this.
In the end, I am just as much who I am, as you are who you are.
Just as in need of acceptance
Just as in need of understanding
Just as flawed. Just as in need of unconditional love.
Trying just as hard to be something
a little better than I already am.

like sugar bee stinging moments

02/07/08

Moments are moments in moments you find significance.
Tiny, tiny, spot-type occurrence synch spirit fire fleeting
they, they.
In a moment, a back turns,
everything changes, love becomes distance, becomes
uncanny in cleaved-apart-ness.
In a moment, a face appears
a freight train runs like mad, uncontrolled, blistering heat
power, power, power, then he reminds you of moments.
In a moment, a phone call.
Then this face is leaning above you and on you
sweet like sugar, with the smile and asking you things
and listening to things, who is this?
It's not the usual; it's such a sudden occurrence.
A sudden occurrence, this face, and deciphering
different words, different phrases, different intonations
different physical contact. A different woman.

These moments like skating on bees, honey and stinging
they buzz and spread and swarm all over.

Your love calls, In a moment, you speak harshly,
remembering the turned back,
but you shouldn't have.
So you do what you always do as a writer.
You sift through the moments.
Like metal detector, fine tooth puzzle pieces, truth seeking freak
you decide to take that last one back.
You write a letter, apologizing, offering openness.
Turns out you were right, she needed you
turned back or no back, twisted round.
It was good that you figured it out.

IT WAS ONE NIGHT: JANUARY

It was one night in January when she told me that she was leaving town for several months. Family that needed help, and they had decided that she was the one since she had no life or commitments to hold her down. I cried for days and asked her to make sure she saw my kids before she left. I wrote sad poems and we spent every moment together for a week trying to make everything perfect before she left. Then, on the day of the most blissful closeness, we got in a fight again. We had been at the Buddhist Temple. Then went to a show in Fort Worth at a douchebag bar I didn't like. We were perfectly in our zone. Roderick met us there. Suddenly, this dude walked by, said a clever word or two, then her back was turned and he had his motherfucking octopus arms all over her. It was the worst fucking thing imaginable! I'd have rather been crucified three times and mocked by the gods, than seen this shit. She claimed it was nothing. That she was just promoting our big benefit show. I wanted to freak out. Roderick would have backed me up, said "it's time" but I didn't. I went out on the curb and sat crying instead. But she still turned it into a scene. As if that was easier than living with leaving as wonderful as things had become. Seemed obvious to many that she'd found a way to push me away. It was raining. She said that if Rod didn't take her home instead of me, she would go home with some guy. He whispered, " Please let me." I walked away. I sat in the rainy street crying. I called a young girl named Amy that had emailed wanting to hang with us. She was a friend of Anson's and had been the reason for our very first fight in November. She talked to me all the way home. Lexy and I barely spoke all week. Rod and I went to a thing in Dallas where we tried to win money from a corporation with a poem, inserting the corporate name. It was horrible. Amy met us and hung out. We sang Karaoke and I thought about kissing her, but didn't, still couldn't. Lexy called to talk about our big show, like it was nothing. We did the show. It was a great success but we were obviously damaged. She called a few days later on the day of the February Mad Swirl. I was angry with her because of something she said. I called back and apologized, turns out someone she knew had died, we talked. I was sick and missed it for the first time in three years. Amy came over and burned a candle in my ear, laid and talked with me.

IT WAS ONE NIGHT: FEBRUARY

It was one night in February, her last Saturday night in town. I dropped my kids off crying because she hadn't come to see them before she left. It really affected them, and me. We did the mic then went to sing Karaoke. It was nice. There was still the tension but she was leaving and we were close, it was good. Then some dude showed up, suddenly. A shitty lame ass weak character. He knew me from the bar scene. She pulled a chair over by her for him in-between us and ignored me again. It was fucking overwhelming. Our last Saturday night, the shitty guy, the kids, all of it! She was in the bathroom, the guy asked if I had an issue. I said, "Look man, nothing against you, she and I have just been through a lot together. She's leaving, my three kids are freaking out, it's very emotional. I need to talk to her. Do you mind not coming to eat with us after closing time so I can?" I was a motherfucking gentleman. Instead, he went outside and told her that I had told him to leave. Not that I had asked simply to have the diner after for personal reasons. But that I had asked him to leave right then. She was angry, said she didn't want to eat with me. I went outside and that piece of shit pussy was standing there. As calm as ice water I said, "Why would you do that? You know that's not what I said? I was asking you a favor as a gentleman about to lose someone he has been through a lot with, why would you do that? " She came out and saw me talking to him and yelled at me in front of everyone! I was speechless, I had almost nothing to say in return. My mouth dried up with anxiety, I could barely react, I was destroyed. Everyone left me standing there except for my faithful friend Rod. I said, "Why would that guy do that to me? "Rod said, "Because he can, that's what guys like that do, fuck guys like us, and you gave him an opening, it's the nature of the douchebag. "I told him that I simply couldn't bear living like this anymore, that something had broken in me, a door had closed and I was different.

On Monday Amy insisted that I needed to go to the mic in Fort Worth even though I didn't want to. She drove out from Dallas and made me go. When we got there, all the poets were there, Lexy was there, Anson was there. It seemed a shock that I showed up with Amy. The only person I had ever seen Lexy express any jealousy over. It was quite the fucking soap opera. I sat in the back corner and cried my eyes out when she played, while Amy held my hand and comforted me. Lexy came over and said, "Are you coming over to drink with me one last time before I go? "A bunch of lame ass Fort Worth musician types she had started bonding with during our apart time were there. A violin player I suspected she had a thing for, had written a piece for. The dickhead pussy fuck that had caused the fight was there. I said, "No" She was upset, said "fine, be that way!" and walked off. Amy went and told her that I was just emotional and that she shouldn't be like that to me. She came and apologized. Said she understood, to call her before she left town. I wanted to. I never did. Amy and I drove off. She asked what I wanted to do. I said go to my regular bar, Cave's Lounge, that I had barely been at in months because Lexy didn't like it there. We went and saw people I knew and chatted them up. Some were freaking out because they hadn't seen me in a while and I had lost 25 pounds (for Lexy). Amy and I went to the store and bought cheesecake and red velvet cake. We ate it in bed and she spent the night with me for the first time. It was the first kiss, first anything I had experienced in months, since I had met Lexy. Two nights after she left I kissed a beautiful friend named Shay, a lot, at the Goth club and spent the night in Lexy's bedroom at Shane's house, but ended up just crying in her arms.

Cheesecake in Bed
02/11/08

Cheesecake in bed?
What a ludicrous set of circumstances
You can't write shit like this.

I will never ever understand people
not as long as I live.
They are like oceans of Karmic waves.
It breaks my heart time and again, the attachment.
Each time I become the motherfucking superhero.
I save the day, make it right.
Then, yesterday's news baby.
As they keep coming, and going again in waves.
It's mad head fuck insane is what it is.
People moved around, sliding fuck goddamn.
My old heart.
I thought I was about to die.
Next thing you know it's cheesecake in bed,
crazy rain drops on the aluminum roof
a game of pool back in my old bar again
where I hadn't been comfortable in a while
everyone's coming up hugging me
shaking the hand ; "You look great man!"
"You've lost some weight man!" "Your hair looks great!"
It's like I've been away or something
but I haven't, just focused on something else
someone else.
"HEY! Who's this hot little dame?"
"Seriously, I don't know, I think she has some urge to save me,
rescue me from a rather public beating I've taken of late "
She brought me some cheesecake and
did some Dr. Phil shit with my best friend.
Sometimes I feel like I'm walking in a movie set
or a lucid opiate dream.
None of the sequences quite make sense
everyone is sitting around this coffeehouse table
and making this crazy art where it all bleeds the fuck out
I don't know, I think I need a new job, a better job
and I need to drink less.

It's all been a little too real in its non-reality of late
or something

It all so painful, this thing we do to each other
to ourselves
I will tell you though
If it's gotta hurt so bad like this
the hot little blond, all smiles
telling me to put the seatbelt on
unlocking the door before I get around the other side
telling me to slow down and take a breath
when I get all worked up.
The cheesecake in bed, and the Red Velvet
mixed with the winter rain
all that wispy silly shit
well, there are certainly a hell of a lot worse ways
to feel better
to feel better
to feel good.
I mean what am I?
Some crazy blessed madman or something?
" Dude, you ARE crazy; you are always like this you know."
Am I? Really? I had no idea,
I always kinda feel like I'm just going along for the ride.

When I exhaled my next breath
a thousand, thousand wild ponies flew out of my mouth
and painted fucked up bright colored pictures
on the wall
of the future
and the past
and things I will never even understand.
ever.

TORNADO GIRL

02/15/08

You came into my life
so suddenly, unexpectedly
and, and, everything
was lifted up and twisted around and
uprooted, like a tornado.
Like this spinning, spinning storm
that lifts and moves
and breathes and lives and feels and speaks
and changes up everything,
my, my, my heart,
my eyes, my time, my hours, my
words, my ideas, my ideas, my days, my friends
my thoughts, my feelings, my views, my
altered views, my altered views and situations.
My work, my work , my art
my art,
all of my words, and time and feelings and art all
lifted up all twisted around and changed all different
All impacted all different now,
all in different unrecognizable places now
like this tornado that is you,
touched down right here
in the middle of my life, my, my,
my heart, my words.
spinning and spinning and spinning
everything all around and
now, when you are gone,
this eerie silence,
everything scattered everywhere
this silence
when you are gone
like this big, wrong, awful emptiness
when you are gone.
like everything is wrong somehow
like everything is undone somehow
out of place out of sorts out of whack
out of synch out of time
like everything is sad and silent
and falling apart somehow
my everything, my everything
all turned upside down.

your words and sentences and voice and ideas
and laughter and jokes and songs and
love and tears
still lingering
in each and every tiny space between
everything I am and think and create and see
I still hear you after everything I say,
I still feel you
I still can, can,
can almost grasp you,
respond to you
answer you,
know what you would be saying in every moment
when you are not here with me.
How could you have become such a part of me
How could you have become such a part of me
How could you have become such a part of
everything I am in so short a time
such an impact,
now a part of me forever, forever
in my. in my,
my heart, my mind, my soul.
twisting me all up like some tornado
twisting and twisting and twisting away
from me, from my world,
left silent, left alone
left hoping, you
have carried something important away with you
something you'll keep
something of me flying away with you as well.
I hope
I hope,
come back someday.

Maybe it Has to Be That Way

02/17/08

It doesn't have to be that way.
It doesn't have to be that way.
Maybe it has to be that way.
Maybe it has to be that way.

One of my closest writer friends, arguably the one
who spent the most time with the two of us,
said the following;

"It couldn't have ended any other way
with the two of you.
Y'all are way too much alike."
(his emphasis on the word WAY)
"Y'all are both very intense and very emotional and
y'all both wear your hearts right out here."
(places his hand upon his shoulder.)
"Yeah, when you're together, and doing y'all' s thing
It's like magic."
(Folds his hands like the church and steeple to demonstrate a point)
"But on the other hand,
when you're working against each other,
butting heads,
it's pure chaos."
(shakes his head, kind of sad like.)

It doesn't have to be that way.
It doesn't have to be that way.
Maybe it has to be that way.
Maybe it has to be that way.

All I know is that now that she is gone
It seems like she emails and calls
everyone BUT me.
My last text was not returned.

All I know is that as it stands now;
The particular things she is angry with me for,
I am one hundred percent unapologetic about.
The particular things that I am angry with her for
She is pretty much clueless and apathetic about.
All I know, is that in all my life

I never met anyone like her, that sometimes
when we would get in what we called
our "best friend zone"
either by ourselves, or in a crowd.
With the tornado that is my mind
and the tornado that is her mind
spinning around at the same time.
Both speaking at one hundred miles an hour.
Both instantly getting what the other was saying.
Communicating in shorthand,
body language, in-jokes
this whole crazy mixed up profound, bleed it out thing.

That when we were in this zone together
I'd never felt more in synch with anyone in my life.
I'd never felt more the same as anyone in my life.
I'd never felt more understood, more real, more on it.
I'd never felt less alone in the universe
than in those precious moments.
More than anything, that's what it was always about.
It, that thing, was like a fucking drug to me,
and I put myself through a lot of suffering
just to keep it going as long as humanly possible.
I just didn't want it to end.

All I know is that all bullshit aside,
I've never in my life felt more like this.
Like I have honestly, in every way,
just lost the best friend I've ever had.
Like I have this huge gaping hole inside me
that is now empty, and throbbing and hollow,
and there are no words to fill it,
and that I don't think I'll ever quite be the same.

It doesn't have to be that way.
It doesn't have to be that way.
Maybe it has to be that way.
Maybe it has to be that way.

Maybe there's a savior and maybe there's not.
Maybe there's a savior and maybe there's not.
In the cold, in the cold, in the cold, in the cold.
In the cold, in the cold, in the cold, in the cold.

A Mess

02/18/08

"It's hard to be mad at you," she said. "I know, I tried it for a while, but there is something about you, it's hard to be mad at you for long. She won't stay mad at you for long. She'll be away and little pieces of you will slip back in and she'll miss you and realize that she'll always love you regardless of how much trouble she went through to push you away. I know because I always will, too." I hugged her very, very close. I was in the car, telling her about how many write me from years ago telling me how wonderful I was, looking back I have some kind of memory shelf life.

As I pulled away, dropping Shay off at her car, hung over in the sun, I waved goodbye.

I called Amy, the silly-hot-sweet-to-me little thing that had also been gracing me with her attentions. Thought about the way SHE feels in my arms. I wanted to see her, breakfast maybe? I was near, but it was too late. It was nice to hear her voice though, maybe later.

I thought about Holly, another I care so much for, sitting in hospital room, in terrible suffering. I wish that I could help her somehow. Be there for her in some real way as she hurts so bad. All I can do is wake up when she calls and needs an ear.

I thought about Thais, my children's mother. "Life is too short" she has said to me three times now. " I would like the children to see you with love in your life again." "Thanks" I say, "that would be grand, but me and you? That kind of fucked me up." "I can see that now," she said. " I don't hate you, I just want you to get better."

The irony being that I would never have even been talking to her If it hadn't been for Alexcie, the closest soul I've ever known, who has pushed me away now, before leaving. It just hurts so bad. This aching hole.

Shay, the insightful girl, my lovely wonderful doll, she laughed at me about it, a little (but with compassion). She said; "I've never seen anyone who can find the broken girls like you can. It's amazing, how you do it, so broken, including me. I think you draw it in because you can't seems to heal from the wife and family yet." She might be right.

I ate at my favorite Thai restaurant for lunch. The lady knows me, she said "By yourself?" With a strange look, because I never am. Last time was with my bestest best leaver. I remember that night. She gave me a good talking to that night. before checking out a venue in Grapevine. Something I never quite figured out turned her mood terrible. Some instantaneous thing turned on a dime. She was always like that, though. Anything could send her emotions off in different directions almost in an instant. I was always, always watching out for her, soothing her, talking her through it, being there for each and every up and down. It sounds like a lot of work but It was familiar to me. Being constantly every day aware of and actively involved in the ever changing emotional states of a woman I love. A lot like the wife, the one who wishes I'd find love again. But they keep running away.

I think about Julie, the pregnant girl, the one who feels trapped. She is a special one. I should have found a way with her. She's really something. But the guy she's with is like some kind of movie villain. She gave me a good talking to the other day, too. Said she had tried to warn me about my pushing away goodbye girl. She had, but who ever listens to anyone anyway?

"You're a mess," my sweet darling Amy keeps saying to me. I'm not quite sure if it's a term of endearment or if she's just wondering out loud If I am irredeemable. But there she is, lying in my arms. Head all tucked up next to me. I suppose it's possible that she actually appreciates me for exactly what I am, maybe. I watch her sleep and she looks like a tiny angel. This lovely energy is just what I need. It's saving me right now. I wish she had been able to eat breakfast with me.

Does she somehow know that I am hard to stay mad at?
That I am loved by many, but able to be tolerated for long by none?
That my soulmate is mad at me and that it's killing me?
That my ex-wife wishes I'd find new love? That I get letters of regret from years and years ago telling me that I was better than most and that they should have been better to me?

Someone should be better to me now instead of looking back. Shay's right, I am a mess. A loveable mess perhaps but a mess. It's just that I'm going to miss my Lexy more than I thought I could ever miss anyone. There will never be another her.

What Am I Supposed To Do Now?

v2 in 02/08 as appears in Mad Swirl issue 6!

What am I supposed to do now?
Return to the bars,
buying drinks for dames for a little attention,
some barely passable hookup now and again,
now ruined, knowing something real?

What am I supposed to do now?
Sit and nod, listen while they prattle on
about lousy corporate jobs
new pairs of shoes
their empty friends
the love of Jesus?

What am I supposed to do now?
Continue with hung over mornings in the cubicle.
Making the lowest wage i've known in 12 years.
Unable to afford car repairs or traffic tickets,
stuff for my children or a roof for a good woman
if such a thing came along.
With no one to understand me,
why this whole thing is all wrong.
Why I shouldn't be here, don't belong here.
Why justice and truth and love and a decent life
is not a Capitalist endeavor,
isn't about money or things
or other peoples expectations.

What am I supposed to do now?
With no one to understand
why I do what I do.
Why the making of ART is the making of love;
love to a woman
love to the self
love to everyone and everything everywhere.
And why that love, that making of art
is more important than anything.
Than all the details of
this ridiculous broken culture.

What am I supposed to do now?
While all the young girlies text one another.

While bad choices are made everywhere.
While the gutless and the weak are elevated to success.
While assholes, wimps and fools get the girl.
While men in uniform tell me
what my business should be.
While hot dog vendors fail to grasp the principle of it.

What am I suppose to do now?
back in the bars
back with empty words
back in the cubicle
back in the car alone, or worse
with someone who barely listens or barely understands.

How to face this indecent numbing ongoing nothingness?!

What am I supposed to do now?
When one who actually understands,
one who is actually just like me,
that I hoped and prayed and waited for
that I thought I'd never find,
has left and gone far away.
When I have to accept that she isn't going to love me.
That despite being more alike, more in synch
than I ever believed possible,
the fatal flaws inside us both
will keep us alone and apart, forever.

What am I supposed to do now
without you.

Words written upon a single tear

02/20/08

is there really love like this?

was there ever
an honest moment?

must time assault us
with round almond eyes.
machine gun words
no goodbyes.

my lost faith.
her lost innocents.
mountain tops
far, far away.

squeezed
like sadness,
into the sky.

The Really Big Show!!

02/29/08

Fire eater, dancing poodles, head in the lions mouth
hi-wire tight rope walker
that's me motherfucker.
A fucking circus act, A really big show.
Repeat performance, uncanny skill, precision
crazy-clown showmanship, OH, How I dig it!
Whiskey a go-go. Go daddy go
do it all the time, yeah, yeah.

The act begins with me
somehow drawing these amazing women into my life.
Different sizes, different shapes,
different ages, different colors
different styles, different beliefs.
The only common factor being
a recognizably strong will and personality.

Then through some strange mystic interaction
these fantastically fabulously bad-assed females
come to see me as this
talented, intelligent, insightful, entertaining
compassionate, honorable, worthy, respectable
gentleman, artist, friend, lover.
Someone worthy of time, energy, trust, emotion, attachment.

OH! It is truly grand indeed! It is, it is, it is.
However this is not the final act.
Not the finale, not the end of the show,
Because in ACT THREE comes the old switcheroo!
Couple weeks, couple months, bunch of years, something.
It starts with something like
"You know what your problem is?"

Then after a while, the female is raising her voice.
yelling a bit, pointing, telling me how it is.
Sometimes big, sometimes small
sometimes private, sometimes public,
but they seem to have always figured it all out.
Exactly what my character flaws are.

Exactly just how fucked up I am.
Exactly what I need to do differently to be somehow right.
To get my shit together, to fix it all up.
To not be whoever it is that I am not supposed to be.
Not doing whatever it is that I'm not supposed to be doing.

It's a farce, a fucked up romantic comedy, a cautionary tale
Shakespearian tragedy, slip and slide serious group therapy
highly entertaining, dramatically enthralling
a really, really big show!
Three ring circus, big top blow out, Chinese acrobatics
High wire tight rope walking jumping falling without a net.
Head in the lions mouth.
come one, come all, come one, come all,
come one, come all, come one, come all,
Watch now, as he begins to learn to laugh at himself.

Maybe You Took too Much From Me?

03/04/08

You've told me that something inside you is off somehow, past stuff maybe? That you walk the world like a zombie, unable to fully feel. You say you're always needing energy from the outside. From music, Art, the feel of certain places and situations. From certain people with energy that you could connect with and feel through. I wonder, do you think you may have taken too much from me? I, who have extreme amounts of unfocused creative, spiritual, mental, physical, emotional, energy bursting from me all the time like an exploding sun, causing near madness for me and sometimes those around me.

Do you think you may have taken too much from me? I did after all offer it up freely, openly, and affectionately. It would make sense, one couldn't blame you if you did. Did you dig down deep and take my energy? I wonder if some of the hundred traits we seemed to share; verbal, emotional, mental, creative, ideological, if some of those might have been you absorbing parts of me. If you still have all those same traits now away from me to the same degree. Even at the end around other people you seemed different, maybe synched into someone or ones other than me, a terrible and lost feeling for me. Like a denied addict. also seeking to absorb energy but only from a strong female cognitive field, and only one at a time. Your's.

I wonder, did you dig down deep into the deepest parts of me, feel what was inside, in your bizarre quest to find those few pure souled people you seek? Like the few you exalted, that changed you. That you wish to somehow emulate. Did you get inside me and judge me by the standard of this quest? Did you take until you reached the core of me, touched my very soul, finding not purity, but struggle? An ongoing never ending battle between light and dark? The edge of madness held back only by a code of honor, sheer will, my ability to love, my art, and my children's faces? A longing desire and an unsettling inner voice that screams more than it speaks softly, as you imagine the voices of beings on a spiritual quest should?

Did I fail to be what you hoped I'd be? Did you find disappointment in my darkness rather than solace in my light? Is that why you turned against and pushed me away and hurt me? Looking for other energy to fulfill you, beautiful liars or maybe other more enlightened souls than my own if you find them? Leaving me empty with a terrible gaping hole where you once were.

It's not fair! I'm a poet, a mad breathing word spitting head spinning poet. Not a goddamn saint, I never claimed to be. I'm just a poet, doing poet things. Wanting to create poet words and poet ideas and poet images. Be loved and understood and connected with and appreciated exactly for who I am , creating and being in this very moment.

Do you think that you took too much of me? Perhaps you drank too deeply of my energy? Down to the core, and then judged me far to harshly when you didn't like the taste at the bottom? We are all of us defined by our struggle, how we react, what we create in each moment, in each day. We are the standards by which we live and conduct ourselves. We are in the end how we treat others. We are what we leave behind us when we go. We are our minor victories and not our failings and should be judged accordingly. Judged by the best we have to offer, not our weaknesses. By our art, and not our sadness. By our capacity to love and not our fear and insecurity. By our dignity, honor, and truth and not our mistakes along the way. My energy is the erratic energy of a poet like many a poet before. I have a purpose and meaning and a value. I have no interest in living up to some standard of another's belief in what my soul should or should not be.

Do you think you may have taken too much from me? One couldn't really blame you if you did, I offer it up so freely, almost uncontrollably, It's not your fault, or if it is, it's at least just as much my fault. Actually, who fucking cares about fault, it doesn't matter.

I'm doing fine, I'm sure you're doing fine. It's just that I really, really miss you, a lot. Maybe we could be friends again someday. In a different way, with different boundaries. If you could be honest and learn not to take so much, and if I could keep myself under control. Hold myself back at least a little bit.

.

I miss my best friend. and don't even give a shit about who was mad at who and why. I just do.

To My Best Friend

03/06/08

I really need you right now.
I know we fought,
some say that we are too much alike
and that it couldn't have happened
any other way. But,
I know there were a hundred things along the way
I could have done to prevent the dynamic of
ending up where we ended up,
and I am very, very sorry.

It's just that
I could really really use my best friend right now.
I need you.
If you were here, you would look me
straight in the eyes
nodding your head
and listen carefully, considering every word I say.
When we first met I was always astounded
that you had just the right words to say.
What I need is your magic words right now,
You know the ones;
"I get it, I get you, we are just the same
I understand you, you are not alone"
Then maybe you could throw in
one of your classics like
"What ever form of self-torture you need
you know I'm always here for you."
Or even better;
"I love you, It can't rain forever"
Jesus, you are brilliant
when it comes to shit like that.
But I forget, you stopped being that way to me
a good while even before you left town
didn't you?

I know.
It's just that I could really really use
my best friend right now.
I'm just saying
I could really use my best friend.
Man, I really could.

A Poet Missing

03/09/08

Ever seen a poet that misses his very best friend, it's no pretty sight. Words running through the mind all the time. All type of invisibly rehearsed I'm sorry-s and if only-s and I wish-s. And when her name comes up, it's long protracted drawn out practiced sentences that make the poet sound emotionally collected not at all basket-case-ish.

Sometimes, beautiful backseat child faces scream out that they miss her, or other poets discuss how much or how little they knew her or wanted to. Or random people at shows asking where. He always nods his head, that's what he does, nods his head. It makes him seem thoughtful and less emotional.

Sometimes other poets though, they see it in the dark red bars, When some funny story is being told and there is a pause at the end where his voice trails off. Even the nodding in those moments doesn't keep the tiny silly tears from welling in the sides of his eyes.

It's a terrible thing when a poet misses the best friend he ever had because poets think too much, and feel to much and write too much and most ironically, no matter how expert they might be with words, no matter how much you would think that they would have the right words for every occasion, even a poet has a hard time conjuring the right words to say I'm really really sorry, to say I miss everything about you now that you are gone, To say, you are still and always will be in my heart.

Sometimes these things are just impossible to say correctly, impossible to form as words that will truly express what burns inside to be expressed.

Ever seen a poet that misses his very best friend? It's a messy and a ridiculous sight, but don't mock, don't point and laugh. These poets, they can't help it, maybe they are born this way.

Stop the Almosting

05/09/08

(a poem written after being unceremoniously dumped by the writer girlfriend I dated for a couple months)

stop almosting me
cruel and stupid gods,
stop the machine
Karma like rotting fruit.

Home alone
all alone
beer with lime
in the night
takes the edge off.

stop almosting me
I tire of living
as a wish upon a wind
as a memory of was
as fire, awful
conflagration of soul
burning tears
I want to cry again tonight
but I haven't drank quite enough.

Haven't actually cried since February
(when SHE left.)
the lack is eating me up
driving me mad
I need doors swung wide open again
but nothing
just this burning pain inside.

Stupid drunken poet.
Stupid gods.
Stupid Karma
stupid machine
stupid always almosting.

death in a paper cup.
is no better or worse
than life as a poet.

Knowing how to feel
how to speak
how to write
how to love
is no better than breathing in
and breathing out.

IT WAS ONE NIGHT; MAY

It was one Saturday night early in May when Lexy suddenly appeared at Mochalux. Devorah was in tears, Opal said, "Who cares." I was nervous and uncomfortable. Our conversation was brief and tense. I thought she would show up the next week, but didn't. I was there with Roderick and one of my very best female friends, Janice, who had just broken up with her fiancé and moved back to town. We'd been hanging a lot. Shane came and asked us to come to a DJ gig he had north of town. We all went over after. Shane pulled Janice aside and asked her not to tell me that Alexcie was back at his house. I'd figured she was staying with relatives. The night before at the bar Shane had asked me for her number, ostensibly to call and see how she was doing. I didn't give it to him. He already knew how she was doing. Janice refused to lie and made him tell me. I had known since Christmas that he didn't have my back. He and I became less and less friends after that because of things involving her. I had taken to heart Devorah's advice. about setting boundaries and having an actual friendship with Lexy, instead of what we always were. I tried, I really tried. I remember our first long phone conversation, I was outside on a Saturday afternoon with the kids. Within a short time we were talking and sharing like before, but I kept strong, kept boundaries, it was OK. We would see each other at shows, drink after, talk nice. But I didn't really call her. I would return her calls, but not immediately. She started bonding instead with Shane. Every time she was around, he was always seemed to be trying to get her to go somewhere else with him, to the Shine. Or talking about stuff they were doing together, gigs he was finding, the kind of stuff we once did. It started driving me crazy, mad with jealousy, she must have known. He must have known, too.

After May Fun City

05/29/08

It's like being back with my fucked up dysfunctional family again, she said; and she's kind of an expert on such things, I think.

There she sat making this joke about the family, and I didn't want to feel that. I kept trying to visualize this thin invisible wall between us keep my heart closed up, keep an arm's length. But the tiny old dysfunctional voices were whispering.

She has no one and nothing and nowhere and I promised to be there forever, and I can be I suppose, but with this wall I need to survive. But it was the same old things, a slap in the head, the kind you would give a dog to keep him under control. Singing my favorite song, watching me sing along.

But I can't let down this wall between us, because then I would feel her and feel our sameness again, and then I would love her and that would kill me, because she doesn't have a goddamn bit of love inside her to give back to me, or anyone really, and that is simply what it is.

Because we're crazy that's why

May was turning to June, it was a Saturday night sitting at our usual tall table at Mochalux. She walked in. I don't know what the deal was, but it was pretty fucking overwhelming. She had her sister and nephews with her so perhaps she had been outside running around with them all day. Her outfit was, well, it was enough to make a marble statue of a blind old man get a boner. It was just this sporty exercise thing, all light gray. It's just that the shorts were so small and tight and the shirt was so small and tight. There was all these smooth light brown legs everywhere. There was all these smooth light brown abs everywhere. My hands were literally shaking the entire evening as she sat next to me. It was almost too much for me to handle. Over-mother-fucking-whelming. We made it through the reading OK, then hit the bar. Some of our Fort Worth poets were out and wanted to get a drink, so we did. Then hit the Pitt Grill after. Towards the bathroom there were about 10 biker dudes that went crazy when she walked in. She was shaken by it. She came over and sat down next to me. Tim Thompson, our Druid Reiki poet walked around and started rubbing her shoulders or aligning her chakras or some shit. All I know is that with the outfit, or almost outfit, and the noises she was making I felt like I was going to release fluids right there in the Pitt. Across the room the bikers seemed worked up as well. Janice called, was getting off at Cave's, I told her I was going nuts she said she was coming. Lexy had to get up and go to the bathroom but was afraid to walk past the bikers. I was getting upset and said "goddamn it I'm gonna have to fight these 10 mother fuckers. She just looked at me silently. Our Druid spoke up and said "Paul, I just want you to know that I don't have your back. "Thanks dude," I said. The other fellows with us said the same. We stood to walk that way, I braced myself for the violence to come. Just then Janice walked in. She looked at me and said "Who the fuck are you about to fight?" I growled "Those fuckers are talking shit about Lexy!" Janice looked and said, "I know those dudes from the bar, sit down, I got it. She walked over to them, pointed, said something about how we were sensitive artists, her friends, and that if they wanted to see something they should look at her tits, and she shook em around a bit. We made it through without incident.

A few days later we were all up at Cave's sitting around the long outside raised area. Lex was at my left. Down a bit and to the right was Brittany, Shane and Rod. The vibe was weird. Brittany was dark. Rod was broody. Lex and I were on a roll. I was paying attention to Brittany for a bit and when I turned back around, Lexy had been engaging in conversation with some drunk dude, 40 something, apparently an ex Navy Seal, or so he said. The topic of the conversation had something to do with him providing her a gun to shoot herself with. He was trying to be clever and hit on her, but she was pretty insistent that the gun was what she was interested in, that perhaps her corpse would be available for a date, but the gun needed to be provided first. His drunk rambling started to annoy her and she started raising her voice. She said " Look, you're just fucking with me! You don't tease a suicidal girl with the offer of a gun but then not provide the gun! You're just getting my hopes up! If you don't have the gun, just go away and leave me alone!" He wouldn't though. She just kept getting more agitated. Finally I intervened. I said " Hey buddy, she said it's time to walk away, step off." He responded, "Oh, so you speak for her now?" I looked directly into his eyes and in my best Hollywood bravado said, " With all that this dame has put me though, you bet your goddamn ass I speak for her!' He was taken aback. She laughed for a second, then looked perplexed like she was thinking over what I had said. I heard Shane, to the right, say " Shit, I better go get Janice; She was working the door. Seal gun man walked slowly away, talking some shit, then Janice came out and tossed him. A short bit later this big tatted up dude came over and put his hand on my shoulder. Then said " Hey man! You are way too big and way too hardcore not to have more ink than that!" It was a ridiculous if innocuous statement. Lexy looked at me waiting for my response. I said in most sincere mockey performance voice, " Dude! That's crazy! You wont believe this, but that is the EXACT same thing I said to your mother last night, before she looked up and said shut up bitch eat my pussy!!" The guys jaw dropped in silent disbelief. Lexy let out what I'm pretty sure way the loudest squealing intense laugh I ever heard escape her face. She almost fell off her chair. Everyone looked around. Then I patted the dude on the back and said "Hey, I'm sorry dude, just funnin ya!, it's all good!" and he walked silently away. To my right Roderick, Shane and Brittany had been watching all this. Shane shook his head and turned to Rod and said "Man, I hate it when they get like this."

What Matters

06/03/08

It doesn't matter
it doesn't really matter
none of it matters.
In the end there is nothing and
so much of this doesn't matter.

Your ideas on linear progression.
Success, moving forward, achievement,
goal chasing, being something,
doesn't matter.
The things we define ourselves by;
possessions,
homes and cars and boats and bank accounts,
titles and positions and influence and occupation.
Doesn't matter.
None of this matters.
It means nothing at all in the end when
it is all said and done.
When the darkness comes.
When all the clock tics and sunrises
have had their way.
It doesn't matter.
Other people's expectations,
how they define you
and allow you to define yourself,
doesn't matter.
What beliefs you profess.
What gods you hold.
What political affiliation.
If you paid your taxes.
Saved for retirement.
Got that promotion.
Doesn't matter,
doesn't really matter.
None of it means a goddamn thing.
Happiness,
living for the moment,
party it up and dig the scene.
How many people you know
How many people you fuck
How many drinks you drink

and drugs you smoke or snort or pop,
it doesn't matter.
It doesn't fucking matter, none of that matters.
All of that is just the hiding.
The living by not living, because you know
that none of it matters.
Art.
Living to create.
Being deeper, more profound
more meaningful, having more substance
more truth,
being a writer
playing the guitar
singing or speaking in front of a crowd,
book signings,
painting a masterpiece,
your name spread around the world.
It doesn't matter.
Art is only passion.
Passion for truth, for life, for connection
for desire, for being,
and all passion fades when
an artist eventually self-consciously
turns the process inwards leaving
only a passion for the art itself.
Creating the never ending logic loop
of a passion feeding upon passion,
with nothing left to be passionate about,
flame burned out.
Sure you might get lucky, create
something that will influence someone somewhere,
which is nice, but it's still nothing in the end
as far as you are concerned.
Just as hollow a death as any other.
None of it matters.
Nothing matters.
It doesn't really matter.
All your pretense.
All your grand ideas.
All your substance and truth and depth.
All you stuff and power and influence.
All your accomplishments,
are nothing.

The only thing there is,
the only thing that is something
the only thing we take from it
as human beings manifest
into a human being culture with absolutely nothing as basis for
even measuring reality at all, without
said culture, other people,
how we reflect our selves onto others.
The only thing that matters is love.
The bits and pieces of love found along the way.
The only truth is love.
True real love is the only real thing that there is.
The rest is bullshit.
Some people might say that love is bullshit,
but they are bullshit,
and all that they say and believe and do is bullshit.
They are just incapable of facing the hard truth
that the only real thing there is,
is something so fundamentally uncontrollable and unquantifiable
as true real human love.
That's it.
The rich man without love is meaningless.
The famous man without love is meaningless.
The successful man without love is meaningless.
The learned man without love is meaningless.
Any artist, any musician, any craftsman
any guru, any thinker, any leader without love
that doesn't know the terrible
brutal bitter wonderful explosive thrilling painful joy
of love, is empty.

The POET.
The poet who has so become the very passion of love itself
and creates himself into a box.
A box where no one else can be,
is the worst most dismal creature of all.
All manner of shadows will dance about him.
All manner of incomplete notions.
All manner of almost loves.
It's like burning forever and never ever burning out.
The sadness is like an ocean,
it's really that bad.
As the ones who should truly love him
fade away, like images from a vivid dream.

June Mad Swirl

I was doing pretty good at keeping some distance between us, but it was hard. Everyone had schooled me when she was gone, on boundaries and standing up for myself. That If I really wanted to be her friend, I needed to try to be her friend and not this relationship that was bound to explode. GOD! I'd had this fantasy the whole time I was dating Shanna. Lexy coming back and seeing this pretty girl hanging on me, hanging on my arms and on my words the way she always did, until she suddenly didn't. I wanted Lexy to see that and think, "Huh, maybe he is a decent man after all. I sure missed out!" I missed it by only a matter of days by the time she walked in I was all broke up and alone again, oddly for the first time since she had been gone, some weird joke from silly gods.

It was First Wednesday, Mad Swirl Open Mic Night. We weren't riding together anymore. She showed, Anson was there, this dame he had been dating, all the usual poet peeps I'd known for years who I'd felt increasingly not close too. I brought Janice, she was interested in bonding with Lexy. I was purposely paying only marginal attention to her, so I have no idea how she got so drunk. I was sitting in the side chairs slightly out of sight conversing with a couple Slam poets. I hear her on the mic, "Paul! Paul! Where's Paul!" I stood and looked to the front. There she was, drunk as shit, that small black skirt all up around her thighs. Jeeezus fuck, she is beautiful, fucked up, but beautiful. "Paul! I can't remember the words to my songs!" She slurred out. Every eye in the room looked to me, some rolling in mute protest at the dynamic they detested. I walked toward the mic and said, "Calm down baby, you're playing one song and singing another, choose one and start slow, I'll sing with you." We sang *"more than this,"* her on the mic and me off to the side until she got the groove." It was quite the spectacle. The Poetry Slam host who had heard my poems about her, but never met her, said "Dude, she is so in love with you, she's just mixed up, scared to feel, something, it's an obvious energy!" I was standing up by her while she finished her set. Anson leaned over to me and said "Tell her that her dress is hiked up! She's giving the whole audience a show!" I laughed, said "Nah! She's rather adorable like that, let her be." Then he said "Man! I hate it when she gets fucked up like this, it's horrible!" I laughed, responded, "Yeah, I find it rather beautiful; I seem to love her even more at her worst." He shook his head.

The next day on Madswirl.com there was her picture. Crooning, in the black dress, all hiked up around the thighs. She looked out of it, but sublimely beautiful, truly poet spank worthy, if you know what I mean.

I Don't Love You

06/08/08

I don't love you
I don't love you
I don't want you walking around,
thinking I love you.
Really you piss me off
about a fourth of the things you say
really, really piss me off
they are so ridiculous,
so infuriating
so frustrating
and I don't mean the deep stuff
I totally agree with you on all that.
I don't mean the philosophies,
the ideas, the feelings the struggles
all that,
we are just the same on all that
exactly the same,
more fucking the same than anyone ever
really.
In fact I mostly believe that I will never ever find
anyone that understands me and really gets me,
not like you,
EVER,
so mostly I'm pretty fucked
and I don't like being pretty fucked.
Mostly I'm pretty pissed off
about being pretty fucked.
So don't go around thinking every thing is OK.
Cause it's not.
It's not just shit you say,
It's the way you hurt me before
It's mostly fine, but it will never be all the way fine.
The way you hurt me before
and the way you hurt my kids
that's what really got me.
Don't get me wrong here, they still love you,
they ask about you all the time, They miss you
They love you more than anyone
that's ever been around me.
But that's them, they are children
Not like me, I'm still upset really.

I mean I know it doesn't seem like it
But I need you, you're the best at what we do
I've ever had.
And as far as the being there to talk to you
when you are depressed,
well, I mean you know, it's hard not to do that
we are the only ones who really get each other
and there might be times when I need you.
And you are fun, I mean
we do have the best times together,

We seem tougher, and smarter and more funny
when we are together than apart
so, I mean how could anyone not want that?
It's pretty awesome,
and it's only painful when
you are saying or doing fucked up shit
right?
So it's no big deal, it's all OK, I think.
Just don't go thinking that I love you
I don't love you
I don't love you
I don't love you
In fact, you really piss me off,
at least a fourth of the time
really, sometimes
I just want to kick your goddamn ass
Really. Don't get me wrong though,
I wouldn't let anyone else hurt you
or disrespect you.
I'd fight 10 biker dudes to defend your honor
in a heartbeat, without hesitation.
I mean , I'd have to.
But don't get the wrong idea here.
Mostly, you just piss me off.
Well not mostly,
mostly I
well,
hell,
you know.

The Darkest Girl Ever

06/11/08

I just want this to all end,
she said
I tire of living this life I am forced to live
all this for a life of nothing
a life I don't even want.
I just can't seem to do it
can't end it,
I wish someone would kill me.

When I look in her eyes
I realize
that I have never forgotten
a single word that she has ever spoken
to me.

I say;
darling, I would gladly kill you
and myself as well
put an end to both our suffering
if only I could be somehow sure
that we could spend
all eternity together in hell.

Realizing, while saying it,
that it was an enormously fucked up
thing to say.

She however, looked at me
as though it was the sweetest
kind and loving thing
she had ever heard.
Awwwwwww.
She tilted her head a bit

We opted for whiskey shots
instead.

Still, there are a thousand possible
tomorrows,
and she never runs out of
things to say.

IT WAS ONE NIGHT: JUNE

It was one night early in June, the 10th, the night before a psychiatrist appointment I had waited so long for. It was a Tuesday night in Addison at a show Anson was involved with. For some reason Lexy returned her focus to me. She bought me beer all night and paid attention to me. The show was lame. We decided to come back to town for last call, do some shots. We made it just in time and threw some down. I felt the powerful desire again to kiss her, sitting on the picnic table behind the Shine. There was this massive pheromone moment, God, we were so close, she is so powerful. It had been so long since I'd felt her that way, so fucking long. I'd been keeping her at arm's length, and even months earlier when we were together everyday, she had been so distant, so casually cruel to me towards the end. I wanted so badly to lean in, take the kiss I had so long craved and deserved. It was all there. She was touching my arms. Feeling them, talking about how much time I must have spent in the gym when she was gone. It was fucking crazy overwhelming! More overwhelming just in that closeness than any of the intimacy I'd known in the months she was gone. But I didn't try or say a word. I wish I had. Why the hell not? We were talking Pitt Grill. Shane came out wanting to get her into the Sunshine bar after hours. Just walked up and said "Paul, you're too drunk, you need to go home, I can only get one person in here anyway, Lexy, you come in." He had no idea how drunk I was or wasn't. It was a statement I would never be un-pissed about. However, she'd been paying attention to me all night and decided to go with me to the diner. It would have crushed me if she didn't. That was it. **I WAS BACK IN.** We were back in our zone.

We sat in the diner and talked about everything. As deep and connected as ever. About what it had been like for both of us apart. I was feeling our energy again, it had been so long. God how I craved her and loved her and missed her! I told her everything. At one point she was lamenting that she would always be alone, that no one could handle her, she said "Even you, you think you want to, but you couldn't handle me!" "I immediately shouted "Oh, yes I can!" We looked into each other eyes for a quiet moment, laughed, then talked all night! I must be the biggest fool alive for not even trying that night, something, a little. I think I have a fear of my own emotions. This is why she and a few others have felt me closed off sexually. They were the ones I really loved. It's easy to hit on a dame you just like a lot, but as much as I love to love it's hard to face it when you're so scared of loss. If only that night I had stepped up, projected the chemistry and been a man. IF ONLY!

The next day, it was as powerful as ever. I was trying to memorize "*What am I supposed to do now*" while sitting in the doctors waiting room. We spoke on the phone. She was in another waiting room somewhere else with her sister getting a sonogram. We cried together on the phone and by the time I saw the doc I was a real mess, got put on meds.

A few days later I texted and asked her if she wanted to go to the movies with my kids. The boys had seen her, but my daughter hadn't. We went, and it turned out to be her birthday. I didn't know. Shane had known and planned a little party at his house, SURPRISE! He didn't call me. During the movie I looked over and saw my daughter in her lap. I remember thinking then, in the flickering light of the screen, what the hell am I doing holding back? With Lexy of all people? My best friend? This is the woman I truly love with all my heart and guts and mind. The one I wish I could be around forever. My soulmate. Sometimes in life, all that matters in the end is that you know you tried your best, no regrets. That image of my daughter in her lap at the movies? That was something I wanted to see for the rest of my life.

My soul turns slightly

06/12/08

Foundation, solid spiritual and emotional foundation. I just realized for the first time that this is what my reflection lacks. She, so easily fed by other's energies, other's ideas, constantly flowing in and out. This explains a LOT. Mixed messages, duel ideas, ever changing notions. I used to blame myself. Vision obscured by my own attachment. But it's real, it's all just as real.. When she is with me, she IS in my zone. She IS mine. What I'm feeling, seeing, hearing, experiencing is real. Checking notes on occasion with others, with the slight mismatched perceptions, is just as real, hence my frustration. Her sliding in and out of my zone. Me wanting her always in there. Always feeling like not enough somehow when she isn't. AH! But me, like a couple others, like HIM, we're solid. Almost way to much so. Unyielding, stubborn, always thinking always considering different directions, but the same spiritual /emotional foundation. Growth is difficult for us, because movement is. Difficult for her, because solid footing is. Too much influence? Back and forth? Is it possible she is incapable of real connection? Any mere friendship? Any simple attraction? We both somehow know that no matter how far apart we are geographically or emotionally, where life takes us, our hearts and souls we will always be bonded somehow. It is a real love. The tragic unworkable-ness of it makes the purity of it no less real.

The Biggest Asshole In The World

06/13/08

I had started dating this girl Shanna
and it was going well, I had high hopes
It was the most sane and comfortable I'd felt in a while.
So I brought her around my children, to see how it would go.
Something I rarely did a few years back when I was first divorced
But these days I do pretty much all the time, they are used to it.
Plus, being around social gatherings, and poetry readings
they pretty much know everyone I am close to anyway.

On this particular day, I really wanted them to like Shanna
because I really wanted it to work out.
She made a nice effort, it was good.
Although she didn't seem to be
the really strong natural with children
that I had imagined her to somehow be, it was still nice.

In the car I asked them "What do you think? Isn't she nice?"
"Yes," they all said, nodding their heads, "she seems nice."
But then my daughter spoke up smiling real loud and said
"But I miss Lexy, when can we see Lexy?"
Lexy had been in my life for a while, then left
leaving me pretty devastated.

I had already brought one other woman around them after that
Amy, who they said was nice,
my daughter had called "kinda crazy"
and had mistakenly called her Lexy quite a few times.
My son had called her "a little too bossy "
Said "It will be a problem."
He is almost never wrong.

But they would never stop asking about Lexy
Like they were remembering as much as I was.
And here I was on this day dating someone very nice,
that I wanted them to really like,
So when my baby daughter brought up Lexy again,
I snapped at her.

I said; "Look dammit stop it! She's not here OK!
I told you she doesn't want to be with us!
She yelled at me and left!

That's just the way it is!
I was asking you about Shanna!"
There was this moment of silence,
and all the smiling and laughing stopped.
My sweet younger son, said "GOD!" To his sister
"Grandma said not to talk about Lexy!"
She looked utterly crestfallen, and said "Sorry daddy."
I instantly felt like the biggest asshole in the world,
making her frown like that, saying that to her.
It was truly awful.
I tried to apologize, make it right,
told her I didn't mean to yell.
My younger son said "Daddy,
I'm sorry Lexy yelled at you and left."
My older son reached over and touched my arm and said
"Dad, I think Shanna is nice, maybe it will work out,
she doesn't seem too bossy, it could work
but you know it's really hard sometimes things seem good at first
but then later aren't, like with you and mom."
I really, really felt like the biggest asshole in the world.

He was right, it was hard, and it didn't work out.

A few months later, when Lexy had returned
and we were very cautiously spending a little time together
here and there. I saw my sons reaction the first time they saw her.
Throwing their arms around her so tight.
Then later I saw my daughter's reaction when she saw her
and it was that same big huge beautiful beaming smile
that she had that day asking for her in the car.
The one I had ruined with my harsh words.
I felt very bad about that day, remembering it then.

All she had wanted was to see someone again
that she really loves,
and ironically the reason I had been such an asshole,
was because that was what I wanted to.

What Am I Supposed to Do, *Now in Pieces.*

06/14/08

*She can't hang around to pick up the pieces, she said.
The implication being that she was somehow responsible
For the pieces I seemed to be in at the time.
But she wasn't.*

*Truth be told, she was very nice an experience.
But at the end, after so many weeks of relative relationship bliss,
the shit she chose to make conflict made it pretty clear that
we were not a match at all. It was a pretty ridiculous a feeling,
being so misunderstood, closed off and judged
by someone I simultaneously felt so close to,
simply for my own views, thoughts, feelings and struggles that
I was looking for connection in sharing,
and a poem in which one line was deemed offensive.
I didn't care much for it, honestly.*

*It's like she, this other one who has always gotten me,
said at the diner one night;
"I know it sucks when someone you're enjoying doesn't work out,
but honestly, you know you could never be with someone
when you have conflict on those kinds of things,
that's too basic for you."
Of course she was right, the REAL irony being
that the pieces in question, the ones I seemed to be in
actually belonged to* ***HER. SHE*** *was the one that had ruined me,
through no fault of her own, I might add, but definitely the pieces
were hers.*

*She had come into my life like a freaken tornado.
She had spent days and hours and weeks with me
always me and her together, way past all my barriers
past all my walls and boundaries, all my thoughts and ideas shared,
all secrets revealed and she didn't judge me or misunderstand me
in fact she completely got me, a fact that she would remind me of
over and over again.
This was the first time in my life I had experienced this.
But, she didn't want me, no need to go into details, she just didn't.
We had fights, and then she left for a good while.*
That *is when I was broken into pieces. Don't get me wrong,
I didn't melt away. Hell, I even spent the night in her room
with a cherished female friend the very night after she left.*

And, I was dating within five minutes, a very nice hot young thing
who was kind to me, but of course, turned out not to get me
within a pretty short time. And then there was her,
and it seemed really good and it was really good.
It felt normal and OK and decent and comfortable
and it was exactly what I wanted. Until, there it was,
The same things I had so frighteningly accurately predicted
in the ONE poem that is the very essence and definition
of the struggle, depression and loneliness that I face right now.
Written months earlier that defines these pieces I seem to be in.
WHAT AM I SUPPOSED TO DO NOW?
About to be published in my favorite magazine.
Submitted months ago.
The words have not left my head for a moment in
the last month or more,
I was reading it over and over in the clinic waiting room
when I finally got my tears back after months of living without.

So there we are, that's the little drama, my little story.
Sitting in the coffeehouse, while this perfectly nice dame
I had a decent time with, but ultimately, just as I had predicted
didn't get me, reads a snarky piece about how she left me in pieces.
While the other, to whom the pieces actually belong.
Who never actually had the guts to give me a chance.
The only one in my life that has ever really gotten me and would
never ever judge me, misunderstand me, or argue with me about
the same old stupid shit, sits right there pretty much oblivious to the
dynamic that she plays such a pivotal role in.

Ironic, but hardly funny, back on psyche meds.
Is this what it's going to be like for me forever?
Perfectly nice dames that come into my life and then judge me,
get pissy and read snarky poems overestimating their own impact,
about me on the mics that I host.
That's two for two this year.

Seriously, is it too much to ask for to meet a woman that I am
attracted to, like these perfectly nice ones. That will at least give me
a chance,
see how it goes, like these perfectly nice ones.
But actually get me, actually ***be*** *like me, actually understand and*
be in synch with me and ***actually listen,*** *creating a mutual bond*
of understanding, sharing, free exchange of ideas.
Complete openness without walking on eggshell shards of glass?

ACTUAL SPIRITUAL COMPANIONSHIP! like her.
Seriously? Is it too fucking much to ask the universe for?
To have this all in one package?
Am I being ridiculous and greedy?

I am fucked, fucked fucked fucked fucked
I will now join the ranks of the many artists I know
older than me, that I respect greatly, who at some point
because of who and what they are had to accept the fact
that they would have a life alone and without love.
Her poem said that my problem was that I had never learned
to live without Love. DO I WANT to learn to live without love?
Is this somehow some admirable thing?
I honestly believe that my capacity to love is one of my greatest
shining strengths as and artist, as a man, as a father, as a human
being living in a world with way to little love in it. Do I honestly
WANT to learn to live without love, Is this a good thing? OR is it just
that now that I am ruined
I have absolutely no choice left in the matter?
Seriously, What am I supposed to do now?

beside xx

06/17/08

I can't shake it, her soul,
unshakable.

Even her Cinderella words,
supposedly forsaken yet oblivious
so oddly sure but unsure.

Even the image of her profile
in theatre flash darkness
is enough.

It rouses my melancholy,
the emptiness of not having.
Wave after wave crashes
upon me,
relentless, cerebral, unforgiving.
Momentary waking euphoria.
Dreams of divine grace man bliss
all brought out and new in dynamic.
And those terrible feelings of death
of wanting to die
of paralyzation in troubadour notions
that death would be preferable
to life without knowing this.

Only
only
to pull her towards me.
The perfect poem.
The perfect vision.
The perfect song.
The one in my soul.
Always beside me
Always beside me
Even if you can’t quite tell.

I LOVE MY GIRLS.

06/18/08

Tuesday, went out to the gig in Addison. Open to poets, but not geared to be half and half the way our gigs are. I ended up not getting to read the stuff I wanted to because it got WAY to late and I had gotten WAY too drunk. Maybe the meds, weird. The night started out awesome. Good energy, great people I love and enjoy. Several of my favorite females that I have been lucky enough to be close to all at the same table, Lexy, Shay, Amy, it was cool. But the energy just got weird. Maybe for me it was the meds. I left and realized I was too fucked up. Shouldn't have been driving. RARE for me, NEVER that far from home. I talked to Janice, she made it to Caves, said try to catch her. Got there, depressed as hell, but she was little help, WAY too drunk herself. Luckily her roommate Jamie, a delightful young lady, kinda took charge. Rod was suddenly there, jealous of everyone else's obliterated-ness I think. But even among good friends the energy of the night was a beast. It got worse and worse. We decided to hit the Pitt. On the way Lexy called, now having the same traumatic return drive from Addison that I'd had earlier. She was having big issues, major tears. At one point talking to her trying to calm her, looking out the window beside me I could see Janice vomiting on the sidewalk. Yeah, something was off, the joo joo was fucked. We got Janice home. By this time, very late, I was talking to Lex in the car and lost her, I panicked, crying, kept saying, I lost her, I lost her, I lost her, I couldn't get her back on the phone. Still on that long ass drive, I felt sure something had happened to her. I was OVERCOME with this fear and sadness that something was wrong, that she was gone, forever, it was awful. Finally I talked to her again, 4 am or something, she wasn't feeling good, none of us were. It was a hell of a night.

The next day, a weird day in the cubicle, taking vitamins, lots of phone calls back and forth. I grabbed the kids and went to Super Salad. Lexy, Janice and Jamie met us there. We talked of the previous night. The weird thing was that as bad as everyone's energy was, the longer we sat there and talked and laughed and joked, the more it all slid away. With my kids there, smart and beautiful and brilliant. We were doing so good we were making a huge loud spectacle of ourselves. Janice suggested we move it to the park. The kids ran around and played. We sat and laughed and told stories and mellowed out. It felt like all the bad energy was completely gone. Here I was with my two most beloved girls, my best friends, this new cool friend, and my sweet beautiful children. It was great. It was one of those moments, the calm after the storm. I was happy that the ones I love the most where able to share the joy of my children with me. It absolutely rubbed off on them. Janice was her normal chatty self. Lexy was even smiling and laughing by the end. My kids love her so much. They are happy with her. She is like family to them. Janice was astounded at the way the boys had argued over who got to sit next to her. From the restaurant to the park each kid rode in a different car. Lexy had Bear, who she always has a special bond with. Whatever she was playing, he asked if he could hear her songs instead, singing all the words. He said "You're my favorite of all!" It moved her to near tears. Touched her, I could tell. It was just a great time. I went back out briefly to take Janice to work, we talked about it. How these times fly by, the good and the bad. so much loss I've known, but even with that, right now, I love my girls, and having them with my kids, it felt like family. It was good.

and I loved you....

06/22/08

It's not your fault
You didn't do anything,
nothing special
It's nothing really.
You just opened your mouth
and I loved you.
Said a bunch of words
and I loved you.
Were kind of silly
and I loved you.
Went to a movie
and I loved you.
Drank too much,
and I loved you.
Made me laugh,
and I loved you.
Were really depressed
and I loved you.
Sang a happy little tune,
and I loved you.
Were very nice to me
and I loved you.
Were mean to me,
and I loved you
Had a crazy brain
and I loved you.
Told sad stories
and I loved you.
Longed for more
and I loved you.
Went far away
and I loved you.
Held small children
and I loved you.
Made me mad
and I loved you.
Talked really loud
and I loved you.
Ate Chinese food
and I loved you.
Touched my hand for a moment

and I loved you.
Nodded your head in agreement
and I loved you.
Cried your eyes out
and I loved you.
Screamed on my voice mail
and I loved you.
Dressed like a whore
and I loved you.
Argued with strangers
and I loved you.
Made me feel real
and I loved you.
Took me around your dysfunctional family
and I loved you.
Spoke in orange yellow streetlight
and I loved you.
Were occasionally ridiculous and infuriating
and I loved you.
Completely ignored me
and I loved you.
Turned to me in times of need
and I loved you.
Controlled the car stereo
and I loved you.
Asked for to go boxes
and I loved you.
Was photographed beside me
and I loved you.
Craved meaning
and I loved you.
Let me take care of you
and I loved you.
Slept curled up in a chair
and I loved you.
Listened to my poems
and I love you.
Were moody
and I loved you.
Were my friend
and I loved you.
Smiled a certain smile
and I loved you.
Felt hopeless

and I loved you.
Made real things happen
and I loved you.
Joked about death
and I loved you.
Liked other men
and I loved you.
Ignored and refused me
and I loved you.
Really, it's nothing
no big deal
Nothing to worry about.
You didn't do anything
It's me, all me,
I couldn't help myself,
I just loved you.

Since Your Return

(Why It's All So Awesome)
06/25/08

I have endeavored toward creating a more mature
boundaries oriented close friendship
and professional relationship.
Drama free has been the motto.
Well, kind of.
We have both been pretty engulfed in drama
just not concerning each other.
No, for the most part we have both been
reasonable and mature towards one another.
Fortunately allowing for us to be very supportive,
both going through some rough times.
A good thing I think, following the advice of a poet,
slightly more experienced and mature.
HOWEVER, all that being said;
I'm pretty sure that if I could have foreseen
one of my supposed closest buddies (rhymes with train)
making you his motherfucking best pal
which feels emotionally more like having my best friend
stolen away than anything I have ever experienced,
at least in adulthood.
Parading you about like some prize.
Taking you around town like some project.
Bragging about you to people, ironically
in a CERTAIN PARTICULAR PLACE
that you actually yelled at me more than once,
for asking you to go to,
but are now getting in with the cool kids in crowd at,
like my *supposed* buddy.
With people coming up asking about you and him
like you were some type of swell unit.
With his constant rubbing it in my face
by always trying to lure you away when you are around our group.
Always telling precious little stories
about all the terrific things he has been taking you to.
Particularly on days when I am lying on the couch
not answering the phone, crying about how much I miss you,
and suffer without you.
You know, SERIOUSLY as fucking AWESOME as all this is,
I'm pretty sure if I could have foreseen this dynamic
I would have said ; **fuck the hell out of maturity,**

Fuck the hell out of sanity.
And I would have immediately upon your return
fallen to my knees in front of you and begged you to let me be your bitch again
promising to be good, to do anything and everything for you
and to never complain about anything ever again.
Seriously, at this point I would have said
fuck maturity and what's right
I would have begged for your time back right up front.

To die

06/26/08

See, the thing is
I would die for you.
I would sacrifice anything, conquer the world
give my last drop of blood. Give up all that I have.
It's not just that I love you, or want you,
it's that you are the most kindred soul
I have ever known.

Given some magic choice of true happiness
for myself, for the entire world, or for only you,
I would choose you without hesitation.
I wish more for you than conceivable.
I wish you enlightenment, understanding,
the gift of true peace and fulfillment.
That all of your lofty goals and desires
were completely fulfilled
all old wounds healed, and that
you were capable of understanding the gift
of true love, the kind of love I hold in my soul for you.

Yet, you see my love as incomplete,
because it grasps. it contains desire.
I am human, no Bodhisattva,
it is the very best I have to offer.
You see the world as offering you nothing pure
nothing real, nothing unconditional.
While I sit hardly able to breathe
not knowing what to do, without you.
You talk of the small number of men
that have treated you with honor and dignity
while so casually omitting my name.
As if my love itself, something I am unable to un feel
is somehow a dishonor.
As if somehow the hundreds of selfish users
liars and object-ifiers
somehow equate to the grandiosity
of my overwhelming burning painful love.

You talk of being alone, and you say it to me
as if we were playing a game.
A game where we pretend that someone somewhere

actually doesn't know how I hunger to devote myself
to your companionship happiness and success.
I know that the demons that eat away at your soul
the terrible void inside, and the challenges you face
merely surviving are not of my making,
have nothing to do with me.
They have other completely different faces.
But I can't help it.
I feel inadequate, unworthy, useless
valueless, purposeless, terribly afflicted
unable to love you
unable to help you
unable to make you happy.
Not even enough to get you by.

I don't know how pure my love is
or how selfless it is,
I just know that I die inside a little more each day
unworthy to live with you
and unable to die for you.

July Mad Swirl

First Wednesday again. Goddamn, the month between seemed like it lasted a lifetime! On meds nearly a month. Lexy and I having developed this being there for each other so much, so supportive, during this time of depression for us both. What an intense month. It seemed like it had been stretched out to a year.

Around the time Lexy had returned I had been talking to Janice's 21 year old roommate, Jamie. This young hip nerdy college intellectual type chick. Very charming. Janice had made me feel guilty for finding her attractive. I remember the day I saw her, Brittany had just come back around, having been dumped. It was only a few days before Lexy returned. Britt, Janice and I were eating pizza. She told me to stay away from her roommate. Instead, I took her to lunch and told her that she was too young for me, that I was into her, and that if she was 10 years older, for sure, but not. No one believed me. They always thought I was trying to get in there. I really just liked the girl and enjoyed talking to her.

By July 2nd, Mad Swirl, Jamie wanted to come with. Lexy called and said that she was sick and wanted to ride with me, wasn't going to perform, but didn't want to miss the family. We all three rode. The girls bonded. I tried to get Jamie to bond with Brittany as well, but she has some spliced tiger DNA. Lexy and I were in our zone. She was sweet, kind, by my side, and calm the entire night. She did drink a LOT, but the weirdest thing she did was this crazy speaking in tongues word vomit thing. It was uber nuts and she later claimed that she didn't do it and that she wasn't drunk at all. Ah! That night, I was so in love with her that night! At Jamie and Janice's place, I had to help her weak little body up the stairway, hands on torso. Outside, after first round break, where everyone smokes and drinks trunk whiskey, we were walking back towards the door. I had some left to go put back in he car. She said "I'll walk with you." I said "Walk with me? I was going to make you do it!" She punched me and said "Shut up!" laughing. We were standing in the exact same spot on the sidewalk where she had asked me in November if I was going to try to kiss her. The sound of her voice laughing was killing me. God I wanted her so bad, she's my entire world, always had been since 10 Mad Swirls earlier.

On the way back from the car her heel broke, she was hanging on my shoulder trying to fix it. Several Dallas poets were near. I could feel their eyes. I looked at Lex and said, "Baby, I love you more than

I've ever loved anyone before!" She smiled and said "Shut up." but it was a slow soft "shut up" with a big pretty smile. I loved her with everything I had.

I'm not sure what the deal was with Anson. Perhaps Lexy being in my zone was bugging him or something, but he zoned in on Jamie. Drank a few drinks, an Apple-teeny if I recall, and started doing the drunk scam thing. It bugged the hell out of me! Why the fuck does he always zone in on women I have feelings for? I suppose I could have said something, he did ask "Is that your girl?" and I'd said, " No, I dig her, we hang out, but she's too young for me." He's never been one for subtlety when it comes to the dames, doesn't get hints, and has a style far too touchy and gropey for my tastes. Maybe it's the additional years, but I always find it better to make them come to me, get in the space, close, words, body language, but keep the touchy feely down until it's the right time, until it's ready. His style is the opposite. All about the hands. It's not pleasant for me to witness, especially when he aims it at someone I dig as well. I make one slight attempt to sit in the way, but she is drunk as shit, and she is reacting to Janice's specific forbidding of her touching him. See, Janice had also found Anson interesting in May when she saw him play at Fun City, also a BIG heart killer for me. I just got up and walked out to the curb and sat down.

In a while, everyone came out. Rod, Lex, Jamie, Anson, apparently I had missed it, lucky me. I was steaming, fuming, burning up. We all walked over to the car. Jamie was drunk as shit stumbling around. Rod carried Lexy, which was weird. I scooped her up and put her in the car, then got Jamie in the back seat. Gave Rod and Anson a silent look of frustration and got in without a word and drove off. On the highway Lexy asked what was wrong. I started raising my voice, "What the fuck do you think is wrong!" She started to raise her voice back, but then stopped, touched my arm and gently said, "Paul, I care about you, I care about what you are feeling and I want to hear, please tell me." I was thrown, flabbergasted. It took the wind out of my fury. Half crying, I said "I'm fucking tired of being second to him! I'm tired of women I care about preferring him over me, it fucking SUCKS!" By this time Jamie was pretty much passed out in the backseat. Lexy put her hand on my hand, and said "You mean Jamie? I thought you said you guys didn't have anything?" I let out this frustrate cry and looked at her and said "It's you! I mean you! It's always fucking about you, everything is about you!" "ME?" She asked, with this weird surprised look as if I'd just popped in from planet Pluto. "Why is it about me? What did I do?" " It's about last year, November and all, when we first met, and you wanted him more than me!" She laughed "Paul, that was so long ago! How can you compare that brief infatuation I had with him to me and you? Everything that we have been through? You are the closest person in the fucking world to me! You know that! Anson is a good friend, but you have to stop comparing yourself, that's your own insecurity, you know that I love you." I was knocked over into stunned silence.

We went to see Janice at Caves, she and I got in this big argument over the phone about how drunk Jamie was. Lexy said the cursing and loud voices reminded her of her family and she would get Shane to take her home if he was in the Shine. I pleaded with her not to go. We drove Jamie back. I had to walk her up the same stairs I had walked Lexy up earlier. It took me some time to clean her vomit off the door step. Lexy and I drove back to Shane's. She made us some noodles and I read her a long letter I had written her a day or so earlier. It was the most gut wrenching profession of love and sadness and desire I had ever written. Basically, bottom line, I just don't want to live without her. When I was done, she said "Damn Paul, that was intense even for you." and held me for a good while. It was the best feeling. Oddly, despite how much she had been sexually charging me of late, especially earlier in the evening, that wasn't there in that moment holding me. Her arms around me, hands on my back. It wasn't attraction I was feeling in that moment; it was just the love, love and safety. I just want her to hold me like that for the rest of my life and never let go. I would do anything for that, from her. Only she won't, no matter how terrific she gets sometimes, how overwhelmingly perfect. She always, always lets go. ALWAYS.

Melancholy Symphony

07/08/08

My guts; all opened up.
Now, I am here before you
praying, that you alter my views,
or better yet that I can alter yours.
I mean just a little, just enough
to move you,
to catch me here, while I fall.

Hold me forever and ever and ever.
Putting things inside you.
Allowing me the luxury of
adoration.

Scrawled sentences that
will never see the light,
of screen or mic.
Here they are;
noodles and truth,
small round table,
every possible fear and insecurity
and all my endless love,
laid out in surrender.

All the dark non-breaths without you
are killing me. They are truly doing me in.

Yet,
Silly crashing moments keep me going.
every moment you
laugh and speak in tongues.
Nod and listen in that certain way.
Allow with grace these torso hands
to guide you up a stairway.
Hands upon shoulder, broken heel.
The way we
shuck and jive one another.
You've got to know that
you're the only one for me
and I for you.
I'm dying here. Truly dying.

Still crying
late in the car with my buddy.
Had to play our poem one more time.
Gasping for air through Shiner Boch tears.
All these prayers on paper like this.
I had to avert my eyes.
The palms of your hands upon my shoulder blades.
I still can't look into your eyes
those times,
when your fingers briefly lock with mine.

I think you get it now,
my madness and sincerity,
that they are intertwined.
Regardless of what others have said of me
in the past,
that you would have ever paid them heed
with innate inabilities to understand me
the way that only you do
and only I do you.

The world is full of critiques.
Critiques of you, critiques of me
critiques of you and I together.
Coming from all directions all of a sudden.
but I don't care, and you don't care
because we have our own problems
and only we know what we are like in
me and you against the world moments.

Can he really not hear my pain?
Can anyone really not hear our pain?
Like a melancholy symphony, together.

I'm falling here I'm falling falling, falling,
and I want to see my children grow up.
I want to see what their faces look like
in five years in ten years
and I want you to be there with us.

Catch me now
and I promise I will hold you up forever.
Softly whispering,
that you were all I needed.

I Possess No Gravity

07/10/08

I possess no gravity, create no orbit
she is not my moon
only a wonderful blazing comet
that briefly lights my sky.

Are the gods so unkind to us?
Do they truly hate us?
A question like 100 lb weight upon the chest
when waking up.
How do we face this alone? She asks.
How do you and I survive this? She asks.
What are we supposed to do?
We were not made for this world, she says.
and she is terribly painfully correct.
What we were made for is each other.
I hold her while she cries the tears of the genuine.
She is my child, my best friend, my mother,
But not my lover, except
in the thousand ways that truly matter.
What is the answer? she asks me,
over and over again.
When the answer is always, always
mere inches away.
Us together.
My hand. My heart. My arms.

I can hold her when she cries,
but not when she laughs
or when she sleeps.
or when she is in ecstasy.
I am not good enough
faulty, unacceptable.
I posses no gravity.
I cannot ever pull her close to me.
Even though together we are perfect,
shining bright,
and apart we may well die.
Her, burning up far far away.
Me fading away sad and lonely
In the darkness of the night.

Not Lonesome

By Ariya (4) and Anando (9) 07/06/08
(written for me and lexy, She sang it while he played guitar)

I am not lonesome with you.
Why wouldn't you want to do stuff with me?
If you do stuff with me, I'll do stuff with you.
In the life I am lonesome by myself.
Why would you never want me?
Because I love you to the moon and back.
And I won't be lonesome when you are back.
Why wouldn't you want me to?
If you do stuff for me, I'll do stuff for you.
In the life I am lonesome by myself.
Why would you never want me?
Because I love you to the moon and back.
And I won't be lonesome when you are back.
I am not lonesome when you are back.

Goodbye again ......

07/11/08

I

You'll still see me.
Maybe I'll come back,
you'll always have a place wherever I am.
You can come see me,
or stay for a while, a few months.
Even bring the kids for a while.
I've got to see them before I go.
We'll get all the kids together this week.
We'll talk regularly.
I just have to do this right now.
I need to.
It might not be forever.

It's just like last time.
Only much much worse.
because now
we have an even greater understanding.
We've grown beyond the ability
to force a conflict and push each other away.
And I have grown beyond the ability
to find something or someone to hide in
when she is gone.

II

What can a decent man do
when he says
"stay, don't leave, let's be together forever.
I will take care of you in every single way."
I will never try to box you in,
only love you every moment for
exactly who you need to be."
But she has to go, apparently.
I'm not good enough to even be here for,
not even close I think.

An Unclear Sign From Cruel Gods

07/12/08

Devastated, that's the only word I can think of, devastated. It's not that she blew me off, not really, it's just that it really, really feels that way. In fact she is more sweet, more kind, more brilliant, more of an incredible listener. More connected to me spiritually, intellectually, creatively, emotionally, functionally, than ever before. Like I say, it's not that she blew me off, not really, it just felt that way. What she really blew off was my emotions, my real gut wrenching feelings. I hadn't meant to go all out like that. The truth is that all that stuff had been in my head, all that "be with me forever," undying love, "let me take care of you always" shit. It was in my head and I guess I had intended to do something with it, but not there, not several beers down at the bar out back on a loud crowded night. It's just that when she said she was leaving me again, like before, that unbearably heavy weight of emotion fell from the sky and crushed me, like before. I suppose that's why it all came out. I felt like it was already too late. Look, like I say, It's not that she really blew me off. She was every bit the best of best friends that any human could hope for. She took my hand, she hugged me, she asked that I come see her, even stay for a long time, months or something. That I should bring the kids up. She said that no matter where she was, I would always have a place with her, anywhere. This doesn't sound like a blow off, but it's like a knife twisting in my poor old heart. What she blew off was just my emotional outburst. I could feel that defensive posture for moment, the change in tone, before I apologized and said that I didn't mean to activate her defenses. At which point she nodded her head and it was OK. See, I love this person more than I ever thought I could love a person. In an all around person way. Not as an idea as others love. Not as someone that should be boxed in and controlled, displayed and managed as previous boyfriends have. Not as an object of selfish use, the way the dozens of freaks and perverts who are pretty much constantly offering her stuff, to take care of her stupid cursed, overly hot ass do. No, mine is the kind of love and desire to nurture and be with, that only a real best friend can have. That's why it hurt. That's why it felt like a blow off, because my thrown out cards on the table drunken near begging was received pretty much no differently than any of those other empty fool's. Thrown in with a dash of you don't really want me anyway you just think you do. (She never believes in someone loving her.) There, my friends we have the recipe for an emotionally devastating blow off. Not that she really blew me off, mind you, she was actually more awesome than imaginable, it just felt that way.

I felt like a walking open wound. Calling up women, old and new, looking for a connection of some sort. What a feeling of desperate aloneness this was. Convinced that the new psych meds I had started were doing me wrong. Leading to a two day ordeal trying to get into see the free clinic doctor, who was quite surprised I think at my emotional breakdown and my stories. Result, add one more med to the mix. I was also facing the wrath of a psychotic hippie suffering from a psychotic breakdown who had decided that I was the Illuminati and was on a citywide crusade to discredit and harass me, multiple phone calls, scenes in public places, it was charming. At one point I changed the mood on my Myspace page to say "CRUSHED" and "HATED BY THE GODS." I feel sometimes like Odysseus struggling year after year to reach my Ithaca, beset by cruel gods for some past hubris. Had an email discussion with an old friend, a woman I loved dearly many many years ago, but like my current crushing reality, was unable to make the connection with. She married someone else, divorced him later, and now lives in New Orleans, remarried again. We bantered back and forth about the gods and if they have any interest in us at all. It was soothing and a little weird. It made me remember how it was, how I was unable to connect with her all those years ago. I projected this scenario with my dearest best beloved now, years from now, same thing, sharing a couple emails, remembering old times, thinking about how I was unable to connect with her. I wanted to die. I really truly wanted to die. This was way more painful an idea than I could sit with, it just was. I feel like I have lived my whole life unafraid to love, to be loved, waiting and waiting for the perfect connection, all manner of memorable attempts at truth. An eight year marriage to a woman I thought was my forever and ever, but tossed me aside like kid's toys in a garage sale. A couple I really connected to on one or two levels. but never being able to pull these shattered pieces into a semblance of a recognizable picture. Now spurned by the ultimate connection, by one who can practically read my every thought. Leaving me behind even now. It doesn't feel like a place to live, to be, it feels like the gods hate me or hate us as she says, either way it's Scylla and Carbides, the unwinnable scenario and I just didn't want to be anymore.

The next day, Janice calls needing a ride. I finish my workout, clean up and go to get her to take her to Cave's, where she works and we all hang out. She's fixing her hair and talking to me, She says in that very loud tough voice that I need to get my ass to Colorado, be there with her, or maybe stay with my old buddy Tom, stay a few months like she said. She says that in the big picture when we all look back, my kids won't fault me for being gone a few months making a last ditch attempt to connect with the woman I am desperately in love with, that I love more than anyone in my entire life ever. That she has seen that my kids love just as much. What am I scared of? I'm scared of everything. Of more pain, of ongoing pain that never ends. I am scared of sadness, but mostly I am scared of myself. That it's me. That at the core of it I am just fundamentally unlovable and will always be this alone. Just then Amy, the dame I dated in February, calls, says she is passing through town and wants to get a drink. I say that we will be at the bar shortly.

We're at Caves. The bar where I have spent night after night since my divorce. Janice is working the door. Something I once did. Where we met in fact, a few years back. Another close female friend, Brittany, is back around. She recently suffered a devastating breakup and was needing a friend. Of course I was there for her, it seems to be what I do. She and I had spent a lot of time together over a year earlier, but true to my pattern I was unable to connect and had to watch her attraction to all sorts of sissy ass bitch men. Eventually, she chose the old flame boyfriend and pretty much blew me off. I say pretty much, because we at some point started sort of a monthly lunch date thing, which was always really nice, and we regularly sent dark poetic snippets to each other via text message. So, I was still in her life a little, enough to be there when she needed a friend. Even at the risk of poking at my old wounds a bit. See, I collect broken girls, a theory that both Lexy and Shay have expressed about me. The funny part being that Lexy is in many ways, despite her brilliance, the most broken of all. So we're at the bar and Amy shows up. For some reason Janice and Brittany don't take a shine to her. We have a drink and some pretty nice conversation. At one point I suggest that we should hookup again one last time, just an unfinished business kind of thing. She asks "WHY? We have no emotional attachment to one another." I say "Well yeah, but we're quite fond of each other, and this is just about unfinished business." She smiles and says "I don't know, it's kind of weird considering we all know exactly who you're in love with, and it's not me." I say, "I dunno, it's just that you were really there for me before, last time she left. I was hurting in a big way and all stressed and balled up with all this energy. I hadn't even kissed a woman in months. You were really there for me, helped me get my confidence back, transition back again. It meant a lot." She laughed, "So you want me to transition you again?" "That sounds kind of fucked up I guess," I say. She looks at me smiling like I am the biggest mess she has ever seen. I walk her out to her Jeep. She gives me a nice long hug, I think about trying to kiss her. Hell, it has been over two months again since I had a kiss, since Shanna abruptly dumped me, and Lexy came back. Two months or more since I have kissed or touched a woman again. But I didn't try, I felt kinda bad about the conversation.

So, there I was sitting near the door talking to this dude. Janice working the door, is sitting with her latest man. She has this amazing knack for finding a new place for her heart whenever she needs one. Sometimes I worry about this, but then I realize that it's probably better than the melancholy bullshit "One love no one else can live up to" madness that I swim in. Really, I envy her. She may be hiding something, but overall she spends a hell of a lot more days smiling than I do. The other, Brittany, my dark soul-ed little poet, is starting to feel the effects of her new meds. Which is great for her. I'm pleased, but a little jealous. I've been on mine two weeks longer, but they aren't doing it for me. She's starting to smile and flirt, very unusual. I'm thinking about nothing but death. I notice like before, the guys she flirts with are in my estimation the most ridiculous kind of dipshits imaginable. The banter is empty and ridiculous. Funny that she'd been taking me to task earlier, for not needing more substance. The old wound bleeds just at little, seeing my pattern. Her, a year or so back. The email girl from years back, and of course as my sweet transition friend had said, " We know who you are really in love with." It was like a giant brick wall on my head in that moment. I've never hated myself and felt more useless and unloved and unwanted in my life. I could hear my ex-wife's cruel words echoing in my head. (you're worthless, no one will ever want you.) I just did not want to live. I thought of my beloved Lexy's decree that the gods must hate us. I thought of the conversation with years back girl, earlier in the day, about the gods, prompted by that. I felt this feeling of utter despair. I prayed and pleaded in my mind, PLEASE SEND ME A SIGN!!! Something! Should I go on??? WHY?? Just at that moment a girl walked in the door. She had been in briefly, earlier, and had asked me if I was still doing open mics. She had been around the bars a while back, and I knew her but only slightly. I got her number and told her I'd call her about some shows. She was young and pretty and I think she must have had few drinks. So here I am, pleading with the gods themselves for a sign and she walks in the door. Walks directly to me, puts her arms around me very tightly and holds me for several moments. I whisper in her ear, "God, how did you know I needed a hug so bad right now?" She holds me tighter still. Then pulls away just slightly, arms still around me, looks in my eyes and says, "You're very handsome you know " and then plants the most sweet soft beautiful kiss I could have dreamed up, right on my lips and in my mouth. Then she held my hand, looked in my eyes, and walked out the door without a word. The dude I'd been talking to said "HOLY SHIT! What the hell did you do to deserve that?" "I don't know," I said "maybe it was a gift from the gods." A sign? If so, what the fuck was it supposed to mean? I sat and thought for a moment, and came up with nothing. I texted my beloved Lexy, she was drinking elsewhere that night. We'd already had two nights that week. I said, "Are you doing OK?" She said " yeah, how about you?" "Middle," I said. My tears began to well up thinking of how much I would miss her again, in so short a time. Janice put her hand on my shoulder and said. "You look like you should go home." "Yeah," I said. Hugged her goodbye. Hugged flirty meds girl and walked out the door. Walking briefly through the bar next door to see if the girl that had kissed me was there, thought, you know, maybe one more or something, but no joy. So I drove home, took my meds and laid in bed staring at the ceiling fan. Mixed up, baffled, lonely, rejected and misunderstood. Then I was asleep.

What I always wanted

07/13/08

I'm not sure why this slight change in dynamic. If something has altered in you with all that you've been through. Or perhaps some minor difference in perception regarding me brought about by something we said or did together. But, there's this new thing.

Now, whenever we start to argue or butt heads a bit, we stop, make a decision to listen to one another hear each other out, and find some resolution. Even if it's to agree to disagree, or to agree in part and discuss more later. The point being that we listen to one another and seek to understand rather than to dominate or win.

This strikes me ironic. Because, now in addition to everything else, all of our sameness, interactions, beliefs, love, appreciation and compassion. To the way we speak to each other, understand and support one another, in good and bad times. In addition to the overwhelming urge I have to love and nurture you, the way that when you give me advice on my children, you are one of the few people I actually listen to, that feels like family.

NOW, on top of all of that, we actually listen and hear one another seeking resolution and understanding over dominance? You do realize that this is exactly what I have struggled to get from every dating relationship and every girlfriend I've had, but they were unable to give? You DO realize that this is the exact dynamic I banged my head against a wall trying to develop with my ex-wife for eight freaking years?! Awesome.

Now that you are about to leave, to not love me and go away again. You have now fully become exactly what it is that I have always wanted.

Nightmare Before Christmas

07/20/08

It's kind of funny,
her favorite all time movie, that is.
I think it must be
Tim Burton's Nightmare Before Christmas.

One of the oddest things about her,
a trait we both share in a big way,
Is that we talk and talk and talk
most of the time,
unless we are mopey
in which case everybody knows it.
Sometimes, when you're always going,
you forget what you've said before
and to who.
I think it's like that when
she tells me about
Nightmare Before Christmas.
She gets this excited gleam in her eyes
while recounting the plot.
What she thinks it means
An outsider coming from this one place
into another.
Yearning for something more.
About the characters, how they meet
where they come from, what they want.
She will smile and laugh when
explaining the funny parts,
Her voice getting higher and faster
Until launching into the final part
where she sings snippets of the songs
in this deliberate cartoon voice, smiling,
Her eyes get large and round.

I have seen her do this entire bit
many times.
I've lost count.
But each and every time
I remain silent, do not interrupt
and give no indication that
I have heard it before.
In fact

I usually maintain facial expressions
that say it is interesting,
new, entertaining,
captivating,
because it is.

I smile and I nod
listening to every single bit.
I laugh at the end and say
"That sounds awesome,
we need to watch that together sometime"
but we never have.

I'm not sure
what else to say about this.
I'm just telling a story
about her.
There are a hundred more.
They are small
and might seem meaningless to you.
But,
when someone
Really means the world to you,
all the tiny stories like this
are not meaningless,

they are everything.

UNDYING LOVE ISN'T GOOD ENOUGH

07/15/08

Damn, that was a lot of kids. We were at Chuck E Cheese's. My three, Lexy and her sister Tonya and her two sons, but she was also baby setting another four or so more. It was fun, the kids had a blast running around crazy, making weird faces on this movie camera thing. My guys are such clowns. It's all about these gold token things there. You need them to play the games. We had a bunch and divided them all up. Nando kept coming up with more somehow. I never ask how. At one point the three grownups were sitting at the table with the pizza. All the kids were running out of tokens. Ariya came over to the table and was trying to charm more out of me. I didn't have any. She was doing this thing with the voice, the facial expressions, blinking eyes, all cute. I told her "Baby, I don't have any more tokens, but you have my undying love!" She got all frown-ey and stomped off in frustration, with a bleh sound!. Tonya pulled out a few tokens and handed them to her. She smiled and said, "I love you daddy!" trotting off! Lexy laughed and said "WOW! The undying love wasn't good enough, but money made her happy!" I said "Hell, just because she's four doesn't mean she isn't the same as every other female! They learn the cute stuff, the voice, the body language early! The manipulation is genetic or something." I was smiling and looking right at her. She said, "I'm not like that! I'm different than other women, I don't do that stuff!" I smiled, Tonya shook her head and rolled her eyes at the magnitude of the statement. After a moment of silence I said, "Hey, when we go to the show tonight, are you going to drive to my place? It's way out of the way for me to head south to Shane's. Her voice got all sweet. Her facial expressions reflexively softer. She said "Aw, c'mon you know I don't like driving, it's not so far! You're better at driving around than me!" I said "OK, baby, I'll come get you, it's OK" She smiled real sweet like. Tonya laughed at me and we shared a knowing look. It was hilarious and profound.

A bit later we were considering the leaving process; Tonya got up to corral the kids. I turned beside me to Lexy and said "Hey, take this." Handing her a $50 bill. She said "What? That's too much! Don't give me that!" I took her hand, did the eyes thing and said "Hey, I love you! Pretty soon you'll be gone, and I won't be able to do my favorite thing in the world, take care of you!" I started tearing up a little. She said "Oh! Don't cry!" I said, "I promise I won't cry, for today!" She took it and hugged me, said "Thank you." It was fucking killing me, her leaving again. No matter how hard I tried, I could not make her change her mind. All this, all these things we do. The many ways our lives are connected together. I couldn't imagine what I was going to do with myself. With my time, my heart, my hours, my money, without her. I just couldn't accept the idea that even with all of this, the art, the family, the support; love and friendship, I just wasn't good enough, my undying love just wasn't good enough, for her to not stomp off in frustration, to make her stay.

Self-Destructive Alcoholic Power Couple

07/16/08

All at once in this terrible crashing moment.
The scenery crumpled, crunching in upon itself.
I am undone.

Trying to get me out of the bar,
can't put your head there, can't sit down there.
They take you off the mic before you are done.
I threaten a heckler from the mic, buy him a shot,
and one for you, only to watch him hit on you.

It's Chuck E Cheese's and all our children's faces.
It's taping up your broken window, and your broken soul.
Taking you to a movie, and holding you when you cry
about how cruel and selfish and dishonest people are
and how alone this makes us both.
It's your drunk ass father threatening to murder my entire family.
It's all the stories of your angry abusive sister.
How awful and cruel and manipulative she is when she drinks.
How she seems perfectly normal until alcohol releases a monster.
A monster that I can literally feel affected your soul.
It's the times when we are perfectly in sync,
playtime with the children, meditation at the Buddhist Temple
long days, close days, philosophical days, funny days, in our zone.
OUR days, it is as though it is too much for us or something.
Then we are drinking, not for fun like everyone else, but to forget.
Your calling me out in front on the mic, not to be "dickie."
Then they are cutting you off.
The show begins, the act out, the shenanigans
but you have me tamed now, I don't react now.
You've trained me not to react, to avoid conflict.
But it seems the conflict we once had, was all I had.
It was a form of self-preservation, some shred of dignity.
Without it I must truly feel the less than nothing I have become.

You slice open your soul and bleed it out.
Like throwing fish to seals, some eat it up
others are dismayed or don't know how to react.
I can see it in their eyes, an uneasiness.
Your back is always to me, always your back.
I'm stumbling around making phone calls,
pleading into voicemails. Until there it is,

we find the sweet spot and I hate myself.
I hate myself. I truly and unreservedly hate myself.
Which is what I was feeling all along,
your behavior just allows me access to those feelings.
As I have allowed you unconditional love to act out against.
Shhhhhhhh! I hear your voice saying,
she is perfectly fine until she drinks.
Like a scattered patched and broken rag doll, a sex toy
arms and legs thrown about,
skirt hiked up to thighs.
Laying in the back seat as my buddy drives.
And there it is again, the sweet spot,
Complete and utter fucking despair.
I let out the biggest most wailing lost depressed cry
I have known in years, everything inside me pouring out.
Your legs up on my shoulders,
I hug your leather boots.
My tears running down them hugging your leg and crying.
I've got nothing I am nothing, Only you.
I am beaten and broken down.
Only your legs upon my shoulders and my broken hearted tears.
Then you lean up, face to face, foreheads together
I can see my own guts in your eyes.
I can feel my tears soaking into your hair.
Hushhh! Stop! Shhhhhh! You say
You promised you wouldn't cry today, you promised.
But it's after midnight I blubber, after midnight.
You open the door while speeding down the highway,
threaten to jump out.
You wouldn't miss me if I died, you say.
Your kids wouldn't miss me, they'd get over it.
You would get over it.
No one needs me.
No one depends on me.
I need you! I need you! I love you! I CRY.
You don't really love me, you say,
looking directly into my eyes.
If I was gone, you'd just love somebody else.
"Fuck you! Fuck you for saying that", I sputter.
You look momentarily lost.
"Ok, well maybe it's just something wrong with me,
that I can't believe it,
that I can't believe in something like that."
SSShhhhh! I hear your voice saying.

She is perfectly fine until she drinks.

You are your father's daughter too, after all,
and in me you've found the perfect love, a best friend
that loves you unconditionally.
That you can push away,
disregard, disbelieve and ignore.
but will always be there for you,
always come back for more.
And I with my razor sharp unconditional love,
have found the way to punish myself
that I had been looking for.
and the way to try to prove myself,
that I so desperately need.

You let me buy you breakfast.
You pay attention to me and slowly
spoon feed my self-esteem back in. Little by little.
With a laugh or a joke, or some kind words.
I push away the fucking painful images of the night.
I swallow the fucking painful feelings of the night.
I can't believe you doubt me after all this time, I say.
Well, you have loved others before, you say.
That girl from the bar, your ex-wife.
Isn't it possible to have loved more than one person
in different ways, but to stil be genuine, I ask?
I don't know, you say, I have never known this kind of love.
I hug you six times goodbye.
You throw your arms around my neck and shoulders
lift your legs and hang on my large frame for a while, laughing.
We smile and say I love you.
You use my name the way you used to.
I practically beg for an opportunity to sit down
and talk to try and prove to you
my genuine sincerity and truth and love before you go.

The circle is complete.
The cycle of abuse, abandonment, and pain
has come full circle.
We two beautiful creative yearning searching souls
who started out together just wanting something real
never managed, it turns out
to be more than that which they cannot escape.
A father's daughter, and a mother's son.

Poison Candy

07/19/08

emotional abuse is
emotional abuse.
sure, it's not Bosnia
its not like them
it's not terrible at all.
it's all honey and compassion
depth and truth
beauty and brilliance
sugar and spice.
But, honestly
be it a
sledgehammer
to the
forehead
or loving the taste
of poison candy
it will kill you
just as dead
in the end.

THE BEST

07/21/08

The best
is going the movies alone.
The best
is having a breakdown in a cubicle
crying on the bathroom floor for 20 minutes.
The best
is the women that come and go
when they find other dudes.
The best
Is going to the bar every night
just to get through the week.
The best
is the pills that make you calmer
but you're not sure is the trade off
with the wild mood swings
is worth it.
The best
is the warning light in the car
that's been on for weeks
and you aint gonna have the money
when whatever it is happens.
The best
Is driving 45 minutes to do a reading
but the guy that invited you
doesn't put you on till after 1am
and by that time you're so drunk
your sad poems make you cry
and fall over chairs and shit.
The best
is when you buy a shot
for some asshole that heckled you,
drink it with the women you love
and the piece of shit
hits on her in front of you
immediately after.
The best
is when your friends are saying
that you have lost your art
because of your love.
The best
is when a girl you barely know

with giant issues
judges your behavior.
The best
is when the ex-wife is living the life
she always dreamed of
with a super terrific awesome guy
proving her theory that you were the
piece of shit holding her back all along.
The best
The very, very, very best
Is when the best friend you have ever had
that you love with all your guts
is feeling like her chest is going to explode
from anguish
while you are
feeling like your head is going to explode
from anguish
but you are alone
and she is not comforting you
and you are not comforting her
only typed text on a telephone because
you are making each other a little crazy.
So that even the only person in the world
that really understands you
that makes you feel ok
just by being around
is sad and alone somewhere else
while you are sad and alone by yourself
writing a poem.
That is the best
it sure is
the best, best
best of all.

SHADOW of Ash

07/22/08

Everything you do affects me.
You are the butterfly
***to my causality*.**

Your eyelids open up universes.
Your horizons are my periphery.

Your voice , in synapse
a chorus of spheres.

The sub-atomic thought moments
that make you
feel alive.

Now inserted
and intertwined
in-between mine.

You are blindingly beautiful
as you explode in time.

I am a man-shaped
shadow of ash
left behind.

Always like a movie

07/24/08

I performed the new piece for the first time. The gut wrenching one that had everybody emailing and calling to tell me how fucked up I am. As if having to go back on psyche meds wasn't already indication enough. The room was full, 3/4 of which I somewhat knew. They'd been gabbing most of the night but this piece drew in every eye and ear. I was really having a weird day. I just changed meds and this one while not making me want to die like the previous, was really tweaking me the hell out. A meth-ey X- ey feeling. I think I upped the dose too early. It came across on the mic. All the anguish and terrible loving of her. She, who can't help but leave in one way or the other, all the time, for months or moments. When I was done I could hear my heart beat in the silent room. The breath of every breathless person. I walked to my seat and sat, all eyes followed with some kind of look; Compassion? Pity? Understanding? Not sure. Roderick nodded in silent approval. Before anyone could speak, Lexy walked in the front door. I had no idea she was coming. Most everyone there must have known who the piece was about because there was this collective gulp and widening of eyes. Devorah, our gentle soul-ed mother figure, leaned over and said "Be strong." I had Lexy's drink ready when she came out of the bathroom. She asked if I was done being evasive. I said "yes" and stood by her side compliantly. I explained how the new meds were freaking me the fuck out. She said she was worried about me. She should be, my mind was like a speeding train. I wanted to go home. Rod wanted to go home, or at least back to Cave's. Instead, she made me stay by her side. It was clear that she had missed me and needed me in the week we had been apart. Since that last terribly travesty of a night. She made us go with her to promote her next show at another place. I handed out a few flyers, it was getting late. I wanted to make last call on home turf. She was annoyed with me, said that she needed a partner that was less selfish and would be more help to her. Rod later said that she was way overly harsh to me. I had a million things I wanted to yell back about what being a partner meant, but didn't. I just said I was sorry and blamed it on the meds and that I wasn't feeling well. That I would do better in the future if she was ever here again in the future that is. She forgave me. Rod drove her car, and we rode back to Caves in silence. I apologized a few more times. Some dude kept following us from bar to bar and calling her to see where we were. He was quiet, I'd met him before. I'd actually recruited the motherfucker at a show when she was out of town. Now the motherfucker was talking to her.

GODDAMN IT! I fucking hate my ironic shitty life! I didn't understand why he was following us. I became convinced that they were saying subtle things in the rare moments he was near. I was sure that she must have been fucking this dude in the week that we had been apart. It just seemed in my mind like there was some hidden thing. It always seems like some hidden thing, but then again I'm crazy, whose to say what's real and what's not when you're in a confusing painful reality. Finally, the motherfucker just disappeared. Still, it was devastating. The bar closed, we were outside. Janice wanted us to wait for her to get off to go eat. Rod and I wanted to sleep. Suddenly, some moronic cheesy little dude was hitting on Lex. She let him. A friend of Jamie's friend. We all went to the diner. My two girls caused a big scene about not being able to substitute menu items, like Lexy usually did. Janice was forceful and tough, Lexy was kind of nuts. She was sure that this life, this world, where menu items could not be substituted, was precisely the kind of world in which she did not want to live. It became a metaphor for everything wrong and indecent everywhere. She said that no one understood. I assured her that I do, I always do. Always me, only me. So we were off to our grand philosophical bonding place. Then we all talked about my children for a long time. How wonderful they are. The dude trying to hit on her couldn't compete with all this, even a little. He was a decent guy after realizing that, it was OK. Janice warned her not to hurt my children again this time by not saying goodbye. She swore that she wouldn't. Went on about how much she loves them, especially my middle one, how they feel like family to her, how she wishes that he was her own child (He could be.), that she loves him that much. She was mine, all mine in those moments, in those sentences, she was mine. She talked to only me. Stood by me. Asked to see the kids before she left again. Wants to do some more stuff with me before. I took her back to her car, Rod, asleep in the backseat by this time. She actually thanked me for hanging out with her. She said that she was very worried about me. I, in my dramatic way, told her that when she leaves a part of my soul will be gone again. It was like a movie. Everything with us is always like a movie.

Don't Laugh At The PITT GRILL

It was just me, Lex and Rod, as it had been many times before. Our regular waitress was there. I'd been late nighting it there with her with other dames long before Lexy, it was comforting. She was a kind hearted older broad. She sat down with us, opposite Lex, beside Rod. She laughed and said "Heard you guys had some controversy up here a couple days ago?" "Yeah," I said, "This other waitress wouldn't give Lex her normal order." "Oh, she's just an uptight bitch!" she said. "She could have done it." Then continued, "I came in the other day and they were all talking about it, said some of my regular customers had caused a scene. I asked who, and they said, you know, that big guy that always comes in with the stripper!" Lexy's eyes grew wide with shock. I mouthed to Rod the words "don't laugh." Lexy said "WHAT! I'm not a stripper! I'm a musician! I dress for performing sometimes, to look nice on stage! I'm not a stripper; I don't look like a stripper!" The waitress just smiled and shrugged her shoulders. Lexy, exasperated, looked at me for support. I said "No darling, of course you don't look like a stripper, that's ridiculous, you look like a very serious artist." "OK then," she said. "Yes, Ok," I repeated with no inflection in my voice. Rod, taking my advice, sat quietly with no expression at all.

Thoughts After Saying Goodbye

07/26/08

I feel like half of my soul is leaving me.
I have never in my entire life felt
as mutually understood.
as connected.
as befriended.
as open and close.
as the same.
as I do with you.
not with buddies. not with girlfriends.
not with family. not with my ex-wife.

Yes, you are quite nuts and have many flaws
but then I am quite nuts and have many flaws also.
That might just be a part of being beautiful
and creative and wonderful.

I love you.
I love you like my best friend.
I love you like a beautiful woman
that I can only dream will
slow down and I love one day
and that I might be lucky enough
that you remember your best friend
the connection that you always come back to.
I love you like family, you are my family.
People like us, we make our own family,
and YOU are my family,
and my children's family.

I will miss you.
I will miss you so much that the words
I miss you seem ridiculously inadequate.
Rather, I breathe and live in your memory.
in all that you have left in me.
You have altered me.
You have truly altered me.

Goodbye my sweet
my dear my best friend.
Goodbye,
hopefully just for now.

Thoughts upon waking up

07/27/08

I immediately feel this tightness in my chest. Open my eyes. This profound feeling of sadness and loss washes over me. I don't think I have ever experienced a feeling like this. I have known all manner of sadness, of loss, of mad desire and frustration. I have sat on a window ledge at a madhouse and known emptiness. I have returned again to watershed despair while Sweetchild Madness swam in grief. I have cried all night in front of a red brick wall knowing that my supposed life's mate and children of my heart and soul and body would be forever locked behind bricks and mortar. I have stood in streets held in tears by poets and friends trying to reach out again. I have fallen into mud puddles while happily ever after and birthday kisses became just another faded dream. I have known sudden death, of cherished buddies, beautiful darlings, and fellow addicts. I have lost property and heart and home to greedy Corporate gods. I have known all kinds of loss and failure and disappointment and almost-ing. But this, this is different.

I could search her out in the next 24 hours, I know where she will be. Maybe she will find time to call me for one last dinner date. But with family and business to tie up, I doubt it. I could go see her play one last time, maybe. But that scenario has a bad association for me, it's all about the place my once buddy Shane took her, when she returned to find all new artistic outlets, pretty much ignoring all the work we had done together previously, after saying things like, "Don't stress, I'm back now we can get things back on track. "Maybe I should swallow that feeling, I have certainly swallowed quite a bit of late. But explaining it to Rod at 4 am last night, he thought, maybe just leave it at that. He said that it was a perfect ending. The perfect conversation at Pitt Grill about all of our times, our feelings, our views, art and politics. The perfect smiles and level headed words. The CD of a local band we saw, I bought her as a goodbye gift. My children, my beautiful children in the car in front of their mother's house hugging her goodbye, saying goodbye. My sweet son, my thoughtful son, emotional daughter. She was such a trooper, not like last time. My daughters big giant "I'm going to miss you so so much" tears. Running off alone down the sidewalk practically screaming in tear filled grief to the door. My four year old daughter able with the purity of a child to express exactly what I was feeling inside. Our final 4 am goodbye in the street. A letting go of expectation in one long hug. Looking in the eyes, the words I love you, with our names, but in a different tone. A tone that says forgiveness of wrongs and gratitude for true connection. An "I love you" that felt like a real goodbye. It was all just perfect, he said. Don't push it. He also said that he can't see this really being the end to the story of our two very unusual souls. That it just feels like there will be another chapter somewhere down the line, somewhere in the future. It just feels like there should be. That she may go far away, find something to latch onto, even find some kinds of connection, but will never find anything as intense as what she experienced with me. Nor will I. This is just one of those times when you have to make big changes, find the stuff that is holding you back and dig it out and overcome it, moving ahead into something else. Or just give it up, let go at last of this terrible thing, this mad delusion we call life. This series of profound attachments that in the end, what keeps us alive.

SAD2008!

07/28/08

In the building, up the elevator, at my desk.
I hit enter to start the computer.
The screen to log onto the network pops up.
It says "Password expires in 2 days,
do you wish to change it now?"
I choose yes.
I type **"GOODBYE0728!",** and verify it.
There are only so many characters one can use,
or I might have typed in;
"I CAN'T BELIEVE YOU ARE LEAVING AGAIN!"
Or perhaps; **"YOU DEVASTATE ME!"**
Or possibly; **"PLEASE STAY!!!"**
Or maybe even;
"I LOVE YOU SO SO MUCH EVEN THOUGH
YOU ALWAYS HURT ME REAL BAD!"
Or go crazy with something like;
"EVERYTIME YOU LEAVE
I FEEL LIKE HALF MY SOUL IS MISSING
YOU FREAKING CRAZY BROAD!"
But no,
there are only so many characters one can use.
SO I settle for GOODBYE, with the date.
Then after a while, that will expire,
she will still be gone and I will want to type;
"STILL MISSING YOU" with that days date.
But that will likely be too long as well.
So I'll settle for; **"SAD2008!"**
and that will be that.

The Night you left me again
07/28/08

I went to the bar to get Janice and have a couple beer. Of course we drank whiskey and got piss drunk instead. I'd stayed in bed all day in the dark, crying until my head was swimming in it. I texted a couple other friends, every one seemed down, there was no solace.

A well spoken black fellow sat next to me and asked why I was drinking like that. We talked about Humphrey Bogart as Rick in Casablanca, and how the only reason for a man to drink like that was loving a woman that you can't have. The kind of woman that leaves you standing in the rain at a train station in Paris. All the open mics in all the world, she had to walk into mine.

Janice was having her own issues, seemingly inconsolable. We left to go to the Pitt. She was crying, carrying a box of pizza and a copy of Siddhartha by Herman Hess. I was crying and thinking about the sound of your voice. How the absence of you getting upset about not being able to substitute menu items at the late night diner, will be a huge gaping un-fill-able hole in my life.

We never made it to the diner. In a few blocks we were distracted by a Karaoke bar. We wandered in, ordered a beer, sang some of the worst Karaoke I had ever sang, to the Beatles *Nowhere Man*, which I found surprising. Janice started talking up everybody in the bar, which is what she does to make herself feel better. I was eyeing the counter culture dames playing pool in the corner, which is what I do to make myself feel better.

Janice did her thing and got me an introduction to the dames. I got them all a beer and did my poet thing. Talked of art, and truth and sadness. Invited them to come see my next show. One was rather pretty, dark hair, glasses , nice shape. She was wearing an olive green skirt exactly the same as one of yours, with that tattered vintage look. I kept eyeing her ass while she shot pool. Imagining fucking her real good from behind in that all too familiar skirt. It was nice to talk to these girls, it made me feel a little bit human again.

Janice came over and said that my debit card had been declined. I knew that I had been over spending in your last week, buying food and drinks, small gifts and flowers. But I didn't think I had emptied it out. We gave the bartender a fake phone number, told her we were going for cash, and walked the tab.

I talked about you all the way back to Janice's place, reading saved text messages and getting teary eyed. When we got there, she thought she might have left her keys at the bar where we just walked the tab. But it was late, and she didn't want to fuck with it.

When I got home, I realized that her keys were in the backseat on top of the pizza box and the copy of Siddhartha. I heated up the pizza and ate it all. It was 3 am and I couldn't stop thinking about you. About how much I would miss you. Your voice, laughter, your face, a thousand great and small things about you. I began to weep huge uncontrollable tears, went to bed and cried myself to sleep.

empty hole

07/31/2008

What is different I think, is this big empty hole. We all have these walls we keep ourselves safe behind. The emotional equivalent of my red brick wall. We don't let people in far enough to hurt us real bad. We are all, the entire lot of us night types, the walking wounded. All the girls I've dated have these walls. All my friends, walls. The VERY few that I have really truly felt for, hell you would need a plan of Greek proportions, un-siege-able. How lonely. I remember my first real post divorce lesson in this, where I was taught this, the first text message dolly. Yeah, I have walls.

But you blew past all that somehow. Odd, because yours seem to be standing up fine. I tried to ask you in a really straight forward fashion really early on not to do that to me. To give me some space, or if you must enter, do so only in the most serious of ways. But something about you, your past, your damage, your needs, your emptiness and what it takes to fill it up. Even with restrictions, labels and terrible wrong ideas about how to be. Even with the pushing and pulling, the basic dishonesty of the pushing and pulling. You still blew past all my defenses. You come and go like it is nothing. Like I will always be there to be what I am. Even when you're here you do it, and I always am.

Now here I am. Empty in the space you leave behind. Feeling every bit 2005 ish, all that and a dance with death. It's so bad, no one even wants to hear it anymore. I have no one to even talk to in this without you aloneness. My fellow artists believe me to have ruined my art over you. Fuck' em though. We will see the collective eating of words. The non-artist types are feeling it, I get feedback. Doesn't make it hurt less though. My running buddies have heard it, same old shit. Basically, I am alone in this aloneness you have left me in. Meanwhile, the ones I am there for, wanted long ago, pretty much do what they always do, find someone else. Same old shit.

Abiding in aloneness, the sound of your voice in my head all day. That's what happens when one is foolish enough to let the walls down, someone else becomes a living breathing part of you and then when they are gone, it is terrible and empty. That's why everyone has the walls, self-preservation. I miss you so much it is like a physical pain. Tears off and on all day every day. Tiny visions of you flash before my eyes constantly. Mostly, I hear your voice; upset, depressed, drunk, serious, all facets of you in all the thousands of hours of freakishly intense interaction we've had. I miss every aspect of you, even the bad parts. I hear your voice when other people are talking. The words that you would be saying, ideas, opinions, your method of interacting. I miss your hands and your eyes. I miss your clothing. I miss you eating. I miss your laughter a lot. I miss that weird sound you make when you get frustrated or excited, worked up. Combined with the things you do with your hands. I miss your hair. I miss your skin. I miss the way you sit, telling me exactly what you are thinking and feeling in that moment just by your posture. Nobody else fucking knows that, can read you like that. You read me too, read me like that, but I'm not so hard to read if you know me, and you do. I miss the way that we agree on a thousand small quirky things, people, culture and the world. About games, competition, art, and bleeding it out. I miss the way you listen to everything I say. Though you're not as well read, when I get started talking you actually listen, and later incorporate things I have said into conversation. I miss the way you forgive me all of my faults, all of my flaws. The way you look me straight in the eyes and just forgive me, like you have no other choice but to forgive me. As if forgiving me is as natural to you as breathing. I miss the way you argue with me, with passion, intensity, sometimes madness. Sure, there are certain flawed areas in your thinking where you just won't budge, but for the most part you argue to understand, not to dominate or to win. It's real. I miss you with my children, playing, at the movies, the park, in your lap. The way you pronounce the word baby to my daughter, and never ever judge them anymore than me, always saying the right things to them. They adore you and look up to you. I miss the way you hurt. You really hurt. Unlike most people you are not afraid to really feel your hurt, like me. You hurt so bad sometimes it affects your entire body, entire spirit, whole being. I miss the way that no matter what, where we are at, when those moments come and you are feeling that pain, that suffering, disappointment and anguish, you turn to me. Always to me. I think I miss being needed by you the most. I am an open book, an open wound, an open soul to you. I have no defenses, no walls, even though you have kept yours somehow. But yours run really deep. Deeper than mine, and with good reason, I get that. So here I am, missing you and having isolated myself with my own intensity. Alone in my aloneness so to speak. I get why no one wants to hear it, or read it, or see my tears. But here I am, missing you. Because somehow, your walls that you have always lived with, allow you to simply go. Mine do not.

I never kissed her

07/31/08

I never even kissed her, not once, not ever.
My soul mate, my best friend,
who I love with all my heart
and soul and guts and everything I had.
Screaming inside me day after day after day after day.
I never even kissed her, not once not ever.
I gently kissed her cheek, her hand
I've held her close, held hands
held her when she cried
Spent hours and days and weeks and months by her side
loving her with everything I had.
Revealing secrets, sharing everything inside.
I've protected her, fed her, supported her
taken care of her,
emotionally, financially, socially, spiritually,
dedicated every possible amount of time
and energy
but never kissed her, not once.
I've been in rooms with her and
looked around
and seen woman all over the room I had kissed.
Good women, decent women, beautiful women
but not that I love like her,
not that I was as anywhere near
as close to as her.
I'd kissed dozens of women in the months before meeting her,
an insane freakish emotional breakdown amount of women,
but never another after meeting her,
at least when she was within a hundred miles
and only then because we had had a fight before she left.

I should have.
I needed to, at least once goddamn it.
To know, so she would know.
There were a few specific times
I wanted to so bad
and was so fucking close, but something always happened.
Or I was just a coward and didn't even try
intimidated by the amount of emotion churning my guts inside.
I only actually asked her once
in all that fucking time, once

and something really fucking stupid happened,
somebody else got in the way.

It's the worst most excruciating painful thing
I can imagine,
not to have kissed her.
To have been so close, so long, so much
so insanely much.
I deserve it
I craved it so, so bad for so so long.
Just one fucking kiss, just one.
I am terrible and weak and un man like.
I would die for just one fucking kiss.
I would give everything I have without exception.
I would cut of my freaking arm
I would sell my soul buy it back
and sell it again
for one fucking kiss
One really, really good long passionate kiss
just so she would know.
Just so she would fucking know.

I have never wanted
anything so bad
in my entire life!

Nothing left

08/01/08

I tell you now,
that I have nothing left in me.
nothing.
no heart, no Soul, no self
no desire, no hope, no endeavor.
I have no room for another love,
not even the capacity to grieve
the one who has left me.
I have nothing left in me.

I have in me
no boyfriend, no husband,
barely any man at all.
no job, no grind, no civility
no false smile, no kind words
no reasonable considerations.
no earning of dollars
no sharing of laughter
no expressions of lust
nothing, there is nothing left
no pretense, no ego, no function
no art, no meaning, no truth,
no clever lines,
no insightful words
nothing to move the reader.
nothing to move the self
nothing to enthrall a woman
nothing for her to return to
as if returning meant anything anyway.

I have nothing.
no fun dad.
no hard drinker
no compassionate friend.
no spirit, no quest, no ideas
nothing.

no books, no microphones,
no dreams
no advice, no encouragement,
no discouragement.

no self loathing, no self love
no love at all
nothing.

no days, no echoes, no time.
no ripples rippling outward
no mind.

no becoming, no unbecoming
I cast no shadow upon the ground.
even my pieces can be broken down.
into pieces, into pieces, into pieces,
until complete and absolute emptiness
is realized and revealed.

I'm telling you here and now
I am empty
there is nothing left in me.
nothing to interest you,
to entertain you
nothing to use, of any use.
I have imploded, fallen apart
melted away and dissolved.
faded away into nothing at all.

She calls to say

08/03/08

Saturday, we're starting the open mic and she calls. This time it's back to y'all. She misses us all. You guys. Look, it's OK to say it, four states away. You miss me. Why wouldn't you miss someone that is there for you all the time in every way? She says she's sure it will be fine. It's awesome there, she is just lonely. Just lonely and missing. I have a great idea on how not to be lonely, stop running away and abandoning people that unconditionally love you. So dumb for someone so smart.

I tell her that I am reading only pieces about how much I miss her. The crowd is small, so I read a bunch. When it's all done I'm more sure than ever that the book is here, that this is a book and it needs to become a book as soon as possible. People are sick of it. They are sick of me and sick of my poems. They are sick of me not valuing mental health above the heart, and above the art. I get it.

Even my friends barely want to talk to me. It actually made me doubt myself for a while. Roderick said, "Look, just for the record, I was never one of those that doubted you artistically. She brought out the very best in you, there is no doubt about that. But she also brought out the very worst in you, I know, I saw it." He is right. She was both the best and worst in me. But aren't the biggest and most powerful things we come across in our lives always like that? Both the best of times and the worst of times? As if somehow it is impossible to have one without the other? From great real unconditional love comes true real suffering. From true real love and suffering comes the meaning of love and true real shining human art. And from true real shining human art comes the openness and understanding of the human experience to be able to actually experience love and truth and suffering. It's all both the best and the worst.

Meanwhile, she is lonely and I am more devastated than I have ever been, wishing I had done more with my past few years. Feeling angry with my ex wife for some inexplicable reason. Not knowing what to do with my heart and time and days. Be OK with myself, some say (of course those that say that never are that). Find someone else some say. You just need to get laid some say. But I don't, none of it. I just need to sit and feel what I am feeling and that is OK this time. It's real. Meanwhile, even though they are all sick of it, I have friends and they love me and they are here for me every step of the way. I may be sad and devastated, but I am not lonely. Going to all the places we always go, not alone. Just without her. It's her, the one who runs away that's alone. It's her that calls and tells me she is lonely. However, one thing I know about her, one unfortunate thing, one terrible thing that I know, she will not be lonely for long. Of this I am completely sure. But I am also equally as sure that there will never, ever, ever be another me, never another that will replace me. Not really, not ever, ever, ever. Not even motherfucking close.

ROCK BOTTOM

08/12/08

I never did it
I never reached rock bottom, I was stuck.
I was afraid.
After years of being less than what I am,
I had no strength
because she had taken every motherfucking ounce of it
and I was afraid.
I'd been there before, and I'd survived each time.
I'd come out stronger each time, but this time
with checkered shirts, an extra 50 pounds,
having begged on my knees,
an entire self-identity of fatherhood,
I was afraid.
Three plus years I hovered in the nether regions but
I never hit rock bottom.
My buddy that took me to the strip club
and bought me drinks and needed a social crutch,
kept me from hitting it.
The hope I held on to that I was still the same
still able to find a woman, maybe in the bar,
that was kind of like her, had a kid or 2,
was real organized, well-spoken,
kept me from hitting it.
All the nights in the bar, working the door
and all the girls that didn't give a shit anyway
kept me from hitting it.
Returning to my open mic host persona from 1996,
kept me from hitting it.
My parents and my children, and them together
kept me from hitting it.
Dating the girl that was once a stripper,
kept me from hitting it.
That beautiful young writer
kept me from hitting it.
The next beautiful young writer
kept me from hitting it.
and the next one and the next one
and the one from a few months back that
wasn't what she seemed,
they all kept me from hitting it.
Two and a half years in a stupid lifeless cubicle

where I didn't hate it enough to leave
but it was barely enough money to scrape by
where I could stay out all night at the bar
come in hung over and vomit-ey and
spend a bit of the day crying on the bathroom floor.
Where the supervisor was laid back and didn't care
as long as work got done and I could come in late
anytime and just work a little later.
This job. This two and half years of absolutely nothing.
This, kept me from hitting rock bottom.
It all kept me floating there, in limbo.
In a place where old friends judge and talk
about how fucked up I am.
About how they can't handle me,
how I make them sad,
and judge and judge and judge
when the truly hilarious part is
that not a god damn motherfucking one of them
is less flawed than me.
In fact an argument could be made that many of them
might be more than equal in the flaws department
and I have never, never, never judged them harshly,
held their flaws up to the light.
Quite the opposite, always keeping my own flaws in mind.
Never getting as good as I give.
Never standing up for myself by
telling my beautiful wonderful creative friends
to go fuck their wonderful selves
kept me from hitting rock bottom.
I was afraid, I was afraid,
I was afraid of rock bottom.
I've never had the strength or the will to face rock bottom
because that succubus Nazi of a wife I had
sucked every ounce of strength out of my soul
by never respecting me for who I am what I need
and what I must go through to grow and thrive.
Thinking only of her selfish self.
Using emotional and sexual blackmail to abuse me.
Using my love for my children to abuse me.
Tossing me into the fucking street,
forgetting all promises made,
It made me weak,
made me nothing, made me afraid.
Made me too much of a pussy to hit bottom.

Never getting the closure to say
fuck you for what you did,
kept me from hitting bottom.
Never fully surrendering to it,
holding onto lies and notions and false hope
and old roles,
and other peoples fucking expectations
kept me from hitting rock bottom.

What was I so afraid of?
rock bottom isn't so terrible really.
It's window ledge at the madhouse.
It's vomit and needles and cold shakes.
It's clock tics like slow motion thunder.
I'm here.
Finally here.
It took her, my one real true for real soulmate.
The only one that is exactly on the same frequency,
that never judged me or held it against me
no matter how many times I tried to show her
the very worst I had to offer.
That lives in the exact same soul space that I do.
That needs the honest healing that only comes
with real true unconditional love as badly as I do
in the precisely exact same way that I do
but being unable to do it.
Feeling her love and acceptance and warmth
knowing with all my heart and soul and experience
that exactly what she wants and needs and craves
is me, in 1997. The man I was when I met the wife.
The man I was on every level, physically,
spiritually, artistically, functionally, emotionally,
but never ever became again being stuck
in the motherfucking quagmire limbo nothingness.
So she leaves, not me but the whole city,
to seek truth and healing elsewhere among others.
THAT is what it takes to hit rock bottom.
A soul mate lost and gone.
Going back on psyche meds
after swearing publicly 5 years earlier that I would die first.
Admitting finally that I just can't handle it myself,
that is what it takes to hit rock bottom.
Being fired from the stupid low paying no pressure job
where I could cry and drink and not give a shit,

that is what it takes to hit rock bottom.
Finding the guts to stand up
to each and every friend and associate that has judged me
and talked shit about me as if I am somehow more flawed than they,
that is what it takes to hit rock bottom
Waking up and realizing that you have nothing and no one
in your room alone, the same old room.
Having nowhere to be, no one to be there with.
Owning almost nothing, no home, no roles
nothing to cling to for reason to live
except for the unfailing need to be at the very least present
for the three best most brilliant children in the world.
That's it, rock bottom.
The kids call my soulmate on the cell phone
"We miss you...we love you so, so much!"
"Give all the kids a kiss for me.. I miss you
It will be ok, it will be ok, WE will be ok, WE WILL BE OK!".
She has made me strong again in some way that
I don't understand, and it hurts like hell.
Fuck it, I'm not scared anymore. I'm here, this is rock bottom.
putting together a book again,
Fuck all expectations and judgments.
This is it, finally, this is rock bottom.

THIS IS NOT MOVING ON

8/20/08

this is not moving on
this is not moving on
crying at TV shows
letters and cash
text messages
This is not moving on
This doesn't feel like moving on

hours and hours
immersed in creating this book
reading and editing and reliving
this is not moving on.

calling when I'm at the bar
calling when you're drunk at 4:30 am
calling when you are depressed
calling when you think I might be depressed.
this is not moving on.

you think our souls are connected
(I already knew that.)
always feeling the same things
at the same time
this is not moving on
doesn't feel like moving on.

going through your black lingerie photos
while we're on the phone
cropping and altering light and shadow
leading the conversation in certain directions
certain words with certain pictures,
certainly doesn't feel like moving on.

crying on the phone
blurting out everything,
you listening closely
saying you are sorry
for every time you've ever hurt me
and really, really, meaning it.
Talking in hushed tones about your feelings,
about me, and about your flaws

how you are closed off emotionally
because of your past
how it's easy for you to take risks in life
but not emotionally
a lifetime scared of emotional risk.
How you admire me for being something
you always wish you could be,
emotionally honest and revealing and full of love
which you already are, you just don't see it.
This doesn't feel like moving on.

Talking late, late into the night
deeper than ever
more emotional than ever
more revealing than ever
as if somehow actual distance
is now our new safety zone
where everything can be spoken
all the pain and fear and dreams and hopes
except for the painful things at the edges,
you never quite speak of
even when you want to,
but it's ok, it’s me, I know you
I already know you, whenever you're ready.
This is not moving on
This feels nothing like moving on.

I can't tell if this is closure
or deeper connection
but this is sure not moving on

We're going to find a way
We're going to get through this.
We'll figure it out you assure me,
Remain positive, we can do this
we'll think positive thoughts
create positive energy
send each other positive messages
there has to be a way to find balance
we will find it
we will both find it.
This is not moving on
This feels absolutely nothing like moving on.

Recommended by 4 out of 5

08/22/08

Even 5 hour long intense
everything possible revealed
holding nothing at all back
crying, mouth dry, reading poems
talking at 100 miles an hour
non-defensive non-judgmental
3 ring circus, everything but the kitchen sink
up till 3:30 am conversation interactions
don't really do anything with us
nothing much, nothing short term at least
maybe some long term cumulative effect.

I mean,
we are already more bleed it out crazy intense
than anyone,
It becomes just a part of us.
there will never be closure not really, not ever.
even in different cities
because no matter how much either of us might seem to
we don't really want it, closure from each other
not even a little.
no matter how much we should
no matter how much
other people think we should,
we are stuck. We are family
forever, even if it kills us.

Even your 25 layers of self-defense denial
run away, crazy justification
that becomes nothing short of emotional abuse
combined with hundreds of miles of actual distance
doesn't change anything.
We are off the Rictor scale you say.
but not perfect in every way.
and there is the rub.
It's cool.
you love me in 4 out of 5 ways
like the gum.
I'm recommended by dentists.
at least those that
have tried Paul.

GRANDE SOULMATE DRIP

09/08

You are like
a Starbucks Grande coffee,
spiritually
in my soul.
You fill me up with this
dark hot
kick it in the ass coffee.
There is no room for anything
or anyone else in this cup.
I can't drink anyone or anything else.
No one or nothing else can drink me.
Our souls are married and bonded
and everyone and everything else
drops away
when we are together,
causing ripples of
friction, jealousy, resentment
and all manner of stupid madness
in all kinds of people everywhere near
for some pretty much inexplicable reason.

I don't really care I suppose
except,
only problem being,
when you fill the Grande Starbucks cup
of my soul
with your burning goodness
you leave room
for cream and sugar.
and you've never added the
cream and sugar.
I won't drink it without
because it's too strong
and frankly a little bitter.

You keep handing me a filled up cup
over and over
saying c'mon drink it.
But I won't
and you get pissy. saying
I keep pouring you this awesome

goddamn coffee
into your Grande Soul,

just shut up and drink it.
But I keep saying
no, I drink my coffee with
cream and sugar,
see,
you leave enough room for it
there in the cup
just enough
and it's not like
as long as you keep filling up
my Grande cup
over and over,
I could actually get any
coffee with cream and sugar
anywhere else
the way I crave it.

So there I am,
best goddamn coffee in town
in my life,
ever, fucking A,
hands down.
A bottomless cup
you keep refilling
dark, bitter, and
and although I love the shit
out of some coffee
It's something
I can't drink
so I have
no coffee at all.

Or maybe being up
all night with you
on the telephone
just makes me think up
some ridiculous shit
in the morning
while ordering a cup.

One Night in August

08/25/08

Some days the mere act of waking up feels like loss. Sunday, got up early and drove Anson back to his car at Caves. He had places to be. I went home and slept until 1:00 pm. Got up, hit the gym. Could feel the misery of soul in body. Hard to lift heavy while fighting back tears. Got home, ate a salad and took the medication. I guess it's helping. It's been a rough week though. fifteen hours of phone conversation with my truest soulmate who left me again, for good this time. I just can't shake the feelings that it's me. That I'm just not good enough. That I'm lacking in ways that keep her from my side where she belongs. This voice in my head replays these messages repeatedly. Not my own voice, it's the voice of one who had promised many years ago, to be with me forever, but had beaten down, humiliated, abused, and abandoned me. The mother of my children. She'd called on Friday morning with threats, name calling, and harsh words. Anson was blown away, said her voice was so aggressive and loud on the phone that he could hear her as clearly as me. We'd been just about to record. He was worried about lack of anguish in the studio. After the ex-wife hung up, he said, lets use this." But the 'this' didn't go away. I didn't leave it in the studio or on the tracks. Sunday, it was still in my head. Still screaming that I was worthless and not good enough. That my soulmate would love me enough, not leave, if I wasn't somehow defective. She called around five, I cried so hard we had to get off the phone.

It's always better at the bar, at least a little. The lights are dim and red. Emotions seem more subdued. I was drinking German beer with two of the possibly most broken hearted love lost drinking buddies I have. One, TJ, the buddy I'd drank with so much when the wife first left, had recently faced a big breakup, sadness was seeping from his pours . The other, Rod, my regular poet drinking buddy whose broken hearted litany deserves to be a novel, a tale that only he should tell. We're doing what such as we do. Drinking, talking of ex wives, lost loves, missed opportunities and regret. I mention that I've sworn off the idea of even being open to dating any women for at least six months. There is some debate as to how good an idea that is and why. Rod jokes that I'll be hitting the porn pretty hard. I tell him "No, I've sworn off porn as well." From these guys, two sets of big round eyes. I believe there was some comment as to "What the fuck?" (He'd been drinking since seven, he said.) I said, " Well, I've still got her black lingerie photos, I've been working with those a bit. Cropping, changing lighting, some really close up stuff. You can almost see vagina. Seriously, they are quite nice." They laugh. At that exact moment my phone rings. I know who it is before looking. That's how we always are. They nod and smile. I answer, "Hold on, let me walk outside. "She says, "Let me guess, you're at the bar? "I step out front, lean on the wooden rail. She tells me of her day. Accidentally falling into a gig. A short set making 40 bucks. I say, "Cool, that's the most you've made for a gig just playing without hosting or anything right? " She says "No, but that's the most I've made just doing originals, so that's awesome, just did five songs!" She was in a good mood. I love her good mood voice. I love her and I love to hear it. I said "That's great, baby! " But I'm also selfish, know the better she does up there, the less likely it is she will ever return. There will be attention, lots of other dudes, connection, and fucking, lots of fucking. And somehow, in some way, they will be better than me, because I am not worthy of her love. At least that's what the ex-wife voice in my head is screaming. She says "Well, I was just checking on you, I'll let you get back to the guys, talk to you tomorrow." "OK," I say, starting to hang up. Then she says "HEY!" "Yeah?" I respond. "I really love you Paul, and I miss you a lot!" I break, start to cry hard. "What?" She says "That's supposed to be positive, I'm trying to send you positive energy and love!" "It is," I say, "I appreciate it, I just miss you so goddamn much I don't know what to do!" "I know, it will be OK." she says. " Really? How will it be OK?" I ask. "I don't know, I just have faith that it will." I let her go, compose myself, struggle the ex-wife voice back down and rejoin my buddies. Sitting between them, I find that it wasn't enough. Tears streamed down my face, big wet ones. TJ reaches over to comfort me, pats my shoulder. The tears don't stop. Rod, drunk and rather profound at times, raises his hands the way he does before making a statement, addresses TJ, "Look, I heard the recording last night, it's awesome, it's powerful, moving. That's what she does to him. Takes his heart out and rubs it on the mic, rubs it on paper, bleeds it out. You can't help but feel it. She has created in him his greatest passion and his greatest art, it's beautiful and real, but here's the downside." Pointing at me, with big thick tears streaming down my cheeks. They both understand. That's what art is. It enables others to truly feel that which they know they should already feel. TJ walks to the bar to buy another round. I notice a glistening teardrop fall from my face into a half empty glass of thick orange gold German beer. It seemed to be about the passage of time.

WOKE UP THINKING BOUT YOU TODAY

08/30/08

You are brilliant and insightful in so many ways. So compassionate, so able to perceive the truths of culture and spirit and art and material concerns. It's person to person where the fatal flaw kicks in.

I wake up, "*You Are My Sunshine*" swinging on the TV. The empty space that was you, particularly awful. Waking realization, transitory anachronism, shampoo bottle. Pages of conflagration of you in me. but precious little me in you. What imprint have I left in you? In your work? No art, minor joy, some small attachment perhaps, replaceable I think. In many ways less than whatever face I imagine next to you now. Touching and speaking with you now. No simple matter for me, one for another. Bottle swap, genital swap, heart swap, why not? One for another, no simple matter, for me. We speak 15 hours in one week. My heart filled even so far away. You couldn't find a job. The roommate up there wanting you out because of your drinkey personality, I can only imagine, but I try hard not to. The next week we barely talk. You've found some work. Someone to fuck you I imagine. Not alone again, no longer needing me. Except on a drunken Wednesday where you call repeatedly blurting out that you love me, on speaker phone in front of everyone over for wine and Bukowski night. That your heart is in different places. Echoing the sentiment from the week before about how much you are feeling the missing of me. How strong our connection, how unexpected.

Unusual for you I think, to feel attachment. I've only seen it in you once. The shampoo bottle in the ex-boyfriend's shower. An image which haunted you. The realization that you were never more than a easily replaceable vagina to him. Most people are like that though, aren't they? It's just that you have so much other truth in you, you shouldn't be. It's your fatal flaw that keeps you alone. I mean never actually alone, but alone in real ways. You have been abandoned in so many ways. Emotionally, functionally, unable to even work legally for a time. You have always had to depend on others to survive. So you evolved this love survival mechanism. Everyone wants to love you and nurture you and take care of you, creating false intense no boundaries intimacy. You get it everywhere, "energy" you call it. But you have had such awful experiences that the fear of true intimacy, trust, and emotional risk, is always at odds with this basic survival mechanism that draws people in. Everyone love me, but I won't love you. That is your mantra. THAT is the nature of your fatal flaw. Men divided into four quadrants, giving only parts of yourself. Broken hearts, disappointment, frustration, bruised egos, shattered friendships, and confusion, is what you leave behind. Too much, too quick, too liberal, too post-modern, too relativistic. Too pragmatic, while oddly so non-pragmatic in every other aspect. That is your survival mechanism fatal flaw. You are so insightful, clever, brilliant in so many ways, that you have reasoned it out. Made something senseless make sense. As you walk though the chaos you leave behind. It must be them instead of me, all of them, you reason. I'm just drawing in a certain type of person. OK.

What about me? Your poet? Drawn to me always it seems as others come and go. Falling away. Telling me that I am closer to you than anyone before. There was always one other but now I equal him. Always scoffing at how I could possibly compare how much I mean to you to these transitory others. You say it's ridiculous. But I'm never good enough to love? Or at least make the slightest open honest effort towards? A try? An honest consideration? Our intimacy, our connection can't possibly be false can it? Having lasted so long and survived so much? You have said that I move you and inspire you in so many ways, bleeding it out, feeling it, creating and struggling for truth, our truth. But what am I to you? Even some barely known violin player was enough to inspire your art. To get you going, turn you on, but he turned you down. He was just a guy that makes some decent music. That's it, nothing special. He was an empty idea to begin with, like all of your false notions, unlike me. Unlike you and I together. You said you had compassion for me and my love for you when he spurned your advances. Something you alluded to, but I had to hear mentioned more from others. As if somehow some dude you barely know not wanting you, reminding you of compassion for me, was supposed to somehow make me feel better? SERIOUSLY!? I don't want your motherfucking compassion. Really, I want your love, your friendship, and companionship. I am not someone that needs your compassion for what I am going through with you. You are not fucking outside of it, somehow above it. It is your dynamic, you constantly recreate it! Tell you what, on the day some fucking violin player has spent a year, thousands of hours, emotion, time, support, is your best friend in your entire life, is told repeatedly for a year that you are just alike, that you are closer and more connected than anyone, have gone though hell and back always unconditionally loving one another even though you put each other through madness, then tell me it reminds you of me. You had a crush on him because of his music. One of the most shallow, meaningless things I can possibly imagine. Yet, he still managed to inspire your art. You were outside of him. I'm not stupid, I know when to walk away from a crush. You are absolutely not, nor were you ever just a crush to me. You feed thousands upon thousands of volts of female energy into me, just not through your vagina, which is reserved I suppose for people you don't love so much? In a different quadrant? Pretty damn fucked up by any standard. But where is my song? What has my supposed value inspired? What effect do I have on you, compared to the hundreds of pages you have created in me? I seem negligible. Some convenient contrivance to some end. When you wake up to some uninspired beautiful liar that you have given your body to, I suspect my love is the furthest thing from your mind.

I'm not really like you in your fatal flaw. It's the one and only way in which we are truly different. That image you had of that shampoo bottle? That is how the entire world looks to me all the time. You and your violin player, and chump ass dudes that follow us around are just the worst of all, because it's you, my soulmate. I suffer more now because of your non-attachment survival love mechanism than I have ever suffered a single person before. There was the wife, but that was also about the children and the role loss. This is overwhelmingly devastatingly all about you. But you, about whom Anson, thinking I was out of earshot, said "Fucking is no more meaningful than taking a drink." Words like an ice pick in my heart that will not leave. Why say your heart is split in different places? Why the 15 hours on the phone? Why tell me how powerful and unusual your missing me is, how it is effecting you. While I'm sitting in a Starbucks, alone, multiple calls in a week. Wondering, burning with searing desire, why we just can't be together. Only to be told that you love me, but only 4 out of 5 ways. Maybe the guys you fuck, that you make carefully sure I don't know about, just get the one way? I'm supposed to feel lucky? I don't feel lucky. Then we barely talk which I know means somebody is around. There is always somebody around. Even during those times for periods of a few days, when I pushed you away for some brief sanity, when I came back, there was always some new fucking idiot hovering around. Your survival mechanism kicking in I suppose, unable to be alone, even for a few days. So now it's only the drinkey overwhelmingly beautiful sounding "I love you's," so loud, emotional and public, so oddly unasked for, that grab my broken heart. So easily offered, I don't get it. This is your thing, how you survive, you move on, non-attachment. Why not just buy another shampoo bottle to replace me? Am I special? Unique? Different? Irreplaceable? Do you really love me in some profound meaningful way that you just can't come to terms with? Is it fucking you up inside to some small degree? A small portion of how it's fucking me up? Or is it just that the emotional uber-supportive unconditional love bleed it out poet role is a difficult one to replace, even up there, but you are seriously shopping around, even now.

Not me though. I'm sitting in it, seriously. I'm way beyond even the illusion of replaceable people now. I'm so real it fucking hurts. So real that I'm going to be alone in real ways, inside and outside now, for a good while. Until, I suppose, something or someone really real genuinely comes along. I'm so real now that even waking up and thinking about all of your terrible painful flaws, doesn't make me love you or miss you any less, not even a little.

******

I write this, I post it, and hardly surprisingly, you call. Not that you are online, you're not. Our connection is faster than DSL. You're depressed and you want to die. You say that you don't think you have it in you to continue on with this emptiness, this meaningless existence. You have now lost touch with even your passion, your music, your art. You feel lost. You're at your new job so we only speak briefly. I try to help, but ultimately one can only offer so much. I offer you every single thing I have, my entire life, all of my days and time and love to heal you, or at least walk beside you holding your hand while we both heal ourselves. I remind you that you promised to give me a chance if you get to the point where you are seriously going to off yourself. "Whatever it takes," I say. Sobriety, therapy, anything, together if you want. Anything for you, unconditional love. I want to be there for you more than anything. I've offered you absolutely everything I have, I don't know what else to say. I can hear the sorrow in your voice, your soul now all bled out. You let me go, get back to work. I'm sure that you will be OK, find something or someone to distract yourself again. I myself am not so blessed though, so easily distracted. I want you more than ever.

Done With Love Poems

09/01/08

I'm done with love poems
I will never write another.
Even though I do it better than most,
I've been told over and over.
Even hardcore feminists have congratulated
my ability to write love genuinely.
It's because I've always been in touch with it.
I've never been afraid to feel it.
I know how to love.
It's not just about want or attraction
or desire or functionality.
It's about compassion and forgiveness and empathy.
A willingness to see the best in someone
not getting distracted by the worst
like so many people living in fear of love do.

It warms my heart remembering all the beautiful souls
I have felt some type, some level, some flow
of love for,
It is a true divine gift every time.

A soul mate though?
That is something different.
It's not even a greater love, not a greater passion
no greater desire,
and certainly not necessarily a greater situation.
It's just something about the connection of souls.
A geometry of interlocking fields of energy.
It is ineffable and inexplicable, poetic, spiritual and profound.
I've only used the word with 3 and
the first two used it first with me.
The first was never meant to be
It wasn't complete, it was pure emotion.
She was too young, it put me in a mental institution
and now she is a lesbian.
The second, I was sure was the real deal
but it wasn't complete, it was conditional.
I married her, had three children
but there were subtle philosophical differences that grew
and in challenging times our love was through.
I never recovered, never regained my center

and when the third, my perfect reflection came along
I was still too broken to make her mine.
If I'd been in better shape, less depressed,
less insecure, less emotional, more confidant,
more in touch with my inner male energy
maybe, maybe, maybe.
But I wasn't, and now she is gone, and I am alone.
And for the first time ever I can remember
I have completely lost any desire to ever again know love.
I'm done with love poems.
I will never again write another.
I possess no want, no need, no desire,
just an abiding emptiness.
As the poet ages
and the decades stack upon themselves
like lettered blocks,
I am done.
A man only gets so many chances.
There will be things to do,
words to create, books to write
undertakings to undertake
life to live, truth to seek,
times to enjoy, I'm sure.
but I have no desire for the love,
or even the simple touch of a woman
ever again.
It is almost a spiritual sigh of relief, in a way
to simply resign ones self
finally, willfully, and meaningfully
to being alone.
There are other things to do
truths to learn
pursuits to pursue
but never another soul mate
she is gone
I am finished forever with love
I will never write another love poem
I am done.

A moment of pretend

09/03/08

"Hey baby, why do you look so sad?" she said, gliding to my table, sitting inches in front of me. "Eh, you know the usual?" I say. "What does that mean?" She smiles, leaning forward, close, stroking her fingers through my beard. "I'm a poet," I say, " a melancholy poet." "Awww," she intones sympathetically while scrunching up her smooth delightful young face. I continue, "Yeah, I was driving by here on the way home from the mental health clinic, crying my eyes out. I thought coming in here and seeing your beautiful smile might make me feel better." She leans in and kisses my face a little, hands above my knees, says "You're so sensitive baby, a sensitive poet, what were you crying about?" "The usual", I say " a dame, art, the world itself." "WOW!" She says, " Who's the dame?" "Well I'm in the middle of putting together this book about how I met my one true soulmate and how she is gone." "Awww! Don't be sad," She kisses my cheek, hands on my shoulders. "I did this thing on the Internet that said that I will have 17 different soulmates in my life!" I laugh a little, "Wow, 17, you're a very lucky young lady, I don't think I am quite so lucky." "Do you have a picture?" she asks. "Yeah," I say, taking out my wallet. "Oh, she's beautiful." She says, "Yeah," I say, "but that's not what it's about, it's her soul and her guts that I love and miss. Actually not miss, we talk all the time, as much as ever, she's just far away, and isn't coming back, so it's confusing and hard." "Are these your kids?" She asks, pointing at the picture. "Yeah, those are my kids." I say. They're adorable!" She moons. "Yeah." I say. She puts out her hand to shake, I take it and kiss it gently, she beams. "What is your name?" she asks. I tell her. She tells me her name. "Could you possibly tell me a different name?" I ask. She looks puzzled for a moment, then asks " Oh, you mean her name, you want me to say her name?" "Yeah" I say. Leaning up and softly whispering the name into her scented soft ear. "OK, baby, sure, in the VIP room then?" "Yeah." I say. She stands, takes my hand, and walks with me to the back area. Her form is perfect, absolutely perfect, she looks nothing like her, but is roughly the same size, and has a similar sweet softness to her voice. Once back there, in a chair, she begins to do the thing they do. All of it. Sights and sounds and scents dancing around in a terrible wonderful arcane bacchanal. Closer, closer, up and down up against me. Wrapping my arms around her, hands on torso. Burning warm perfect smooth, I gasp for breath. My heart races like time and regret and age. Holding her tight, I kiss her shoulder, her neck, her face leans up, hair against my chest, and kisses my mouth. She stands, faces me, everything in my face, in my eyes, all of it. All the things that are supposed to mean something, from someone that is supposed to mean something, in a perfect world. She leans in, breath on my face, face against my face, her hair falling on me, the rhythm of our breathing completely different, like jungle screams and ancient ritual death. Her tongue caresses my ear, my earrings in her mouth, then she says it, she whispers the name. Softly and gently, exactly the way I will gasp it out someday, like Citizen Kane on my deathbed, with my dying breath, my final thought, my final word. She says her name into my ear with an exhale, with a grunt like sigh. "Alexcie!" I grasp her, pull her close, very firm. My face into her naked breasts, breathing out in loneliness, loss, betrayal and desperation, I weep. My tears on her soft bare flesh, a flesh that one could almost imagine has never known suffering. Not like her. I cry and cry and she holds me tight. "Shhhh! Shhhh! It's going to be OK," She assures me, in a soft voice, holding me in soft hands, pressed against soft nakedness. My eyes are closed tight, and in my imagination, she looks like somebody else entirely. She stands, dresses, I hand her a crumpled bill. "You shouldn't be so sad" she says. "You seem like such a sweet guy, a sensitive poet." She laughs a little. "Don't worry, the world is full of beautiful girls!" "Sure it is," I say, "Thanks doll, you're a real sweetheart, just what I needed." She smiles really large, exceedingly young and exceedingly beautiful. I am absolutely certain that she has no idea whatsoever what an awful painful thing it is to truly love. She embraces me again one last time, kisses me small on the mouth, and I walk away, out and under the bright clear Texas afternoon sky.

Abandonment in Three Acts

09/04/08

It really hasn't even been a year yet? Thirty days away from a year? Just the other day you were saying how bizarre an idea that is. How in so many years past it seems like nothing happened, seemed stagnant, but this year has had so many eras to it, so much has happened, so much impact it seems like forever, like there is no way that it all fits into one year.

ACT ONE:

Our first act was the most intense thing that ever happened to me, at least since my marriage. Every day all the time, hours and hours. The emotion that you poured into me consumed and overwhelmed me. I was your non-sex boyfriend in every freaken way. I took care of you and supported you in every way. I never wanted that. I loved you almost immediately, hell, immediately. I know love at first sight is like an infatuation, but as we bonded and became closer than I'd ever been to anyone before, even my wife, I realized that we were soulmates. Exactly, astoundingly, alike inside. But there is a lot going on inside you, a lot of layers, a lot of dragons to fight. A lot of disconnect between your feelings, actions, decisions, 4 quadrant categorizations, survival mechanisms. My fatal flaws, your fatal flaws, the fear of emotional risk thing. A whole book's worth of WHAT THE FUCK. I caught some sense of this early, not the full deal, that's overwhelming and had to be experienced, both the joy and suffering known, to understand. I saw something though. I was more honest with you than I've ever been with anyone. More mature right up front. Calm, easy, " I have feelings, and these feelings will grow if we continue this level of intensity." You had the boyfriend you lived with, but he was invisible and you always talked about how it was almost over. So it wasn't hard to pretend. But then Anson came around, he was hanging on you, flirting with you, right fucking in front of me! It was the most unbearable demeaning thing. To be second to the invisible is one thing, but to be so invested in time, energy, and emotion, and be third. Too much. I asked you. I laid it out calmly. But you wouldn't listen. There was the female emotion, and I do love you, so I caved, we continued. We continued because it was good for you, you got what you needed, what you wanted. It was never what I wanted. It was never about me. You are the absolutely best friend, most common soul, best everything, ever, but being a non-sex boyfriend, all that time, energy, emotion, consuming me, keeping me from absolutely any other life, was never what I wanted. By that I mean it really truly is what I wanted, but with someone who loves me enough to be with me, treat me like a decent man. And by someone, I of course mean you. But it is what you wanted. So we continued and it slowly destroyed me bit by bit. Led me to near madness. Not because it was awful, sure, reading all this, it seems like there are some awful parts, and there were. But it was only so awful because it was so wonderful. The majority was wonderful. It was the very best and you were the very best. It was impossible to walk away from. When you decided to leave for Colorado, ostensibly to help your sister, by that time I was completely living and breathing you. If you had been fucking anyone else in that period from the boyfriend breakup up in November until the time you left in February, you kept it hidden from me. I didn't really pry, because I was insane with attachment and felt like I was going to die from anguish half the time. We were together the vast majority of the time. On certain nights though, I would lay in bed all night without sleep, agonizing, going insane, tormented about what you might be doing with your vagina that night away from me. It was unimaginably awful. I should have walked away, at least put some distance, stood my ground, but I love you so much I couldn't. If I had a face, if I had known or seen another that you allowed to have you. If there was a face to that terrible image always flashing through my mind of some strange dude pounding away at your pussy, it would have been enough. Enough to turn me. Enough pain to force me to create distance and find myself again. You always knew this. Almost a year, knowing all your stories of your past sexual liberalism, some enough to literally make me cry. Soul destroying stories I was forced to endure regarding the subject. You must have been out there. You must have been fucking. But you never mentioned a single name to me. I've never seen a face. Never described a night or a situation. If there was one, and if it was anyone remotely in our town, our scene, or at some music show I would have possibly come into contact with, you must have made some special powerful effort to convince that person or persons to never give up the secret to me in any subtle or overt way. What an effort it must have been to maintain such cloak and dagger bullshit, A STAGGERING EFFORT, at least in my imagination. Who knows, maybe it's all in my head. That's what happens when you spend day after day month after month, with a female you love that doesn't respect you, involved in every way except the one that makes things real, you go crazy in your head. It's a big part of what kept me locked in limbo. We had these couple big fights before you left. It was all getting to be too much, as much as I love you, as much as I had come to rely on you and exist in you, the dishonesty that was always at the edges was too much. Let me be clear, EVERY fight we ever had was one hundred percent about this dynamic of sexual dishonesty. Either subtly or overtly. We are a perfect match in every way. Without this, your fatal flaw, if we had really been together, who we are as people, we would have nothing to fight about, even small disagreements would be easily overcome. We would be the perfect smooth, loving, communicating relationship. It would be bliss. It was at times, without other's influence. But we weren't together. Bottom line, I told you from the beginning what I didn't want, but you said take it anyway, and I did, because I love you. We had those fights, it's weird because we have talked all about it now. Completely one hundred percent forgiven each other. Water under the bridge. Come to an understanding and closeness that far surpasses anything before. But you can actually remember those nights entirely differently than they happened. Not see the subtle dynamics that you possibly unconsciously manipulate with your body language and actions. Probably, it comes back to the unspoken words, hidden faces. But I am your whore, your intellectual whore. You use me for everything inside me but always keep the doors open to use others for whatever they have too. You say that you give to anyone only what they inspire in you, as little or as much. You say that my jealousy is ridiculous, that I am a forever, a bigger deal than almost anyone. There was always one other from your past, that you rated higher, but hardly see, not like me, I imagine there is some reason for that. I hoped and prayed that you were keeping me around for a reason. Because I sure as fuck wasn't just another random buddy, I saw those come and go. Every single decent insightful person we came across thought for sure positively that our dynamic was that of a relationship. A loving romantic relationship. That was the energy you always gave me, maybe it's what you do to keep from giving it to whoever the faceless people are. I always felt that with everything you channel into me all the time, there must be a reason. This period of finding yourself that I must endure, this searing dishonesty that I must endure in order to come full circle and embrace my true love, flaws and all. Knowing a happiness that would be salvation for us both.

INTERMISSION:

You left, you were gone for just over two and a half months. I was fucking devastated. Speaking of fucking, I thought you must have been, probably a lot, up there. There were small hints later. Sentences that slipped out. But I never asked and you never ever offered names or details. Kept the silence going. Not me, I told you every detail. I was honest with you from the start, and I was honest with you about what I did when you were gone. When we had our fights, there was a sweet young girl that was near, and for whatever motivation inserted herself into the equation. She had already been around and associated with Anson, our musician pal that had originally inspired my first attempt at truthfulness. She basically saved me. I remember Devorah, one of our poets, congratulating me back then. Telling me that she thought I would fall apart when you left. I would have. This pretty young naked girl sleeping next to me, buying me cake and small toys was the only reason I didn't. I don't believe in that, I have never believed in that, hiding in someone, replacing one person for another not to feel the loss. But I did it. I did it because she was sweet to me and you had devastated me more than anyone before. She made it easy, I didn't have to work at it. I think she felt kind of sorry for me, seeing what you and I went through. It didn't last of course, such things rushed into rarely do.

And it's not like people that are like me, like us, inside, are terribly common. It's not like you were ever out of my heart for a moment anyway. I spent a week alone after her, with all of you rushing back in. This sweet girl and I had just broken it off, but I was suddenly missing you, only you, everything about you, all the things I hadn't felt. I tried to call you a couple times, but didn't answer when you called back. Wrote a few poems. A writer girl from the open mic gave me a smile, it had only been a week since the last one, but I jumped on it, worked hard to make it happen. Called, talked her up, did the charm thing, and we spent the night together our first date. Within a week we were calling each other boyfriend and girlfriend. something I'd not done since my divorce. But, the missing of you was terrible and I needed to feel normal again. She was very nice, kind, an interesting girl. Being with her was extremely comfortable, soothing. It was the opposite of you in every way. It was exactly what I needed, to feel like a normal man for a while again. To feel wanted. But it was all rushed. That's the problem when you are trying to hide from feelings, that is what you do, you rush into the hiding without taking the proper time to get to know what you're rushing into. You judge by things on the outside. Turns out we had some pretty big philosophical differences and it ended, a little over two months. The obsessive fantasy I had of you coming back and me having this pretty girl hanging all over me, saying, Look! Look! See?? I am a fucking man! Why didn't you ever treat me like a man!! Well, it didn't happen. I missed it by a matter of days before you were back.

ACT TWO:

Suddenly you were back. It was early May. You called Shane and asked him to put you up again, he did, and he lied to me about you being back in town and at his place. Our friendship never recovered. I miss him. We became friends again, nice friends, but I kept walls up, a little distance, something you recently told me was stupid and made you mad at the time. I struggled and struggled to be an actual friend and business partner and not an intellectual whore, not a no barriers caretaker non-sex boyfriend. You bonded with Shane instead, and he took you to music shows. You kept telling me not to worry about our shows now that you were back. That we would work together to get everything back on track. We never did though, you ignored them in favor of new stuff that you and Shane went to, It sucked, a lot. By early June though, everything went back to full 'us' mode. In many ways double the intensity, double the connection. I was going through a lot getting back on medication, experimenting with several types. You were going through a lot just trying to figure out how to survive. We were there for each other 100 percent. It was beautiful. I thought it was impossible to love someone as much as I had loved First Act You, but I was wrong. Second act you got into my heart even deeper. Your experiences away had changed you somehow, you were even better than before. There was still that dishonesty though, and as close as we became, as understanding and bonded in so many ways, you still in your flawed fears, were able to acknowledge only this, that what we were only this intellectual whoredom. I was willing to be open and patient, living in hope. But you decided to leave again. Some fucking dude you had met up there left a comment that he was looking for roommates. I watched as you slowly convinced yourself day by day, that it was terrible here. That there was no future for you here. It was the excruciatingly painful. Having the person you love most in all the world, that you center your existence around, slowly convince herself that your life together is worthless and she should leave town for good! I tried everything. I became more insane in my emotions. The thing that probably drives more of a wedge between us than brings us together. I was exactly back in the place I had been in January. You leaving, and me freaking out, only loving you even more than before. Which I hadn't imagined possible. I begged you like a fool to stay, to be with me, to marry me. But you always said the most ridiculous things about "life taking you somewhere" and it is just fucking impossible to argue logically with such illogical meaningless bullshit. The only thing that took you anywhere, was your un-dealt-with issues, shaky logic, and your foot on a gas petal. I did everything I could. We could have fought again, but we didn't. We both made special efforts not to. You still did some of the same bullshit before leaving. Almost exactly the same, time and pattern wise actually. But I sucked it up. You were kind and compassionate and said goodbye. You said goodbye to my children this time as they cried in the street in front of their mother's house. Then later that night to me, driving off for what may well be the last time I ever see you, July 27th 2008. It would have been easier if we had fought again, but we didn't.

ACT THREE

The third act is weird because you were gone. I never saw your face after July 27th. Through the middle of August we spoke here and there, but not intensely. I messaged you that I love you and missed you to keep me in your mind, but tried to be low key, let it all play out. It felt like we would remain in contact, but slowly grow apart. A very sad thing, but I am a grown up, despite how fucking crazy I have acted with you. Plus, I held on to some hope that you would learn whatever lesson you were trying to teach yourself so far away, realize I was the only real one, and come back to me, someday. Some friends hung out with me, fellow poets. I had these several day ongoing text message conversations with a very sweet Buddhist girl, helpful in getting my mind off you and adjusting to the thought of moving on. Not trying to hide or date right away, but actually feel loss and heal this time, do it right. Make friends with females, have some solid positive supportive friendships. Think about dating a little again in a few months. Start slow, do it right this time. One drunken Saturday I was with Shay, a close female friend with some unresolved connection between us from a couple years back. She means a lot to me, and it's tempting sometimes to try to get into her when I'm feeling like this. We had spent the night together the night you left the first time. I'd wanted to feel that then, but I really appreciate her and wouldn't want that with her unless it was real, not just hiding from something. I ended up crying in her arms about you that night in February instead. This night in August we got close, talked some big words and it seemed like we were heading that way. Then something happened. She did something that reminded me of you, something involving Shane and the bar. An unresolved pain and resentment between us. I kind of freaked out. I was an asshole to Shane and pushed Shay away.

Almost immediately after, you started calling. A LOT. You were looking for a job really hard and it was eating away at you. Anson had been up there with you doing shows, and god knows what else, but had come back. The roommate you have up there had told you that you needed to find another place to live, something about your "drinkey" behavior. Again one of those things I really couldn't bear to hear about as my imagination went wild. You were down. We spoke every day. Sometimes several times a day. Several hours long into the night on several occasions. Everyone else dropped away again. I was at Starbucks one day and you were telling me how unexpectedly huge your missing of me was. How you don't normally have this kind of attachment, but you and I are special, we relate on so many multi-levels it's hard to be without once you have had it. All these revelations came to you without me influencing or trying to, just letting go to the universe. The weirdest part of act three, the phone weeks, was the open honest intensity. Like there were even less barriers than before because of the distance. We talked about everything. All that we had been through before, feelings, our history, all of it. All of it except for any specific stories about who had ever had your pussy. You did say however, that you couldn't do it anymore, that something had changed in you and you had become like me. Only true connection, even love, will have you now. That you were finally looking for something real. I was beside myself screaming inside that you had to come back and be with me. That I AM your something real. I've proven this! That you had to marry me, be together always. Be a family with my children, loving each other forever! You apologized to me sincerely for all the times you ever hurt me. It was so overwhelmingly emotional these days. I walked around crying all the time. Pretty soon **I was back in a third time**. In that heightened emotional madness that only you create in me. Calling when we were having wine and Bukowski night, drunkenly blurting out the I love you's on speaker phone. How much you miss me, our friends, thinking of us. Having wine and Bukowski without you. You went through this bad depression on and off every few days. I actually got you to promise me, to swear that you would NEVER off yourself without giving me a chance first. Coming back and being with me, trying it for at least six months rather than death. I know you meant it too, because you actually mentioned it to Anson later, even if jokingly. I joked that it was progress, a relationship with me now ranked above an untimely death. It's progress! We became emotionally closer than ever before over the phone. During this act you said things like, you miss me more than you ever miss people, and that you were surprised. That with me and our friends you felt like you had a feeling of family. Something you never had, and you were missing that up there, feeling alone. That I was irreplaceable. That your heart was in two places. That talking with me was the only bright spot of your day. On and on with wonderful things like this. On three different days you actually asked me to live with you, that we could be together all the time, that you would be in my children's life, but you still wouldn't agree that you would be with me, no specifics, but you, I assumed, would still be fucking other guys, I said "You know that won't work, I've never lead you to believe that would work." I said "Be with me, and I'll leave here, come up there and leave my kids, at least for a while, to see, for us to be together." The aloneness you felt without me, you were trying to find away around it I suppose, without "changing us." We said I miss you's and I love you's so much it was overwhelming, everyday all day. It made me CRAZY. Why wouldn't you come back and be with me! YOU HAVE NOTHING AND NO ONE REAL UP THERE! Even if you do, it's not better than me, not better than here. I pleaded, I begged, marry me, let's be together forever! I love you unconditionally. All past struggles behind, me and you forever. It's because you are looking for this perfect man you say. There had to be this perfect connection on five different levels. You give me credit for four. One kind of shaky, which hurts. But that three, you say, are **off the Rictor scale!** More connection than you have known in your life. Closer than anyone. In the past even in the closest times there was always that one painful qualification, that one dude I never actually met who was number one. Then finally you conceded that although he had been closer, more connected, in some ways, I was closer and more connected in others, so it was about even. I was now in a tie as the closest most connected person you have known in your entire life. Only, he doesn't want you, keeps you at some arms length even though you are friends, rarely sees you and doesn't speak with you every day. While I am capable of unqualified adoration every day. Drawn to each other always.

It was then I realized that there was no way I could ever love another again. It was Sunday night and we spoke of the nature of love and replaceable people. The day before on Saturday had been your most depressed and suicidal yet up there. I told you that your idea of true love, the irreplaceableness, that you love that person if they are there or not always and forever. That was us, that was me. I told you that I love only you forever and that I wasn't going to be with anyone else and if you don't come back for a year, or two years, I'll still be here waiting for you and loving you. Alone, loving only you. That if you never come back and never find me again, I will be alone forever forsaking everything because nothing else can ever compare to the one true soulmate, to real unconditional love. I want nothing else now. On Monday I got up and drove way across town. Anson and I had been working together on a book and spoken word CD project. I wrote a poem about never writing another love poem. It felt OK. We recorded for several hours, made a copy of the first draft manuscript, had lunch and great conversation about art and life. It was a good day, I was feeling OK with the idea of just being alone. Late that night I went to the bar with Rod and started throwing them down. Anson called, had been reading the manuscript. He was emotionally affected by it. Not just in the literary sense that I had hoped, but very personally, digging up certain days and times that the had played a part in. He apologized for a particular time that he felt my pain had been his gain. We talked about some things. It really dug it all up for me. He and I talking about it like that. Not like characters in a book, but us and what we went through with you. The things that you do, but don't seem to realize, or don't want to realize. The insane emotional tornado that is you. I had no idea that the manuscript would fuck him up like that, and that fucked me up. A little bit later you called, I was good and drunk by then. I can't remember the beginning of the conversation's start, but you said that we would have to start talking less, that you were pushing me away because your heart was in two places and you were having trouble moving forward. MOVING FORWARD!?!? The person who had called me two days earlier depressed wanting to die up there, hating the meaningless new job, the lack of connection, the lack of family, missing me, telling me I was the closest person in her life, now within a day you were pushing me away and moving forward!? I was drunk and it was unbearable, I screamed on the phone, not angry, but pleading. I fell to my knees on the ground in front of the bar, screaming on the phone. The door guy came out, people were all around, I was screaming " NO! NO! NO!! I LOVE YOU I LOVE YOU!! I LOVE YOU! STOP IT! There is no forward there, you are fucking unhappy there, you have been calling me for weeks, you are alone, how fucking ridiculous is this, I love you!!! I LOVE YOU! You are my family! My kids are your family! My friends are your family! I AM YOUR FAMILY!! I LOVE YOU!! Please come back! This is your home! I am your home!" I was on the ground sobbing in the parking lot in front of dozens of people, it was beautiful. You said "I'm sorry, I didn't mean it, I'll deal with it, figure out a way," and we got off the phone. I went in and drank some more with Rod, a lot more. It was dollar well night and we both hurt ourselves. We went to the diner and you weren't there. In fact you weren't anywhere. You were just this far away voice with all these contradictory feelings, motivations, and drives.

I went home and I wanted to fucking die, what you said, what he said, all the other stuff in my life, money, no job, ex-wife, vodka, it was all too much. I got the big knife, a clean cut like Brittany always talks about. I sat with the knife pressed to my wrist until 5:30 am. Why can't I do it, why can't I do it? It hit me. This true love thing, this unconditional love thing. I can't even kill myself because of you. I love you so much that even if you never want me, I still have to be here in case you need me. I have to live in case you ever need me. That is what love means. It means not only forsaking all others, and the self, but even forsaking the idea of not self, of not being. I was screwed. I love you too much to live without you and I love you too much to die for you. Unless you die first, which of course you promised me a chance before that happens, so that is it. Right then and there in that moment I realized that all thoughts of death needed to be expelled from my head. That I need to find some kind of way to survive, even alone, because I know that as long as you live I will never do it. I sent you ass loads of text messages begging you to come back. So many messages that you got upset because they kept waking you up. You called and complained, I was in the bathroom and missed your call. I called you back on the way to the mental health clinic. You were cold and it was obvious you were upset and pushing me away. YES, I went crazy on the messages, but why do you think I was so fucking crazy? Look at what you did to me! You can't be that oblivious! You said, "I love you, I have compassion for what you are going though, but It's making it hard for me to move forward, to have a life up here." It was too much, you had spun everything around and closed off again. Like January, found an excuse and pushed! It was overwhelming. After two weeks of bonding, closeness, all the words, the emotion, your sadness, neediness, depression, back to me. That's when it hit me, in the car, it wasn't really about that. It was about your need, always about your need. You needed me, so you drew me back in. Now, new job, meeting new people, maybe the roommate isn't pissed anymore, for now, got over it, but you just don't need my energy at the moment. That's what moving forward means. In my mind I imagine you fucking somebody new, some faceless dullard, the same old image.

So that's it then? Act three? Now I'm stuck in the headfuck all alone. The people I was reaching out to two weeks earlier back-burner-ed again, like always, for you. I am sitting in this unconditional love for you, not wanting anyone or anything else. You somehow managed to spurn me again for a third time without even coming back. My freaking out wasn't some selfish thing all about me. It was about you, what you're going through. Depression, loneliness, all the things you expressed for two weeks? Suddenly, it's as though I'm acting out some drama on my own? I'm furious! You are not outside of this, That is why in the middle of August, after being gone for a while you needed me again. It's your dynamic. Always recreated endlessly. Push and pull. I cry in my doctors office, she says we need some space to work on ourselves, or no matter what happens we will never be any kind of real support for one another because we will always keep being there for each other, loving each other, then hurting each other. It's awful. I drive by the all nude strip club. Talk to a stripper into whispering your name in my ear. Crying hard on her naked breasts. The next night I go out and drink alone. Act 3 seems to be over. 2 weeks of intensity, the tornado that still spins from far away. From a week of friendship and love and missing, to an emotional suicidal Saturday, to a Sunday where you finally place me as the closest person in your life. I finally understand and verbalize to you the nature of true love forsaking all others. To a Monday where you say that you are pushing me away. To a Tuesday where your voice is already cold and distant. There is the honest undeniable influence of another voice I am not seeing. In the word choices, in the inflection and the sentences repeated in a certain way. Something we have talked about. Conversations with someone else are influencing you away from me and away from our world. You have run away and let someone else in. Which, I suppose I already knew was happening, just these last two weeks were so overwhelming I couldn't help but give that one hundred percent to save us, to love you, one last time. It's not just that this last act with you hurt more than the previous two, it's that in real deep meaningful ways **it hurt more than anything ever**. Despite all the flaws, I have never loved anyone as much as I have loved you, and I have never loved you as much as I did in those last few weeks of August, from far away, on the telephone.

She Is Gone

So now that she is really gone
not half way gone
not far away but still talking everyday gone
but gone,
heart in one place gone
moving forward somewhere else gone
not returning messages gone
getting energy from someone else gone.
It hits me like a brick in my throat
a splitting apart of my heart
an emptying out of my intestines
She is gone.

I have a beer at the bar
and she is gone.
read poems to a crowd
and she is gone
sell my blood
and she is gone
eat lunch
and she is gone
hug my children
and she is gone
an unusual amount of time alone
and she is gone
make a right turn on to Cooper street
something I see reminding me of something interesting
turn and look at the empty seat
and she is gone.
Ray LaMontagne playing at Starbucks
and she is gone
sad, needing someone to talk to
and she is gone
see a girl in a tattered green skirt
and she is gone
up late talking online
and she is gone
wake up in the morning
and lie there in bed thinking about her
and she is gone
her songs in the car
and she is gone

an entire book of it
and she is gone
Dave Matthews in the locker room at the gym
and she is gone
applications for shitty jobs
and she is gone
put pen to paper
and she is gone
cry a hundred thousand mournful tears
as if somehow enough tears
might make a difference
enough poems
enough words, enough typed messages
enough prayer, enough self-abuse
enough want, enough desire, enough love
but she is gone

her heart is in one place now.
but mine is all scooped out.
she is moving forward now
but I am stuck
swallowing fire
fiend-ing and falling apart
she is gone
was I that replaceable?
being never quite enough anyway,
only loved 4 out of 5 ways
but still her closest connection ever?
is there anything left of me in her?
still in her mind
still in her heart
now apart
is it even a struggle at all, leaving?
or is someone else's energy enough?
is it all the same,
different face,
different place,
different name?
is it even hard for her at all now that,
she is gone?

agony

09/08

The agony of love,
how terrible it is.

The pain of truly being alive.

Troubadour suffering,
denied sight of the beloved.

Empty silent nights.
Every aspect
pounds and rushes.
flowing through the entire body.
Wildfire
memory.
A sweet pain in
every terrible breath.

sadness seeping in around 7:30

9/08

it's getting me.
all day its been ok
but just now, 7:24 pm
it's getting me.

remembering our raised voices.
repeatedly playing back these
crazy drunken voicemails.

"Fuck you for not being there when I need you!"
"Don't pretend you don't know!
I need you right now!
I need my best friend on the fucking planet!
fuck you for not answering!
answer the Goddamn motherfucking phone!"
sad girl tears. screaming.

She's no better at this shit than I am
she pretends to be, but she is a liar
a drunken liar.

I've been ok all day
but at 7:35pm
it's getting me.

The difference between strippers, best friends, and other dames

09/08

Strippers are like regular women
but different, more uninhibited
so it's a test,
see what you still got.

Strippers will always touch your arms and shoulders
They are real big on your shoulders
always lingering on the shoulders
taking the time to feel the size and mass.
And the upper back,
something you have focused on for a good while now.
but especially the triceps
always the triceps.
The triceps are always the biggest draw.
They like your beard, they play with it
and your hair, especially when it's sticking up
They pay attention to the earrings
and always, always want to look at the tattoos.

This is similar to bar cougars
late at night, when you work the door at the bar
Pretty much the same things
but more sloppy, less practiced than strippers.
And regular drunk bar girls will
Behave the same to a lesser extent.

Not to mention that
all of the above to one degree or the other
will find you charming, clever, witty
sweet, and funny.
All big positives,
except that you only exhibit these traits
when not depressed over some terrible heartbreak
which you are a lot.

Best friends are different,
they are like normal girls in most ways.
Initially they will scruff your hair
Touch your arms a lot,
but in a way that is more subtle,

but you notice, because you are aware of such things.
They will also put their hands on your chest
while speaking, a lot, but casually,
like it's a thing two dudes might do,
even though that's ridiculous.
But then, when they see how nice you are
And sweet and kind, and that you do everything for them
you lose your man-ness
and become kind of this asexual bitch
that is there to take care of all their needs
while they serve pussy out to whatever
dipshit has the right angle when they are drunk.
It sucks.
But sometimes,
if you fight and are apart for a while
when they come back
they will touch you again, special attention to the arms
and make statements about
how you must have been in the gym a lot
while they were gone.
It seems cool, but
you will likely fall back into your bitch pattern again.
And she might have just been reeling
from some freaking violin player she had a crush on
turning down her advances
because he felt like she was
kind of a drunk whore, which obviously
makes her feel pretty bad and
even though you think she is kind of a drunk whore too
she is your best friend after all
and you can't help but be in love with her anyway
because you know her really, really well
and think that she is completely awesome in every other way
except for the drunk whore thing.
Its all pretty fucked up and painful
you're the bitch
she's the whore
It will probably end up fucking you up so bad
that you will seek out an afternoon with a stripper
just to see if you still have any man left in you at all
and yeah, it seems like maybe a little
so much so that the second stripper
gave you all this free attention
and talked about art and poetry and singing

and wants to come see one of your shows, maybe perform
which is awesome,
because she is way hot and kissed you a little
and held you, and listened to your story
about your best friend
and had some pretty decent insight
Then texted you saying that
she was looking forward to hanging out soon.
So, you feel a little like a man again
even though you still can't stop thinking about
how you wish that the best friend you ever had, the drunk whore
would stop being so fucking stupid
and come back and be with you, and marry you
It's the worst thing ever,
but at least the afternoon with the stripper
makes you feel a little bit less like knifing your goddamn self
than you did before.

fallen into disrepair
09/08

somewhere in there
falling into disrepair
my belief.

that anything anywhere is
real or right.
any man is decent,
any woman virtuous.

my heart is breaking.
my soul is tired.
my body ready
to let it all go.

Somewhere in there
falling into disrepair
my hope.

That things will ever get better.
Ever be different.

It's not so much that
I lost my way
as everyone has spun me
In different directions
blindfolded
mocked
bloodied with a spear in the side.

Somewhere in there
falling into disrepair
my ability to love.
I had one last chance

she thinks I'm a joke
someone to be managed
delicately
lied to and misled.
Unconsidered,
pushed and pulled when needed.

Somewhere in there
already fallen into disrepair
is me.
Everything is broken
or bleeding
or running away.
Entropy
drips from my eyes.
Time eats me like a cancer.
Friendship burns
like
the fires of hell.

Somewhere in there
is an empty space
where something used to be
but isn't now.

There's nothing.
Less than nothing.
No need for anything
left
at all.

Deconstruction of Emotional Pain

09/08

There are parts of me that are hurting
that she simply does not possess.
That he does not possess.
That many do not possess.

Misshapen internal organs.
Unnecessarily mutated brain lobes.
Weird heart palpitations.

There are things in me
in unimaginable pain
like they can't imagine.

But I'm all crazy, right?
Much for mocking,
worth something
but not worth great art
or any type of dedication

Don't ever fucking tell me that I'm special
Don't wonder out loud to me
in honey sweet voice
how I could compare myself
to him,
or some other him,
with curvy crooked words like
fishing hooks.

What does closest even mean?
Two atoms that mushroom explode
each other?
Two forgotten mutts
stuffed into a cage?

It's all a grand deviation
from sensibility.
Irradiated fantasy
A kick in the nuts nightmare.

Leaves and trees may
possess energy

but they don't
posses the capacity to love
like I once did.
Before her words
induced absolute relativism

a post-modern selfish symphony
ABC
take care of me
EFG
you're so special
to me.

Everyone cries at the solo
sung out to the room,
at the end-
baby.

There are parts of me hurting
that she cannot imagine.
Because someone
took those parts away from her
a long time ago.

Let me share something
important here:

A PATHOLOGY
is not the same as
a PHILOSOPHY.
One can be embraced
the other
must be overcome.

Mistaking the two
is sure fire easy way
to cause someone you love,
that loves you
one hell of a lot of pain.

Especially when
one purposely seeks out poets
with a propensity
for bleeding it out.

Come Undone

09/08

Nothing ever happens
Anywhere
Anytime
Nothing at all
Birds don't sing
The sun don't shine
Elephants forget
Cars don't start
Bees are cut off at the knees
Eyelids never blink
Flowers hang unbloomed
Cats don't scratch and claw
Silent death never comes
Men don't cry
Thunder doesn't follow lightning
It's always empty in the sky
All the grass is brown and dead
Politics stays the same
White noise static on the television
The national anthem is never sung
No one eats pie or cake or pizza
Candle wax doesn't melt
Babies aren't born
Men in horned rimmed glasses never sneeze
Volcanoes lie dormant
Rabbits eat their own feet
Movie sets are empty, no one yells "action" on them
Race horses fall over
Time flows down a drain
Hairstyles never change
Policemen sit silently, not eating donuts,
not writing tickets or laughing at your expense
White lace dresses tatter
Bowling balls wobble
Gum is spit out
Unsmoked cigars sit smoking
Girls don't flirt
Whoops don't holler
Grasshoppers won't hop
The far off sounds are coming from nowhere
No one wins a medal, or first prize or second prize

or no prize
Writers tap there pens relentlessly then
fall Christ-like backwards in work chairs
Clowns don't cry
Fools are suffered lightly
Glass eyes don't see
Blues songs aren't sad
Everything yellow disappears
No one gets on an airplane
There are no regrets
Martyrs can find no martyrdom
Monsters aren't frightening
Childhood is a walk in the park
Wheels won't turn
Hummingbirds kill themselves old school Japanese style
Fortune cookies are empty inside
Cheaters prosper a little
Hats blow off heads
Turtles stack upon turtles in a pyramid
Fish cannot breathe
Monkeys stop fornicating
Limestone doesn't taste like lime
The whole dark world stands still mid jack-off
Ticket takers won't take tickets
Flies on the wall don't even give a shit about what's being said
Liars lose their inertia
Honey tastes like piss
Guns misfire
Eggs crack open of their own volition
Carousels won't spin
Angry people sit down with head in hands
Moths surround the ankles
The ketchup won't pour out
Entropy sings like Christmas carols on small children's lips
Nothing ever happens
Anywhere
Anytime
Anything at all
And you don't love me
And you don't love me
And you don't fuck me
You don't fucking fuck me
You fucking fuck other people
But not fucking me

Bugles blow mournful
Every living tiger screams
Fire burns the head of a match
And you won't stop leaving
One way or the other
With your body
With your face
With your words
With your pussy
Your pussy won't fucking stop leaving
Your heart
Your love
Your connection to all things great and small
It just won't stop leaving
over and over and over
Like trains at a train station
Particles of light
Turning pages in a book
I can't see your fucking smile
somebody is fucking you now
Ripples in a pond
Butterflies in spider webs disintegrate
Icicles fall stabbing baby lizards in the eye
The universe is flaccid
No one even bothers to masturbate anymore
Pancake syrup down the side of your face
The waitress at the diner offs herself
Phones don't ring
Prodigal sons never return
Pedophiles sip cocktails and smile
at new years eve celebrations
Planted seeds grow Karma like rotting fruit
Demons go unfought
Prophets predict the worst scenarios
Sleep is now a wicked enemy
Poems fall apart
Every single fucking poem falls apart
Inkless pens
Shit from the ass
Stupid languages
Words don't mean shit when twisted around like
quantum folly bullshit bluster
And you don't love me
And you won't love me

You won't love me
You won't fuck me
only fools to which you are nothing.
only fools to which we are nothing.
Everyone goes back to full time jobs.
We all give up the ghost, or the dream, or the secret
secrets, secrets, secrets,
motherfucking secrets!
Perverts, liars, fucking cunts
every last one of you
Return to the same as before
Except for me, disabled now
Everything back to what it was
You back in your place
Everyone back to their place
Someone yells action
Frozen time resumes
Nothing happened
Nothing happens
Nothing ever happens anywhere
Nowhere
No time
No one
Nothing at all
Nothing at all
Nothing at all

10/01/08 Wednesday

It was an intense period. I had the house to myself for 10 days while family visited family. Usually Janice comes by, some of the other friends, but most were unavailable this time. Roderick was around some. Mostly, I spent the week with Anson. He was here for a few days, ate lunch with the kids on Friday, then came back on Monday and was here until Thursday morning. We got deep into it, discussing everything. Art, culture, ideas, the spirit, religiosity, making it. We worked a lot on the book and CD projects. He turned one of my poems into a song purely on a whim. He played it at a gig he was doing at The Grotto in Fort Worth. A place I had been to with some Fort Worth poets, but became a sore spot in Lexy's second act because it was the place she and Shane had found where she put her energy instead of our gigs, and of course she met **OTHER PEOPLE THERE**. Anson's show was great. He called me up in the middle of it to perform T*he GRIND*, it went well. Then he played the song from my poem. It was awesome. Rod and I left a little early and went to Caves to see Janice, then back home. Anson met us later. We all fell asleep in different rooms. At 5:30 in the morning I was awakened by the sound of Anson's phone in the living room, he didn't pick up. My phone rang next, I knew it was Lexy. I picked up. She was drunk as hell, walking around the streets of Denver to 7-11 for some food. We talked; I told her how much I missed her. I'd been texting her all night telling her how cool the show was and how Anson and I were doing that thing on stage where we played off one another's intense energy. Something we'd done twice before when she was still in town. I guess it affected her. She was lonely, said she had no support, no family, no feeling of belonging up there. She said that she was going to send two bus tickets, one for me and one for Anson, to come up there together. I told her that I would come, but not at the same time as Anson. She was furious. She yelled at me intensely and for a long time, told me that I was selfish and only ever thought of myself. What about her? What she needed, wanted, us both. I had to calm her for over 30 minutes, drunkenly telling me that my love wasn't real. That I say I'll do anything for her, but my actions are different than my words. That I am not real. I had little sleep; Friday with the kids was rough.

On Monday and Tuesday when Anson returned we talked about a lot of stuff, she came up a lot more. Things slipped out on both sides. It was not awesome, details I didn't want I shut out, but confirmation of my worst fears, of behaviors when I'm not around, was awful. The images in my mind were assaulting me. Her words from Friday morning were assaulting me. Janice, Rod, Anson and I met Tim Thompson and Crystal, our Fort Worth poets, at The Grotto. Everyone was psychoanalyzing me and everyone else. I just kept drinking hard until it hurt, trying to get rid of these terrible images in my head.

On Tuesday Anson and I drove to Plano to a gig that I thought was happening but wasn't. We hit this little music coffeehouse mic in Dallas instead.

Wednesday night was the Mad Swirl. I'd missed the previous one, second time ever. Some old peeps had been really shitty and negative to me, I couldn't take it. Not with everything else happening. I was going to skip this one as well, but Anson talked me into it. He said we would go first to the music mic across the street, then drop over and back. It was the same music mic that exactly a year earlier had been cancelled and moved to Halloween, that we had gone to. Which was the reason that Lexy and her sister Tonya had walked across the street to the coffeehouse to see if anything was going on, had met Johnny O. by the bathroom, and been invited to the Mad Swirl. The night we met. It had been 12 Mad Swirls since we met. Our calendar anniversary was two days away, but this was our open mic anniversary. I asked Johnny O. to put Anson and I on the list together. Anson asked what I had in mind; I told him that we were going to bleed our souls out in honor of Lexy, and we did. I read three pieces about her, Her Soul Bled Out, Grande Soulmate Drip, and I Loved Her Before and After. Tears like a dirty death river flowed down my face. It was the most emotional I had ever been on a mic. The most emotional anyone had ever been on that mic. Anson played with me in perfect unison. I walked off gasping for breath and he jumped right into a mournful soulful song dedicated to her, incorporating the words from two of her songs and one of my poems. He followed with a Ray Lamontagne song that she loves, and then hit the roof with a third. We blew the fucking place away. The emotion, the synergy. Strange how this had come around, he and I working together, this shared energy originating with her. We bled our souls out for her; the entire audience was drenched in blood that night.

Later, at the Pitt Grill, Anson, Rod and I were walking up to the door when she returned my call. We were drunk as hell and babbling on, she wasn't, I think. I went on about the show, a couple other people had texted her about it. Anson told her it was an incredible unrepeatable performance. She seemed sad, said "What's up with you guys having so much fun without me?" I laughed! I said, "Baby, you're missing the point. We bled our souls out FOR you, not without you. This was my present. The emotional intensity you love and crave more than anything. This was for the year that we have lived through together. It's anything BUT without you. Truth is I'm never without you. I'm a completely different person now. You are in my in every moment, every breath, every day, every thought, every feeling. I live in you. Even gone months now I'm never without you for a second, and this night was dedicated to you!" I drunkenly said, "I love you," and hung up the phone. We ate and laughed and talked very loud about love and loss and dames, the way mad drunk men and artists do. She wasn't there, but she was.

Anniversary Poem

10/02/08

I miss Lexy, I miss Lexy, I miss Lexy
because she is beautiful!
beautiful face, beautiful heart, beautiful form
beautiful voice, beautiful soul!
I miss Lexy, I miss Lexy, I miss Lexy
Because she is brilliant, insightful, and fun!
I miss Lexy, I miss Lexy, I miss Lexy
because she is my favorite person!
because I am in love with her!
because I want her more than I've ever wanted anyone!
I miss Lexy, I miss Lexy, I miss Lexy
because she is my best friend!
I miss Lexy, I miss Lexy, I miss Lexy,
because I just feel better when she is near!
Her voice Her words Her ideas
I just feel whole when we are together!
I miss Lexy, I miss Lexy, I miss Lexy
because she understands me!
because I understand her!
because we understand each other!
I miss Lexy, I miss Lexy, I miss Lexy
I fall to my knees and pray that she truly love me someday!
that we will be together!
that she will be my lover!
that she will FINALLY forsake all others!
I miss Lexy, I miss Lexy, I miss Lexy
I like talking to her!
I like what she has to say!
I like being around her!
I just really really like her!
I miss Lexy, I miss Lexy, I miss Lexy
She is my soul mate
I feel like half my soul is missing when she is far away!
I miss Lexy, I miss Lexy, I miss Lexy
she is the one I like to listen to!
she is the one I want to spend all of my time with!
it's her face that I want to see every single day!
I miss Lexy, I miss Lexy, I miss Lexy
I hear her voice in my head see her face in my mind,
remember everything about her all the time!
I miss Lexy, I miss Lexy, I miss Lexy

because she is wonderful and beautiful and brilliant!
insightful and compassionate and amazing and fun!
and I love her!
I love her! I love her! I love her!
I miss Lexy, I miss Lexy, I miss Lexy
because my life is incomplete
and sad and lacking and empty,
when she is not here with me!
I miss Lexy.

A Text Froze Shoulders Over

From the moment we met
you knowingly connected our souls.

Every single decision-
every action since,
has spiritually affected me.

By now
it has become easier for you
to simply blow me off as crazy.
Mock me,
rather than own any connection
to your "Best Friend's"
suffering.

A denial so thick-
you now barely give a shit.

The mechanism
in which you need a caretaker
for your heart
while you shield it from those
you deem worthy of your vagina-
had spurned my spirit
into an abiding
self-loathing.

THE REPLACEMENTS

Who are they now?
What are their names?

Who is buying your drinks,
driving you around,
sympathetic when you are sad?

Who is eating your cooking,
listening to your views
being told that you and they
are just the same?

Who are they now?
What are their names?

Who is your new best friend?
(The one you carefully hide shit from.)
Who is providing a roof over you head?
Who are you fucking?
Who is your pal that you keep around
while you fuck someone
in the other room,
that dies a little inside
each time?

Who is just like you?
Who is closer to you
than anyone ever before?

Have they heard the percentages?
Have they heard the sad stories?
Have they told you theirs?

Have they heard you sing melancholy
about how you've
never known love?
while
Fighting back tears,
breathing shallow and short
desperately imagining that
they will be the one
that finally breaks through?

Who are they now?
What are their names?
Have they tried anything new?
Who is hearing your one-thousand "I Love Yous "
only to be told in stupid confusion
that "I love you"
even a thousand times
doesn't mean "I love you"
it simply means "I love you"
after all,
haven't you explicitly stated
that you've never known love?

Who is bringing you stuff?
Talking for hours upon hours?
Taking you places?
Foolishly letting their children
fall in love with you too?

Who is it that can't stop crying?
Who is saying goodbye?

Who are they now?
What are their names?
Do they also want to die?

I'd ask if they were as good as me,
as good as all of us,
as brilliant and talented and noble
and compassionate and powerful and real.

But it's likely
that when it comes to replacements,
I was one too.

We are all just replacements.
It's insane,
and likely all just the same

You Run Through People

you run through people
you run through people
you run through people like
blood runs through veins
like tigers run through jungles
like terrible thoughts
run through my mind.

some you don't care about
some you care about
some you use, manipulate
some take care of you
some keep you alive

you run through people
you run through people
some here
some there
a lover
a fuck
a best friend
a pal
a drink
ENERGY
a place to stay

some you don't love
but they love you
some you want
but they don't want you
some you might love
maybe
but you run away

you run through people
you run through people
you run through people like
water runs in a river
like days running away
like someone screaming crying with
the devil at their heels

you run
you run
you run through people
and you cut a path of destruction

like
a bleeding wind
like
confusing half-truth sorrow
like broken hope.
another group
another face
another name
no lasting bonds
another place

all the same
all the same
all the same
it's just survival
it's just the demons
never catching on.

you run through people
like a hot knife through the imagination
like a melancholy song
like wasted life
like one hundred thousand desperate tears
like sadness that never stops

you run through people
you run through people
you run
from yourself.

This, My Friends Is What They Call Closure

"I just want something real he said, I just want something real. "
-opening lines from *Spiritus Veritas,* October 2007

Then why? Why would someone just wanting something real, spend an entire year deeply emotionally involved with someone willing or able to give him everything but? It's not about her inability to hear me say what I want or don't want. It's not about her classifications, labels, separations, categories and safety zones. Avoiding emotional risk by separating emotion, sex, friendship and love. It's not about her 'I give different people what they inspire in me.' flawed thinking justifications. It's not about using or manipulation or dishonest misdirected sexuality. It's not about if she is consciously aware of what she does or if it's a subconscious survival mechanism. It's not about her demons, things she cannot face, or proclamation of never having known true love. It's not even about alcoholism or clinical depression. All of that, every bit of that, is all related to her fatal flaw, but it's not the point. As much as I want it to be. To quantify it and make it solvable. The question is, why someone that just wants something real, would allow someone, even someone brilliant, wonderful; with insanely synchronistic spiritual and philosophical commonality, to channel massive overwhelming amounts of female, sexual, emotional, spiritual, non-vaginal, relationship level energy into him for an entire year without being willing or able to be in a relationship. It would be nice to say that it's all about friendship, closeness, connection, or even eternal romantic optimism. But why would someone wanting something real put his entire life on hold? All personal, social, romantic, artistic, spiritual aspects of life? It's not about friendship. True friendship doesn't consume people. It's not about her fatal flaws at all. I meet plenty of flawed people all the time and they don't dominate a year of my life. I simply walk away, or love them with some distance for who they are. It's about my own fatal flaw. Why the very first times I heard her singing about her never having known true love, I felt the overwhelming urge to love her. Whatever it is that drives me to think that I can figure her out. If I can do just the right thing, say the right thing. If I can prove myself somehow. If I possess more endurance, more truth, compassion, honor, morality, than most. That I will finally get the love that I need and deserve and crave. To be somehow whole. From someone that I love, admire, respect and desire but is incapable of giving me what I need because of their own flaws. The damage that their lives have created in them. It's about me. Any other man might have just walked away. Any other man might have just been a friend, with some distance, without letting her feed so much energy in and take so much out. Funny, I can remember her telling me about a few of these, and that they are the ones she longed for. Someone with more confidence, less need, and without a superhero savior knight in shining armor complex. It's about my fatal flaw, not hers. They just happen to fit nicely together, just as much as the push us apart.

It's my fatal flaw that kept me in a miserable marriage, at least the last few years. Thais grew to despise me because I wouldn't ever give up. She had given up, and she wanted me to, but I wouldn't. That is why it ended so badly. Why she abused me, insulted me, destroyed and betrayed me. It was never because she was a bad person, she's not. She is the mother of my children, I genuinely loved her. It was because something inside her had caused her to give up on our marriage, but I wouldn't cooperate. She tried to make me, but I wouldn't. Something inside me wouldn't let me. It's the same. Lexy is not Thais. They are extremely different, but similar in some ways. In many ways Lexy is everything I wanted Thais to be that she wasn't. Her personality, ideas, social and spiritual beliefs. A hopeful idealistic artist rather than a failed one, bitter about art. An introspective communicator. She is like me, my best friend. I married Thais, We felt like best friends at first but it was always based on her idea that I supported all of her views without contradiction. We had children, and I spent eight years doing everything possible short of killing myself to make her happy, I loved her very much. But in many real, deep, spiritual, meaningful ways I love Lexy even more. But like Thais, she can't or won't give me the unconditional love I need. And just like Thais, no matter how hard I work at figuring out all the complex psychological dynamics, I can't seem to make it into a happily ever after. Only she with equal belief and effort, could create something real with me, as an equal in every respect partner. Part of my flaw is that when I really, really love someone, I become blind to certain aspects of them. There is a certain type of behavioral duplicity/disconnect in Lexy, just like there is a certain different type of behavioral duplicity/disconnect in Thais. In both cases I was blinded by love and unable to admit it. I'm pretty sure that in some way, it is this very flaw in me that actually creates this abuse dynamic. Even though I am what they want, it makes me somehow not quite what they want. I love them with all of my heart and crave their love in return, but on some level, in some way, through some subtle dynamic, what I am asking for is abuse, not love. I guess I need to figure out how to stop asking for abuse.

Like Thais, my relationship with Lexy always seemed written by the fates. Based on these uncanny situational synchronicities. Even the freakish unusual series of events that had to all fall into place for us to meet. The things that got her to that spot on that night, being so much alike, being in the emotional and life situational places that we both were in. Living close enough geographically, even though where we met was far away. So many synchronicities throughout. Once, we were eating at the Mongolian Grill. We'd been at the plasma center all day, arguing back and forth the way couples in relationships often do. The meal was done, we got our fortune cookies. She always shuffled them and put them out for me to choose. We had the exact same fortune, something I've never seen happen, but it happened with us that day. They read; "You owe someone you love an apology." We laughed and apologized for the day. Perhaps it was ultimately bigger than that though, maybe it was big picture.

Lexy, If I had been stronger, I would have stood my ground and become an actual friend to you and not a weak intellectual whore. Or had I been stronger you may have seen me as more of a man. People always say that women don't love a man they can walk all over, that they can't respect. Maybe I would have inspired that in you, that final thing we lacked, that 5th element. I could have been the best lover, boyfriend, even husband, you could dream of. The way I always wanted to be. I would have been enough to fulfill you. You wouldn't have fallen into depression and suffering. Fallen so deeply and desperately back into your addictions and self-destructive behaviors to fill the emptiness inside. But I wasn't, I failed you, and that is my fatal flaw. You are my best friend, I love you, always. If you ever find your way to actually being something different with me than what we were, whatever that might be, I'm here. If you ever find your way back onto an actual spiritual path, a path of recovery from your addictions rather that insane indulgence in them, I'm here. If you ever find in your heart that some small part of the love you had for me was actually real and wish to fight your demons rather than drown them, I am one hundred percent here. It's true, I fucking hate it but it's true. If you truly love someone, you must let them go, set them free. If it's meant to be, really is that fate thing, they will return. Maybe having learned and experienced what it is they needed. I pray that you survive the experience.

You are like a butterfly my soul mate. A sublimely beautiful brilliant, wonderful, damaged, alcoholic, butterfly.
I'm sorry.

Master Time Travel

What do you want me to do?? She asks.

I call her from the parking lot of the bar.
Drunker than drunk, alone and crying like dirty death
haunted and beset by
images, words, feelings, and regrets.
I'd feel bad about calling her in such a state
except she does the same to me, so I don't.
She asks the question,
" what do you want me to do?"
" what do you want me to do?"
" what do you want me to do?"
I have no answer but sobs and silence.

The next day when I hurt so bad I can barely move
an entire day of aching heart, aching body, aching soul.
Lying in the solitude such days bring, I find an answer.

I WANT YOU TO MASTER TIME TRAVEL.
Turn back time, make days rewind,
bless us both with a one year do over.

THIS TIME:
When you leave him you have no regrets.
When you look at me, you know
When we spend days and hours and weeks, you know.
You give yourself freely and openly and unreservedly
to me, because you just know.

THIS TIME:
You are ready to face the demons and fight
with me by your side.
You love me as only a best friend can
and we are stronger, nothing can stop us, together.
You are honest. You take emotional risk.
You are not afraid. You give us a real chance.

THIS TIME:
Not another motherfucker touches you.
Take back every hand and mouth and body part
every single goddamn one after the day we met.
I'll take back my few as well.

Because this time we are destiny, meant to be
and we abide in love and support and bliss
with only each other and no other.

THIS TIME:
We never fight about stupid shit.
You never leave
You never come back, then leave again.
We continue our gigs together better than ever.
We do everything successfully together.

THIS TIME:
Every single "I love you" you've bestowed upon me
isn't vexed with qualifications, recriminations
and defense mechanism justifications.

THIS TIME:
We move in with each other and love each other.
We focus on our art together, creating and
making books and recordings,
write poems and songs and sing them and
scream and cry and laugh them out together.
Nothing gets us down or stands in our way
because we have each other always in all ways.

THIS TIME:
Sometime around the third month we realize
that we need to both stop drinking so much
so we go to 12 steps, or therapy, or the Buddhist temple
or something, or maybe it just happens naturally
but were not afraid to do it,
to face the things inside that haunt and hurt us
that we always try to drown and hide from,
because when we walk hand in hand facing every day together
aint nothing for us to be afraid of
we've got each other. Forever.

THIS TIME:
We do it the way it was supposed to be.
Our destiny, our shining enlightening healing truth
our something real for you and me.

THIS TIME:
We do it all right, the whole thing

and by now we are happy
sublimely superbly happy
and you are not far away
and we are neither of us sad, dark, lost, or alone.

What do I want you to do?
I WANT YOU TO MASTER TIME TRAVEL!
Take it all back, make it right!
And this, this ridiculous existence we struggle through
Will be little more than some bad barely remembered
accidental mistaken fucked up alternate time line.
a major edit, a complete rewrite
happy endings all around
Hell, we'll even throw in some joy
for all the friends we love as well.
So do it!
MASTER TIME TRAVEL,
Turn back time
Before it's too late
I'm waiting and waiting and waiting for you here!
Please, I love you, I love you, I love you,

Should Have Been Me

You finally got to the point where
you are trying to get some help
which is great
but it won't work, not yet
you're not quite there yet
and the odds are against you
you need someone that loves you
at your side supporting you,
it should have been me.

You finally listened to someone
telling you how crazy your behavior is
it should have been me.

You give out parts of your self
to too many people
in drunken madness
even those WAY off limits,
all of them, every goddamn one of them
should have been me.

You are desperate and sad and alone
and want someone to fill that void
to be with you, get you through
satisfy you
it should have been me.

You could have gotten better
in a years time could have found truth
and healing
love and companionship
instead you've gotten much worse
fallen prey to the worst of your nature
instead of the best
given in to vice and addiction
sadness confusion and misery.
The beast now has free reign.
You could have been a great artist
now you've lost your soul.
You could have been loved
now you're alone
in all the ways that matter.

You could have had family,
children and close friends that love you,
now you have only yourself.
You could have finally had
a place to truly belong
but you ran away.
You could have gotten better
instead you got much worse.

Don't you see?
There should have been
somebody there for you
to save your soul
to make it right
to keep you safe
help you along the path
to love you unconditionally
and help you become whole...

Don't you see?
That somebody,
should have been me.

The Impermanence of The Rose

There is a single perfect
RED ROSE
on the bush in front of my bench press.

I can't stand it,
this RED ROSE,
this symbol of love.
Perfectly bloomed,
mocking.

The women in my life
have mostly proven
their hearts elusive.
Although, there are a few that fill me
with words.
Loving me, I'm special, connected, close
the only other one except for him.
(there's always a him.)
I'm not sure what good any of this does me.
I still awake in terrible darkness.
I still have no one to cut
the RED ROSE for.

Of course it's my own fault,
I know.
My heart is unendingly permanently unmanageably
STUCK,
having met my one true soulmate.
Who has at last it seems, no longer needing me,
cast me aside.

I would cut the rose and drive it to her now
were she within a hundred miles.
Although, she wouldn't appreciate it anyway.
That's the single way in which we differ,
her romantic pragmatism.

She would look at the RED ROSE
and not see love's beauty,
only death and decay.
Now plucked from it's bush, dying that much faster.

In Buddhist temples,
flowers are offered to images of the Buddha
in honor of his teachings on impermanence.
Celebration of the Dharma, the truth.

But she sees only death,
only the impermanence of the ROSE
not the Dharma, not the truth
not the love that lies behind it.

Odd, I think,
that one such as she
would be so mired in awareness and grief
surrounding
the impermanence of something beautiful.
When loving her
is the greatest lesson in impermanence
that I have ever endured.

I'd still give her the RED ROSE
anyway,
even though
with what life has taken from her,
she is unable to fully appreciate it.
Even though she destroys me with her
Inabilities.

Yes,
I'd still give her the ROSE
and the LOVE.

Epilogue, or The Final Alternate Ending

01/01/09

As the first light of a new year slips through the dusty yellowing blinds, the blue of new time mixing with the gray of old, I sit faithless. Ruined, a shadow, an echo. Dwelling of course on the company and times of one year ago now. Why am I up so early? First moments, first light, first day? What fight what struggle? Sadly, the same un-won one.

I thought I had the ending perfect, the symbol of the rose, the lack of closure as closing. But metaphor aside, a story I suppose isn't told until its all told. My editor, Crystal, upon editing the full manuscript for the book you hold, beseeched me to write an epilogue. She said the rest must be, had to be, told. So I sat with that in my mind for days and weeks until the dawn of same old something new, a year, to arise still full of Red Bull, to type, if I still can, if I still have such a thing in me.

It was like a verbal strangulation. I was sitting at the bar recounting the artistic mad sad joy that was the Mad Swirl in October, the anniversary night. When Janice looked directly at me and told me something. Something she believed I needed to know. Of course, like on previous nights, she was right, She, like I, doesn't sit well with lingering dishonesty. So she told me something. She later said that she felt I would never walk the path of healing or letting go, until all illusions were shattered. But that night, I made her take it back, say she might be wrong, and drank a lot. I called Lexy from the parking lot, about which the next day I wrote '*Master Time Travel*' It was the last time I spoke with her. I fell into a great depression, internalized it, started eating a lot. That week, I had the book cover image of her tattooed on my chest, over my heart. My beautiful scar.

There had been some weird nights with Brittany after Lexy left. Once, drunk at the bar, this dude friend of Janice's decided she would be his crushing crush. Britt laid in the street insisting that someone run her over with a car. No one did. She cried over her ex. He called, and Janice cursed him out. But by this point a few weeks later, in this new level of depression, I was alone scrolling through my phone and saw a Brittany text message; "I love you Paul." There were also a few from Lex, various professions of love and suicidal intent. I wrote a bit about this, It reminded me of a moment in 2005 with my Sweetchild Madness, having not seen her for so many years.

She had leaned across a table drunk as hell, kissed me and said "Paul, you know I've always loved you!" My response was "Ok, but what good has your love ever done me?" Haven't seen her since, unfortunately. So, I wrote a bit about 5 different women that have used the words "I Love you" with me and how little good that's ever done me. I posted it. Brittany wrote me saddened and wanted to take me out to the bar and to eat. A few times that week in fact. One night she told me that other than her ex, I was the only person in town that had ever mattered to her, that she cared about. It was as though she had upped her game to match the now absent Alexcie. She sounded like her and was even using certain key words, something that did not escape me. Why? I wondered, do I draw such things to me? And why do I love these damaged manipulative dolly's so? A night or 2 later, in a group, drunk at the Pit Grill, she really let it out, I'd asked Anson to watch. His jaw dropped as she, kissing on me, said "Paul Loves me! I know he does, I know I'm second to Lexy, but that's OK, I can deal with that." Brittany had never shown me this love. Every time I'd ever felt It and tried, she rebuffed me and preferred to simply take what she could from me and move on to the next moron. It was her I'd had in mind when I told Lexy early on, that I never, EVER, wanted to be an Intellectual Whore.

A few nights later I'm watching her flit around at the bar, guy to guy. We are about to leave, Anson, Rod and I. Janice tells me that her talkey pal had told her that Brittany said that I freak her out. Quite a different slant. Janice is furious. She says that she is tired of girls like Brittany and Lexy manipulating me and being dishonest with me. One thing to my face, another behind the back. And that it needs to all be out. I say, "Fuck this!" Start walking back in. They are all trying to block my way and grab me, except for Anson. Who looks at everyone and says "Why are you holding him back?" They stop. I walk back to Brittany, who is the middle of making this young dude cry. I can see it in his eyes and the look on her face. I grab her, pull her aside. I wanted to be harsh, but I couldn't. I say; "Right now, you are just the same as Lexy and I don't need that. I love you, but you have some serious fucking issues!" She looks at me blankly as says "I Know that!" I walk away.

In the car I say "Damn, that felt good, was liberating, but that was just a practice run!" Anson looks at me and says "I need mine" I tell him "No, not tonight," but he insists. We then have a rather loud lengthy discussion. We go inside immersed in emotional intensity and it all starts to come out. Everything he knows about Lexy that I didn't. Fatal flaw four quadrant shit. Full on murder of my soul shit.

Things done and lied about, other people coersed into lying, and things said about me. Mocking levities that stab and never ever EVER go away. It was a hell of a night and it continued on until the sun came up. Anson and I both crying big awful tears curled up in a ball upon the floor. The kind of night that changes everything. The next couple days neither of us wanted to talk to Alexcie. She left her last voice mail; ***"Where are you? Why aren't you picking up the goddam phone? I really need you! I'm losing my motherfucking mind, and no one is picking up the phone! I could really use someone to talk to! Why aren't you picking up the goddam phone?!"***

I spent an evening on the town with Shane and we worked everything out. Unfortunately, I found that he had been coerced to dishonesty as well. I explained all the things he did that had been things I never would have done had the dynamic been reversed. He listened, he understood, and we were able to salvage the strong bond of friendship we once had, despite what her dynamic had done to us.

A week passed, it was a hard week and I was drinking hard. I was alone at the house for several days and Anson was over a lot. He kept telling me I needed to slow down on the drinking but I couldn't. It was her on my mind all the time, all of it. It was killing my guts. At one point wondering if I should chill for a while I let it go in a prayer to the universe, asking for a sign. A bulletin appeared on Myspace, saying that Tuesdays were now $2 any kind of shot at the bar for all current and former employees. It seemed like the sign. Anson, Rod and I had a gig that night at a college in South Dallas, then we went to the bar. I started in, determined to drink away all thoughts of Lexy. My love for her, my disappointment in her, my apparent crucifixion. By the time I ran out of money, I was making out with some dame, possibly two, to buy me drinks. I was slobbering falling down slurring out "I'm a whore now, now I'm a whore, this is how it feels." Frankly, it's all a little blurry, especially after that point. The next thing I clearly remember is being at home on the kitchen floor with a large kitchen knife in my hand and blood on my wrist. I just remember thinking that I can't live with her, this new to me version of her, but I love her so much that I don't want to live without her! Anson wrested the knife from my hands, keeping me from doing too much damage. I lay crying balled up on the floor screaming WHY? WHY? WHY? He texted Lexy, saying "Paul is the worst I've ever seen him, I'm considering calling the police." She texted back simply "Call the police." Rather than facing, owning up to how she had hurt me, she had cut me out of her heart. She now, truly, no longer gave a shit. The next morning I called my ex-wife Thais, crying. I said "Look, I know I've been waiting all this time for you to apologize, but maybe it's me, maybe I should as well. I finally met the one person who truly gets me, that I truly love, and I am not good enough for her. She has lied to me and utterly abandoned me. I was not good enough for her, I failed her. I can't help but think that I must have failed you as well, and for that I am truly truly sorry." To my astonishment, she was compassionate. We spoke at length. She pointed out for the first time in years, that I had some good qualities. We agreed that we should meet for lunch soon, the kids as well. That night was the Fun City Open Mic. It was a good one, the energy was powerful we did our thing quite well, all of us. I didn't drink.

Friday at noon, Anson went with me to a 12 step meeting. It was excruciating and hard to sit through, there in the same room I had lived in for a year so many years ago. We picked up the kids from school. In the car, I said, "Hey guys, how would you like to sit down next week with your mom and I and have lunch? They all said "NO, NO, NO," They didn't want to see a fight. Nando said "Tell you what, you guys all eat lunch together, I'm catching a bus to Colorado to stay with Lexy!" It was cute, but after a dozen more mentions of Lexy, Anson gave me this look as if finally understanding how big a part of my life, and my children's, she had become, and how difficult this was going to be.

I texted her, saying "I think the time has come for us to take some time apart and not talk." She returned "I agree, you are experiencing a level of insanity I cannot deal with." (She had latched on to the idea of my tattoo as insanity, an excuse to not face her own.) I returned "We are hilarious; funny, I think, that with the patterns you experience, you would call me crazy, I would hope that someday, rather you would say sorry. I'll never be unkind to you. I'll always love you, goodbye." I blogged the following;

"I know why it happened.... I know damn well why.....demons gone far too long unfought....WE MUST FIGHT OUR DEMONS!! regardless of where they began.... because the sad sad truth is that if we don't..... then they defeat us...and we become demonic..... and the demonic have but one purpose.... to spawn demons in others..... THIS is the cycle of human suffering I've never quite experienced it in this way before.... this up close.... this painfully personal.... not only that.... but

the hidey holes of all my fought but not yet defeated demons have been stirred.....I am now in charge of feeling all of my own demons.... as well as the ones she has put in my care.... her own."

On Monday, Janice called and wanted me to come hook up with some dame. She said it would make me feel better. I hadn't been terribly social. I'd made out with 5 or 6 dames in September or so, when Lexy and I started pushing apart, but 2 were strippers and the one drunk bar girl I spent the night with, turned into more of a sweet hold me while listening to Emo music me kind of thing I went to the bar to meet the hookup. I didn't know the girl, but to my surprise, I knew the face. Years earlier when Thais had first left me, my friend TJ and I had discovered the bars together and plopped ourselves down in them. I remember one of the first nights. Me, wondering how I would ever find it in me to meet women. There were three fucked up barflies at the bar. We decided that we were going to embark on a mission to hook up with barflies. Years later this girl Janice was hooking me up with was one of the original girls in the bar that night. There was some type of cosmic symmetry in play. Some message that some cycle was complete. I took her to Rod's, I wouldn't have sex with her, but promised her cunnilingus. She was drunk as hell and swigged some of Rod's Nyquil. I was sober, she was flatulent. She was just a nice troubled dame needing some solace as badly as I was, I made her feel a little better for a while, she thanked me. But, as I snuck out and drove home, I realized that this would never be for me again. Not only was I was ruined from anything real, but from anything half-assed as well it seemed.

That Friday I picked up the kids and we met Thais for lunch. It went smoothly, it was OK. I'm pretty sure her new husband was nearby in case of any issues. Sitting there with her for the first time in 4 years, I could still remember all the reasons I had been so angry with her, the personality traits, they were there. But somehow along side that I could suddenly remember the reasons why I had loved her so much as well. It was surreal. I talked about Alexcie, and the book. We talked about the kids. It was nice. I could tell though, that part of it was sympathy, that on some level she had suddenly realized how much I have been suffering, first over her, and now over Lexy. I'm pretty sure that what I saw in her eyes was sympathy. The next week I had this weird experience where I went into the garage and unboxed all of my stuff that had been stored in boxes for a few years. I set up all my Buddhist stuff in my room and felt like something was different, some part of me reclaimed. I brought in all my books and organized them. I brought in all my photo albums, went to the store and spent hours scanning photos from my past and posting them all up on Myspace. Many people from my past commented and chatted about them. Something had come back in, big love, big history, but also big grief.

I spent a few nice nights hanging out with Julie. I never tried to hit on her, even though I really wanted to. My self-esteem was pretty destroyed. Plus, her story is just as crazy as mine and she was suffering just as much. We were really there for each other on a couple nights, in a big way. It helped us both start to address the grief for real.

I spent a lot of November sick, barely worked out, and by the end of the month I was 30 pounds heavier than when Lexy left. I'm glad she has never come back, I couldn't bear for her to see me now, I just couldn't.

As I finished this story up, I read it to Janice, she burst into tears and said that she didn't want to be like Lexy, no matter what. Was tired of being a woman that runs from love. She had a guy in Arkansas that is her soulmate. Everything about the way she describes him, is exactly how Lexy and I are. She had read "HER SOUL BLED OUT" and cried, and said "I don't want to be like Lexy, I'm going to let myself love and be loved. Stop running away and stop hurting men along the way." She called the guy and he came and got her right then, now she is in Arkansas planning a wedding. I'm happy for her, I envy her, her soulmate, mine so far away.

Lexy has gone to a few meetings up in Denver, considering dealing with the drinking, or so I hear. I have to feel that she has been influenced by me, and that feels pretty good, even if it isn't quite sticking yet. I can't help but feel that she should be here with me, and we should be doing it together, it just doesn't seem right, seem fair. It's not. I hope she makes some progress, wherever she is.

I wrote this poem in December;

Only a Winter Memory

It's small odd things that remind me of her,
and make me miss her.

Walking outside wearing my long black overcoat
for the first time this season.
It was Winter,
when we were first close.

Walking alone in the long coat
eyes half-closed,
I feel her presence beside me.

I drive by a small Italian café
I've been meaning to check out for a long while.
In my mind, we are eating there.

I haven't had a regular lunch date
with her gone.

I check the Internet for her,
but nothing.
Only she and I together, from before.
As if she ceased to exist as an artist
without me.
Caught in something else.
Some labor, less of love.

There is someone,
somewhere,
doing something,
that bares her name and face.
This, I know.

But that person has done and said things
that are not her.
It's as if she no longer exists.

Was she ever real?

Was she created,
and did she create herself for me?

Among brown crunchy leaves,
bare trees and clear skies,
gray empty streets,
deep dark black private nights.

Me, flowing around in my long black coat
like Bella Lagosi's cape.
Her, only a heavy sweater
some cute stylish hat, beaded jewelry,
laughing, talking and crying,
eyes so wide,
voice so alive with possibility.

Does that woman of my dreams,
the answer to my prayers,
no longer exist?

Was she only that person there, then,
for me, in a Winter
forever only a memory.

For me, depression is like a snowball rolling down a hill, it gets worse and worse exponentially. I have no idea if the meds really help or not. As far as Lexy, all I know is that despite everything I fucking miss her. Not a day goes by that I don't think of her, and not a day goes by that I'm not angry with her, somehow at the same time, I miss her with everything I have inside me. I found a new therapist, a dame, she seems well trained and insightful. She listens and doesn't judge. I have high hopes. She says that I'm not crazy. That anyone faced with someone they truly love behaving the way Lexy does, saying the things she does, should be greatly affected, it's normal. She says that her behavior, her patterns are in no way atypical of someone who has faced the type of things that she has faced. That it seems like I did the best I could, but never had a chance. She keeps saying that it's not my fault, it's not my fault. Maybe someday I'll actually believe it.

Is this how the story ends then? Me, a few months sober, walking into a therapist office? I suppose so. I walk in. I sit down. She says "You seem really upset, tell me about it, why are you here? Hands shaking, voice cracking, tears streaming down my cheeks, I look at her and say; I met this dame at an open mic. She is a singer. I fell desperately in love with her. She is my soulmate. She became my entire life, but in the end she didn't want me. Now she is gone. I have lost her forever...

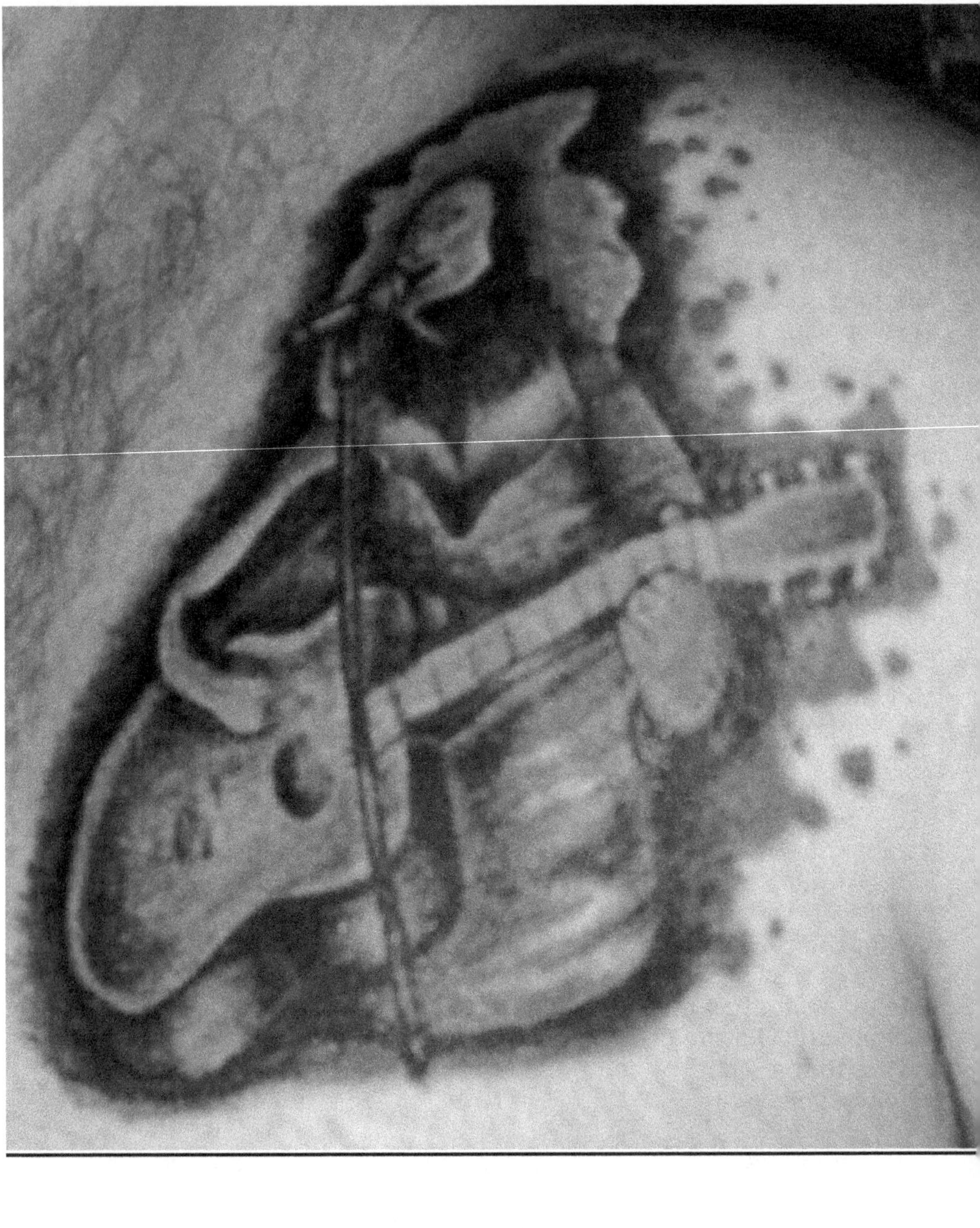

The Last Poem I Wrote For Her

Loving her was like loving fire.
Hot, beautiful and primal,
a terrible burning in the heart.

Not like loving earth,
something solid,
a place to stand,
to plant the feet
and grow things.
A love to live upon.

Nor was it like loving air.
Something you can breathe in
and relax surrounded by.
Like a cool evening breeze
that blows on through
lending a certain comfort
along it's way.

It wasn't even like loving water
drank in
swallowed up
a love that satiates,
can be survived upon
that cools, revives,
is the essence of life.

No,
loving her was like loving fire
and loving fire
is a madness.
You want so badly to touch
it's amazing incomprehensible
irresistible flame,
but it's fire,

and even a lovely gentle fire
does but one thing,
consumes that which feeds it.
It only destroys.
Because that's what fire does.
No matter how exquisite
beautiful, enthralling or powerful,
It burns.

Loving her was like loving fire
and it consumed me
and scarred me
and burned away at my soul
until I was all burned up.
like a walking volcanic phantom,
sweltering ash in her wake.

Paul Sexton is a poet and writer that resides in Arlington Texas. He has three beautiful, clever children. He has been performing, hosting, and lecturing for events in bookstores, museums, colleges, festivals, coffeehouses and bars since the mid 90's. His work has been published both online and in print, and he has sold numerous books through small press. Shaman Noir, broken romantic, unyielding idealist. Paul believes, "one must first create the poet to create poetry." Currently, he is working on Spoken Word performance recording projects, a novel, and a selected anthology of past works.

www.ingramcontent.com/pod-product-compliance
Lightning Source LLC
Chambersburg PA
CBHW031942080426
42735CB00007B/230
* 9 7 8 0 5 7 8 0 1 4 5 3 1 *